Integral Education

SUNY series in Integral Theory

Sean Esbjörn-Hargens, editor

Integral Education

New Directions for Higher Learning

Edited by

Sean Esbjörn-Hargens
Jonathan Reams
Olen Gunnlaugson

Cover image of the chair from iStockphoto © Vinko Murko

Published by
State University of New York Press, Albany

© 2010 State University of New York

For information, contact State University of New York Press, Albany, NY
www.sunypress.edu

Production by Diane Ganeles
Marketing by Michael Campochiaro

Library of Congress Cataloging-in-Publication Data

Esbjörn-Hargens, Sean.
    Integral education : new directions for higher learning / Sean Esbjörn-Hargens,
Jonathan Reams and Olen Gunnlaugson.
        p. cm. — (SUNY series in integral theory)
    Includes bibliographical references and index.
    ISBN 978-1-4384-3349-3 (hardcover : alk. paper)
    ISBN 978-1-4384-3348-6 (pbk. : alk. paper)
    1. Education, Higher—Aims and objectives—United States.   2. Education, Higher—
United States—Philosophy.   3. Educational change—United States.   I. Reams, Jonathan.
II. Gunnlaugson, Olen.   III. Title.

    LA227.4.E835 2010
    378.73—dc22   2009052828

10 9 8 7 6 5 4 3 2 1

Contents

III   Case Studies

IV Looking Ahead

Figures

Acknowledgments

When the idea for this book first materialized three years ago in conversations between us, there was a recognition that this book was waiting to be written. The rich and increasingly diverse interpretations of integral education needed to be gathered and woven together as a way of strengthening this field in the making. By calling upon the visionary and trail making roles of our colleagues, our intention has been to bring together a compelling opening statement for integral education as a field of study.

We wish to thank all our colleagues and associates for the chapters they have contributed to this volume as well as SUNY Press for their leadership in supporting the emerging field of integral studies. We also wish to thank Jennifer Gidley and Gary Hampson for their original impetus for a scholarly book on integral education. As well, we wish to express our gratitude for those involved in the annual Next Step Integral education seminar. These important seminars have been a seedbed for much that is now growing in this new field. A deep bow goes to the California Institute of Integral Studies, John F. Kennedy University, and the variety of institutions around the world that are supporting the emergence of integral education. We also are thankful to Ken Wilber for the role he has played in provocatively taking integral studies to the next level. Most importantly, we thank our students who have all too often been the "guinea pigs" in an exploratory process and have allowed us to experience the fullness and freedom of integral education. It is this direct experience of the value of an integral approach to education that has been the primary inspiration for putting this volume together.

Integral Theory in Service of Enacting Integral Education: Illustrations from an Online Graduate Program
  Sean Esbjörn-Hargens, John F. Kennedy University

Earlier versions of this chapter appeared previously as:
Esbjörn-Hargens, S. (2006). Integral education by design: How integral theory informs teaching, learning, and curriculum in a graduate program. *ReVision: A Journal of Consciousness and Transformation, 28*(3), pp. 21–29.

and

Esbjörn-Hargens, S. (2007). Integral teacher, integral students, integral classroom: Applying integral theory to graduate education. *AQAL: Journal of Integral Theory and Practice.* 2(2), pp. 72–103.

The Complete Yoga: The Lineage of Integral Education
   Jim Ryan, California Institute of Integral Studies

Originally appeared in *ReVision: A Journal of Consciousness and Transformation*, Vol. 28 No. 2, pp. 24–28.

Integral Transformative Education: A Participatory Proposal
   Jorge Ferrer, Marina Romero, and Ramon Albareda, California Institute of Integral Studies

An earlier version of this chapter was originally published in *Journal of Transformative Education*, Vol. 3 No. 4, October 2005 pp. 1–22.

The Emergence and Characteristics of Integral Education

An Introduction

Sean Esbjörn-Hargens, Jonathan Reams,
and Olen Gunnlaugson

It is mid-morning in a college classroom with a view of the surrounding hills reflecting soft light into the otherwise stark room. The professor is aiming to help his students find their way through the various theories they have been exposed to over the last four weeks of this course. One young woman raises her hand and asks in earnest seriousness, "But which is the best theory?" He is stopped short in that moment. He realizes that he has projected a variety of assumptions about what these graduate students know and how they know it. Her question invites him to reflect on what is needed in order to help her learn, rather than simply teach what he knows. He proceeds to convey the benefits of relating to the strengths and limits of various theories rather than simply adopting any one of them. Even then he recognizes that there is so much implicit in what and how he is teaching. In particular, he is faintly aware of the range of worldviews that exist within the students in this classroom and feels the challenge of trying to create an educational space that is sensitive to and challenging of these various modes of understanding reality and our relationship to it. How does he simultaneously acknowledge her desire to have a single theory be the "best" one and to point out there are more complex ways of relating to the range of theories, frameworks, and approaches available to us.

Reflecting on that moment, he comes to realize how much he has been inspired by a notion of education that aims to integrate a wide variety of educational influences and perspectives. He also realizes that he is still early in the process of realizing the potential that such an integrative, or integral approach to education holds. Like many educators, he finds himself on a journey into a territory where the contours and landmarks are changing as the world around us changes. The maps he has for this journey are themselves in transition, as well as shaping the territory in the process. His desire to manifest an integral pedagogy has set him on a course that involves map-making in a landscape in flux, and finding good companions for the journey is important.

The book before you is the outgrowth of a three-year long conversation, and of gathering colleagues to share their ideas, reflections, and stories about integral education. As this landscape is still in its formative phases, our intent has been to introduce the emerging principles of integral education and the range of frameworks used to embody these principles. We also want to lay some groundwork for expanding the conversation in ways that convey our and the authors' particular views and relationship to integral education and integral studies.[1] After some deliberation, we chose to focus on exploring integral education within formal and informal contexts of higher education and adult education, in part because of our own professional settings but also from the shared recognition of the importance of bringing together the conversations and research of our colleagues. In addition to this focus we feel that this volume serves educators in other educational contexts such as outdoor education, the development of professional trainings, assessment of educational effectiveness in high schools, and overseas field courses.

Designations such as *alternative, holistic,* and *transformative* have been applied with increasing frequency to educational theories and practices in recent years. Thus there are a number of substantive approaches to education that find expression in contemporary schools, including those informed by the metaphysical perspectives of philosopher-sages like Rudolph Steiner (1965, 1967, 1983, 1997), Alfred North Whitehead (1929), Jiddu Krishnamurti (1912, 1953, 1974, 1975), and Sri Aurobindo.[2] There are also a growing number of schools along the entire spectrum of education (from elementary school programs to doctorate degrees) that provide various expressions of alternative education in action. These approaches are often referred to as *holistic* and are associated with the educational approaches of individuals like John Dewey (1975) and Maria Montessori (1916, 1965, 1973). Lastly, there are the *transformative learning* approaches connected to the research of Jack Mezirow (1978, 1990, 1991). Often, these approaches are contrasted with the more *mainstream, conventional,* or *traditional* forms of education, which tend to focus on the acquisition of knowledge, development of cognitive skills, and individual achievement. This division in educational approaches has many sources and a long history (Crain, 2000; Forbes, 2003; Miller, 1997).

To our thinking, these efforts indicate pathways and initiatives that are working toward actualizing valuable and timely ideals of education. While there is an acknowledged overlap between such approaches and what we present in this book, we feel that there are also important distinctions and points of departure that merit identification and further exploration.

Academic discourse on *integral* education has thus far been largely absent from mainstream educational literature, as well as from leading conferences and publications in holistic, transformative, and other modes of progressive education. In the last few years this has started to change through various seminars, conferences, and academic publications all focused on integral education (see below). These represent the diversity of thought and exploration fueling what we perceive as an emerging field. We are convinced that integral approaches to education will contribute to the field of education at large. We see a growing need for frameworks that can unpack and articulate better distinctions around a comprehensive range of pedagogical issues. These frameworks need to be able to hold a variety of tensions in a dynamic balance, as well as be inclusive of diverse ways of engaging in educational endeavors. There are a number of creative tensions that lie at the foundation of an integral approach to education such as adhering to traditions while also emancipating ourselves from their constraints; the study of established forms of discourse and thinking outside the proverbial box; specializing in disciplinary distinctions and building bridges across domains of study; and cultivating contemplative dispositions while rolling our sleeves up as we jump into action.[3]

Holding these tensions in mind, the goal of this volume is to offer an overview of the current landscape of integral education, pedagogy, and curriculum from a variety of perspectives coming from leading researchers and practitioners working in integral education. Our aim is to make this research more accessible to both academics and educators and we anticipate that the initial readership of this book will include academics, educators, consultants, students, and others with an existing interest in integral education. Our intention is for this book to act as a resource to serve broader communities of university educators who may not be aware of what an integral approach to education encompasses, yet are actively searching for innovative and comprehensive solutions to the educational challenges they face. We also look forward to the prospects of this book being adopted for curricula relating to innovative approaches to education. Finally, our hope is this volume will contribute to the further development of integral education as a field of study (as well as to other emerging integral approaches in and across other fields of theory-practice).

The Emergence of Integral Education

A number of self identified integral projects and initiatives have played an important role in preparing the soil for integral education to appear in different settings. A number of chapters present some of these projects, from nineteenth century initiatives to the ongoing 40-year history of the California Institute of Integral Studies. More recently, a variety of endeavors have surfaced that have taken an explicitly integral approach to education.

At the end of 2005 and in the beginning of 2006, *ReVision* published a two-part issue on integral education, from a primarily Aurobindoian perspective, entitled "Revisioning Higher Education."[4] In the fall of 2006 John F. Kennedy University began offering an accredited online graduate level certificate and a Master of Arts degree in Integral Theory, with an explicit commitment to principles of integral education.[5] In June of 2007 the *Journal of Integral Theory and Practice* (JITP) published a special issue devoted to integral education from a Wilberian perspective with applications and case studies aimed at character education, high schools, colleges, and graduate universities.[6] Since August of 2007 there has been an annual five-day seminar on integral education held on beautiful Whidbey Island in Washington State.[7] In August 2008 John F. Kennedy University hosted the inaugural biennial Integral Theory Conference, which showcased numerous presentations on integral education as well as panels with some key figures in the field.[8] Over the last few years a number of articles on integral education have been published in various academic journals. (In addition, there is currently a non-academic anthology on integral education in development focusing on a K-12 audience).

All of these initiatives together have contributed to a dynamic conversation and engaged exploration about the nature and potential of integral education. Our individual involvement with these efforts has fostered a desire to contribute further to the development of the field by putting together this anthology. We feel this volume is timely because there has been a growing interest in an integral approach to education as evidenced by these and other initiatives. Yet the field is still nascent, working to clarify its own boundaries and struggling to gain broader acceptance and legitimacy. These challenges are further complicated by the diversity of labels under which this approach has arisen around the world. Thus, our hope is that this collection of voices will help expand the ongoing conversation and offer inspiration to fuel new directions and research within this emerging field.

In particular, we aim to accomplish this objective through chapters that provide an overview of the historical context, examples of distinct approaches, and case studies as well as reflections on future directions for integral education. It is important to us to provide a volume that conveys a reflective process of emergence for the whole field so that integral education can grow to become more diverse without losing touch with an interest in establishing grounds for a greater basis of unity and shared vision. Thus, part of our inquiry has explored the characteristics that distinguish an integral approach from neighboring approaches with similar mandates (e.g., holistic approaches) as well as more conventional and mainstream approaches to education.

Characteristics of Integral Education

Integral education is an emerging field that draws broadly from an array of mainstream, alternative, and transdisciplinary sources of knowledge. As a result we are reluctant to posit a singular or overarching definition of integral education. Rather, we are interested in encouraging multiple, even contradictory approaches, to integral education. Such diversity is, we feel, essential to the deeper process of clarification and articulation of what lies at the heart of integral education. It also provides room for things to be permeable and messy. This diversity is not only reflected in the breadth of chapters presented, but also emerges from the range of views and experiences we as editors bring to the process. Our dialogue as editors, and those with our authors, has helped to identify key characteristics common to many self-identified as well as parallel integral approaches to integral education. Thus, we have identified a number of foci, commitments, or elements that enact integral education. These include the following:

- *Exploring multiple perspectives*: Our view of integral education is that it avoids splitting complex issues into simple binaries; paradox, contradiction, polarity, multiplicity, and dialectics are invited, cultivated, and embraced. Reality is multidimensional and as a result we need to include the insights and truths from myriad perspectives as they all have something to offer a more complete understanding of any topic or phenomena. This integrative process often does not lend itself to (re)presenting a clean well-organized single reality.

- *Including first-, second-, and third-person methodologies of learning and teaching*: We recognize the simultaneity of subjective, intersubjective, and objective aspects of reality and the need to make contact with these aspects with domain appropriate injunctions and criteria. Thus, combining learning modes like artistic expression, participatory inquiry, and empirical analysis is commonplace in integral education.

- *Weaving together the domains of self, culture, and nature:* Our experience has led us to valuing how these respective areas fit together and can be integrated. These three domains serve as an integral checks and balances system that minimizes excess in any particular area.

- *Combining critical thinking with experiential feeling:* Every action has an explicit or more often implicit logic behind it. These logics are affective as well as cognitive, requiring a commitment to intellectual rigor and the grounding of such rigor in direct knowing and embodied experience. Thus, an ongoing effort is made to ground conceptual distinctions within our lived experience and shared resonance with others.

- *Including the insights from constructive-developmental psychology:* We see a central role for developmental approaches that recognizes that individuals—students and teachers—are at different stages of growth in their personal and educational journeys. The more we can inform our classrooms by these insights the more contexts we can provide to engage with this vital transformative potential.

- *Engaging regular personal practices of transformation:* We can each engage in various practices to participate in our own "interior" growth allowing us to embody more perspectives through various practices of "body, mind, and spirit." There are all kinds of informal and formal techniques for exercising our embodiment, awareness, and presence—the more we develop each of these the more open we are to learning.

- *Including multiple ways of knowing:* We recognize that not only do we all develop, but also we develop along multiple pathways of being (e.g., cognitive, emotional, moral, kinesthetic, transpersonal). Each of these pathways provides us with a distinctive way of knowing and learning that is irreducible and therefore needs to be honored on its own terms and included as fully as possible. This includes a multidimensional view of humans that honors body, heart, mind, soul, and spirit.

- *Recognizing various types of learners and teachers:* The comprehensive nature of an integral approach also embraces the complexity that various typologies add to the picture. Issues of learning styles, personality types, pedagogical styles and more lead us to be aware of the need to appeal to multiple modes of learning and expression.

- *Encouraging "shadow work" within learners and teachers:* We also have learned the importance of students and teachers becoming more self-reflective and increasingly aware of their trigger points—what makes us reactive, dismissive, or shut down to ideas and other people. By learning to look at what we do not want to see in ourselves (and others) we become more compassionate and open to learning. This is an ongoing process of owning our projections, minimizing idealization, avoiding the tendency to split things into good and bad, catching ourselves when we are rationalizing away our responsibility and so forth.

- *Honoring other approaches to education:* We feel that one of the attributes of integral education is that it is committed to being knowledgeable about the strengths and limits of conventional, alternative, holistic, and transformative approaches to education. Each of these approaches has valuable contributions to make toward a more integral approach.

These ten characteristics represent some of the central features of our present understanding of integral education. They are neither mutually exclusive nor exhaustive. Different approaches to education in general and integral education in particular interface with this list in a variety of ways: some adhere to all of them, some emphasize various characteristics more than others, and some only illustrate a few of these. Nevertheless, these characteristics offer a provisional overview of the distinct elements that characterize educational approaches as *integral*. In calling attention to these characteristics, our interest is also to further distinguish integral education from neighboring approaches such as holistic education. While holistic approaches may share a number of the characteristics above, there are important differences, which this book hopes to further clarify. In inviting authors to contribute to this book, we encouraged them to reflect on and introduce new distinctions relevant to integral education that they feel optimally serves their objectives and experience.

Overview of the Book

The opening section of this volume provides a background on the development of the early initiatives in integral education, tracing historical roots and emergent branches. Next we focus on the theoretical foundations and distinct approaches of integral education, including; *integral pedagogy* (perspectives on the process of learning/education); *integral curriculum* (perspectives on the implications for teacher education and course design); and modes of *integral learning and inquiry* (explorations of the role of transformation and development). We then proceed to showcase applications of integral education, addressing case studies within post-secondary settings including online education. Finally, we include chapters that address the hopes and concerns for establishing integral education as a field, specific educational implications, and methods of assessment for integral approaches and research, followed by exploratory perspectives on the future of integral education.

Section I: Historical Contexts

Integral education is informed by a rich variety of historical sources. The most common historical association is with India's philosopher-sage Sri Aurobindo (1872–1950). While this is an important association, our aim in this section is to situate integral education within a broader historical context. In acknowledging the myriad historical currents feeding into integral education, we feel that a richer conversation can emerge that will help carry integral education into our present moment and beyond.

Gary Hampson opens this section with *Western Islamic and Native American Geneaologies of Integral Education*. In this chapter he unpacks a range of meanings of the term integral and applies a scholarship of integration to reveal the deeper historical roots underlying integral education. After a brief exploration of Amerindian notions of integral education, he traces a lineage of educational thought and practice beginning with Plato's Academy, through the Islamic Aristotelian and Medieval renaissances, and into the Italian and German Neoplatonic renaissances. He concludes by describing how this lineage relates to current higher educational practices as presented in the rest of this volume.

Next Hampson joins Markus Molz in the combined contribution *Elements of the Underacknowledged History of Integral Education*. In this chapter they begin by picking up the thread at the stage where explicit use of the term integral education came about. They have uncovered a series of educational ventures from the mid-nineteenth to early twentieth centuries that took the ideas and ideals of integral thought and created educational systems, practices, and schools that were innovative and in many cases left a lasting impact on a wider strand of educational practice.

We conclude this section with an chapter by Jim Ryan, *The Complete Yoga: Lineage of Integral Education*. Ryan presents the educational vision of Haridas Chaudhuri and its roots in Sri Aurobindo's *integral yoga*. He outlines the three features of Chaudhuri's approach and how these are illustrative of the ideals of the California Institute of Integral Studies. In doing this Ryan provides us with an important window into one of the most influential historical streams of integral education.

Section II: Distinct Approaches

There are a number of different integral approaches to education available today, such as those inspired by; Sri Aurobindo's metaphysics and integral psychology (e.g., The California Institute of Integral Studies), Ken Wilber's Integral model (e.g., the Department of Integral Theory at John F. Kennedy University), Rudolf Steiner's esoteric philosophy (e.g., the Waldorf education system), and William Torbert's developmental action inquiry (e.g., the Department of Organizational Transformation at Boston College). Each of these competing and complementary approaches is an important part of the emerging conversation of what traditions have constituted and are presently informing integral education.

In this section we showcase several of the well-known approaches (mentioned above) as well as some emerging ones. We begin with Sean Esbjörn-Hargens' *Integral Theory in Service of Enacting Integral Education: Illustrations from an Online Graduate Program*. In this chapter, he presents both a general overview of integral education based on the five elements of the AQAL model and a specific case study of a graduate level program based on and in Integral Theory. In seeking to articulate both general principles and concrete details of integral education, he has sought to give voice to an Integral approach that is robust enough to withstand the rigor of graduate and postgraduate level research while also being adaptable to the demands of different fields of study across the education spectrum.

In *Integral Transformative Education: A Participatory Proposal* Jorge Ferrer, Marina Romero, and Ramon Albareda provide an introduction to their participatory model of integral transformative education. This approach draws from all human dimensions: body, vital, heart, mind, and spirit within a process of inquiry and integration. They outline two additional approaches to integral education in order to draw a contrast with their own proposal, which is symbolized by the "integral creative cycle" of the four seasons. They conclude by outlining five basic features of integral education and then go forward to explore the challenges and prospects of such a participatory approach.

Next, Erica Steckler and William R. Torbert provide an overview of an approach to integral education based on action research in *A "Developmental Action Inquiry" Approach to Teaching First-, Second-, and Third-Person Action Research Methods*. Steckler and Torbert present us with a wonderful examination of the application of decades of research into a developmental action inquiry approach to education. Through describing three detailed incidents in Torbert's Action Research Methods PhD course, they illustrate how first-, second-, and third-person action and inquiry can interweave to generate single-, double-, and triple-loop feedback that can cultivate real-time awarenesses in both researchers and leaders.

In *Teaching Integratively: Five Dimensions of Transformation*, Roben Torosyan looks deeply into the question of what it means to teach integratively. He examines Lauer's five dimensions of living and learning and draws out novel comparisons with other leading developmental models to help learners consider multiple perspectives and apply learning concretely to personal, professional and civic life alike through various applied examples.

Concluding this section, Matthew Bronson and Ashok Gangadean team up in *Encountering the (W)hole: Integral Education as Deep Dialogue and Cultural Medicine*. Here they model "deep dialogue" through a notation system that Gangadean has developed and uses to explore integral themes of educational inquiry. Their approach combines global philosophy and linguistic investigation in service of meta-cognition. In the process, they surface a number of considerations and cautions around any integral endeavor.

Section III: Case Studies

Having presented five distinct approaches to integral education we now turn our attention to more explicit applications of integral principles to education. In this section we have seven case studies, which explore integral education in a number of contexts: online, non-academic, contemplative, assessment, science, and health. We begin with Ed Sarath's *Jazz, Creativity, and Consciousness: A Blueprint for Integral Education*. Sarath recounts an emergent model of integral curriculum that was central to a program he developed in Jazz and Contemplative Studies at the University of Michigan. His chapter explores the implications for embracing epistemological diversity—that is, first-, second-, and third-person perspectives on meditation, improvisation, and coursework and how this enriched view has brought about a more integral expression of jazz education.

Next, in *Grounding Integral Theory in the Field of Experience*, Terri O'Fallon presents a case study of the application of integral thought at *Pacific Integral*, a graduate-level professional leadership development program near Seattle, Washington. The article showcases the deep learning behind the task of embodying integral principles and theories and how they led to insights concerning the relationship between state-stages and structure-stages of development. The chapter illustrates the transformative potential in working with key principles of integral education within a cohort group of professionals.

Then, Moshe Renert and Brent Davis present their work in *An Open Way of Being: Integral Reconceptualization of Mathematics for Teaching*. They use an Integral framework to analyze past and current research of mathematics for teaching and contend that Wilber's Integral Methodological Pluralism is a suitable methodology for investigating the multiple layers and potentialities of this complex human activity. They conclude by discussing some of the implications for teacher education entailed by an integral reconceptualization of *mathematics for teaching*.

In *Written in "Three Voices:" A Turn Toward Integral Education*, Irene Karpiak explores the pedagogical significance of integrating the objective, subjective, and intersubjective dimensions of integral education and development in her writing courses at University of Oklahoma. Karpiak structures these three perspectives through the voices of the Artist, Scientist, and Philosopher and provides examples of how her students practice related writing exercises as a means for promoting integration within their understanding of course content and their development as writers.

Next, Joel Kreisberg takes us into one of his courses through *Integral Education, Integral Transformation, and the Teaching of Mind-Body Medicine*. In this chapter, Kreisberg presents how he has used three different integral formats to engage students in embodied learning of mind-body medicine: Murphy and Leonard's Integral Transformative Practice, Dacher's Integral Health Assessment, and Wilber's Integral Life Practice. Through these frameworks, students explore their own psychological and physical well-being directly through first-, second-, and third-person perspectives. Kreisberg's resulting assessments provide educators with a number of considerations for using similar frameworks in their own classrooms.

In *Matching Educational Intentions with Assessment: Using an Integral Map*, Nancy Davis takes one aspect of Wilber's AQAL framework, the quadrants, and describes how it has helped her and others she works with to disentangle various complex and even unrecognized issues in assessment. Her chapter shows how this can connect educational intentions with appropriate assessment strategies and methods through learning to ask the right questions in the right contexts.

Then in *Expanding our Vision in the Teaching and Design of University Science,—Coming to Know our Students*, Sue Stack narrates us through an examination of reforming physics teaching in Tasmania, Australia. Stack's stories and reflections reveal the deep, complex, and multi-layered challenges being faced. By focusing on a few incidents, she allows us to feel into the depth of thought and capacity required to begin figuring out how to support such educational reforms in the systems and people we work with.

Section IV: Looking Ahead

In our last section, we have a number of chapters that speak to various considerations practitioners of integral education will want to be cognizant of as the field continues to emerge. The chapters in this section provide a unique perspective on the nascent field of integral education and establish possible directions for the field to take in the years ahead.

The first chapter is Katie Heikkinen's *Integral Mind, Brain, and Education*. In this chapter, Heikkinen presents how the emerging field of Mind, Brain, and Education can benefit from an Integral approach. She uses Wilber's Integral model as a comprehensive framework to support this new field in its goals of exploring the connections between educational, biological, and psychological sciences. In particular, she draws on Integral Methodological Pluralism to illustrate the relationship between various research approaches and the classroom.

Next, Carissa Wieler presents her *Embodying Integral Education in Five Dimensions*. In this chapter she draws on a number of educational contexts—formal and informal—to reflect on some of the key components of integral education. She takes us on a multi-layered journey of her own inquiry into the nature of being an integral student. The questions she raises and the insights she obtains along the way serve to invite us into our own exploration of all things integral, asking ourselves "am I fully engaged in my own learning?"

Then in *Opening Up the Path of Integral Education*, Olen Gunnlaugson reflects upon his previous integral assessment of the former holistic approach that guided *Holma College of Holistic Studies* in Sweden from 1996 to 2001. He revisits the integral perspective that emerged during the transition year to *Holma College of Integral Studies* in 2002–2003 and addresses the shortcomings and learning of this implementation phase. He then closes with questions and considerations for the development of future integral educational initiatives.

Next, Markus Molz's *Contemporary Integral Education Research: A Transnational and Transparadigmatic Overview* surveys a great portion of current strands of integral education, focusing on European researchers and practitioners. This takes the previous historical thread in the opening chapters and brings it into the current day, revealing the breadth of work going on within the notion of integral education and parallel developments. His contribution can serve as a nexus, linking likeminded theorists and practitioners and raising our vision of how integral education currently exists to a significantly broader horizon.

In *Spirituality and Integral Thought in Higher Education*, Jonathan Reams asks respected educational researcher Alexander "Sandy" Astin to reflect on his long career in relation to integral approaches. In this conversation, Astin surveys a number of forces at work in higher education in America today and how their trajectory opens up the potential for higher education to move into a more explicitly integral direction. In addition, he discusses his recent research project on spirituality in higher education, and how the findings emerging lend further support for the principles of education that an integral approach brings.

Last we have Jennifer Gidley's *Evolving Higher Education Integrally: Delicate Mandalic Theorizing*. In this piece, Gidley presents a display of integral thought from her long research into understanding the core elements of an integral approach to higher education. She briefly describes two dimensions through which integral education theory could be broadened and deepened, the temporal and spatial, and then goes into depth around a third, the pedagogical. She identifies four core pedagogical values—love, life, wisdom, and voice—and shows how they enable theoretic coherence to emerge between a unitive centre and the pluralism of the periphery.

Coda/Afterword: Concluding Meta-Reflections

We conclude our introduction with a few words from our own meta-reflections on the volume as a whole. Our intention here is to pull together several of the threads that emerged throughout this volume and point to some of the key areas facing integral education that remain to be explored. We also wish to leave you with some thoughts for moving through the volume.

First, we want to direct your attention to some of the meta-issues that we feel will be central to the development and evolution of integral education as an academic field within higher education. One of these challenges is how integral education as a *field of study* will require the careful unpacking of relationships between what can at times be casually held and often enmeshed understandings of integral as; a theory, a meta-theory, a model, or a meta-framework (i.e., AQAL). A prime example of this involves challenges posed by the evolving relationships between the work of Ken Wilber and other theorists who have either developed integral ideas of education in parallel or built upon his work.

A second challenge revolves around what we feel to be a primary distinguishing factor between holistic and integral education—the exploration of how best to work with developmental models and theory in a classroom setting. How can we engage multiple perspectives in order to build bridges from where students are and how they think to their next steps? What kinds of tensions exist between our desire to tell students all we know and their desire to learn what they feel they need?

The third challenge we perceive is about integral injunctions—actual individual and group practices for educators and students. In other words, how can any or all of this be put into practice? What kinds of limitations do we encounter in doing this, as well as in the concepts themselves?

Finally, we wish to leave you with a couple ideas for being mindful of the process involved in engaging an anthology like this. First, we recognize that it can be challenging to absorb and digest the contents of such a volume. Given this, what does it take to move through the process of encountering new perspectives, wrestling with them, taking in parts that resonate while holding a critical stance to others, to practice, experimentation, and moving toward embodiment? How can you as a reader support yourself through what this book stimulates? Second, it is clear to us that as an emerging field, integral education has no simple definitions, clear prescriptions or 10 easy steps to follow. How can you draw from the various chapters here and add your voice to the growing conversation of sorting out how we can better serve the deep callings that motivate us as educators? With that in mind, we invite you to dig in and explore these *new directions for higher learning*!

Notes

1. Throughout this volume we use *integral studies* to refer to the broad field of integral thought that includes both established and emerging approaches. We will allow the context of each article to determine if *integral* is being used in a general or in a particular sense (e.g., Wilberian). In alignment with the style guide of this series we have chosen to use "Integral Theory" (with capitalization) to designate a Wilberian usage. Likewise we will be capitalizing "Integral" when the usage is Wilberian and paired with terms like "Integral model," "Integral approach," and "Integral map." This is because Ken Wilber has explicitly named his body of work "Integral Theory" and many authors in this volume predominately use these terms in this way.

However, we still feel that "integral theory" (without capitalization) is a legitimate usage to refer to a more generic collection of theories, models, and ideas that are "integral" in focus. Nevertheless, in this volume we will be using "integral studies" to signify the broad field of integral thought that includes well established as well as emergent approaches. Furthermore, our usage of "Integral Theory" (with capitalization) should be read in a broad Wilberian sense to mean beyond Wilber but anchored in the AQAL model he has developed and its associated distinctions.

We want to avoid a Wilber-centric discourse for a number of reasons. Toward this end, in Chapter 3 by Jim Ryan, we have retained his capitalization of the Aurobindoian terms "Integral," "Integral Philosophy," "Integral Yoga," and "Integralists." We do this to acknowledge the Aurobindoian tendency to also capitalize "integral" in these sorts of ways and to serve as a counter balance to a Wilber-only standard of capitalization. For us the academic value of using capitalization in this way is to signify a specific usage of "integral" that refers to a particular corpus of theorizing and application.

It is important to us to support a plurality of integral streams of thought, especially in a dynamic new field like integral education. Thus, throughout this book we will not be capitalizing "integral education" even when used in an Aurobindoian or Wilberian context since this volume is explicitly using "integral education" in a broad way that includes these contributions but is not constrained by them.

2. It is worth noting that there are at least three different books with the title "Integral Education" coming out of the Aurobindoian context. The first one is a short book, less than 100 pages, that was published in 1952 and compiled by Indra Sen entitled *Integral Education: In the Words of Sri Aurobindo and the Mother Selected from their Writings.* Thirty-five years later Raghunath Pani published *Integral Education: Thought and Practice* (1987). This is a comprehensive study (over 600 pages) comparing the National education policies of India with Sri Aurobindo's contemplative approach. Most recently, Partho (2007) has published *Integral Education: A Foundation for the Future.* Partho describes the intent of this volume as providing "a personal Aurobindonian critique of integral education and not to present Sri Aurobindo or [the] Mother's thoughts on integral education" (p. xvi).

3. For a more detailed description of these distinctions see Murray, 2009.

4. These two issues contained twelve articles, seven of which used "integral education" in their titles. This collection (guest edited by Matthew Bronson) showcased a variety of considerations and approaches to integral education (especially the Aurobindoian perspective). Three of the articles published in this two-part issue have been revised and published here.

5. In addition to these online offerings, JFKU has offered a Master of Arts in Integral Psychology on campus since 2002, which is based on Sri Aurobindo's Integral Yoga and Wilber's Integral Theory. In addition, JFKU is now offering an integral psychotherapy track in their counseling program. JFKU currently has around a dozen core faculty and another dozen adjunct faculty who are exploring themes and issues related to integral education. Through its academic programs, hosting the biennial Integral Theory Conference, and housing the Integral Research Center, which is conducting original longitudinal integral research on education effectiveness, JFKU is currently playing a formative role in exploring, implementing, and enacting integral education at the graduate level.

6. The seven articles in the issue are arranged in a chronological order based on the age group each author-educator teaches. Thus, as you move through the issue, you can experience the full range of application of an Integral approach to education: moving from the character education of elementary and middle school to the homerooms of high school to the majors of undergraduate campuses and the professional preparation of graduate universities.

7. The annual seminar is organized by *Next Step Integral.* Each year there are over 40 attendees, over half of which are educators who present their insights on innovative ways to approach integral teaching and learning.

8. At the 2008 conference there were 16 presentations on integral education, many which had important implications or contributions to the conversation on integral education. Also there was a panel devoted to exploring education from an integral perspective and one devoted to the relationship between Integral Theory and academics. With over 500 people in attendance most of whom are involved with education or academics in some form (e.g.,

of the 100 presenters 75 of them had terminal degrees), this became an important event for integral educators.

References

Bronson, M. (Ed.). (2005-2006). Revisioning higher education parts 1 & 2. *ReVision* 28(2–3).

Crain, W. (2000). *Theories of development* (5th ed.). Upper Saddle River, NJ: Prentice Hall.

Dewey, J. (1975). *Experience and education.* New York: Macmillan.

Forbes, S. (2003). *Holistic education: An analysis of its ideas and nature.* Brandon, VT: Foundation for Educational Renewal.

Krishnamurti, J. (1912). *Education as service.* Adyar, Madras: Theosophical Publishing Society.

Krishnamurti, J. (1953). *Education and the significance of life.* New York: Harper & Brothers.

Krishnamurti, J. (1974). *On education.* Pondicherry, India: All India Press.

Krishnamurti, J. (1975). *Dialogue on education.* Ojai, CA: Ojai Press.

Mezirow, J. (1978). *Education for perspective transformation: Women re-entry programs in community college.* New York: Center for Adult Education, Teachers College, Columbia University.

Mezirow, J. (1990). *Fostering critical reflection in adulthood: A guide to transformative and emancipatory learning.* San Francisco: Jossey-Bass.

Mezirow, J. (1991). *Transformative dimensions of adult learning.* San Francisco: Jossey-Bass.

Miller, R. (1997). *What are schools for? Holistic education in American culture* (3rd ed.). Brandon, VT: Holistic Education Press.

Montessori, M. (1964). *The Montessori method.* New York: Schocken Books. (Original work published 1916).

Montessori, M. (1965). *Dr. Montessori's own handbook* (1st ed.). New York: Schocken Books.

Montessori, M. (1973). *The absorbent mind.* Madras: Kalakshetra.

Murray, T. (2009). What is the integral in integral education? From progressive pedagogy to integral pedagogy. *Integral Review,* 5(1) 96–134.

Pani, R. (1987). *Integral education: Thought and practice.* New Delhi: Ashish Publishing House.

Partho. (2007). *Integral education: A foundation for the future.* New Delhi: Sri Aurobindo Society.

Sen, I. (Ed.). (1952). *Integral education: In the words of Sri Aurobindo and the Mother selected from their writings.* Pondicherry, India: Sri Aurobindo International University Centre.

Steiner, R. (1965). *The education of the child in light of anthroposophy.* London: Rudolf Steiner Press.

Steiner, R. (1967). *Discussions with teachers.* London: Rudolf Steiner Press.

Steiner, R. (1983). *The essentials of education* (J. Darrell, Trans.). London: Rudolf Steiner Press.

Steiner, R. (1997). *The roots of education.* Hudson, NY: Anthroposophic Press.

Whitehead, A. N. (1967). *The aims of education.* New York: The Free Press. (Original work published 1929).

I

Historical Context

Western-Islamic and Native American Genealogies of Integral Education

Gary P. Hampson

> Through the power of its music, through the dialectic of its juxtapositions, through the pressure of its metaphors, through the variety of its registers the [new] poetry comes to enunciate its meanings.
>
> —Abbs, 2003, p. 108

Introduction

What apt meanings or identifications can be given to *integral education*?[1] To address this question one might imagine a dimension of semantic possibilities ranging from the contracted to the expansive. The former might involve (i) restriction to integrative notions arising from the lineage of one author such as Aurobindo or Wilber; (ii) restriction to explicit usage of the term *integral* itself—thus for instance including Bakunin, Maritain (Molz & Hampson, current volume), Soloviev, Sorokin and Kremer (1996) but excluding pre-1997 Wilber and various holistic educators and; or (iii) restriction to a default, loosely pragmatic, cluster of ideas where identification might be made more in relation to, say, the signifier *holistic* than *anarchist*, *Catholic*, or *indigenous*. Such contracted interpretations could be understood as pertaining to a modern worldview which de facto moves toward prosaic, instrumental closure of the literal and/or conventional (regardless of discursive use of such terms as "integral" or "postconventional")[2]—an *economical* perspective (in deference at least to Occam's razor) on what could potentially be usefully true or appropriate. Such interpretations no doubt have validity for certain contexts. However, given the heterogeneity of both the use of the term and also that potentially signified by such uses, explorations involving more *expansive* accounts would appear to be in order.

The current chapter (as with the theorizing in this volume of, for instance Gidley and Molz) offers such a narrative, one aptly understood in relation to Boyer's (1990) "scholarship of integration," in this instance specifically regarding a postformal approach to integral theorizing (Hampson, 2007) through which a more radically "poetic" invitation toward integral/education is enabled. This invitation can be seen to facilitate a form of "deep dialogue" (Bronson and Gangadean, current volume) regarding integral education theorizing via the algorithmic metaphor "integral *as x*" (e.g., "integral as synthesis of spirit and reason"), whilst re-prioritising integral's etymological foundation of "pertaining to a whole"—"an integral *x*" (e.g., "an integral education"); noting differentiation from the non-specialised usage regarding its sister denotation, "*of* a whole"—"integral *to x*" (e.g., "creativity is integral to a good education"). Through the post-Wilberian notion of *types* of integral,[3] and through extending the postformal (metaphoric) template of *thinking ecologically* (Hampson, 2007), the notion of an ecology of integrals (Hampson, 2007) (or "an integration of integral views"—Gidley, 2007b) can be further elaborated and applied. This allows for both a geographical variety of integral education "noetic ecosystems" across cultures, and also historical depth—or genealogy—for each ecosystem (noting that such evolution may be marked variously by growth, disjunctures, stabilities, complexities). Such a genealogical configuration may be seen as forming a complex relation to that integral theorizing which involves non-complex models of socio-cultural development (such as non-interpenetrating configurations of *traditional-modern-postmodern*).[4] Cross-pollination (among other relationships) may not only be seen within such ecosystems, but also between them, such as the Indian-Western case of Aurobindo. Moreover, the notion of integral itself can be understood as a noetic ecology (*integral as involving a particular set of dimensions and their interrelationships*), thus the entire picture can be seen as a holarchical one, where holarchy is interpreted by way of Koestler's (1967) original understanding rather than Wilber's (1995) less heterogeneous variation.

From this theoretical orientation, two case studies (one minor, one major) are explored. The minor elucidation is that of the ecology of Native American (Indigenous American or Amerindian) integral education; the major, a genealogical identification of Western-Islamic integral education up to the early nineteenth century (for later developments, see Molz & Hampson, Molz, and Gidley, current volume). "Western" and "Islamic" are cohered here because Western education has been intimately woven not only from Greek and Roman culture but also through Classical Islam. Regarding the university, for instance, Islam scholar George Makdisi identifies no less than "eighteen substantial affinities between the Islamic and the occidental patterns of the organization of learning and their transmission through institutional arrangements" (Rüegg, 1992, p. 8); in short, "the Muslim university (*madrasa*) was the archetype for the European university (*studium general*)" (Hilgendorf, 2003, p. 67). Although Western-Islamic and Amerindian integral educations arise from different genealogies, interesting synergies or harmonics can be seen between the two. Regarding Western-Islamic integral education, a schema of types of academic thought is posited including two integrally-identified *evolving* types, namely, Neoplatonism and Aristotelianism. These are interpreted as broad attractors rather than containers, thus encompassing such major "varieties" as Hermetic Neoplatonism and Thomist Aristotelianism; the narrative thence explores the *intertwined* genealogy of Neoplatonic and Aristotelian integral education. It is noteworthy that the following integral authors have all been identified as Neoplatonic: Steiner (Gidley, 2007a), Aurobindo (Mayer, 2002), Gebser (Combs, 2005), Wilber (Kealey, 2002), Gangadean (Klostermaier, 1997), and Laszlo (Abraham, 2006). In this way, a historical grounding is given to the discourse, one indicating a rich spiritual-philosophical heritage, a living ecosystem with both agentic singularity and healthy noetic diversity.

Native American Ecology of Integral Education

Gregory Cajete (1994), a Tewa from Santo Clara Pueblo, founding Director of the Institute of American Indian Arts and Associate Professor of Education at the University of New Mexico, presents a compelling account of Amerindian education philosophy, one he describes as "an ecology." In relation to educational discourse, I present a reading of his theoretical contribution—an exemplar of "the fecundity of the individual case" (Jardine, 1998)—as follows.

Somewhat analogous to Ancient Greek *paideia* (see *Antiquarian Origins* below), the purpose of Indigenous American education involves attaining knowledge, seeking truth, and developing wisdom and completeness. A key understanding is *mitakuye oyasin*: a Lakota phrase meaning we are all related. In service of Life, it is founded on a set of principles, theoretically formulated by way of interpenetrating conceptual maps. A core map involves four quadrants around a central region, with an area below and one above. The four quadrants are the "cardinal orientations of indigenous creativity" (Cajete, 1994, p. 158), oriented toward Artist/Poet (illumination, insight), Philosopher/Teacher (preparation, immersion), Shaman/Priest (incubation), and Warrior/Hunter (evaluation), respectively. These four involve such disciplines as theology, philosophy, depth psychology, social psychology, human ecology, ecosophy, biology, and herbology. The center is "the place of emergence" comprising "the nature and dynamic expression of creative thought as expressed in the arts and sciences" (p. 203). Below are the geosciences; above, cosmology and astronomy. Foundational characteristics include:

1. *Interconnectivity*—including that between: inner and outer; individual and collective; nature and cosmos; science, art, and spirituality; environmental, human, and noetic ecologies;

2. *Vertical depth*—in terms of both developmental levels and semantic holarchies;

3. *Art and language as expressions of the soul*—"art as a way of wholeness, creativity, and orientation" (p. 158) for "identity and aesthetics" (p. 182); the sacredness and power of language and thought; and

4. *Respect for diversity among individuals, cultures, and species*—including the authenticating of the sanctity of each person's unique singularity, and resultant social contribution.

Capturing a postformal understanding, Cajete notes that "each foundation of Tribal education is exquisitely complex" (p. 39) partly in that they contain each other and operate in reference to a context-dependent dynamic harmony which sometimes involves considerable disturbances—a "tearing apart" or "wounding"—for further development or evolution. Regarding pedagogy—both "informal" and "formal"—Cajete identifies a plethora of features including "facilitating human potential through creative transformation" (p. 27) via an organic series of developmental stages to levels beyond ego, and "the integration of mind, body, and spirit through a dynamic and complex set of activities" (p. 82) involving a valuing of the heart and the body (embodiment through knowledge-action nexuses including work and sport). He also substantively addresses ethics and morality, critical thinking, holonymy, a Goethe-like "cultivation of all one's senses" (p. 33), and narrative methodologies. Further, he examines the complex inner-outer complementarity of teaching and learning where the former in part comprises a context-dependent "communicative art" attendant to *readiness to learn*, whilst the latter involves "subtle, yet deeply rooted, universals" (p. 30). Finally, he uses an organic approach involving a dialectic between learning and surrender such that busyness for its own sake does not constitute effective learning. To call upon the words of integral education theorist, Jennifer Gidley (2007b): "There are indigenous and traditional people on every continent who may know more than modernist western science can imagine" (p. 198–9); "this is not a regressive romantic plea. . . . It is a conscious integral philosophic stance towards a new cosmopolitanism" (p. 199). Building upon this—and, in so doing, problematizing *simplistic* phylogenetic notions—the above account surely opens up the fruitfulness of exploring the stronger metaphor of *integral as indigenous*.

Western-Islamic Genealogy of Integral Education

Regarding Western-Islamic integral and integral education, the terms[5] have been variously configured by different authors at least since the early nineteenth century, including Fourier's 1829 harmonic education (Molz & Hampson, current volume).

Similarly, Russian scholar John Randolph (2007) identifies that Nikolai Stankevich, originator of the 1830s Stankevich Circle in Moscow—from which sprang the "Westerner" (anarchist-idealist) and "Slavophile" (*sobornost*-idealist) nineteenth-century Russian integral groupings—was a "system-builder" (p. 178), "attempting to work out an 'integral worldview' (*tselostnoe mirovozzrenie*)" (p. 178, n. 13). But from where do such interpretations of integral as these arise? Historian Charles Taylor provides an important clue in his work on Hegel and other German humanists. He identifies Friedrich Hölderlin's philosophizing, for instance, as involving a dialectic between Kantian subject and Spinozist substance, "the two ideals of radical freedom and integral expression" (Taylor, 1979, p. 8). Elsewhere he refers to the "… integral realization of reason" (Taylor, 1979, p. 102) as an attractor beyond utilitarianism, whilst "integral truth" is used in relation to Hegel's Idea which simultaneously involves self-knowledge and self-creation, "both knowledge of itself as other; and also realization of itself as something independent of itself" (Taylor, 1975, p. 335). Such examples point to the identification of integral as pertaining to the late eighteenth- and early nineteenth-century nexus of German humanistic philosophy, a nexus itself capable of being identified as (Hermetic) Neoplatonic in its broadest sense (see, e.g., Magee, 2001). *Integral as Neoplatonic* is thus enabled, indicating the antiquarian "origin" of integral education.

Simultaneously, another antiquarian integral stream may be identified: *integral as Aristotelian*. The comprehensiveness and logical consistency of Aristotle's "complex and multifaceted" systematic cosmology—a "synthesis of his many predecessors' insights" (Tarnas, 1991, p. 64) includes address of transcendence and immanence, the construction of noetic ecologies of both substance and causation, and the seeding of developmentalism. Manifestations of Aristotelianism comprise (secular Islamic) Avicennist and Averroesian, and (Christian) Thomist Aristotelianisms, the last (Aristotle's works as interpreted by Aquinas in the thirteenth century) being carried primarily by Catholicism, as exemplified by Jacques Maritain's early twentieth century integral education (Molz & Hampson, current volume). This accords with the general signification of "integral" in Catholic discourse as pertaining to Aquinas—see, e.g., Jeffries (1999).

The interweaving streams of Neoplatonism and Aristotelianism can be understood in relation to an integrative schema (itself potentially identified as integral theorizing) involving four types of academic thought through history. The other two are comprised of *atomist-technicist-empirical* (partly corresponding to a characterization of nineteenth century Anglophone "science") and *contingent* (partly corresponding to a characterization of what is conventionally understood as the arts and humanities). Space does not permit here an in-depth discussion of this schema (adapted from Schmidt-Biggermann, 1996); nonetheless, mention should be made both of the overlapping nature of Neoplatonic and Aristotelian integrals and also of their apt inclusion of features of the other two streams. The significance of contingent history, for example, is implicit in the current chapter (and, e.g., valorized by Aurobindo 2003, p. 361). Indeed, interest in the history of ideas is a Neoplatonic one (see below). Given that Aristotelian and Neoplatonic themes figure strongly in the history of Western education—particularly that of the university and academy—a rich account of this branch of integral education can be narrated, one involving a series of renaissances—Islamic Aristotelian (c. 9th century); European Aristotelian (12th century); Italian Neoplatonic (15th century); and German Neoplatonic (18th century). Given the poetry of this three-century cycle, one wonders what the twenty-first century holds.

Antiquarian Origins

In the fourth century BCE, Plato's Akademia offered a *paideia* (a term and theme which was to reappear in different guises through history such as *encyclopaedia* signifying a *paedia* pertaining to the whole)—a "liberal" cultural and moral education (for the ideal citizenship of free men)—comprising gymnastics, music, and grammar until age 20; science as arithmetic, geometry, astronomy, and musical harmony (ages 20–30); and philosophy (30–35) (Abelson, 1906, p. 2). Although Plato's pupil, Aristotle, devised a somewhat different philosophy, his (albeit less hallowed) Lyceum (also known as *the peripatetic school of philosophers*) was similar to Plato's Academy (Abelson, 1906, p. 2), although it was "more inclined to lectures and instruction than to discussion" (Kyle, 1993, p. 82) and also "was the first to make a collection of books for his school" (Kyle, 1993, p. 82)—a library—thus seeding the self-sufficient educational facility (Kyle, 1993). Both schools were regarded at the time as more complete than the basic Greek education of gymnastics and music. Heralding the quasi-autonomous socio-noetic location of *academia as (relatively) beyond the melée of ordinary discourse* (a location currently under attack by the economicist paradigm), they were located just beyond the city walls of Athens as "an explicit attempt to shelter inquiry from the politically destabilizing effects of the public exercise of reason by the Sophists" (Fuller, 2001, §2, ¶11). Plato's Academy lasted until the first century BCE, with a second Platonic Academy flourishing between the second and sixth centuries CE (O'Connor & Robertson, 2004). The fate of Aristotelian peripatetic schools beyond the first century BCE remains uncertain.

Islamic Aristotelian Renaissance

Although this antiquarian situation heralded modern Western education, the route—following the demise of the Roman Empire—was to be through the Islamic world. Indeed, the Classical tradition—largely that of Aristotle (Burrell, 1998)—was passed on and developed through Islamic civilization for over half a millennium (during the European Early Middle Ages) mostly before uptake by Europe again in the twelfth-century medieval renaissance. Islamic education flourished, partly through an approach oriented toward an integral ecology involving "the search for Truth (*haqq*), proper action (*Alim*), spirituality (*iman, nur,* and *huda*), ethics (*ulama*), and wisdom (*hikma*)" (Hilgendorf, 2003, p. 63) within an emphasis on *community* (as exemplar of The Good). Mosque schools abounded, whilst higher modes of analysis were found in the universities, the *madrasa*, which emerged as an institution in the eleventh century in Iraq (Huff, 2003). In the latter were made "advanced discoveries in … geometry, astronomy, geography, medicine, optics, and physics, plus comprehensive contributions in theosophy, philosophy, and encyclopedic compilations" (Hilgendorf, 2003, p. 63) forming "a virtually complete body of specialized scientific information, without question the most complete store of knowledge of the natural world [humanity] had yet compiled" (Goldstein, 1995, p. 92).

Such a complete body of knowledge can be seen as an outcome of the Aristotelian-integral impulse. Islamic history scholar Toby Huff (2003) identifies this Islamic learning system as pertaining to a whole, noting that "from the eighth century to the end of the fourteenth, Arabic science was probably the most advanced science in the world, greatly surpassing the West and China" (p. 48). Acknowledging the importance of the Arabic incorporation of the Hindu numeral system in the development of science, he even identifies that, "the planetary models of Copernicus, appearing 150 years after the time of Ibn al-Shatir, are actually duplicates of the models developed by the Marâgha astronomers" (p. 51).

In terms of educational practice, Abdesselam Cheddadi (1994) forwards the notion of lifelong learning (learning as pertaining to the whole human lifecycle) in Islamic education—noting the phrase from *cradle to grave* as being attributed to Muhammad. At the same time he acknowledges the Graeco-Roman heritage of Classical Islamic educational theories, identifying that they pertain to the whole human—a person "considered in every aspect of his or her being" (p. 2)—and in terms of reaching toward "the perfection proper to [a person's] nature" (p. 2), indicating a nuanced developmental schema. Educational principles include "the restrained use of authority … the need to awaken the [student's] interest, the value of example, and progression in learning. Above all, they insist on the importance of the pedagogical relationship" (p. 2). Here, both the regard for the timeliness of a student's learning and also the I-Thou (Buber & Kaufman, 1921/1970) nature of pedagogy—referring to the pertinence of character (*Bildung*'s "beautiful personality") in both student and educator—resonate with various contemporary integral and holistic pedagogies. They also stand in contrast to the contemporary prevalence of economistic and behaviorist implementations. Cheddadi specifically relays the understandings of fourteenth-century savant sociologist and educator, Ibn Khaldun: that, as antecedent to the unorthodoxly expansive temporal structure of Steiner's integral education curriculum—and in contrast to modern mainstream curricula's fragmented time allotments—Ibn Khaldun warns against teaching two or more subjects in a simultaneous fashion so as to facilitate a deeper understanding of a subject's interconnectivities or integrality. Poetically echoing later integral iterations such as *Bildung*, he theorizes learning in terms of the acquisition of a *habitus*, where "habitus are like gradually formed 'colours' of the soul" (Cheddadi, 1994, p. 2). As an educational whole—through curricula, pedagogy and institutional practice—the Aristotelian integralism of Islamic universities thence became the template for the European university. But it was to take on a new twist: Thomism.

Medieval Aristotelian Renaissance

The European universities of Bologna, Paris, and Oxford were instituted some three centuries after the (presently still-existent) Al-Qayrawan university was founded in 859 CE in Fez, Morocco (Najjaar, 1958). Goldstein (1995) extols: "It was only after the School of Chartres had established its new natural philosophy that European scholars were plunging into the Islamic heritage with full enthusiasm … the effect was an intellectual stimulation without parallel" (p. 93). The possibility for such enthusiasm toward this Islamic Aristotelian integral orientation had been facilitated over a century earlier first by the synthesis of faith and reason by Anselm of Canterbury, the "father of scholasticism" (Asztalos, 1992, p. 410) (*integral as synthesis between faith and reason*) and later by the radical educational thesis proposed by Hugh of Saint-Victor Abbey in Paris. He proffered that we should "learn everything" (Tarnas, 1991, p. 175). *Integral education as university* and *integral/education as encyclopaedic* thence took root in Europe. Tarnas (1991) articulates:

> The purpose of the seven liberal arts—the *trivium* (grammar, rhetoric, and dialectic) and the *quadrivium* (arithmetic, music, geometry, and astronomy)—was to "restore God's image in us." From this new commitment to learning arose the composition of the great medieval *summae*, encyclopaedic treatises aimed at comprehending the whole of reality. …This same educational conception became the basis for the development of universities through Europe. (p. 175)

Classical ideas were central to the conception of the university. From the outset, they had the Neoplatonic Aristotelian task of realizing their underlying idea or entelechy (Rüegg, 1992). The ideal comprised an ecology involving such features as love of learning, breadth of curriculum, integrity, clarity, humility, solicitude and collegiality. By comparison, it is hard to see how such an integral ecology is not being lost in the contemporary economicist climate. Is the university no longer aiming to fulfill its potential?—a pertinent question given that notions of community and integrality are infused within the very term "university," a term derived from *universitas magistrorum et scholarium* meaning "a community of masters and scholars." *Universitas*—which may signify either *society, community, guild*;

or *whole, universe*—is itself derived from *universus*—"the whole taken together," "all turned into one." Both roots can be seen to bear intimate relations with the integral quest such as through the powerful vector, *integral education as knowledge integration necessitating a scholarly community.*

Gradually, however, two social currents emerged in response to this integrative impulse. The first involved an intensification in the direction of the secular (objectivity-oriented) Islamic-Aristotelian heterodoxy influenced by Ibn Rushd (Averroës), "Aristotle's greatest Arabic commentator" (Tarnas, 1991, p. 175). The second—a Christian Augustinian current (carrying in part the profundity of subjectivity—see, e.g., Abbs (2003)—but also a fixed and relatively unsophisticated Platonism)—substantively opposed this scientific direction. Thomas Aquinas integrated these two steams (Thomist-Aristotelianism), an interpretation which initially carried much weight (with strong influence at least until the Renaissance, then less so as befits the demise of Catholic influence). The Church, however, "sensing the secularising threat of the pagan Aristotelian-Arabic science, of an autonomous human reason and its embrace of profane culture" (Tarnas, 1991, p. 192) increasingly prohibited the interest in integrating spirituality with natural phenomena. In so doing it intensified the rift between religion and science, dismembering the integral impulse and unwittingly help eventually form the bittersweet revolutionary sensibility of the Enlightenment and subsequent ongoing restlessness of modernism. This was not, however, before a renaissance of a different kind, one so great as to be identified in retrospect as the key social catalyst for the integral-aperspectival structure of consciousness (Gebser, 1949/1985)—a structure still emerging as is evidenced by recent academic interest in integral studies, including this very narrative. The social rebirth in question was the Hermetic-Neoplatonic Italian renaissance, often referred to as simply The Renaissance.

Italian Neoplatonic Renaissance

Whilst Aristotelian developments had been taking place in Classical Islam and medieval Medieval Europe, Neoplatonic-integral had been evolving in the Byzantine Empire; Professor Richard Hooker (1996) describes how

> the Byzantine Neoplatonists carried on the work of synthesizing philosophies—the most crucial of these was the synthesis of Platonism with Christianity. In the fourteenth and fifteenth centuries, the most active of these Neoplatonists was Gemistus Pletho. He is most significant for the Italian Renaissance for he visited Italy and introduced the Italians to Byzantine Neoplatonism. (n.p.)

The offering included works by Plato hitherto unknown in medieval Europe. The net result catalyzed such a flourishing that a cultural discontinuity—a new golden age—was perceived to be happening by those involved at the time (Rüegg, 1996). This spiritual humanism involved both a new awareness of self and a new academic paradigm of questing toward things-in-themselves through philological historical discovery (Rüegg, 1996). The Florentine Academy—set up by ambassador and patron Cosimo de' Medici, directed first by Marsilio Ficino and later by his disciple Francesco Zanoli Cattani da Diacceto, and including such philosophers as Giovanni Pico della Mirandola—spearheaded a classical rebirth. It firmly established perspectivality (Gebser, 1949/1985) whilst simultaneously facilitating the social genesis of the integral-*a*perspectival structure of consciousness through perspectivality's intensification as exemplified by the work of Leonardo da Vinci's pupil, Jacopo da Pontormo (Gebser, 1949/1985).

The original understanding of the academy, like the original notion of the university, was also infused with the value of community, as Marian Ciszewski elaborates.

> Like Plato, Ficino opened his home to his friends, *whom came to be called academics* ... . Among the "co-philosophers" and "brothers in Plato" as Ficino called them, we find not only philosophers, but also poets, rhetoricians, lawyers, politicians, priests, physicians and musicians. (Ciszewski, italics added)

This was a veritable ecology of humanity within academic embrace. Ciszewski goes on to identify two main motifs in Ficino's creative philosophical work. The first "was a thought borrowed from Gemistus Plethon, that from Hermes to Plotinus there is a single great philosophical and theological tradition of eternal wisdom (*prisca theologia, catena aurea*), which Ficino tried to make agree as much as possible with orthodox Christian thought" (Ciszewski, n.d.). This was synergistic with the theory and practice of *friendship as love* (philia), which itself can be identified as part of an ecology of love comprising eros, agape, and philia (noting here that philia might be a valuable addition to Wilber's (1995) love schema which comprises only eros and agape).

The second theme was that "Plato's and Aristotle's philosophies are in real agreement and harmony (they agree as to principles, and disagree only in verbal formulas)" (Ciszewski, n.d.)—a Neoplatonic interpretation regarding the intertwinement of these two streams (as per the current chapter). Contemporaneously—from the time of the Vatican librarian Agostino Steuco—this ecology of syntheses was known as the *philosophia perennis* (the perennial philosophy) (Schmidt-Biggermann, 1996)—a narration involving the mystery of God from a human perspective such that "divine wisdom can only be understood analogically" (p. 519). (Thus potentially adding to the potential significance of poetic metaphor through a quintessentially transcendent vector). *Philosophia perennis* is a signifier which plays an iconic role in much integral and holistic discourse. This resurgent realization involved an integral expressivity reborn, hitherto neglected by medievalism: New loci of meaning were found and expressed both visually and aurally, philosophy was spiritually enriched, inner and outer connected, the empirical and historical integrated, whilst the *poiesis* of "art" and *poetics* of "science" formed a dynamic integral dialectic—all leading to educational programs pertaining to conceptions of the whole (Rüegg, 1996)—a wellspring of integral.

German Neoplatonic Renaissance

Three centuries later, a further iteration of the Neoplatonic-integral impulse took place, this time in Germany. This spiritual (neo)humanist orientation can be variously seen through baroque, classicist, romantic, idealistic, and anthroposophical moments, involving such figures as Leibniz, Herder, Goethe, Schelling, Hegel, and Steiner, with their "radical epistemological perspective" (Tarnas, 1991, p. 433). Educational manifestations here include those of Humboldt and Schiller outlined below. A closely related *post*-Hegelian—decidedly Russian—manifestation involves the "great synthesis," of "integral knowledge," *sobornost* (spiritual community) and Sophiology of the Russian Slavophiles, notably Soloviev (Bischof, 2005, p. 286). An etymological connection here can be seen among *wisdom as Sophia, wisdom as identified in postformal literature* (e.g., Sternberg, 2000) (e.g., and the terms *philosophy, anthropo-sophy* and *eco-sophy*. The philosophical fallout from Hegel was far from linear, however; other vectors included socialist/anarchist-integral education (Molz and Hampson, current volume), Steiner's integral education (Gidley, current volume) and Dewey's dialectically-influenced approach.

An influential educational text within the fertile nexus of German humanism was Friedrich Schiller's *On the Aesthetic Education of the Human* (Schiller & Snell, 2000), which sought to unite the contingencies of experiential life with the *form* through the notion of "living form," realized in the *play* of aesthetic unity "beyond the seriousness of effort" (Taylor, 1975, p. 37). Calling upon the ideal of expression theory, Taylor (1975) identifies

> an expressive harmony in which natural desires and the highest human forms are effortlessly united in a single élan. This is freedom, in the sense of integral, undivided, unconflicted self-expression. It is all this, the effortlessness, harmony, free creativity, which Schiller wants to convey in the word "play." (p. 38)

This interpretation could be summarized as *integral as creative play*. Another integral vector is Schiller's concretization of *humanitas*: the quest for the synthesis of reason and sensuality in the harmony of each unique personality (Holborn, 1964).

Inspired in part by his friends Schiller and Goethe, Holborn (1964) indicates that Neoplatonist Wilhelm von Humboldt devised an integrally-oriented educational approach for Prussia, notably for the new University of Berlin in 1810—an approach which was to have profound effect on the development of the modern university. Appointed by the Prussian government (1809–1810) to oversee the reorganization of education, Humboldt initiated a tripartite system as follows. The pedagogical approach of Johann Heinrich Pestalozzi—a holistic if didactic ideology of "head, hand, and heart"—became influential in elementary education (p. 473). In secondary school education his influence took the form of humanistic *gymnasia* (similar to British grammar schools) and the more practically-oriented *realschulen*. For higher education, it was that

> the new idea of a university was presented in a philosophical form by Schelling in 1803. Science (*Wissenschaft*) was conceived as a *universitas*, an organic totality of knowledge. Special studies had to be pursued in the light of a single all-embracing truth. (p. 479)

Berlin University was founded in 1810, heralding a new era of academic freedom: "The German universities, entering upon a century of productive scholarship and research unequalled in any country, exercised an influence far beyond Germany" (p. 484). "Education was directed toward the acquisition of philosophical wisdom, individual moral distinction, and artistic taste" (p. 478). Notable characteristics of Humboldt's philosophy included:

- re-establishing the medieval unity of knowledge but with the Enlightenment's understanding of the autonomy of human reason (p. 480);
- emphasising creative spontaneity rather than rationalism or pragmatism (p. 480);
- identifying the interrelationship between teaching and research (p. 480);
- identifying the interrelationship between *praxis* and *theoria* (Oelkers, 2001, p. 81);
- valorising all experience (not just scholarship) in order to develop good character or a "beautiful individuality" (Oelkers, 2001, p. 81);
- noting that "historians should endeavour to describe the working of ideas behind the events of history" (Oelkers, 2001, p. 82); and
- valorizing the theory of *Bildung*.

The last item—currently receiving considerable traction in the philosophy of education[6]—is understood by Oelkers (2001) as partaking of neither the *tabula rasa* theory of Locke nor of the *innate nature* theory of Rousseau; rather, "that experience of finding out what are the 'imprints of humanity and humanism' in the experience of life, while excluding everything that is 'mechanical'" (p. 81); self-causation; cultivation, not instruction; the *true art* of character building, where "'character' refers to the *singularity* of the individual that will learn by himself only what is homogenous to his inner form" (p. 81, original emphasis).

Meanwhile, Wilhelm's brother, Alexander von Humboldt, also contributed to this integral wave through developing "world physics." Alexander's "*Kosmos* (1845–62), which was read all over the world, absorbed an encyclopaedic knowledge of science into a panoramic view of the universe," (Holborn, 1964, p. 528) a view intimated by this chapter's panoramic regard for integral education.

Openings to Dialogue

Education exists to set up a conversation down the ages and across the cultures, across both time and space.

—Abbs, 2003, p. 17

In toto, the above narrative identifies a pre-industrial genealogy of Western integral education as it journeys via Classical Islam; it also offers a reading on Native American integral education. A postformal approach to integral education theorising—in this instance, one adopting an ecological (e.g., genealogical) and poetic (e.g., etymological, metaphorical) sensibility—can facilitate fecund interpretations of integral education. Such openings to dialogue can supplement, problematize, and/or re-orient default interpretations including the loosening of the undue semantic grip of such terms as *traditional, postmodern,* and *integral*: integral approaches to education are neither new nor limited to Western cultures. Both the maneuver of meta-coherence as well as numerous contemporarily-identified integral education features can be found throughout Western-Islamic history, features interestingly synergistic with indigenous American integral education (whilst noting that contingent differences also exist across time and culture: the situation is complex). Features variously include aesthetics as paradigm, *Bildung*, breadth of understanding, care, community (intellectual and societal), complexity, depth (historical, philosophical, semantic), contemplative dwelling, creativity, ecosophy, embodied participation, ethical orientation, expressivism, freedom, friendship, *habitus*, harmony, an I-Thou pedagogical relationship, imagination, interconnectivity, knowledge–mystery dialectics, life, love, metaphor, nuanced developmentalism, perennial philosophy's cosmic ontology and four fields of knowledge (Schumacher, 1977),[7] play, potential, readiness to learn, spiritual philosophy, transdisciplinarity, the unique character of our singularities, unity-in-diversity, and wisdom. These can be identified as largely postformal modalities, which in turn can be seen to inform contemporary postformal pedagogies (Gidley, current volume). Regarding the Western case: through identifying integral education as Neoplatonic and Aristotelian a rich history opens up pointing to a correspondingly fertile spiritual-philosophical heritage—one in relation to which contemporary understandings may be located.

One such contemporary integral understanding is that offered by Brent Davis's (2004) exquisite genealogical ecology of metaphoric templates regarding teaching philosophies. One aspect of interest here is his identification of the ancient Greek (Neoplatonic and Aristotelian) concept of *gnosis* from which *knowledge, notion,* and *noosphere* are derived. Gnosis refers to big-picture thinking—"matters of existence and questions of meaning" (p. 26), pointing toward "wisdom and ethical action" (p. 30). Unlike the rather semantically monotonic *knowledge,* "inherent" within gnosis is a dialectic between certainty and uncertainty: knowledge and mystery in one complex unit. The term thus facilitates dialogue with contemporary interests such as Roben Torosyan's (1998) *undecidability.* Gnosis is associated with *poiesis,* the etymological root of *poetic,* and as such stands in contrast to the *tekhne* (technology) of *episteme* (epistemology) (Davis, 2004) with which it should dance in balanced relation. Given the contemporary overdetermination of epistemological/technical know-*how* over the know-*why* of gnosis, perhaps suitable (dialectical) "cultural medicine" (Bronson and Gangadean, current volume) might be to revitalize the notion of *gnoseology* as apt complement to *epistemology.*

Such an idea need not be tethered to a pre-evolutionary interpretation of metaphysics, but could rather position it in generative dialogue with postformal understandings (such as suggested by Alfred North Whitehead's writings); indeed, an evolving metaphysics "expanding the space of the possible" (Davis, 2004, p. 184) would be in keeping with the tenor of Hermetic-Neoplatonism[8] offered here. Gnoseology could be adopted as an innovative vector for research, and integral education theorizing could become as creative, contingent, careful, and complex as the education it seeks to promote.

Notes

1. This chapter will foreground higher education; although, as befits an integral approach *integrating* educational levels, other levels of education will not necessarily be excluded. Regarding "x as y" phrases, (e.g., *integral as indigenous*) my intention and use of italics sits in relation to Lakoff and Johnson's (1980) writing, specifically their discussion of metaphors.

2. See, e.g., Hampson (forthcoming).

3. Extending AQAL *types* beyond Wilber's own usage.

4. E.g., Gebser's identification of the Italian Renaissance as catalyst for the *integral-aperspectival* structure could be understood as foregrounding *integral as Hermetic-Neoplatonic.*

5. Interpreting *integral* as denoting worldview or similar ("an integral *x*").

6. See, for example, the special issue of the *Journal of Philosophy of Education* (2002) *36*(3).

7. Schumacher (1997), for example, forwards Plotinus' and Aquinas' understanding of *adequatio* that the different levels of being (physiosphere, botanosphere, zoosphere, and noosphere—to extend Wilberian terminology) require corresponding human epistemological modalities. Schumacher similarly elucidates at length "The Four Fields of Knowledge" which, as Gidley (2007b, p. 44, n. 96) indicates, corresponds to Wilber's later iteration of *the four quadrants*.

8. A difference can be seen in this regard between Platonism and Neoplatonism: unlike Plato, "Plotinus seems to accept Heraclitus' position that the everlastingness of becoming is expressed in the form of an endless cosmic flux" (Stamatellos, 2007, p. 127).

References

Abbs, P. (Ed.). (2003). *Against the flow: Education, the arts and postmodern culture*. London; New York: RoutledgeFalmer.

Abelson, P. (1906). *The seven liberal arts: A study in medieval culture*. New York: Columbia University.

Abraham, R. H. (2006). The new sacred math. *World Futures, 62*(1 & 2), 6–16.

Asztalos, M. (1992). The faculty of theology. In H. de Ridder-Symoens (Ed.), *A history of the university in Europe. Volume 1: Universities in the Middle Ages*. Cambridge, UK; New York; Port Melbourne; Madrid; Cape Town: Cambridge University Press.

Aurobindo, S. (2003) *The complete works of Sri Aurobindo. Volume 1: Early cultural writings*. Pondicherry, India: Sri Aurobindo Ashram.

Bischof, M. (2005). Verdansky's noosphere and Slavophile sobornost. In L. V. Beloussov, V. L. Voeikov, & V. S. Martynyuk (Eds.), *Biophotonics and coherent systems in biology*. New York: Springer.

Boyer, E. L. (1990). *Scholarship reconsidered: Priorities of the professoriate*. Lawrenceville, NJ: Carnegie Foundation for the Advancement of Teaching; Princeton University Press.

Buber, M., & Kaufman, W. (1923/1970). *I and thou* (W. Kaufman, Trans.). New York: Touchstone.

Burrell, D. (1998). *Platonism in Islamic philosophy*. Retrieved 20 July 2008, from http://www.muslimphilosophy.com/ip/rep/H001.htm

Cajete, G. (1994). *Look to the mountain: An ecology of Indigenous education*. Durango, CO: Kivaki Press.

Cheddadi, A. (1994). Ibn Khaldun. *Prospects: The quarterly review of comparative education, XXIV*(1/2).

Ciszewski, M. (n.d.). *Academy Florentine*. Retrieved 25 July 2008, from http://ptta.pl/pef/angielski/hasla/a/academyflorentine.pdf

Combs, A. (2005). Inner and outer realities: Gebser in a cultural/historical perspective. *The Journal of Conscious Evolution*, 1.

Davis, B. (2004). *Inventions of Teaching: A Genealogy*. Mahwah, NJ; London: Lawrence Erlbaum Associates.

Fuller, S. (2001). Strategies of knowledge integration. In M. K. Tolba (Ed.), *Our fragile world: Challenges, opportunities for sustainable development.* Oxford, UK: EOLSS Publishers (for UNESCO).

Gebser, J. (1949/1985). *The ever-present origin.* Athens, OH: Ohio University Press.

Gidley, J. (2007a). Educational imperatives of the evolution of consciousness: The integral visions of Rudolf Steiner and Ken Wilber. *International Journal of Children's Spirituality, 12*(2), 117–135.

Gidley, J. (2007b). The evolution of consciousness as a planetary imperative: An integration of integral views. *Integral Review, 5,* 4–227.

Goldstein, T. (1995). *Dawn of modern science: From the Ancient Greeks to the Renaissance.* Cambridge, MA: Da Capo Press.

Hampson, G. P. (2007). Integral re-views postmodernism: The way out is through. *Integral Review 4,* 108–173.

Hampson, G. P. (forthcoming) Futures of integral futures: An analysis of Richard Slaughter's analysis of causal layered analysis. *Futures.*

Hilgendorf, E. (2003). Islamic education: History and tendency. *Peabody Journal of Education, 78*(2), 63–75.

Holborn, H. (1964). *A history of modern Germany: 1646–1840.* Princeton, New Jersey, Chichester, UK: Princeton University Press.

Hooker, R. (1996). *Neoplatonism.* Retrieved 21 July 2008, from http://www.wsu.edu/~dee/REN/NEOPLATO.HTM

Huff, T. E. (2003). *The rise of early modern science: Islam, China and the West.* Cambridge, UK; New York; Melbourne; Madrid; Cape Town; Singapore; Sao Paulo; Delhi: Cambridge University Press.

Jardine, D. W. (1998). *To dwell with a boundless heart: Essays in curriculum theory, hermeneutics, and the ecological imagination (Vol. 77).* New York, Washington D.C./Baltimore; Boston; Bern; Frankfurt am Main; Berlin; Vienna; Paris: Peter Lang.

Jeffries, V. (1999). The integral paradigm: The truth of faith and the social sciences. *The American Sociologist, 30*(4), 36–55.

Kealey, D. (2002). Neoplatonism in transpersonal psychology: The thought of Ken Wilber. In R. B. Harris (Ed.), *Neoplatonism and contemporary thought (Studies in Neoplatonism). Part two.* Albany, NY: State University of New York Press.

Klostermaier, K. K. (1997). The hermeneutic center. *Journal of Ecumenical Studies, 34*(2), 159.

Koestler, A. (1967). *The ghost in the machine.* London; Melbourne; Sydney; Auckland; Bombay; Toronto; Johannesberg; New York: Hutchinson and Co.

Kremer, J. W. (1996). *The shadow of evolutionary thinking.* ReVision, 19(1).

Kyle, D. G. (1993). *Athletics in ancient Athens* (2nd ed.). Leiden, The Netherlands: E.J.Brill.

Lakoff, G. & Johnson, M. (1980). *Metaphors we live by.* Chicago: Chicago University Press.

Mayer, J. R. A. (2002). Plotinus' Neoplatonism and the thought of Aurobindo. In P. M. Gregorios (Ed.), *Neoplatonism and Indian philosophy.* Albany, NY: State University of New York Press.

Magee, G. A. (2001). *Hegel and the hermetic tradition.* Ithaca, NY: Cornell University Press.

Najjar, F. M. (1958). The Karaouine at Fez. *The Muslim World, 48*(2), 104–112.

O'Connor, J. J., & Robertson, E. F. (2004). *The academy of Plato.* Retrieved 25 July 2008, from http://www-groups.dcs.st-and.ac.uk/~history/Societies/Plato.html

Oelkers, J. (2001). Wilhelm von Humboldt. In J. A. Palmer (Ed.), *Fifty major thinkers on education.* London; New York: Routledge

Randolph, J. (2007). *The house in the garden: The Bakunin family and the romance of Russian Idealism.* New York: Cornell University Press.

Rüegg, W. (1992). Themes. In H. d. Ridder-Symoens (Ed.), *A history of the university in Europe. Volume 1: Universities in the middle ages.* Cambridge, UK; New York; Port Melbourne; Madrid; Cape Town: Cambridge University Press.

Rüegg, W. (1996). Themes. In H. d. Ridder-Symoens (Ed.), *A history of the university in Europe. Volume 2: Universities in early modern Europe (1500–1800).* Cambridge, UK; New York; Port Melbourne; Madrid; Cape Town: Cambridge University Press.

Schiller, F., & Snell, R. (1795/1954). *On the aesthetic education of Man* (R. Snell, Trans.). New Haven, CT: Yale University Press.

Schmidt-Biggemann, W. (1996). New structures of knowledge. In H. de Ridder-Symoens (Ed.), *A history of the university in Europe. Volume 2: Universities in early modern Europe (1500–1800).* Cambridge, UK; New York; Port Melbourne; Madrid; Cape Town: Cambridge University Press.

Schumacher, E. F. (1977). *A guide for the perplexed.* New York: Perennial.

Soble, A. (1999). *Eros, agape and philia.* St. Paul, MN: Paragon House Publishers.

Stamatellos, G. (2007). *Plotinus and the presocratics: A philosophical study of presocratic influences in Plotinus' Enneads.* Albany, NY: State University of New York Press.

Sternberg, R. J. (2000). Intelligence and wisdom. In R. J. Sternberg (Ed.), *Handbook of intelligence.* New York: Cambridge University Press.

Tarnas, R. (1991). *The passion of the Western mind: Understanding the ideas that have shaped our world view.* London: Pimlico.

Taylor, C. (1975). *Hegel.* Cambridge, UK; New York; Oakleigh, Melbourne; Madrid: Cambridge University Press.

Taylor, C. (1979). *Hegel and modern society.* Cambridge, UK; New York; Melbourne: Cambridge University Press.

Torosyan, R. (1998). Undecidability in quantum physics, chaos theory, and deconstruction: Implications for politics, ethics, and society. In S. P. Kodish, & R. P. Holston (Eds.), *Developing sanity in human affairs.* Westport, CT, USA: Greenwood.

Wilber, K. (1995). *Sex, ecology, spirituality: The spirit of evolution.* Boston: Shambhala.

Elements of the Underacknowledged History of Integral Education

Markus Molz and Gary P. Hampson

Introduction

This chapter seeks to facilitate adequate breadth and depth in integral education theorizing through identifying hitherto underacknowledged yet pertinent historical streams (focusing on mid-nineteenth to mid-twentieth centuries) which have explicitly embraced the term integral education. Emphasising leading protagonists, prioritization will be given to socialist and Catholic integral education streams, with additional mention of the (perhaps more familiar) Aurobindean and Gebserian threads. These—along with other integral approaches such as those in relation to Steiner (Gidley, 2007; current volume) and Sorokin (Jeffries, 1999; Snauwaert, 1990)—may fittingly be viewed as part of an ecology of (variously overlapping and particularised) integral education streams potentially in "deep dialogue" with each other. Such identification can form part of a yet larger picture including an extensive global history of integral education incorporating the contemporary situation.

Socialist Integral Education

Early use of the term integral education can be found in the approaches of a few French and Russian socialists.

Charles Fourier (1772–1837), Victor Considérant (1808–93), Jean-Baptiste Godin (1817–88)

Fourier, a founder of the socialist movement, had developed a system of harmonic education by 1829. Attendant to gender equality, inter-individual and social differences, it was built upon his *Theory of the Four Movements*—"social, animal, organic and material" (Fourier, 1808/1996, p. 3)—which included a notion of cultural evolution through several phases (involving both construction and destruction) beyond the already-achieved level of civilisation, altogether effecting a "transition from social chaos to universal harmony" (Fourier, 1808/1996, p. 4). He lucidly critiqued formal educational practice, noting that its "methods lack emotional and spiritual dimensions" (Fourier, 1829, Vol. 1, p. 196).[1] His educational approach instead was based on an understanding of the developmental needs of the person in relation to the community, including the idea that manual skills should be learnt before the child "receives *integral* education according to the whole range of available methods, from which it can choose without being subjected to the system of any given sophist" (Fourier, 1829, Vol. 2, p. 47, original italics). The basic principles of Fourier's educational vision—summarized by his disciple Victor Considérant—were that,

> education should be: universal and not elitist; suited to vocational calling and not arbitrary; convergent and not divergent; active and not passive; composed [regarding body and soul] and not simple [i.e., not only intellectual]; integral and not partial; developmental and not constraining. Through these conditions education will be unitary and attractive. (Considérant, 1844, p. 48)

The industrialist Jean-Baptiste Godin was inspired by Fourier's vision of workers' communities. From 1859 Godin created an unprecedented architectural, economic, and socio-cultural synthesis of a Fourier cooperative community around his expanding plant for heating stoves in Picardy, France. Long before a nationwide system existed, Fourier implemented a fully-fledged social security system including free health care, child care, and education. A sizable proportion of the plant's surplus was spent on cultural events and the education of community members of all ages. Godin's (1871) *Social Solutions* provides an account of the various facets of this outstanding experiment of life, learning, and working in this "social palace" (which was to last for several decades). The approach to education in this Utopian community is reflected in the chapter titled *Integral Education* and each of the subsequent chapters which elucidate a particular level of this approach—according to age cohort. Godin summarized the purpose of education as seeking to realize for all people "the integral culture of the human spirit by the integral culture of the entire species" (Godin, 1871, p. 558) guiding us toward generative lives.

Paul Robin (1837–1912), Mikhail Bakunin (1814–1876), Piotr Kropotkin (1842–1921)

Having resigned from the restrictive French national educational system, passionate teacher Paul Robin became involved with the International Workingsmen's

Association (IWA) in which Fourier's ideas circulated along with those of Karl Marx and Mikhail Bakunin. Bakunin invited Robin to become his successor on the editorial board of the Swiss socialist journal *Egalité* (Douyère-Demeulenaere, 1994) in which Bakunin proceeded to publish two articles on education in 1869. In the second article he claimed, "we seek equality and, because we seek it, we must also seek integral education, the same education for everyone" (Bakunin, 1869). Human equality, liberty, diversity, and solidarity were seen as mutually dependent; he stressed the need to abolish the differentiation between blue- and white-collar work types of education, aligning with the words of Kropotkin: "We advocate the *education integrale*, or complete education, which means the disappearance of that pernicious distinction" (Kropotkin, 1898/1912, p. 369, original italics). Bakunin upheld "the Platonic ideal of education as freedom from illusion" (Suissa, 201, p. 640), identifying freedom in relation to the spontaneity of life whilst opposing alienation—notably that of state and church (Walicki, 1977). In this period, Robin wrote IWA conference reports on integral education, publishing three articles (1869, 1870, 1872) in the *Revue de Philosophie Positive* (*Journal of Positive Philosophy*). The Marxist stream of the IWA, however, increasingly dominated the socialist movement, and *anarchist* socialism—including Bakunin and Robin—became excluded.

In 1880, Robin became the director of a radically co-educative[2] orphanage and school in Picardy, and implemented his vision of integral education. Inspired both by Fourier/Considérant and by Comte's scientific positivism (Demeulenaere-Douyère, 1994), Robin took care to alternate and interweave physical, craft-based, intellectual, aesthetic, and moral education inside an intentional educational community in which adults and children were living, eating, working, learning, and celebrating together. Inspired by Kropotkin's core idea of mutual help and communal spirit, elder children tutored younger ones in return for supportive activities. Major characteristics of this approach included developmentalism, student-centeredness respectful of individual freedom, self-expression and self-realization, integration between school and community, equal opportunities, and bottom-up (participatory) organization; whilst religious education was eschewed or dealt with comparatively (Demeulenaere-Douyère, 1994; McLaren, 1981). Robin's school became an international attraction, leading him to run teacher training seminars on site and elsewhere in France and Belgium.[3] They became the seed of the Association Universelle d'Education Intégrale (AUEI), which was founded in 1893 by Paul Robin and others. Education, according to the AUEI's manifesto was, *inter alia*, one "which strives for the parallel and harmonic development of the entire being" (quoted in Demeulenaere-Douyère, 1994, p. 414). "The programme which corresponds to this idea can be resumed in one [sic] word: *of all*. Of all science and all art not vague glimmer, but solid and precise notions" (p. 416). Although the Church eventually conspired to effect its unwarranted closure, Robin's influence maintained currency through the likes of Sébastien Faure, Célestin Freinet, Francisco Ferrer (who catalysed the Catalan "modern school" movement), and the highly successful Maria

Montessori movement. Overall, Robin significantly contributed to the formation of the Education Nouvelle (a still-operative alternative education movement), and set theoretical and practical precedents for such figures as Gramsci, Piaget, as well as feminist education. Contemporary research on anarchist education includes that of Gallo (1995), Heinlein (1998), and Suissa (2006).

Catholic Integral Education

Meanwhile, another explicitly-termed *integral education* became established from an antagonistic even if somewhat overlapping quarter—that of Catholicism. This type of education can be understood as forming part of the longer history of the Thomist Aristotelian stream of integral thought (Hampson, current volume), within which the spiritual evolutionary theory of Pierre Teilhard de Chardin may be located.[4]

Jacques Maritain (1882–1973)

The use of the term in this context dates back at least to that of Jacques Maritain and his adage, *integral education for integral humanism* (Maritain, 1943). Maritain "was raised in a socialist environment and very early on determined that he would give his life for the cause of the proletariat" (LaFountain, 1999), so it is not unlikely that Maritain acquired the term integral education from the socialist context while giving it a broader, spiritualized meaning. As a student, Maritain experienced a spiritual crisis and converted to Catholicism. He became a disciple and later critic of Henri Bergson, and developed a friendship with the Russian philosopher Nicholas Berdiaev who may be considered—like Bergson—an early integral thinker. Maritain held professorships in both France and the United States, publishing extensively—gaining considerable international academic and clerical reception—across major fields of philosophy including the philosophy of education; he also participated in the drafting the Universal Declaration of Human Rights.

Maritain critiqued the hegemonic tendency to elucidate the *means* of education whilst substantively underacknowledging its *ends* or purposes (Maritain, 1943). Rather, a spiritual-philosophical grounding was seen to be required: "The complete and integral idea of man[5] which is the prerequisite of education can only be a philosophical and religious idea" (Maritain, 1943, pp. 6–7). Maritain's integral humanism "seeks to bring the different dimensions of the human person together, without ignoring or diminishing the value of either" (Stanford Encyclopedia of Philosophy, 2008). The primary goal of education is "human awakening" (Maritain, 1943, p. 9) "through knowledge and wisdom, good will and love" (Maritain, 1943, p. 11) necessitating evolutionary hierarchies and multi-layered knowledge integrations (Maritain, 1932/1995)—a significant antecedent to Wilber's (1983) *three eyes of knowledge.*[6] "The whole work of education and teaching must tend toward unity, and not to spread out; it must strive to foster internal unity in each person" (Maritain, 1943, p. 45)—a cohering "liberal" education for all. Indeed, "to introduce specialization in this sphere is to do violence to the world of youth" (Maritain, 1943, p. 64), whilst the humanities curriculum are identified as requiring an opening up to the plurality of cultures and religions (D'Souza, 1996, Gallagher & Gallagher, 1978). Maritain devised four pedagogical vectors: (i) help children grow spiritually by making them aware of their own resources; (ii) focus on inner depth: the internalisation of educational influence and the liberation of the intuitive power; (iii) counter dispersion, nourish unification; and (iv) teach in a vitalising and liberating manner (Maritain, 1943). Maritain envisaged a new social order regarding the common good of humanity as a whole (Maritain, 1936) in accord with "truth, knowledge, goodness, and beauty at all levels of reality, material and immaterial" (D'Souza, 1996, p. 508).

Alexis Carrell (1873–1944)

The term integral education was also adopted by an occasional acquaintance of Maritain, Alexis Carrell, Nobel Prize winner and controversial eugenicist who proffered that we need a

> . . . complete renovation of our educational system. We must show every child that any existence . . . becomes radiant when it is illuminated by an ideal of beauty and love . . . What is the use of developing science, letters, art and philosophy if society is disintegrating? If our civilization is to survive, we must all be prepared to live, not according to ideologies, but according to the order of things . . . We . . . need to substitute *integral education* for the exclusively intellectual type on which we have hitherto concentrated . . . It is important to give neither spiritual nor physiological training the supremacy hitherto accorded to the intellectual. The task of the professor of integral education in every school will be to build up complete human beings . . . The aim of integral education is to prevent man from becoming dehumanized."
> (Carell, 1952, pp. 192–193)

Plínio Salgado (1895–1975)

A further—more authoritarian—expression of integral education occurred in Brazil in the 1930s. Dissatisfied with both individualist and Marxist approaches to modernization, Plínio Salgado founded the Açao Integralista Brasileira (AIB) in 1932 as a means for social and political activism, targeting the creation of a strong Brazilian nation rooted in Catholicism. The movement purportedly attempted to avoid "struggles between provinces, between classes, between races, between groups of whatever nature" (Salgado, 1937, p. 174). In the programmatic "integral directives" distributed in 1933 from the central to provincial offices, the "integral unity" of the "integral state" was thought to be assured by means of a strong central government and a corporatist representation of all social units. *Educação integral* here was seen to play a key role, comprising the joint mission of family, church and nation-state (understood as a society of families), embedded in a hierarchical worldview. By 1937 this movement claimed to operate more than 3,000 schools and community centers with the intention to additionally create "universities inspired by the principles of an integral philosophy" (AIB, 1933). "The idea of integral education for the integral human being was a constant in the integralist discourse" (Cavalari, 1999, p. 46), referring to both the whole human being (physical, intellectual, civic, spiritual) and the entire society (including physical, scientific, artistic, economic, social, political, religious aspects) (Cavalari, 1999). Political change eventually led to the movement's demise.

As a whole, though, Catholic use of the term integral education thrives. It is contemporarily used in such contexts as educational institute names, seminars titles, and mission statements. Contemporary Catholic educational researchers include Broedel, 2007; Bucher, 2007; Hancock, 2005; and those contributing to Hunt (2000).

Aurobindean Integral Education

Aurobindo Ghose (1872–1950), The Mother (1873–1973), Indra Sen (1903–1994), Haridas Chaudhuri (1913–1975)

A further still-contemporary interpretation of integral education is that stemming from Aurobindo Ghose (Sri Aurobindo). Following an education at Cambridge University, substantial engagement with political activism in India, and a brief role as secondary school teacher, Aurobindo re-oriented his life toward spiritual philosophy, developing *integral yoga*. *Integral* here derives from the Sanskrit *purna* meaning "complete" (Ryan, current volume). Aurobindo (2003) talked and wrote extensively on education throughout his life, although it was his spiritual partner, Mirra Alfassa/Richard—"The Mother" (1978/2002)—who explicitly named his approach "integral education," an identification further developed by Indra Sen (1952) and Haridas Chaudhuri (1977). The Mother created the Aurobindo Ashram school in 1943 (later to become the Aurobindo International Centre of Education) and conceived the idea of Auroville as a social laboratory for the future of humankind. Sen and Chaudhuri brought Aurobindo's integral philosophy, psychology, and education to the Academy, whilst Chaudhuri—whose PhD was entitled "Integral Idealism" (Subbiondo, 2005)—founded in 1968 the largest and longest-standing integral education institute, the California Institute of Integral Studies (CIIS).

As critical contrast to the hegemonic confusion between education and "the acquisition of [a narrowly defined] knowledge," (Aurobindo, 2003, p. 359) Aurobindean integral education addresses the conjunction of our physical, emotional, mental, and spiritual dimensions (Aurobindo, 2003; Chaudhuri, 1977) requiring intercultural and interreligious promotion (Ryan, current volume) in a spirit of equality, and a balanced individual lifelong self-educational process across and beyond all knowledge boundaries. "Integrality of education is conceived as a process of organic growth . . . dependent upon each child's inclination, rhythm of progression and law of development" (Raina, 2002, p. 376)—a freedom against "coercion, mindless test taking, and rote learning" (Ryan, current volume, p. 51). Aurobindo (2003) enunciated three principles of teaching, namely, that (i) nothing can be taught (*teacher as helper* rather than *teacher as instructor*); (ii) each person has their own type of development: it is "barbarous" to hold a pre-arranged idea regarding a student's learning direction; and (iii) one should work "from that which is to that which shall be" (p. 384).

Joseph Subbiondo, currently president of CIIS, forwards Chaudhuri's understanding that Aurobindo's approach addresses the quest to cohere Western and Eastern, left brain and right brain styles of thinking. He also forwards Chaudhuri's summation that Aurobindo gave "the world a complete art of integral living" (Chaudhuri, 1997 quoted in Subbiondo, 2005, p. 21) through nondual spiritual philosophy.

For further contemporary (Anglophone and non-Anglophone) discourse on Aurobindean integral education, see e.g., Adams, 2006; Axer, 1983; Das, 1999; Pani, 1987; Ranade, 2007.

Gebserian Integral Education

Jean Gebser (1905–1973)

The last stream outlined here regards that of integral cultural theorist Jean Gebser who left Germany as a young man to live a somewhat unsettled cosmopolitan and polyglot life across numerous countries. His ideas developed during the 1930s and 40s culminating in the publication of *Ursprung und Gegenwart* ("The Ever Present Origin") in 1949. Using a deep historico-philosophico-cultural approach, he identified the integral-aperspectival structure of consciousness (as the concretion or integration of preceding macrohistorical structures), a mode catalysed by the fifteenth-century renaissance—the "European experience of Bildung" (Gebser, 1956)—developing notably throughout the twentieth century alongside the previous mental-perspectival (still dominant) structure. Although a senior official in the Spanish Ministry of Education for a short spell, he wrote little on education. Nevertheless, as his work concerns a meta-perspective on the evolution of consciousness, it can be interpreted as offering integral education theorising a deep schema of worldview change for both culture and individual alike (Gebser, 1949/1985). Regarding considerations of the future of humankind stemming from such a perspective, Gebser identifies adult learning as playing a key role, and transcends the more restricted view of *education as necessarily involving institutions* to *education as life experience* (Schulz, 1965). As an exemplar of this view, he was invited to lecture at numerous universities and was even invited to take a chair at the University of Salzburg despite lacking high school qualification. He evolved the notion of *Bildung* to the yet more complex *Bewusstseinsbildung* where "the notion of *Bewusstseinsbildung* encompasses the integration of the results of the different academic disciplines and the integration of the different stages of life, through which we become free and open" (Schulz, 1965, p. 8).

Regarding the contemporary situation, Gebserian integral educational discourse can be found in both German (e.g., Bärtschi, 1998; Frei, 1985; Girg, 2007; Möhring, 1996), and English (e.g., Gallant, 2006; Gidley, 2007; Lozano & Mickunas, 1992; Murphy, 1988; Neville, 1999, 2001; Robinson, 2004).

Futuring the History of Integral Education

A rich plurality of integrally-minded education approaches can be identified throughout global history, including those explicitly using the term integral education. The above narrative makes a substantive contribution to the latter through elucidating underacknowledged threads.[7] Interpretations have varied widely from anarchist to authoritarian, from secular to spiritual, from philosophy to practice. Taken together these streams offer insights into the potential breadth, depth, and dangers of integral education, and can assist in the facilitation of cohering the current disconnection among integral approaches.

Available to us now is surely the genesis of an emerging unity-in-diversity of integral education streams, within a dynamic ecology of integral approaches. In order to embrace such a situation, we would need to duly acknowledge temporal trajectories, conceptual shapes, and practical implications relating to the various streams, noting that each stream has its own historical, cultural, and philosophical context, each with its own strengths and blind spots. Although they may seem from a certain perspective to be queer bedfellows, it is surely through such transversal juxtapositions that transformative learning both within and across the various integral education communities may be catalyzed. Apprehending the limitations of each integral approach can help us recognize the dangers of undue contraction (on whatever grounds). Taken as a set, they foreground the importance of interlinking individual emancipation, pedagogical innovation, revolutionary vitality, evolutionary thinking, spiritual tradition, and political action. An interpretation of integral education arising from the current historical overview can be characterized as involving the following themes:

1. A lifelong and lifewide practice across formal and informal learning opportunities;

2. Engagement with dimensions and aspirations of the whole human being in a dynamically harmonious way;

3. Cultivation and facilitation of inner qualities (for all ages and in all domains of life);

4. Connectivity, such as that between disciplines; occupations; cultures; theory and practice; private and public; beauty, truth, and goodness;

5. Engagement with the challenges and opportunities of the given era (regarding, for example, governance, technology, social justice, ecology);

6. Respect for the evolving freedom and uniqueness of the learner— education as self-determined, unfolding in an emancipatory way along individual trajectories;

7. Facilitation of a non-dogmatic, critical, experimental, and experiential enjoyment of being, becoming, doing, relating, and caring.

The last three points stem from a non-authoritarian interpretation of integral education. As such it indicates the possibility of tension between freedom-flow and a fixed ideological interpretation of an integral (education) theory.

Notes

1. All non-English quotes translated by Markus Molz.
2. Co-education was still illegal in France.
3. Professional education for practicing teachers had not yet been institutionalized.
4. Regarding de Chardin and education, see e.g., Collins (1973), Kim (2005), White (2008).
5. Historical wording has been maintained: *man* is to be interpreted as *humanity*.
6. Wilber does not reference Maritain in this regard.
7. It seems somewhat ironic to us that those who originated the term *integral education*—namely, anarchists and Catholics—are insufficiently credited for it; conversely, Aurobindo and Gebser did not foreground the term (although they wrote about *integral*).

References

Açao Integralista Brasileira. (1933). *Diretrizes integralistas.* Retrieved 2008/10/17 from www. integralismo.org.br?cont = 123&vis

Adams, A. (2006). *Education: From conception to graduation. A systemic, integral approach.* PhD dissertation, California Institute of Integral Studies.

Aurobindo, S. (2003). *The complete works of Sri Aurobindo. Vol. 1: Early cultural writings.* Pondicherry, India: Sri Aurobindo Ashram Press.

Axer, J. (1983). *Integrale Erziehung. Ein pädagogisches Konzept auf der Grundlage der Philosophie Sri Aurobindos.* Köln: Verlag Wissenschaft und Politik.

Bakunin, M. (1869). On education II. *Egalité.* Retrieved 2008/10/17 from www.spunk. org/texts/writers/bakunin/sp001401.html

Bärtschi, C. (1998). Pädagogische aspekte im werk Jean Gebsers, *Schulpraxis, 3,* 19–25.

Broedel, W. (2007). *Kritische Bildung—spirituell konzipiert.* PhD dissertation, University of Salzburg.

Bucher, A. (2007). *Wurzeln und Flügel. Wie spirituelle Erziehung für das Leben stärkt.* Düsseldorf: Patmos Verlag.

Carrel, A. (1952). *Reflections on life.* London: Hamish Hamilton.

Cavalari, R. M. F. (1999). *Integralismo—ideologia e organização de um partido de massa no Brasil* (1932–1937). Bauru: EDUSC.

Chaudhuri, H. (1977). *The evolution of integral consciousness.* Wheaton, IL: Theosophical Publishing House.

Collins, P. M. (1973). Teilhard de Chardin and Christian schools. *Educational Theory, 23*(3), 267–276.

Considérant, V. (1844). *Théorie de l'éducation naturelle et attrayante, dédiée aux mères.* Paris: Librairie de l'école sociétaire.

Das, M. (1999). *Sri Aurobindo on education.* New Delhi: National Council for Teacher Education.

Douyère-Demeulenaere, C. (1994). *Paul Robin (1837–1912): Un militant de la liberté et du bonheur.* Paris: Publisud.

D'Souza, M. O. (1996). Educational pastiche versus the education of natural intelligence and the intellectual virtues according to Jacques Maritain. *Educational Theory, 46*(4), 501–510.

Frei, L. (1985). *Die Anthropologie Jean Gebsers und ihre pädagogische Relevanz.* Masters thesis, University of Zürich.

Fourier, C. (1829). *Le nouveau monde industriel et sociétaire Vol.1 and Vol.2.* Retrieved 200817 from http://classiques.uqac.ca/classiques/fourier_charles/nouveau_monde/fourier_nouveau_monde_1.pdf and . . . /fourier_nouveau-monde_2.pdf

Fourier, C. (1808/1996). *Fourier: The theory of the four movements.* Ed. and trans. G. S. Jones & I. Patterson. Cambridge, UK: Press Syndicate of the University of Cambridge.

Gallagher, D. A. & Gallagher, I. (1976). *The education of man: The educational philosophy of Jacques Maritain.* Westport, CT: Greenwood.

Gallant, A. (2006). *Imagination: Resuscitating education.* Paper presented at the 3rd International Conference on Imagination and Education, Vancouver, Canada. Retrieved 2008/10/17 from www.ierg.net/confs/viewpaper.php?id = 234&cf = 3

Gallo, S. (1995). *Educação anarquista: um paradigma para hoje.* Piracicaba: Editora UNIMEP.

Gebser, J. (1949). *Ursprung und Gegenwart.* Stuttgart: Deutsche Verlags-Anstalt. Authorised English translation (1985): *The ever-present origin.* Athens, OH: Ohio University Press.

Gidley, J. (2007). The evolution of consciousness as a planetary imperative: An integration of integral views. *Integral Review, 5,* 4–226.

Girg, R. (2007). *Die integrale Schule des Menschen. Praxis und Horizonte der Integralpädagogik.* Regensburg: Roderer.

Godin, J.-B. (1871). *Solutions sociales.* Paris: Le Chevalier.

Hancock, C. I. (2005). *Recovering a catholic philosophy of elementary education.* Chicago, Il: Newman House Press.

Heinlein, M. (1998). *Klassischer anarchismus und erziehung. Libertäre pädagogik bei William Godwin, Michael Bakunin und Peter Kropotkin.* Würzburg: Ergon.

Hunt, T. C., Joseph, E. A. & Nuzzi, R. (2000). *Handbook of research on catholic education.* Charlotte, NC: Information Age Publishing.

Jeffries, V. (1999). The integral paradigm: The truth of faith and the social sciences. *The American Sociologist, 30*(4), 36–55.

Kim, B. Y. (2005). Teilhard de Chardin and holistic education. In J.P. Miller (Ed.), *Holistic learning and spirituality in education.* Albany, NY: SUNY, pp. 79–86.

Kropotkin, P. (1898/1912). *Fields, factories and workshops: or industry combined with agriculture and brain work with manual work.* London: Thomas Nelson & Sons.

LaFountain, P. (1999). Jacques Maritain (1882–1973). In *The Boston Collaborative Encyclopedia of Modern Western Theology.* Retrieved 200817 from http://people.bu.edu/wwildman/ WeirdWildWeb/coursesdictionary/mwt_themes_730_maritain.htm

Lozano, E. & Mickunas, A. (1992). Gebser and pedagogy: The integral difference. In E. M. Kramer & A. Mickunas (Eds.), *Consciousness and culture: An Introduction to the thought of Jean Gebser.* Westport, CT: Greenwood Press, pp. 179–200.

Maritain, J. (1932). *Distinguer pour unir, ou Les degrés du savoir.* Paris: Desclée de Brouwer. 2nd English translation (1995): *Distinguish to Unite or Degrees of knowledge.* (Collected Works Vol. 7). Notre Dame, IN: University of Notre Dame Press.

Maritain, J. (1936). *Humanisme intégral. Problèmes temporels et spirituels d'une nouvelle chrétienté.* Paris: Fernand Aubier. 2nd English translation (1968): *Integral hHumanism: Temporal and spiritual problems of a new Christendom.* New York: Scribner.

Maritain, J. (1943). *Education at the crossroads.* New Haven, CT: Yale University Press.

Marshack, D. (1997). *The common vision: Parenting and educating for wholeness.* Peter Lang.

McLaren, A. (1981). Revolution and education in late nineteenth century France: The early career of Paul Robin. *History of Education Quarterly, 21*(3), 317–335.

Möhring, M. (1996). *Von der Umweltbildung zur ganzheitlichen Bildung als Ausdruck integralen Bewusstseins.* PhD dissertation, University of Bremen.

Mother, The (1978/2002). *On education.* Collected Works of The Mother. Vol. 12 (2nd ed.). Pondicherry: Sri Aurobindo Ashram Trust. Retrieved 2008/10/17 from www.sriaurobindoashram.org/ashram/mother/downloadpdf.php?id = 12

Murphy, J. W. (1988). Computerization, Postmodern Epistemology, and Reading in the Postmodern Era. *Educational Theory, 38*(2), 167–283.

Neville, B. (1999). Towards integrality: Gebserian reflections on education and consciousness. *Encounter: Education for meaning and social justice, 12*(2), 4–20.

Neville, B. (2001). The body of the five-minded animal. In S. Gunn & A. Begg (Eds.), *Mind, body and society: Emerging understandings in knowing and learning.* Melbourne: University of Melbourne, pp. 57–64.

Pani, R. (1987). *Integral education: Thought and practice.* New Delhi: Ashish Publishing

Raina, M. K. (2002). Profiles of famous educators: Sri Aurobindo (1872–1950). *Prospects: The Quarterly Review of Comparative Education, 32*(3), 373–383.

Robin, P. (1869/18/72). De l'enseignement intégral. *Revue de philosophie positive,* V, VII, IX.

Robinson, P. (2004). Meditation: Its role in transformative learning and in the fostering of an integrative vision for Higher Education. *Journal of Transformative Education, 2,* 107–119.

Ranade, S, (2007). *Introduction to integral education: an inspirational guide.* Auroville: Sri Aurobindo International Institute for Educational Research.

Ryan, J. (current volume). *The complete yoga: The lineage of integral education.*

Salgado, P. (1937). *A doutrina do Sigma.* Rio de Janeiro: Schmidt.

Sen, I. (Ed.). (1952). *Sri Aurobindo and the Mother on education. Compilation of essential writings introducing integral education.* Pondicherry: Sri Aurobindo Ashram Trust.

Schulz, G. (Ed.). (1965). *Wege zum integralen bewußtsein. Eine festgabe für Jean Gebser zum 20. August 1965.* Bremen: Putscher.

Snauwaert, D. T. (1990). Toward a prophetic mythos: purpel and sorokin on culture and education. *Educational Theory, 40*(2), 231–235.

Stanford Encyclopedia of Philosophy (2008). *Jacques Maritain.* Retrieved 2008/10/17 http://plato.stanford.edu/entries/maritain

Subbiondo, J. (2005). An approach to integral education: A case for spirituality in higher education. *ReVision 28(2),* 18–32.

Suissa, J. (2001). Anarchism, utopias and philosophy of education. *Journal of Philosophy of Education, 35*(4), 627–646.

Suissa, J. (2006). *Anarchism and education: A philosophical perspective.* London: Routledge.

Wexler, J. (2005). Toward a model of integral education. *ReVision, 28*(2), 29–34.

Wilber, K. (1983). *Eye to eye: The quest for the new paradigm.* Boston, MA: Shambhala.

White, S. R. (2008). Multicultural visions of globalization: Constructing educational perspectives from the East and the West. *Interchange, 39*(1), 95–117.

The Complete Yoga

The Lineage of Integral Education

Jim Ryan

The word "integral" has entered the vocabulary of higher education. It has no single definition, admitting of a myriad of meanings and understandings in practice. But many in the West respond to the word nearly instinctively, as if it provides a resonance of possibility that is lacking in contemporary experience, not only in the educational realm. For the purposes of this chapter, I will use the meaning of the word Integral as it is inflected in the Integral Philosophy and Integral Yoga of Dr. Haridas Chaudhuri, who drew his central insights from the Indian sage Sri Aurobindo and from the ideas of Sri Aurobindo's spiritual partner Mirra Alfassa (referred to as The Mother. Also referenced as M. Richards.) (I term these three and their followers as "Integralists.") Taking Chaudhuri's notion of Integral for this discussion on education is by no means arbitrary. Chaudhuri founded the California Institute of Integral Studies in San Francisco in 1968, a graduate school, which was dedicated to the ideal of providing an integral education in the West.[1]

The word, Integral, in the tradition of Sri Aurobindo and The Mother is a term that comes from the Sanskrit word purna, which means complete. When Sri Aurobindo examined many of the ancient yogas of India, he found that each focused on a particular aspect of the human being. One yoga might focus on the physical body (hatha yoga), one might focus on the emotional (bhakti yoga), one might focus on a factor of knowledge (jnana yoga), or one might focus on action (karma yoga.) Sri Aurobindo, acknowledging and affirming the positive elements of these many yogas, endeavored to develop and practice an "Integral Yoga," a "Complete Yoga," that would serve the complete human being.

I will not dwell here on certain of the basic and unique philosophical assumptions that Sri Aurobindo and The Mother made. I will touch on them only later, in order to put them in proper context. For now let me summarize the notion of education that began its development with Sri Aurobindo, continued forcefully with The Mother, was adopted and formed in practice in higher education by Chaudhuri, and which has lived, sometimes hidden and sometimes overtly, at the California Institute of Integral Studies since Chaudhuri's death in 1975.

There may be numerous facets to the ideal integral education, but three stand out. Firstly, the Integralists believed that education should be of the whole human being; it must involve the physical, the emotional, the mental, and the spiritual. Secondly, it must be global and have reference to the, "total human situation" (Chaudhuri, 1977. p. 78). Thirdly, it must attempt to surmount the contradictions and antagonisms inherent in ordinary human cultural and philosophical positioning.

In regard to the education of the "whole human being," the elements of the physical, emotional, and mental education as outlined by the "Integral tradition," as defined here, are fairly easily translatable to innovative Western educators. I will outline these briefly later. But the usual stumbling block among educators in the West would be with the word spiritual in the litany. For the secular minded this word may sound too religious or too New Age. Naturally, words like, "the Divine," or, "God," (also, of course, "Goddess") which Dr. Chaudhuri, The Mother and Sri Aurobindo freely used would alienate the secular academic even further. Both The Mother and Chaudhuri, however, made efforts to be clear about this word spiritual, which stands for something that is, in the end, indefinable. They took pains to make the concept more accessible to the more secularly inclined, as neither of them saw a definite demarcation between what should be considered spiritual, and what should be considered secular.

In regard to the spiritual ideal, The Mother talked about a person's, "frame of consciousness beyond the frame of his ordinary life" (Aurobindo and Richards, 1966. p. 72). She states in regard to the spiritual that:

> This discovery very generally is associated with a mystic feeling, a religious life, because it is religions particularly that have been occupied with this aspect of life. But it need not be necessarily so: the mystic notion of God may be replaced by the more philosophical notion of truth and still the discovery will remain essentially the same, only the road leading to it may be taken even by the most intransigent positivist." (Aurobindo & Richards, 1966. p. 72)

The Mother goes further.

> The starting point is to seek in yourself that which is independent of the body and the circumstances of life, which is not born of the mental formations that you have been given, the language you speak, the habits and customs of the environment in which you live, the

country where you are born or the age to which you belong. You must find, in the depths of your being, that which carries in it the sense of universality, limitless expansion, termless continuity. (Aurobindo & Richards, 1966. p. 74)

She also says.

Through space and time many methods have been framed to attain this perception and finally to achieve this identification. Some methods are psychological, some religious, some even mechanical. In reality, everyone has to find that which suits him best, and if one has a sincere and steady aspiration, a persistent and dynamic will, one is sure to meet in one way or another, externally by study and instruction, internally by concentration, meditation and revelation and experience, the help one needs to reach the goal. (Aurobindo & Richards, 1966. p. 50)

In the simplest terms The Mother sees the goal as acquiring the capacity to know the, "the truth of our being, that is to say, the one thing for which we have been really created . . ." (Aurobindo and Richards, 1966. p. 49).

Chaudhuri (1966) invited, ". . . all men, believer or disbeliever, theist or atheist, to embark upon the voyage of life with total concern for the truth" (p. 28). Chaudhuri developed a notion of "universal religion" which was religion in name only. It was in fact a concept that included and transcended all religions, so that honest seekers of truth could join together without division. He called for three principles:

(1) A sincere search for the supreme truth and the ultimate meaning of life. In conducting this search, all biases, prejudices and preconceived notions must be set aside. Critical inquiry must be combined with radical open-mindedness. (2) A spirit of loving co-operation with fellow beings in the search for truth. It is by virtue of working together toward the common destiny of human welfare and progress that the bonds of universal love can be more and more strengthened. Active transformation of life and society in the light of truth. (3) A resolute will not only to know the truth but also to live up to the vision of truth. Such a resolution would naturally involve the willingness to make sacrifices for progressive transformation of life and society in light of the truth. (pp. 28–29)

These views of The Mother and Chaudhuri make a bit clearer what is meant by spiritual in the Integral tradition that they represent. The concept is spacious and inclusive, transcending religion and religions. Chaudhuri (1966) understands that, "An Atheist may be nearer god than a theist," (p. 28) and that, "A courageous agnostic may be a far more sincere spiritual seeker than a pious devotee whose loud professions of faith may be only a mask for his laziness or hypocrisy" (p. 28). He invites both theist and atheist on the quest for truth. The Mother also makes clear that, ". . . everyone has to find that which suits him best" (p. 50).

The statements quoted from The Mother and Chaudhuri were recorded during the 1950s. There are some obvious limitations to them, if we wish to define "Integral" in its widest scope of inclusiveness. Though remarkably open, they betray a bias toward Hindu notions of godhead. Buddhists particularly might find elements in the definitions of spiritual of both thinkers not always congenial. Also, because of their language of "universals" and notions like, "supreme truth," which again have Hindu roots, their philosophy, on its surface, would not meet well with postmodern thinking, which often emphasizes the deconstruction of the notion of the universal. Finally, the emphasis on "progress" and evolution is not a feature of Eastern philosophies, generally. However, the other two principles of integral education that are found in this tradition, outlined below, provide an internal corrective to such missteps (which are obvious to us now only because we have the wider angle of history and knowledge.) The other principles, which are still developing in practice in the Integral tradition inspired by these thinkers, reinforce the central thesis that Chaudhuri (1966) brought forward in regard to not only spirituality, but also to inquiry into anything in an Integral way: "In conducting this search, all biases, prejudices and preconceived notions must be set aside. Critical inquiry must be combined with radical open-mindedness" (p. 28).

Returning briefly to the other elements of the "education of the whole human being," we are on less abstract ground. The idea that education of the physical body is essential to a fuller human education accords with the Greek view, which is still quiet influential in Western cultural thought. Sri Aurobindo, The Mother, and Chaudhuri all understood that learning how to condition and keep tuned a healthy, vital human body was an essential part of the full education of a person. At the Sri Aurobindo Ashram in Pondicherry south India everyone participated (and participates) in rigorous cultivation of the physical body as part of Integral Yoga. Beyond simple exercise, they called for an "evocation of the potentialities" (Bhattacharya, 1952. p. 126), a "fullness of capacity" (p. 134), and a "totalness of fitness" (p. 134). We might consider some of the work done by Michael Murphy (who was a student of The Mother and Chaudhuri) on the body and sports and the work done by somatic psychologists as pointing toward this notion of bodily development that goes quite a bit beyond mere physical exercise. In the case of the Integralists it was understood that the body was a nexus of action of the Divine. However, bodily awareness, care, and health certainly provide the basis for a fuller education of the person, whether this belief in its "Divine" aspect is shared or not. In the West this has been understood for growing children, but has been nearly completely neglected in regard to adults.

Emotional education is the second realm of integral education as defined by these thinkers. The technical term used by all of them was "education of the vital." The Mother called the education of the vital, "perhaps the most important and the most indispensable" (Aurobindo and Richards, 1966. p. 62). The point is that for the human being, after the physical, the vital or emotional arena is the most difficult. In fact, one could say that if human beings could really begin to master the vital arena, the arena of emotions and passions, every aspect of human life on the planet would alter for the better.

A thorough exploration and understanding of a person's reactions, impulses, passions, and emotions is called for by The Mother and the Integralists. The approach is definitely yogic in that they expect a yoga-like attention to be brought to every aspect of the emotive life. But the yoga here is not a suppressive or an ascetical yoga. It is a yoga meant to clarify and bring to an almost aesthetical perfection the realm of feeling. Both The Mother and Sri Aurobindo were very active in the arts, particularly poetry and painting, and they saw engagement with the arts as crucial for education of the vital. This realm of the human being is educated then by creative art, by nuanced understanding of psychology, and by aware focus on the feeling realm of the human being. These realms may incidentally be included in mainstream educational strategies, but they are not comprehensively engaged. The hope here would be for a refined, sensitive, and powerfully moral human being to emerge from "vital education."

The education of the mental called for by the Integralists is, for the most part, understandable in generic terms. There is an emphasis on freedom in the learning process that most liberal educationists would endorse. Coercion, mindless test taking, and rote learning are all condemned. Because of the emphasis by the Integralists on an indefinable transcendent, however, the mental is not given supreme status as it is in the academic realm generally. The aim is always higher values, not merely mental facility. This results in a thinking process that focuses carefully on the dialectic of thought. The Mother herself advises to think in terms of thesis, antithesis, and synthesis. She urges that the mind be trained to envision an antithesis to each thesis that is developed. When this is done she urges a mental practice of envisioning a higher synthesis. She urges that the ambit of the mind be gradually and progressively expanded so as to encompass ever larger conceptual frameworks, based on this method of "uniting contraries" into more comprehensive syntheses (Aurobindo and Richards, 1966. p. 50). I will return to this element of the Integralists approach to mental education when discussing the final educational principle dealing with surmounting contradictions.

In conclusion, in this discussion of these four aspects of the human being which must be addressed in an "holistic" education, it must be understood that these domains are always, "interdependent and interpenetrating" (Aurobindo and Richards, 1966. p. 57). In the integrated human being they are to be developed to work in harmony toward the person's highest aspirations and most vital expression of life.

A second principle of integral education that was championed by Chaudhuri (1977) and The Mother called for a global education that made reference to the, "total human situation" (p. 78). Chaudhuri thought of an, "International Community Education," with the goal of "human unity" and "global peace" (p. 83). In different contexts he emphasized a list of principles that were important, among these were (1) Promotion of intercultural, interracial and inter-religious understanding; (2) Acceptance of ideological diversity within the global unity of human-kind; (3) Affirmation of the intrinsic dignity of all individuals, men and women, everywhere in the world; and (4) The essential equality of all races, and peoples and nations of the world.

Education for Chaudhuri meant taking into account the whole world. He did not in his books theorize as extensively on this issue as with other elements of his understanding of education, but the California Institute of Integral Studies as he developed it had a very wide academic reach, far beyond its basic East-West philosophy concentration. Theses and dissertations were done over many years on the politics, economics, anthropology, sociology, and area studies of many nations of the world. The bottom line was that he understood the crucial importance, in a developing global context, of mutual understanding between cultures and nations. One of the primary motivations for his establishing of the Cultural Integration Fellowship (founded in 1951, it still flourishes in San Francisco) was to work toward what he called cultural integration, a term which meant not eliminating diversity in cultural expression, but bringing it under a synthetic understanding which would allow people to embrace difference.

Along a line that ran parallel to Chaudhuri's, The Mother in 1952 theorized about an "International Centre of Education," (originally an idea of Sri Aurobindo) that would work toward "a collective reorganization [of human conditions], something that would lead toward an effective unity of mankind" (Aurobindo and Richards, 1966. p. 102). She imagined an educational center where people from all countries would share their arts, music, architecture, dress, games, food, etc. She thought that,

> A synthetic organization of all nations, each one occupying its own place in accordance with its own genius and the role it has to play in the whole, can alone effect a comprehensive and progressive unification which may have some chance of enduring. (p. 103)

She continued,

> The first aim then will be to help individuals to become conscious of the fundamental genius of the nation to which they belong and at the same time to put them in contact with the modes of living of other nations so that they may know and respect equally the true spirit of all the countries on the earth. (p. 104)

Naturally, this internationalist ideal was firmly joined with her understanding that both communal and individual progress must proceed simultaneously. She imagined in this international center that the individuals would all be in search of their highest spiritual development, while they worked toward collective "unification." Part of the purpose of the international Utopian experiment, Auroville, which was established in 1968 in south India by The Mother and the Pondicherry Sri Aurobindo Ashram, was to join these two ideals.

To put it most simply, the ideals of education of The Mother and Chaudhuri, under this rubric of global education, meant an emphasis on unity in diversity. The ideal was a progressive effort to surmount individual, cultural, and national differences by adopting a view that saw in all such oppositions the possibility of a deeper complementarity and the possibility of a synthesis at a higher level of what originally appeared opposed. This is, in effect, the application of Indian spiritual understandings of non-duality to everyday existence and life, but whatever its genesis it lays out a progressive and inspiring ideal for human education.

The final element of the scheme of integral education of the Integralists that I am emphasizing here is the attempt to surmount the contradictions and antagonisms inherent in ordinary human cultural and philosophical positioning. This may well be the most subtle and difficult of the elements of the Integral tradition to grasp, yet I feel it may be the most significant. I am certain it is inspired by a mystic vision for lack of a better term, which is not accessible to many—the non-dual vision that the Integralists relentlessly used to engage difference. (But never to eliminate difference!). There are parallels in certain postmodern thought and in work such as that of Edgar Morin, which I shall not engage here. Because of the mystic commitment of the Integralists, who saw (more correctly "realized") an overarching unitary Reality that brought everything together, they were always aware of the relativity of any intellectually formulated view. This lead at crucial junctures of their thought to a quite distinct sense of "truth," one that directly contradicted Aristotle. The Mother once made the startling statement that the opposite of anything that is true is also true (Satprem, 1979, p.172).[2]

This is the crux of it. If we understand that everything that contradicts our views in the human context is a complementary truth that must be comprehended by us at a more spacious level, we can then explain why it was that the Integral tradition as taught and practiced by its premier American exponent, Dr. Chaudhuri, was so open and expansive. It offers to the educational environment a completely unique embrace of difference and contradiction that I believe is a powerful healing force. When at the mental, at the intellectual, and more importantly at the emotional and vital level, we can cognize and feel in the contending opposite idea or feeling an identity with our own, we cross a threshold of consciousness from which there is no going back. This is one of the reasons why I suspect that even the fundamental philosophical notions of the Integralists such as the notions of evolution, Divine Unity, etc., need not be seen as barriers to being a follower of the Integralists' path. Some have theorized about a notion in mental terms of warm thinking, which combines a spiritual aspiration with thinking, to change the way ratiocination is done. In the case of the Integralists, I would like to suggest a notion of vectors of truth which may, in worldly terms, sometimes conflict, but which must all be susceptible of a final "resolution" in the human heart and consciousness. This then brings us to a place where we are bound to embrace every aspect of the human being, every aspect of the world, and every contradiction as the highest exercise in education.

Notes

1. The original name of the school was the California Institute of Asian Studies. The school became the California Institute of Integral Studies, when it became accredited in 1980. I am not claiming, here, any perfection of the Integral ideal (however defined) in this school, but I do believe that the central conceptions of this concept of "Integral" do deserve attention in the field of education.

2. The full quote is: "When one thing is true, you can be sure that its opposite is also true. And when you have understood that, you have begun to understand."

References

Aurobindo, S. & M. Richard. (1966). *Sri Aurobindo and the Mother on education*. Pondicherry, India: Sri Aurobindo Ashram.

Bhattacharya, P. K. (Ed). (1952). *Scheme of education*. Pondicherry, India: Sri Aurobindo Ashram.

Chaudhuri, H. (1966). *Modern man's religion*. Santa Barbara: J. F. Rowny Press.

Chaudhuri, H. (1977). *The evolution of integral consciousness*. Wheaton, Ill.: Theosophical Pub. House.

Satprem. (1979). *The Mother or the divine materialism. Part I*. Paris: Institut de Reserches Evolutive.

II

Distinct Approaches

Integral Theory in Service of Enacting Integral Education

Illustrations from an Online Graduate Program[1]

Sean Esbjörn-Hargens

Both mainstream and holistic approaches toward education have much to recommend. Thus, it is unfortunate that proponents of alternative education all too often pit themselves against traditional education. As a result, they often overlook the strengths of traditional models and fail to see their own holistic blind spots. Likewise, mainstream education often views itself immune to any insights coming from the holistic approaches and refuses to admit its own limits. Consequently, we are left with two fragmented, partial approaches—each equally incapable of providing a meta-perspective on education. What is needed is an integral educational approach that honors the strengths and limits of both mainstream and alternative educational approaches and is therefore more capable of situating these general philosophies and the programs that embody them into a more comprehensive framework that facilitates a dynamic learning environment.

In this chapter, I will focus on a particular approach to integral education by introducing distinctions based *on* Integral Theory that are used in an online graduate program *in* Integral Theory. Integral Theory is both the context and the content of the program. In other words, Integral Theory is used to enact an integral educational context that explores Integral Theory. Integral Theory is a post-metaphysical approach to knowledge synthesis that is based on the AQAL ("all-quadrants, all-levels") framework, its five elements, and Integral Methodological Pluralism (IMP) (see Wilber, 2006). As a result, Integral Theory provides a comprehensive means of integrating the four dimension-perspectives of objectivity, interobjectivity, subjectivity, and intersubjectivity (and their respective levels of complexity) with the major methodological families (e.g., phenomenology, empiricism, structuralism, hermeneutics, systems theory, etc.) in such a way that avoids postulating pre-existing ontological structures. Thus, Integral Theory is interested in the participatory relationship through which multiple ways of knowing the myriad dimensions of reality occur through various methods of inquiry. When applied to education, this Integral approach is designed to offer an effective means to combine the best of both conventional and alternative approaches in a particular form of integral education

A central goal of this chapter is to outline how the five elements of Integral Theory can provide a useful and comprehensive approach to enacting integral education especially at the graduate level. To accomplish this, I will outline four aspects of each element, for a total of twenty, and demonstrate how this heuristic offers a template for an Integral approach to education through supporting the development of integral teachers and students alike. After introducing each element I will depict the possibilities of integral education by drawing on brief examples from the Master of Arts in Integral Theory program at John F. Kennedy University. I am the founding chair of this program, which is explicitly based on Integral Theory and its associated AQAL model (see appendix for its program learning outcomes) This chapter will serve as an invitation to other educators and students to explore how elements of Integral Theory might support their own efforts toward embracing more inclusive, comprehensive, and integral approaches to education. The breadth of Integral Theory introduced can benefit different approaches and levels of education by inspiring educators to reflect critically on missing elements of their curricula and expanding the pedagogical modalities in their repertoire as well as support what they are already doing. Even a partial implementation of ideas from Integral Theory can result in educational experiences that allow students and teachers to see, feel, and experience more of reality in the classroom. Many of the suggestions and examples throughout this chapter could be recalibrated in order to be developmentally appropriate for other ages and education programs (e.g., K through 12 or undergraduate) The integral vision outlined in this chapter would necessarily look and feel different at various levels of psychological development and within various curricula. It is my hope that by sharing how I have used Integral Theory to inform my own educational efforts, I will inspire other educators to use the AQAL model in creative ways to accomplish integral education.

Integral Theory

Today's academia is characterized by disciplinary turf wars and clashes between traditional, modern, and postmodern perspectives. In response Integral Theory offers a framework that is the result of over 30 years of cross-cultural and post-disciplinary scholarship and application As a result of its applicability across, within, and between disciplinary boundaries, Integral Theory has been widely applied by individuals associated with over 35 professional fields, including art, business, research, ecology, medicine, consciousness studies, religion, criminology, psychology, healthcare, nursing, politics, and sustainability, to name a few

Often represented by the acronym AQAL, Integral Theory's signature phrase "all-quadrants, all-levels" is shorthand for the multiple aspects of reality recognized in an Integral approach (Wilber, 1995). According to Wilber, there are at least five recurring elements that comprise an Integral approach: *quadrants, levels, lines, states,* and *types.* These five components represent the basic patterns of reality that recur in multiple contexts. To exclude an element in any inquiry or exploration is to settle for a less comprehensive understanding or a reduced participatory engagement with reality. In contrast, by including these basic elements, an integral practitioner ensures that he or she is considering the main aspects of any phenomena: all-quadrants, all-levels, all-lines, all-states, and all-types.

The first element, all-quadrants, refers to the basic perspectives an individual can take on reality: the interior and exterior of individuals and collectives, which is often summarized as the following four dimensions—experience ("I"; subjectivity), culture ("We"; intersubjectivity), behavior ("It"; objectivity), and systems ("Its"; interobjectivity) Each of these perspective-dimensions is irreducible and has its own validity claim (i.e., truthfulness, justness, truth, and functional fit) and mode of investigation (see Fig. 1). The quadrants provide a particularly helpful

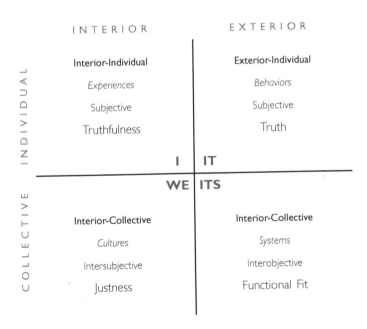

Figure 1. Some Aspects of the Quadrants

lens for educators to understand their own role in the classroom. For example, if you are a teacher, you have the "I" of your perceived embodied self, the "We" of the intersubjective relationships between yourself and the students, the "It" of your own actions and behaviors in class as well as the activities you have students engage in, and the "Its" of the educational system with its rules, policies, and institutional dynamics.

The next four elements of the Integral model arise in each of the four quadrants: All-levels refers to the occurrence of complexity within each dimension (e.g., the levels of physical complexity achieved by evolution in the behavior quadrant); all-lines refers to the various distinct capacities that develop through each of these levels of complexity (e.g., the developmental capacities of cognition, emotions, and morality in the experience quadrant); all-states refers to the temporary occurrence of any aspect of reality within the four quadrants (e.g., weather states in the systems quadrant); and all-types refers to the variety of styles that aspects of reality assume in various domains (e.g., types of festivals in the cultural quadrant).

Because each element is understood to be part of each and every moment, Integral Theory claims that if an approach to education excludes any of these components, it falls short of a truly Integral approach. Integral Theory assigns no ontological or epistemological priority to any of these elements because they co-arise and "tetra-mesh" simultaneously While Integral Theory provides a particular way of including these five elements, it recognizes that other approaches to education can achieve this without adhering explicitly to the AQAL model[10]

Integral Education

Over the last decade, there have been a number of milestones in the application of Integral Theory to integral education. In 1995, Ken Wilber published his groundbreaking 800-page tome *Sex, Ecology, Spirituality*, which ushered in the "all-quadrant, all-level," Integral approach. Shortly after its publication, individuals began applying the AQAL model to many fields and disciplines, including education[11] The Integral model provided these educators with a viable way of bringing together the best aspects of both conventional and alternative approaches, as well as highlighting the limits of each. The previous dilemma of how to choose between mainstream or holistic education programs or to try and assemble piecemeal aspects of both gave way to an interest in exploring how the meta-framework of the AQAL model could provide a more comprehensive and effective way to build upon these differing approaches.

Integral education then attempts to combine the best of traditional approaches with the insights of alternative ones. It provides both academic rigor that develops the rational mind for critical inquiry and connects students to their preverbal bodies and transpersonal Spirit through experiential and collaborative inquiry. Whereas conventional approaches tend to emphasize the objective dimension of empirical science and rationality, and holistic approaches tend to highlight both the subjective dimension of expression and self-inquiry and the intersubjective dimension of collaboration and meaning-making, an Integral approach includes and values all three dimensions: objective, subjective, and intersubjective[12]

In fact, one of the key principles of my conception of integral education is the recognition that these three dimensions can be seen in how the teacher, the students, and the classroom all co-arise and enact each other. If one of these components of the educational space receives substantially less attention than the others, then a teacher's attempts at an integral education will fall short of the AQAL integral ideal. Integral teachers should strive to simultaneously attend to (1) their own subjectivity and "vertical" transformation through such practices as self-inquiry, meditation, shadow work, and embodied exercises; (2) the intersubjectivity they share with their students through such practices as reflective dialogue, collaborative exercises, perspective taking, and providing presence while others speak; and (3) their classroom through such practices as arrangement of seats/tables, use of space, structure of each class (e.g., rules and roles), opening windows, use of visual aids and handouts, assignments, and length of breaks.

Thus teachers aspiring to embody the AQAL model proposed here should recurrently attend to these three dimensions: opening oneself to being continually shaped as an integral teacher (the "I"); supporting and challenging students to be integral students (the "We"); and recreating class structures into an Integral classroom (the "It/s"). Each of these three spheres has the capacity for vertical development. Teachers (and students) can individually develop toward worldcentric and post-rational capacities within multiple lines of psychological development (cognitive, emotional, interpersonal, moral, kinesthetic, etc.). Students in a course or program create a culture—a "We" space—that can also develop along a continuum from egocentric narcissism (e.g., "We are not going to do what the teacher says!") to ethnocentric herd mentalities (e.g., "We will do what the teacher expects or what our parents and friends think we should do.") to expressions of worldcentric per-spectivalism (e.g., "We will keep many perspectives in mind and do what serves ours and others' own growth within multiple dimensions."). Classroom structures can also develop along a spectrum that supports and correlates with the vertical transformation of individuals and the group. On one end of the spectrum, you have authoritarian structures (e.g., rigid rules, teachers with unilateral power, and teachers serving as expert), and on the other end you have Torbert's (1991) liberat-ing structures that support group-reflectivity through multiple feedback loops and dynamically evolving part-whole relationships. You can have an integral classroom but lack integral students; you can be an integral teacher but not have an integral classroom, and so on. Thus, an Integral approach to teaching as I am defining it aspires to coordinate and attend to all three, which in turn helps create the condi-tions of a dynamic, transformative space.

This triadic approach is relevant to education in myriad contexts and is currently being applied to every level of education from kindergarten to graduate school[13] As a way of illustrating in more detail what an Integral approach to education consists of, I will now examine education in light of the five elements of Integral Theory, providing concrete examples of what an integral teacher can be aware of in cultivating an integral learning context for students and creating an integral classroom. As mentioned above, there are many ways to include these five elements, what follows will serve as an illustration, not a paradigmatic example. Also, the inclusion of these five elements is scalable and therefore can be as simple and straightforward or as complex, ambitious, and detailed as one likes. In fact, this scalability is what makes the Integral model useful in being adaptable to various contexts.

The experience at JFKU has shown many of its teachers and students how the Integral model provides an effective template to design pedagogy, classroom activities, evaluations, courses, assessments, and curricula. Drawing on the five elements of quadrants, levels, lines, states, and types, an instructor can be sure to include more essential aspects of educational space than most current approaches.

For the purposes of this chapter, I will be broadly defining integral education as follows: an approach to education that (1) integrates the strengths of traditional, modern, and postmodern educational theoria and praxis by incorporating first-, second-, and third-person perspectives and methods, and (2) is committed to vertical growth and horizontal integration within both students and teachers. This definition is meant to capture the essence of an AQAL approach to education but also be spacious enough to allow for various non-AQAL approaches. In other words, I want to propose a general definition that can support conflicting but generative approaches within or outside of an AQAL context. The point is there can be many ways to accomplish the goals of Integral Theory without necessarily adhering to the current presentation of the AQAL model. For example, one of the main aims of the above definition is the avoidance of the kinds of splitting all too often associated with both mainstream and alternative approaches, which fail to hold the dignity and disaster of each other, various disciplines, and different worldviews. On the one hand, we do not want to short-circuit how the field of integral education might express itself. On the other hand, there is value in making clear the guiding principles that distinguish the approach to integral education presented in this chapter from some of the other approaches that also call themselves "integral." With that in mind, we can now examine the twenty aspects of integral education I have identified that can result from using Integral Theory.

Twenty Aspects of Integral Education

The Integral model provides an effective template to design pedagogy, classroom activities, evaluations, courses, assessments, and curriculum. Drawing on the five elements of Integral Theory, an instructor can be sure to include more essential aspects of educational space than most current approaches. These elements can be used to generate an integral analysis so that instructors can quickly assess themselves, their students, and current courses more effectively. But just what, exactly, does integral education and instruction consist of?

One answer is all four quadrants of the AQAL framework, four general levels of developmental altitude in each quadrant, four lines of psychological development, four states of awareness, and four general typology approaches to learners—one per each quadrant. By drawing on at least four distinctions within each element you provide yourself with an even number of checkpoints to ensure that you are staying in contact with a manageable amount of irreducible aspects of reality. Admittedly, this is an ambitious template. While it is ambitious, there are a growing number of educational programs like those at JFKU that are striving to successfully include and apply these 20 aspects (four kinds of each of the five elements) at the graduate level.

In covering all these aspects, Integral approaches to education can continue to expand and incorporate other aspects and dimensions as is appropriate for each context, such as types of religions or cultural lines of development. Of course, further distinctions within all the elements are encouraged and can be incorporated into various educational settings. These 20 aspects can be applied to the teacher, the students, and the classroom. For the purposes of this chapter, I will only provide a brief overview of these 20 aspects in order to give you a sense of the potential of this framework. Along the way I will illustrate ways the Integral Theory program at JFKU works with these aspects at various scales: classes, courses, curriculum.

Quadrants

Using the first element of quadrants, an Integral approach to education recognizes that any educational moment contains four irreducible dimensions: educational behaviors, such as reading, writing, lecturing, and sitting in chairs; educational experiences, such as imagination, emotional reactions, intuitions, thoughts, and insights; educational cultures, such as what is appropriate to say in class, shared meaning between students and faculty, and group values; and educational systems, such as financial aid structures, program curriculum, grading rubrics, and school policies. Each of these four dimensions is always present whether a teacher is preparing lessons at home, students are chatting in the hall, or the school is closed for the holidays. By recognizing that every moment in the classroom contains these four dimensions, you, as a teacher or student, can begin to consciously interact with these aspects for a deeper communion with reality and a fuller capacity for responsiveness.

Within each dimension, integral education recognizes that there are at least three broad levels of complexity that can be loosely correlated with body, mind, and spirit (see Fig. 2). For example, within educational experiences, a teacher can give an assignment that invites students into (1) exploring the felt-experience of their bodies, (2) engaging a theory with their critical mind, or (3) noticing the ever-present Witness of their own awareness.

These 12 foci serve as a summary of the essential dimensions of an AQAL approach to integral education. These 12 components can also be reframed as forms of engagement. In other words, not only can these 12 aspects represent the essential goals of a course or program (e.g., to be ethical, to be experiential, to be practical), but they can be seen as the various modes of interaction and ways of knowing the world. For example, as a teacher or student, you can ask, "In what ways does my course support _____" (insert each of the 12 ways of knowing in Figure 2).

Each of these ways of knowing transcends and includes the terms listed in their respective quadrant (see Fig. 3). Thus, an AQAL approach to integral education can be summarized as one that is accomplished through the four activities of: Integral Action (UR), Integral Inquiry (UL), Integral Participation (LL), and Integral Dynamism (LR). In this context, integral education becomes a commitment to continually engage in action in the world as skillfully as possible; inquire into one's interior space along the entire spectrum of experience; participate compassionately with a variety of worldviews; and support the health and dynamism of all global systems.

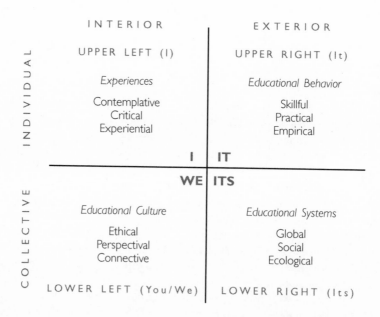

Figure 2. Twelve Foci of Integral Education

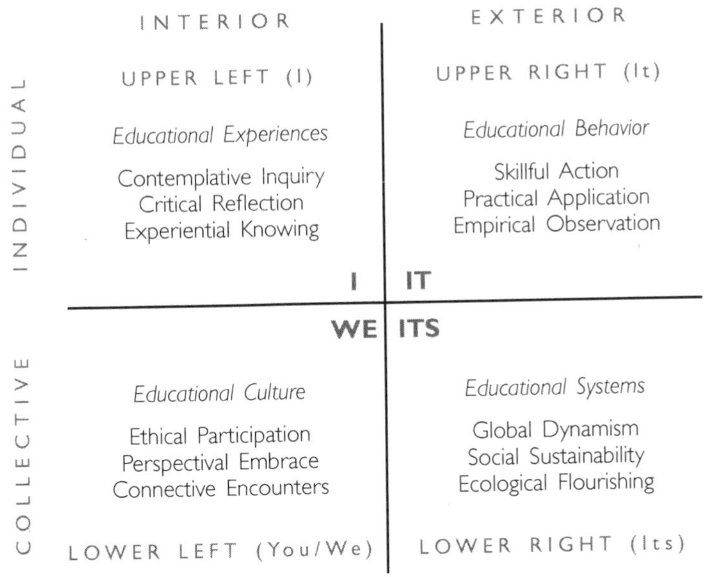

INTERIOR   EXTERIOR

UPPER LEFT (I)   UPPER RIGHT (It)

Educational Experiences   *Educational Behavior*

Contemplative Inquiry   Skillful Action
Critical Reflection   Practical Application
Experiential Knowing   Empirical Observation

I | **IT**

WE | **ITS**

Educational Culture   *Educational Systems*

Ethical Participation   Global Dynamism
Perspectival Embrace   Social Sustainability
Connective Encounters   Ecological Flourishing

LOWER LEFT (You/We)   LOWER RIGHT (Its)

INDIVIDUAL (left margin, vertical)
COLLECTIVE (left margin, vertical)

Figure 3. Twelve Ways of Knowing

The quadrants are used in a variety of ways within the JFKU Integral Theory program. They are an explicit part of two of the five Program Learning Outcomes (PLOs) (see appendix). I used them to build the curriculum, making sure the program has four to five courses focusing on content associated with each quadrant. Many course assignments use them such as "integral journaling" in Developmental Psychology (Esbjörn-Hargens, 2006) and feedback/data analysis in Integral Life Practice Inquiry (Golin, 2008). We also use them to help design the two annual four-day residential gatherings—making sure we are attending to all four domains. We also employ the quadrants to identify lines of evidence for our ongoing self-study process as part of our accreditation.

Levels

In Integral Theory, levels can refer to either the general altitude of development across multiple lines or specific levels within a given line. In the context of the 20 aspects of an AQAL approach to integral education, levels refers to four general levels of altitude that occur in each of the quadrants. Using Wilber's (2006) color spectrum these are Amber, Orange, Green, and Teal. Other altitudes are important but given that these are the most common levels they receive particular focus here. These four levels are associated with the four most prevalent worldviews: traditional, modern, postmodern, and integral. Each of these worldviews has its own preferred behaviors, experiences, culture, and systems.

Thus, integral education includes these four levels and their correlates in all four quadrants as they occur within the teacher, the students, and the classroom. For example, a teacher might commonly have Teal-integral experiences of inhabiting multiple perspectives, live in a small town embedded in an Amber-traditional culture, and teach in a Orange-modern school system, where she is expected to perform Orange-modern educational behaviors (lecture for most of the class, give multiple choice tests, etc.). A detailed description of these levels in the context of education (e.g., traditional educational experiences, modern educational experiences, etc.) is beyond the scope of this chapter. However, I want to discuss one area that focuses on the value of recognizing these four general levels in students' experience.

I believe it is important for integral educators to continually ask themselves how to teach in a way that could help their students transform vertically toward post-rational modes of being. According to Kegan (1994), there are five basic developmental levels or "orders of consciousness" that define how a person knows the world or constructs reality. The first three levels are similar to those found in today's child and adolescent development texts: 1st order (ages 2–6 yrs), 2nd order (6–teens), and 3rd order (teens and beyond). Most adults (>80%) in developed nations reach at least the conformist or 3rd order of consciousness, where a person is able to internalize a value system, understand and respect the needs of others, and think abstractly.

In addition to the three commonly accepted stages or orders of consciousness development, Kegan's research demonstrates the existence of two others—4th and 5th orders. At the autonomous or 4th order of consciousness, a person becomes "self-authoring"—that is, they become capable of constructing their own value systems as opposed to operating within the value systems given to them by their culture, family, or place of work. At an integral or 5th order (Wilber's vision-logic), they begin to bring together and synthesize many different value systems into coherent and meaningful wholes. Kegan correlates the 3rd, 4th, (4.5), and 5th orders of consciousness with traditional, modern, postmodern, and integral worldviews.

This developmental sequence is essential for an AQAL approach to integral education because it means that even if a teacher is at the 4th or 5th order of consciousness, many of their undergraduate and graduate students will be transitioning between 3rd and 4th order.[14] Not to mention that integral content generally demands a 5th order of consciousness in order to be fully grasped both conceptually and in an embodied way. An important question that emerges is: How do we as educators work creatively with this situation and avoid placing students in over their heads? By creating an integral classroom, university teachers can support and challenge their students to develop beyond their 3rd and 4th order selves in order to more fully experience and embody 4th and 5th order integral capacities.

In light of the dynamics outlined above the JFKU Integral Theory program has recently began working with Theo Dawson and Zachary Stein of Developmental Testing Services to research and build a new developmental measurement: Lectical Integral Model Assessment (LIMA). LIMA is part of the program's ambitious iTEACH project.[15] One of the main goals of this psychometric is to identify how students at different levels of psychological development interpret and apply the Integral model. In so doing we will be able to identify the developmental learning sequences related to Integral Theory and be able to adjust our curriculum and pedagogy accordingly. As such, we will minimize the conditions that put students "in over their heads" and in turn help our students apply Integral Theory (PLO 4—see appendix). In addition to these uses of levels in the program, there is an emphasis on cultivating students capacities to understand and "speak to" the value systems of the major worldviews mentioned above (PLO 1—see appendix).

Lines

Since Howard Gardner published *Frames of Mind* (1983), the notion of multiple intelligences has received considerable enthusiasm within mainstream educational circles. In Integral Theory multiple intelligences that are known to demonstrate vertical growth are called developmental lines. There are over a dozen developmental lines that have been researched (Wilber, 1997). While there are lines of development in all the quadrants, there are at least four main developmental lines within an individual's interior that integral education should take into consideration: cognitive, emotional, moral, and kinesthetic[16] Each of these four capacities of an individual's self-system allows them to grasp a different aspect of reality: Cognitive line: grasp of the (inter)objective realm, including sensory input, perspective taking, and interconnections between phenomena; emotional line: grasp of the subjective realm, including feelings and impulses, internal sensations, and phenomenological awareness; moral line: grasp of the intersubjective realm, including interpersonal obligations and responsibility, duty, and compassion; and kinesthetic line: grasp of the somatic and physical realm, including physical sensations, hand-eye coordination, and bodily movement.

By developing these four capacities we serve ourselves in multiple ways and provide an ongoing integrative process between essential components of the self-system. There are many ways, as I will demonstrate, that these four aspects of the self-system can be exercised and honored in education. Other important lines are the interpersonal, spiritual, aesthetic, and self-identity lines[17]

Lines of development are used in several noteworthy ways within the JFKU Integral Theory program. First, students are continuously engaged throughout the program's classes and activities in their own Integral Life Practice (PLO 5—see appendix). Integral Life Practice exercises all four of the major lines discussed above as well as others through a variety of combined practices and injunctions (see Golin, 2008; and Kreisberg, this volume, for a more detailed description of ILP). Also, faculty members are expected to be working with a robust ILP of their own, making the program a dynamic practice community where daily and weekly practice are supported. Second, as part of the iTEACH project, students and faculty are assessed along multiple lines (e.g., ethics, interpersonal, reflective judgment, emotions, and ego identity). This is done to provide direct feedback on where people's growth edges are as well as for curriculum development.

States

Numerous states of embodiment, consciousness, and awareness occur within the educational context. Teachers and students often experience such ordinary and non-ordinary states as insight, confusion, joy, presence, hurt, clarity, embarrassment, fatigue, hunger, and so on. It is important to be aware of the occurrence of states and the role they play in and out of the classroom. By working actively with various states, the transformative space and translative capacity of the classroom can be increased dramatically. Integral Theory has spent a lot of time exploring the role of states in relationship to levels and lines (Wilber, 2006). There are at least four main categories of natural states of consciousness that are acknowledged and included in integral education. The first three are those states associated with waking, dreaming, and deep sleep: *gross-waking states* that take physical reality as its object such as the experience of the world through the five senses and physical impulses and sensations; *subtle-dream states* that take the subtle realm as its object such as visualizations, imagination, reverie, dreams, emotions, images, and the experience of luminosity; *causal-formless states* that take vast openness as its object such as formlessness, certain types of spaciousness, vast openness, and the experience of emptiness (shunyata). The fourth category is *witnessing states*, which can take any state as its object and witness it such as the capacity for unbroken attention (gross), lucid dreaming (subtle), or formless absorption (causal) (Wilber, 2003b).

According to Integral Theory, each of these interior states has an exterior body associated with it. For example, a dreaming state is connected to the subtle body. Thus, by including these various states, an integral educator is also including the major bodies that the esoteric traditions recognize and work with. An AQAL approach to integral education also takes the position that ever-present Nondual awareness is the ground of all states. These various states (and their accompanying bodies) can be included in numerous ways in education through various exercises and practices (e.g., body-based meditations and movement exercises), homework assignments (e.g., journaling about one's experiences while doing some chi gong exercises), and group activities (e.g., t'ai chi).

States are used throughout the JFKU Integral Theory program. Almost every course has a weekly meditation or practice that is some form of state-training. Some courses spend a lot of time working with states—such as Integral Zen's requirement of several hours of zazen practice each week, Phenomenological Inquiry's utilization of small groups to explore our direct experience of first-person embodiment, or Integral Ecology's use of 18 practices for cultivating integral ecologoical aware-ness. Also, the program provides students and faculty with a list of 10 awareness practices that are expected to be used both in and out of class. This list includes such practices as embodied reading, presence, reflective dialogue, witnessing, and perspective taking—each of these works explicitly with states in various ways.

Types

The last element of the AQAL model is types, which is often used to include masculine/feminine and/or personality types. There are many types of learners and various cartographies that map their learning styles. These typologies range from well-documented gender differences, to the equally popular triad of visual, auditory, kinesthetic/tactile learners, which can be expanded into the five sensory represen-tational systems of neurolinguistic programming (NLP), to the sophisticated nine type personality system of the Enneagram, or the sixteen Myers-Briggs personalities. While awareness of all these and the many other documented approaches to learning can enrich education, integral education recognizes at least one main category of learning styles per quadrant: sensory styles of learning in the Upper-Right quadrant (e.g., NLP); personality styles of learning in the Upper-Left quadrant (e.g., the Enneagram); gender styles of learning in the Lower-Left quadrant (i.e., masculine or feminine); and preferred narrative styles in the Lower-Right quadrant (e.g., first-, second-, and third-person narrative structures of communicating).[18] By being aware of and including these basic categories of learning types, educators dramatically increase their capacity to be aware of their own type strengths and weaknesses in each of these areas, to be more effective in the classroom through well-designed activities, and to be more responsive to students and their diverse needs.

Types play a valuable role throughout the JFKU Integral Theory program. The typology of choice within the JFKU Integral Theory program is arguably the Enneagram. Students take a course in the Enneagram at the end of their first year and its language and system are often utilized in other courses. Faculty build and deliver their courses in ways that appeal to multiple learning styles and personal-ity types. Many courses require students to weave together first-, second-, and third-person narrative styles in their weekly assignments and final papers (PLO 2—see appendix)

In summary, by applying the AQAL framework educators can become more integrally informed in their practice, in turn better serving the enactment of them-selves, their students, and schools. The 20 aspects of integral education outlined above provide a bridge between Integral Theory and educational practices. These 20 aspects can be adopted for a variety of educational goals and situations. For example, they can serve as a basis for developing more integral theories of learning and teaching, developing teacher training programs, establishing new classroom activities, articulating an integral educational philosophy, putting together curricula, creating integral education policies, guiding research on educational effectiveness, and exploring how the educational environment can be used as part of Integral Life Practices.[19]

Enacting Integral Education

With its many elements and distinctions Integral Theory helps to enact a multidimensional learning environment that brings us into a fuller engagement with the major aspects of reality and allows a variety of ways of knowing and being. Drawing on Integral Theory, an AQAL approach emphasizes a number of commitments which serve to enact integral education: (1) The best components of both conventional and alternative approaches to education can be integrated into a fuller, wider, deeper, more transformative educational space that is integral in its curriculum, pedagogy, evaluation, assessment, and methods of inquiry. The AQAL model is a helpful and a comprehensive framework capable of accomplishing this task. (2) The teacher, the students, and the classroom can engage transformative and translative processes through various practices of awareness, interaction, and organization. It is of utmost importance that the teacher continually engages in his or her own transformative and integrative practices, such as meditation and shadow work, in order to better stabilize post-rational modes of being and knowing. (3) The educational space has four irreducible dimensions that are all equally important and must be included in multiple ways: subjective experience, objective behavior, intersubjective culture, and interobjective systems. (4) Each of these four dimensions has depth and complexity that develops over time; this development can be facilitated. In particular, integral teachers need to monitor how they are meeting their students where they are developmentally and not placing them in over their heads. (5) It is crucial to attend to the multiple developmental lines in teachers as well as students. This involves understanding the complex relationship between the capacity to take multiple perspectives (the cognitive line), interact in meaningful ways with others (the interpersonal line), and engage in worldcentric ethical action (the moral line). (6) Teachers must recognize and work creatively with the many natural and non-ordinary states of embodiment and awareness that they and their students cycle through in response to class content and activities. The more that teachers can support students in accessing various gross, subtle, causal, and witnessing states, the more fluid they will be in their own embodied awareness. (7) Because there are many types of learners and dimensions of learning, an educator needs to work with multiple typologies in order to provide the most responsive and effective educational space. Key typological categories to use include the five senses, gender, personality, and preferred narrative style (i.e., first-, second-, and third-person).

These seven commitments represent a foundation upon which additional insights, understandings, and distinctions can be placed. As stated above, integral education emerges from a desire to: engage in action in the world as skillfully as possible; inquire into one's interior space along the entire spectrum of experience; participate compassionately with various worldviews; and support the health and dynamism of global systems.

Conclusion: Integral by Design

In this chapter I have discussed how educators can use the five elements to transform themselves, serve their students, and create multidimensional learning environments. I have provided a number of illustrations for how each element is being used in JFKU's online graduate program in Integral Theory. These elements are being used to design curriculum, program learning outcomes, evaluations, course delivery, original educational research, weekly assignments, ongoing awareness practices, and residential gatherings. Through such examples I have demonstrated how the five elements of Integral Theory serve to create a uniquely comprehensive and dynamic approach to education; one that enacts integral instructors, students, and classrooms.

Hopefully educators who would like to better serve the transformation of themselves, their students, and the planet will find inspiration and practical suggestions for expanding their teaching repertoire and learning practices to include some of the integral modalities described in this chapter.[20] A careful incremental approach toward re-thinking and re-feeling curriculum in integral terms needs to honor the unique context in which each educator plies her trade, and thus a comprehensive implementation of an AQAL approach to integral education will be of interest only for the self-chosen few. This description of how Integral Theory's comprehensive ideas and formulas translate into practice itself has been offered as an example of integral praxis. By showcasing aspects of a thriving program that is integral by design I hope to have contributed to the broader discourse on integral education. This chapter has been put forth as an invitation for educators to venture more often into new ways of thinking and perceiving: reflecting on the enactment of themselves, their students, and their classrooms.

Acknowledgments

I would like to thank my students and colleagues at JFKU, Fielding Graduate University, and Integral Institute for their support in exploring more Integral approaches to education. Also I would like to thank Matthew Bronson, Olen Gunnlaugson, Alfonso Montuori, Frank Poletti, Matt Rentschler, and Zachary Stein for helpful suggestions on earlier versions of this chapter.

Appendix: JFKU Integral Theory Program Learning Outcomes

1. Graduates will be able to communicate to/with the value schemas generated by traditional, modern, and postmodern levels of worldview.

2. Graduates will be able to take/write from first-person, second-person, and third-person perspectives as differentiated phenomena available to all humans.

3. Graduates will be able to use/employ multiple methodologies as defined by the quadrants and zones of Integral Theory.

4. Graduates will be able to apply the five elements of Integral Theory: quadrants, levels, lines, states, and types.

5. Graduates will be able to successfully engage in an ongoing Integral Life Practice as defined by Integral Theory.

Notes

1. This chapter is a revised and updated version of Esbjörn-Hargens, 2006 and 2007.

2. For an overview of integral theory see Visser, 2004, and Esbjörn-Hargens, 2009. For another example of Integral Theory applied to a graduate program in Integral Psychology see Part 2 of Esbjörn-Hargens (2007).

3. Unless otherwise noted by context I will use "integral education" to refer explicitly to an AQAL approach to education (i.e., education informed by Integral Theory). By doing this I hope to differentiate this approach from the many that sometimes identify themselves as "integral" but often, in my experience, leave out too much to seriously be considered integral in a general sense (i.e., all inclusive or comprehensive) or Integral in a particular sense (i.e., the AQAL model). Integral educators Jorge Ferrer, Marina Romero, and Ramon Albareda (this volume) identify three approaches to integral education: mind-centered; bricolage; and participatory. I am in substantial agreement with Ferrer and associates that the bulk of current approaches to education that identify themselves as "integral" are of the bricolage type and therefore deceptive because they "can create the false impression that one is actually engaged in integral learning simply because of the relative attention paid to other dimensions of the person—especially in contrast to traditional mind-centered education" (Ferrer et al., p. 85). To this taxonomy, I would like to add AQAL (e.g., approaches that use Integral Theory as a guiding framework for pedagogy, inquiry process, curriculum study, evaluation, and methodology). AQAL approaches to education build on this participatory vision by providing a comprehensive meta-framework that can more effectively accomplish

their goals of integrating "the horizontal and vertical dimensions of integral education" (Ferrer et al., p. 84). In general I feel that Integral Theory's post-metaphysical position is deeply resonant with Ferrer's participatory vision.

4. This program began in 2006 (in partnership with Integral Institute) and consists of a one-year, 10-course, 25-unit certificate and a three-year, 30-course, 68-unit Master's of Art degree. Currently the program has 100 students (one of which has a chapter in this volume: Carissa Wieler) and 18 faculty (four of which have chapters in this volume: Katie Heikkinen, Joel Kreisberg, Terri O'Fallon, and myself). See endnote 5 of the introduction for an overview of some of JFKU's other Integral offerings. Also, in 2006 Integral Institute partnered with Fielding Graduate University (FGU) and began offering a three-course certificate and an Integral Studies track in a Master's of Organization Management and Development. In 2008, Allan Combs at CIIS established an Integral Theory (i.e., AQAL) track in the online doctoral program in Transformative Studies.

5. For seven articles presenting Integral Theory being applied to different levels of education see the special issue of *AQAL: Journal of Integral Theory and Practice* (Summer 2007). This issue provides an initial exploration of what integral education can look like at various levels of school, from kindergarten through doctorate programs. Additional articles on Integral Theory and education include: Combs 2008; Fisher, 2003; Friesen & Wight 2009; Gunnlaugson, 2004, 2005; Golin, 2008; Lauzon, 1998; Loubriel 2009; and Marrero 2007. Recently, Fisher (2007) posted a 65-page annotated bibliography that documents over 132 citations of Ken Wilber in the education literature over the last 25 years (1982–2006). This valuable resource provides a helpful overview of the key authors who draw on Integral Theory either in passing or as a primary basis for education. Visit the Integral Research Center for a document that contains abstracts for around a dozen MA theses and PhD dissertations on education using Integral Theory (http://www.integralresearchcenter.org/sites/default/files/Dissertations-Theses.pdf). For some examples of different levels of schools using Integral Theory see endnote 13.

6. The Integral model is post-disciplinary in that it can be used successfully in the context of *disciplinary* (e.g., helping to integrate various schools of education into integral education); *multidisciplinary* (e.g., helping to investigate educational phenomena from multiple disciplines); *interdisciplinary* (e.g., helping to apply methods from ecological science to educational assessment); and *transdisciplinary* (e.g., helping numerous disciplines interface through a content-free framework) approaches. See Wilber (1999–2000 and 2003a) and Visser (2004)

7. See the *Journal of Integral Theory and Practice* for examples of the wide ranging applicability of the Integral model Currently, of the many integral fields emerging, next to integral psychotherapy, integral education is likely the most well established in terms of published articles and a network of practitioners.

8. The quadrants can represent both the basic perspectives any individual can take on something (i.e., a quadrivium—four views) and the basic dimensions of an individual. So while artifacts such as a tables and chairs do not have all four quadrants (i.e., dimensions) they can be looked at from the four quadrants (i.e., perspectives) (Wilber, 2006).

9. For an understanding of this co-arising, see Wilber's most recent work on post-metaphysics and Integral Methodological Pluralism (Wilber, 2001, 2003a, 2006).

10. For example, while Ferrer, Romero & Albareda's approach (this volume) is not directly inspired by Integral Theory, it does represent a compatible version of integral education by including the five elements of the AQAL model (also see Gidley's discussion of

Steiner education, this volume). Ferrer and associates accomplish this by including quadrants through their discussion of the horizontal dimension of education; levels through their discussion of the vertical dimension of human complexity; lines through their discussion of the various developmental capacities of students and teachers (e.g., "interpersonal skills," "emotional skills," etc); states through their inclusion of "special states" of consciousness; and types through their discussion of masculine and feminine principles in education. Their chapter is a great example of how one can accomplish integral education without having to draw explicitly on Integral Theory or its framework. Likewise, Ferrer and associates' example illustrates that the five elements of Integral Theory can be basic (and intuitive) aspects of any approach that is committed to being integral. What Integral Theory provides is an explicit way of both including these elements in any approach and understanding the many complex ways these elements relate to each other. Thus, one does not have to subscribe to the AQAL model or all its tenets to accomplish the kind of integral education Integral Theory is committed to achieving. However, there are unique benefits and features afforded an integral education that draws explicitly on the AQAL model.

11. Also noteworthy in the history of integral education is that on July 20–22 of 2000, Integral Institute, which was founded in 1999, hosted its first meeting on integral education. This gathering brought together 50 educators who had been using Integral Theory in their departments, programs, classrooms, and courses.

12. For simplicity I am using "objectivity" to represent both the UR quadrant of objectivity and the LR quadrant of interobjectivity.

13. There are currently a number of other schools from elementary to high schools that are informed by Integral Theory. In Mt. Airy, Maryland, the Misty Mountain Montessori Education Center, is exploring an Integral approach to Montessori education. They are expanding the Right-Hand quadrant focus of traditional Montessori programs (i.e., cognitive development in relationship to social and environmental factors) to include more Left-Hand quadrant elements, often associated with Waldorf schools (e.g., imaginal, creative/artistic, explorative, and cultural dimensions) (see Wheal, 2007). In Tucson, Arizona there is El Pueblo Integral, a small K-12 school that combines Integral Theory with Paulo Freire's approach to education. Nearby in Phoenix, Arizona is the Metropolitan Arts Institute, a college prep charter high school that combines Integral Theory with Howard Gardner's research on multiple intelligences and student learning styles. In addition, there are many undergraduate university courses throughout the world that teach Integral Theory or draw on some of its key principles and apply them to some context such as art, ecology, or writing. At the graduate level, there are the programs at JFKU, CIIS, and FGU.

14. Kegan (1994) points out that when an individual is at any level, 50% of their meaning-making will issue from that order of consciousness and 25% from both the level below and above.

15. iTEACH stands for: Integral Transformative Education Assessment for Curriculum Research. The Integral Research Center is in the process of designing and launching an ambitious longitudinal study using methods from all eight zones of Integral Methodological Pluralism to assess the transformative effects of integral education. We are using over a dozen established assessments. Lots of innovative programs (both mainstream and alternative) highlight how transformative their educational programs are for their students. We do not doubt these claims; in fact we feel the same way about the online program in Integral Theory. However, we want to really find out "In what ways do our students transform?"

Do they, over the course of three years of coursework, actually demonstrate some vertical stage development (e.g., exiting Kegan's 3rd order and stabilizing 4th order) or is it just horizontal development (e.g., increased access to emotional content). And even if it is just horizontal development, what aspects are developing? In short, we do not only want to tell everyone about how transformative this program is, we also want to demonstrate the exact ways it is transformative. We plan on using the results of this ongoing study to improve the developmental potential of our curriculum. So we will be adjusting our program making it even more conducive to psychological transformation and growth. For more information on the iTEACH project visit http://www.integralresearchcenter.org/action.

16. Based on current research (see Wilber, 2000a), Integral Theory posits a necessary but not sufficient relationship between several developmental lines. In particular, the cognitive line (i.e., perspective taking capacity) has been demonstrated to lead the interpersonal line, which in turn has been shown to lead the moral line. This also makes logical sense. For example, one has to be able to hold something in awareness (cognitive line) before they can hold it in relationship to another person (interpersonal line). And the capacity to hold that object in relationship to another person is necessary before one can hold that relationship within a moral context (moral line).

17. Of particular importance in Integral Theory is the self-identity line and its capacity for postautonomous ego development (see Cook-Greuter, 1999).

18. Other recognized approaches to learning style include Kolb's, Herrmann Brain Dominance, and Felder-Silverman's (for an overview of all three see Felder, 1996).

19. I would like to thank Zachary Stein for mentioning several of these potential outcomes.

20. It is worth noting that nearly half of this volume (e.g., this chapter, all seven of the case studies in section III, and three of the chapters in section IV) draws heavily on or are deeply informed by Wilber's corpus and its resulting Integral Theory. This highlights how practical, scalable, and influential Wilber's writings have been to the emerging field of integral education. These 11 chapters as well as the 29 sources named in endnote 5 provide a wealth of material on how various educators have translated the distinctions of Integral Theory into concrete educational realities.

References

Cook-Greuter, S. (1999). Postautonomous ego development: A study of its nature and measurement. (Doctoral dissertation, Harvard University, 1999). *Dissertation Abstracts International, 60*(06), 3000.

Combs, A. (2009). Reflections on online integral education: The learning community as a vessel for transformation. *Journal of Integral Theory and Practice, 4*(2), 1–12.

Esbjörn-Hargens, S. (2006). Integral education by design: How integral theory informs teaching, learning, and curriculum in a graduate program. *ReVision: A Journal of Consciousness and Transformation, 28*(3), 21–29.

Esbjörn-Hargens, S. (2007). Integral teacher, integral students, integral classroom: Applying integral theory to graduate education. *AQAL: Journal of Integral Theory and Practice, 2*(2), 72–103.

Esbjörn-Hargens, S. (2009). An overview of integral theory: An all-inclusive framework for the 21st century. Integral Institute Resource Paper # 1 (24 pages).

Felder, R. M. (1996). Matters of style. *ASEE Prism, 6*(4), 18–23.

Fisher, R. M. (2003). "Lighting up" the integral: A critical review of Ken Wilber's philosophy and theories related to education. Unpublished manuscript.

Fisher, R. M. (2007). *Ken Wilber and the education literature: Abridged annotated bibliography.* Retrieved August 23, 2008 from http://www.pathsoflearning.net/resources_writings_Ken_Wilber.pdf

Friesen, E. & Wight, I. (2009). Integrally informed journaling for professional self-design: Emerging experience in a graduate program context. *Journal of Integral Theory and Practice, 4*(3) 59–86

Gardner, H. (1983). *Frames of mind: The theory of multiple intelligences.* New York: Basic Books.

Gebser, J. (1985). *The ever-present origin* (N. Barstad & A. Mickunas, Trans.). Athens: Ohio University Press. (Original work published 1949)

Golin, C. L. (2008). Integral life practice inquiry: An integral research approach to personal development. *Journal of Integral Theory and Practice, 3*(1), 163–183.

Gunnlaugson, O. (2004). Towards an integral education for the ecozoic era. *Journal of Transformative Education, 2,* 313–335.

Gunnlaugson, O. (2005). Toward integrally informed theories of transformative learning. *Journal of Transformative Education, 3*(4), 331–353.

Kegan, R. (1994). *In over our heads: The mental demands of modern life.* Cambridge, MA: Harvard University Press.

Lauzon, A. (1998). Adult education and the human journey: An evolutionary perspective. *International Journal of Lifelong Education, 17*(2), 131–145.

Loubriel, L. E. (2009). Integral music performance and pedagogy: A post-secondary performance and education model. *Journal of Integral Theory and Practice, 4*(3) 87–107.

Marrero, F. (2007). An integral approach to affective education. *AQAL: Journal of Integral Theory and Practice, 2*(4), 1–23.

Torbert, W. (1991). *The power of balance: Transforming self, society, and scientific inquiry.* Newbury Park, CA: Sage.

Visser, F. (2004). Ken Wilber: *Thought as passion.* Albany, NY: SUNY.

Wheal, J. (n.d.). *The times, they have a-changed: An integral perspective of the Montessori method in the 21st century.* Retrieved August 22, 2009 from www.mistymountain-montessori.org/integral.html

Wilber, K. (1995). *Sex, ecology, spirituality: The spirit of evolution.* Boston: Shambhala.

Wilber, K. (1997). *The eye of spirit: An integral vision for a world gone slightly mad.* Boston: Shambhala.

Wilber, K. (1999–2000). *The collected works of Ken Wilber (Vols. 1–8).* Boston: Shambhala.

Wilber, K. (2000a). *Integral psychology: Consciousness, spirit, psychology, therapy.* Boston: Shambhala.

Wilber, K. (2000b). *A theory of everything: An integral vision for business, politics, science, and spirituality.* Boston: Shambhala.

Wilber, K. (2001). *On the nature of post-metaphysical spirituality.* Retrieved November 18, 2003, from http://wilber.shambhala.commisc/habermas/index.cfm

Wilber, K. (2003a). *Introduction to excerpts from volume 2 of the Kosmos trilogy.* Retrieved November 18, 2003, from http://wilber.shambhala.com

Wilber, K. (2003b*). Excerpt G: Toward a comprehensive theory of subtle energies.* Retrieved November 18, 2003, from http://wilber.shambhala.combooks/kosmos/excerptG/part1. cfm

Wilber, K. (2006). *Integral spirituality: A startling new role for religion in the modern and postmodern world.* Boston: Integral Books.

Integral Transformative Education

A Participatory Proposal

Jorge N. Ferrer, Marina T. Romero, and Ramon V. Albareda

The real voyage of discovery consists not in seeking new landscapes, but in having new eyes.

—Marcel Proust

Introduction

Our main intention in this chapter is to introduce a participatory approach to integral transformative education in which all human dimensions—body, vital, heart, mind, and consciousness—are invited to cocreatively participate in the unfolding of learning and inquiry. After some preliminary considerations about the basic elements of an integral curriculum and the "horizontal" and "vertical" dimensions of integral education, the first part of the chapter situates our participatory perspective in relation to two other approaches to integral education: mind centered/intellectualist and bricolage/eclectic. In the second part, we present the basic contours of a participatory model of integral transformative education using the organic metaphor of the four seasons. We also stress the importance of integrating "feminine" and "masculine" principles in whole-person learning and outline several basic features of integral transformative education. In the third part of the chapter, we discuss several challenges for the implementation of integral transformative education in modern academia and suggest that these challenges can be seen as precious opportunities to reconnect education with its transformative and spiritual roots. We conclude with some reflections on the transpersonal nature of human participatory inquiry.

Before proceeding further, however, it may be important to stress straight-away the eminently theoretical character of this chapter. The following reflections emerge from many years of pedagogical experimentation at various institutions of alternative adult education such as the California Institute of Integral Studies, San Francisco, and the ESTEL School of Integral Studies, Barcelona.

Integral Education: Elements, Dimensions, and Approaches

Elements of the Integral Curriculum: Content, Training, and Inquiry

Before we start our discussion of integral education, it is important to distinguish among three basic elements of learning or three types of pedagogical empha-sis—*content, training,* and *inquiry*—and situate them in the context of an integral curriculum.

The element of content refers to the presentation, explication, discussion, analysis, critique, comparison, and/or integration of information (i.e., facts, ideas, theories, models, approaches, traditions, etc.). Historically, content-based learning has been the mark of mainstream Western education. It can be extremely creative as well as "integral" in the sense of working with or toward integrative frameworks, approaches, and understandings (e.g., synthetic thinking, multiperspectivism, inter-disciplinarity, cross-cultural studies, etc.).

The element of training focuses on the acquisition of specific skills and capabilities at all levels: for example, technical skills, research and writing skills, clinical skills, interpersonal and emotional skills (e.g., group dynamics), dialogical and argumentative skills, postformal and complex thinking skills, somatic/pranic skills (e.g., through yoga, sensory awareness, or tai chi chuan), and contemplative skills (e.g., meditation classes).

The element of inquiry focuses on the facilitation of pedagogical spaces that foster individual and collective inquiry into focused topics, questions, or problems. This dimension can be accessed using (a) mental/verbal approaches, such as dialogi-cal inquiry, argumentation, transdisciplinarity, and so on, or (b) multidimensional approaches, such as supplementing mental/verbal approaches with others that engage the voice and wisdom of the body, the vital, the heart, intuition, special states of consciousness, and so forth.

Let us now offer some general thoughts about these elements and clarify their significance in a graduate-level integral curriculum.[1] First, these three categories are not mutually exclusive, and it is obvious that most traditional and alterna-tive educational practices engage all three to some extent (except, in most cases, multidimensional inquiry approaches). Second, all three pedagogical forms are equally important elements of education and learning, and different courses can naturally stress one or several of them, depending on their aim and focus. Third, we believe that as learners move from school to college, from college to university, from undergraduate to graduate education, and from master's to doctoral levels, there needs to be a gradual but increasing shift of emphasis from an educational praxis that is based mainly on content/training (arguably more appropriate for children and young adults requiring epistemic foundations) to one based mainly on inquiry/training (arguably more appropriate for adults who aspire to contribute new knowledge or practical service to the world). In the latter, many of the training programs may take the form of (a) acquisition of practical skills (e.g., technical skills, organizational skills, clinical skills), (b) acquisition of facilitation skills (e.g., interpersonal skills, emotional skills, leadership skills), and (c) acquisition of skills that can be used as inquiry tools once learned (e.g., meditation practice, somatic techniques, complex thinking). In practical terms, this means that a graduate-level integral curriculum might include a creative mix of a few foundational content-based courses (especially at the master's level), some training-based courses of the types appropriate to each program's focus, and many inquiry-based courses of both verbal/mental and multidimensional types. Of course, different courses could combine these elements creatively in numerous ways.[2]

Horizontal and Vertical Dimensions of Integral Education

Perhaps the simplest way to start exploring the idea of an integral education is in terms of the discipline's *horizontal* and *vertical* dimensions. As Judie Wexler (2004) succinctly put it, the horizontal dimension refers to "the way we integrate knowledge" (i.e., content, training, and mental inquiry) and the vertical dimension to "the way we integrate multiple ways of knowing" (i.e., special trainings and multidimensional inquiry). These dimensions can cross-fertilize and shape each other in complex ways; for example, to engage in certain forms of transdisciplinary inquiry may call for multiple ways of knowing, and to include multiple ways of knowing in the learning process may call for transdisciplinary approaches to inquiry.[3] Let us look at each of these dimensions in more detail.

The horizontal dimension is intimately connected to what, in the 1990 Special Report of the Carnegie Foundation for the Advancement of Teaching, Ernest Boyer called the "scholarship of integration." According to Boyer (1990), the scholarship of integration emerged from the increasing need of many researchers to "move beyond traditional disciplinary boundaries, communicate with colleagues in other fields, and discover patterns that connect" (p. 20). "Interdisciplinary and integrative studies," Boyer added, "long on the edges of academic life, are moving to the center, responding both to new intellectual questions and to pressing human problems" (p. 21).

In general terms, horizontal integral scholarship can be of four types: (a) *disciplinary*, or aiming at the integration of models, theories, schools, and so forth, within a single discipline of knowledge (e.g., integration of object-relation models in developmental psychology; structuralism, feminism, and critical theory in sociology); (b) *multidisciplinary*, or the study of any given phenomenon from multiple disciplinary perspectives (e.g., the study of human consciousness from the perspectives of neuroscience, cognitive psychology, phenomenology, and mysticism) (see, e.g., Klein, 1990, 1996); (c) *interdisciplinary*, or the transfer of principles or methods from one discipline to another (e.g., methods of nuclear physics to medicine; somatic techniques to spiritual inquiry) (Lattuca, 2002; Nicolescu, 2002); and (d) *transdisciplinary*, or an "inquiry-driven" integrative approach that creatively applies any relevant perspective across disciplines (i.e., transcending the disciplinary organization of knowledge) with an awareness of their underlying paradigmatic assumptions and the practice of "complex thinking" (Montuori, 2004; Nicolescu, 2002).

Two important qualifications: First, any of these horizontal approaches potentially involve the integration of various research methodologies and techniques (e.g., qualitative and quantitative; phenomenology and electroencephalography), epistemic standpoints (e.g., emic and etic; first-, second-, and third-person), and epistemologies (e.g., Buddhist and Western science). Second, all types can have two chief orientations: (a) basic, or aiming at the conceptual integration of two or more authors, approaches, theories, models, schools, or disciplines (e.g., the thought of Jung and Campbell; feminism and critical theory) into a more encompassing integrative framework, theory, or new discipline; or (b) applied, the use of already constructed integrative frameworks as a tool to study, situate, critique, interpret, understand, or develop transformative action regarding any phenomenon (e.g., using Ken Wilber's four-quadrant model as a lens to study the various theories of art interpretation).

Horizontal integrative scholarship can be motivated by the following nonexclusive regulative goals: reconciliation/harmonization (e.g., apparently contradictory data or conflicting views are reconciled within a larger vision or integrative framework); holism (e.g., addressing the fragmentation of knowledge that is the fruit of the hyperspecialization of modern science and academia); multiperspectivism (e.g., deepening our knowledge about any subject or phenomenon by applying different perspectives, models, fields of knowledge); creation of new fields of inquiry (e.g., psychoneuroimmunology, ecofeminism, psychohistory, neurophenomenology); and fostering cognitive and psychospiritual development of researchers and readers (e.g., multiperspectivism and transdisciplinarity have been associated with postformal forms of cognition such as Gebser's "integral consciousness," Morin's "complex thinking," Kegan's "fifth order consciousness," or Wilber's "vision-logic," some of which are considered fundamental stepping stones toward transpersonal and contemplative ways of knowing).

Although further methodological clarity about the horizontal dimension still is needed, we believe that the greatest challenge of integral education lies in the facilitation of the vertical dimension of learning: multidimensional inquiry or integration of multiple ways of knowing. It is essential that contemporary holistic educators address the vertical dimension of education for at least three reasons. First, the presence of this dimension can facilitate not only an existentially meaningful integrative framework for students' academic pursuits but also the ongoing integral transformation of students, faculty, and institutions. Second, the practice of multidimensional inquiry constitutes the real cutting edge of integral education; after all, horizontal integrative scholarship is already common practice in many mainstream educational programs, departments, and universities—as the aforementioned Report of the Carnegie Foundation showed almost 15 years ago. Third, as we elaborate subsequently, the incorporation of the vertical dimension can reconnect education with its transformative and spiritual potential. Therefore, although we do not underestimate the importance of horizontal integralism, the rest of this article focuses on the vertical dimension and explores a number of challenges involved in its implementation. But let us first offer a brief taxonomy of integral approaches to education.

Approaches to Integral Education: Mind-Centered, Bricolage, and Participatory

Although most holistic educators agree about the need to incorporate all human dimensions into learning and inquiry (e.g., Hocking, Haskell, & Linds, 2001; Miller, 1991; Miller et al., 2005; O'Sullivan, 1999; O'Sullivan, Morrell, & O'Connor, 2002; Rothberg, 1999), the practical efforts to materialize this vision tend to crystallize in three different approaches: mind-centered/intellectualist, bricolage/eclectic, and participatory. We will look at each of them independently, but it should be obvious that, in actual practice, these approaches can be combined in multifarious ways.

The mind-centered/intellectualist approach

This approach is based on the intellectual study and/or elaboration of integral visions or understandings. It uses the intellectual tools of mainstream education (e.g., logical analysis, rational argumentation, synthesis of the literature) to reach a more integrated understanding of the topic of study and can include fundamental questions such as the nature of the human being, life, reality, or the cosmos. It is usually—although by no means always—offered in the context of a traditional pedagogical methodology (i.e., magisterial lectures, textual research, teachers' assessment of learning through written essays, etc.). In other words, the mind-centered approach to education is "integral" in its object of study but not in its pedagogy, methodology, or inquiry process. In terms of the conceptual distinctions offered previously, we could say that the mind-centered approach focuses on the horizontal dimension of integral education and neglects the vertical one.

Although the intellectual engagement of integral understandings is clearly an important corrective to the usually fragmented nature of Western education, the reduction of integral education to merely intellectual activity generates a deep incoherence that can effectively undermine its transformative and emancipatory potential. Essentially, an exclusively or eminently intellectual approach perpetuates the "cognicentrism" of mainstream Western education in its assumption that the mind's cognitive capabilities are or should be the paramount masters and players of learning and inquiry.[4] A common consequence of this reduction is the confusion of an expanded intellectual understanding with genuine integral knowledge. Most phenomena studied in the human and social sciences (and arguably in the biological and physical sciences as well) partake to some extent of different nonmental dimensions (material, energetic, emotional, spiritual, etc.), and therefore an eminently mental approach is likely to lead to partial understandings and even significant distortions.

This problem becomes heightened in the study of human spirituality. Most spiritual traditions posit the existence of an isomorphism or deep resonance among the human being, the cosmos, and the Mystery out of which everything arises ("as above so below," "the embodied person as microcosm of the macrocosm," etc.) (see, e.g., Chittick, 1994; Overzee, 1992; Saso, 1997; Shokek, 2001). Therefore, the more dimensions of the person that are actively engaged in the study of the Mystery—or of phenomena associated with it—the more complete our knowledge will be. In our view, this "completion" should not be understood quantitatively but rather in a qualitative sense. In other words, the more human dimensions creatively participate in spiritual knowing, the greater will be the dynamic congruence between inquiry approach and studied phenomena and the more coherent with, or attuned to, the nature of the Mystery will be our knowledge (Ferrer, 2002, 2008a; Ferrer, Albareda, & Romero, 2004).

The bricolage/eclectic approach

What characterizes the bricolage approach—by far the most widespread in "alternative" educational institutions—is the incorporation of experiential moments or practices (e.g., movement, meditation, ritual) into an essentially mind-centered education or the eclectic curricular offering of courses that engage the other human attributes (e.g., tai chi for the vital/prana, somatic techniques or hatha yoga for the body, meditation for spiritual consciousness). Note that although some classes may engage, and to some extent develop, the nonmental dimensions, these dimensions rarely if ever are part of the substance of the educational process (e.g., inquiry tools into subject matters, evaluators of inquiry outcomes), which is mainly planned, conducted, and assessed from the perspective of the mind. The bricolage approach can take place in the context of both traditional education (not aiming at integral understandings) and mind-centered integral education (which studies or attempts to develop integral visions).

In terms of the conceptual distinctions offered above, we could say that this approach engages the horizontal and vertical dimensions of integral education in an unintegrated and ultimately deceptive way. It is unintegrated because the intellect is not working in collaboration with the other ways of knowing in the context of a creative cycle of integral learning and inquiry (see next section for an illustration of what such collaboration may look like). And it is deceptive because it can create the false impression that one is actually engaged in integral learning simply because of the relative attention paid to other dimensions of the person—especially in contrast to traditional mind-centered education.

Although the bricolage approach constitutes an important advance in relation to mainstream education, it is important to distinguish between genuine integral growth and a process of integral training regulated by mental parameters (see Ferrer, 2003). Most important in the present context, it is crucial to distinguish between the eclectic engagement of the nonmental human attributes as supplements of learning and their integrated creative participation at the various stages of the inquiry and learning process. The bricolage approach, despite its many advantages over a purely intellectualist education, remains fundamentally cognicentric.

The participatory approach

The participatory approach seeks to facilitate the cocreative participation of all human dimensions at all stages of the inquiry and learning processes. Body, vital, heart, mind, and consciousness are considered equal partners in the exploration and elaboration of knowledge. In other words, this approach invites the engagement of the whole person, ideally at all stages of the educational process, including the construction of the curriculum, the selection of research topics, the inquiry process, and the assessment of inquiry outcomes.[5] The novelty of the participatory proposal is essentially methodological. It stresses the need to explore practical approaches that combine the power of the mind and the cultivation of consciousness with the epistemic potential of human somatic, vital, and emotional worlds. In terms of the conceptual distinctions offered above, we could say that the participatory approach aims at the synergic integration of the horizontal and vertical dimensions of integral education as well as at the coherent alignment of the verbal and multidimensional inquiry modalities.

As should be obvious from this brief presentation, we do not consider the participatory approach merely one more alternate perspective. On the contrary, we passionately believe that, if skillfully implemented, it constitutes a richer, more natural, and more transformative integral educational praxis. In the same way that Sri Aurobindo—the originator of integralism in India—distinguished between a spiritual liberation of consciousness in consciousness and an integral transformation that entails the spiritual alignment of all human dimensions, we differentiate between an educational process regulated by the conscious mind and one organically orchestrated by all human attributes. What is more, we propose that a participatory approach is not only more satisfactory but also more natural and coherent with the multidimensional nature of the human being. If it does not look natural at first, we suggest that this may be attributable to the dissociated "second nature" embedded in the modern Western individual. We will return to this crucial issue later in this chapter.

But the fundamental question, of course, is how to implement in practice participatory approaches in modern academia.[6] To begin exploring this question, the next section uses the organic metaphor of the four seasons to illustrate a possible way in which the various human dimensions can participate in a complete cycle of creative academic inquiry. Our intention in this presentation is not to offer a paradigmatic model for others to follow but rather to provide a possible general orientation whose ultimate value needs to be assessed by both teachers and students as they attempt to cultivate more integral approaches to academic work.

A Participatory Model of Integral Transformative Education

The Four Seasons of the Integral Creative Cycle

Whether in nature or in human reality, a creative process usually unfolds through several general stages that correspond roughly with the seasonal cycle of nature: action (Autumn, preparing the terrain and planting the seeds; the body, studying what is already known about a subject matter, i.e., the body of literature); germination/gestation (Winter, rooting and nourishment of the seed inside the earth; the vital, conception of novel developments in contact with unconscious transpersonal and archetypal sources); blooming (Spring, emerging toward the light of buds, leaves, and flowers; the heart, first conscious feelings and rough ideas); and harvest (Summer, selection of mature fruits and shared celebration; the mind, intellectual selection, elaboration, and offering of the fruits of the creative process).[7] Let us briefly look at each of these seasons and how they can be appropriately supported in the context of academic work (Fig. 4).

Autumn: The body, planting, action

In many lands across the globe, Autumn is the time to prepare the soil for the new harvesting cycle. The soil is scrabbled, cleansed of old roots and stones, and, if necessary, fertilized. Then the new seeds are planted in the soil.

In the human creative cycle, Autumn is the time for preparing the physical body to be a solid and porous receptacle for the germination of new vital seeds.[8] It is important to release the body from accumulated tensions to make it more open and permeable. It is also essential to relate to the body as a living organic reality that holds meaningful contents that cannot be intentionally accessed through the mind or consciousness (Ferrer 2008b).

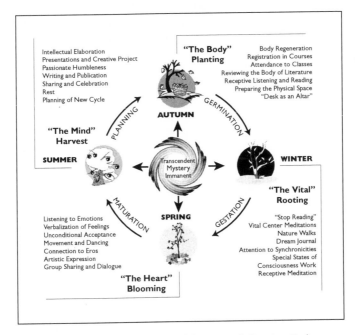

Figure 4. The Four Seasons of the Integral Creative Cycle.

Academically, this is the time to take actions such as enrolling in stimulating courses, attending lectures, and reviewing the body of the literature—which can be approached as a set of potentially seminal works with the power to impregnate the vital seeds of many individuals. During lectures, dialogues, and readings it is crucial to cultivate an attitude of receptivity, as if one were planting seeds in one's inner soil. This is also the time to prepare the physical space in which the creative process will take place; for example, cleaning and organizing the office space and, as Deena Metzger (1992) beautifully puts it, preparing the desk as an altar—as the bride chamber for the beloved (i.e., the muse, the daimon, or the creative wellspring within).

The task of the mind at this stage is to support appropriate action by engaging behaviors such as those that create optimum conditions for listening to the body, actualize physical structures, and search out new resources. This is also a time for the mind to let go of old ways of thinking so that it can support and recognize the novel fruits of the new creative cycle. During Autumn, the mind can stagnate the creative process if it spends too much time wondering about the ultimate outcome of the inquiry or tries to predetermine its development or arrive at its own answers before the stages of the creative process have had the chance to unfold. Autumn is the season to trust the body, to support the structural dimension of reality, and to rely on the power of action.

Winter: The vital, rooting, gestation

Once the seeds have been planted, there is not much else for a cultivator to do. Winter is essentially a time of waiting, of darkness, of silence, and, most important, of gestation. It is imperative to stop the activity of Autumn so that the planted seeds can do their own autonomous work: splitting open, rooting in the soil, and getting fed by earth's essential nutrients.

In the same way that a germinated seed first grows toward the darkness of the soil to be nourished and develop roots that are the necessary base for the upward growth of the plant toward the light, in the human being an activated vital seed first plunges into the depths of the personal and collective unconscious. Like the roots of the trees in a forest, human vital depths are interconnected in the unconscious, where they can be nurtured not only by the collective wisdom of human heritage but also by the generative, immanent dimension of the Mystery. This contact between the vital world and immanent Mystery makes Winter an especially sacred season that needs to be properly honored. As with the dormant appearance of nature in Winter, it may appear to the conscious mind that "nothing is happening" at this juncture of the creative process, but it is important to remember that tremendously powerful and creative forces are actually at play in the darkness—forces that will eventually catalyze in Spring not only the regeneration and blooming of life in nature but also the emergence of the creative impulses in the human soil.

In academia, Winter is a time in which it may be important to stop reading or assimilating further information in any other way. The process of creative gestation requires its own inner space, which is facilitated by silence, interiorization, and stillness. Not knowing how to accompany appropriately this stage of gestation, too often students—especially at their dissertation stage—paralyze the creative process by their inability to stop reading. (This obviously has implications for the sequence of readings required in academic courses). The conscious mind, not able to "see" in the darkness of this stage, can easily believe that in order to move ahead it has to continue incorporating new theories and ideas. Obviously, there will always be important essays or books to be read, but in the same way that we need to stop eating to facilitate an effective and nourishing digestion, it is necessary to stop reading in Winter for an adequate gestation of the creative impulse. Appropriate activities during this season are not those seeking to find immediate answers but those that support the alignment of the mind/consciousness with the process of gestation. It is crucial to cultivate a sense of trust in the natural processes that are taking place within our creative matrix during this season, much as a pregnant woman must trust the gestation of a fetus. Some examples of supporting activities include keeping a dream journal; taking nature walks; working with special states of consciousness; practicing receptive forms of meditation such as vipassana, wu-wei ("without doing"), or shinkan taza ("sitting only"); cultivating visionary imagination; doing symbolic work; paying attention to synchronicities in everyday life (including "that book that fell from the shelf"!); and engaging in practices that facilitate an embodied contact with the vital center or *hara* as the physical/energetic container of the creative pregnancy.

In Winter the mind needs to cultivate an attitude of patient receptivity, not knowing, and humble respect. It is important to develop patience and receptivity toward stages of the creative process whose rhythm and unfolding elude the mind's intentional control. Respect and not-knowing naturally emerge from the mind's recognition that "something" is happening beyond what it can see directly. And humility is borne out of the awareness that, although the mind can be present to the process, the creative dynamism has no need of its powers at this stage. During Winter, the mind can abort the creative cycle if—out of ignorance, impatience, or mistrust—it attempts to take control of the process and/or get to know prematurely the nature of the still embryonic creative drive. It is as if a farmer, not trusting the chthonic process of the seed, anxiously digs the soil to "see" what is happening or to actively help the seed to grow. Winter is the season to cultivate a patient receptivity toward the unknown and to trust in those aspects and stages of life that transcend the intentionality of the human mind and consciousness.

Spring: The heart, blooming, diversity

Spring is the season for the shameless blossoming of newly regenerated life. It is a time of spontaneity, contrasts, and celebration of diversity; a time for the sprouting of buds and the blooming of flowers; a time of tremendous fragility and intensity and, if the conditions are appropriate, of countless surprises.

In the creative process, Spring is the season to open the heart, breathe deeply and widely, listen to one's affective world, and make room within so that the raw sensations associated with the upwelling creative energy emerging out of the gestation process can be organically incorporated as emotions and feelings. This is the stage of first contact with and embodiment of those creative impulses gestated in Winter. This can be a time of joyful exhilaration in the wake of the fresh contents emerging from within—a time in which it is crucial to avoid the mental temptation to prematurely assess what is emerging. At the end of the season, it is important to let go of those developments which, like Spring flowers, were temporary manifestations of the creative process and start contemplating those that remain and may become fruits in the Summer.

In academic work, the first part of Spring calls for activities that support the embodied magnification of those first creative energetic blossoms, including physical games that involve movement and dance (like "dancing one's research question") and sensual/sexual explorations to awaken and integrate the erotic power of life into the inquiry process. The importance of Eros and sexuality in a genuinely creative process cannot be understated.[9] Eros is the creative power of Life in its primordial, undifferentiated state, and sexuality is one of the first soils for the organization and creative development of such primary energy in human reality. That is why it is so important that sexuality is an "open" soil based on natural evolutionary principles and not on fears, conflicts, or artificial impositions dictated by the mind, culture, or spiritual ideologies (Romero & Albareda, 2001). The second part of Spring calls for activities such as somatic expression, verbalization of feelings, embodied practices that facilitate listening to emotions and feelings (see Ferrer, 2003), and artistic expression (music, painting, sculpture, plastic arts, poetry, singing, etc.). Peer-group work becomes central at this stage, because it provides a social context for nonjudgmental contrasts and cross-fertilization among incipient creative expressions.

Two qualities are essential for the mind to cultivate in Spring. The first is an attitude of genuine curiosity by which the mind looks at the emerging contents as if it were the first time that it sees them, avoiding their codification through previously learned conceptual schemes or theories. The second is an attitude of unconditional acceptance and support of all the budding contents. At this stage, the creative process can be aborted if the mind projects its previously learned schemes or theories onto what is emerging or if it prematurely judges their value. Spring is not the season of the mind but a time to trust the heart and unconditionally support its processes.

Summer: The mind, harvest, celebration

In Summer, some flowers have matured into fruits and some of those fruits become ripe. It is the season of harvest, celebration, sharing, and gratitude. It is also a time to rest, to peacefully contemplate the new seeds contained in the fruits, and to plan another cycle for the following Autumn.

In the creative process, the "fruits" represent the ideas or expressions selected for further elaboration and refinement. If the mind has accompanied the entire process with the appropriate stage-specific attitudes of a sensitive farmer, it will easily discern at this stage those fruits that are mature and deserve further consideration. Summer is the season of the mind—a time for the intellectual/aesthetic elaboration of ideas. It is also an auspicious time to open oneself to the transcendent dimension of the Mystery, which can now illuminate the mind with insights that may enrich the refinement of the creative fruits.

In the academic system, Summer is the season to focus on the articulation of ideas with clarity, beauty, elegance, precision, and sophistication. It is also the time to dialog with others about one's ideas in order to polish them in both substance and verbal/nonverbal expression. Putting those ideas into writing or other expressive means is a further step in the materialization of the creative process. Ideally, the writing style should be coherent with the original creative impulse so that the words embody the message without distortions. This is the season to contrast one's fruits with already existing developments and ideas, that is, with the fruits of the creative process of others. (In mainstream education, those contrasts occur long before the creative process has delivered mature fruits, and although this may be helpful at times, it may also endanger the process, leaving students feeling a lack of confidence that can lead to a compensatory mental reformulation of already existent ideas). It is also the time for the sharing of refined ideas through class presentations, written papers, or other creative projects—and it may be important to explore different modalities to convey those ideas (visual, aesthetic, dramatic, etc.). A further stage in this process could be the publication of the fruits of the season in magazines or journals and/or their presentation at professional conferences or public events. Finally, this is the time to raise new questions, plan a new research cycle, and explore avenues for further inquiry that may awaken new vital seeds within ourselves and others.

In Summer we reach at last the season of the mind. If the mind has been in contact with the multidimensional nature of the creative process, the attitude that it will naturally display in the presentations of the fruits will be one of passionate humbleness. It will be passionate because the ideas will be grounded in somatic, vital, and emotional experience. And it will be humble out of the recognition that the ultimate sources of the creative process transcend both mental structures and personal individuality; in other words, they are both transcendent and transpersonal. Learners can then feel that they have been both the gardener and the soil of the creative process while simultaneously being aware of the many participating elements that have collaborated in the unfolding of that process (body, vital, heart, mind, and consciousness; the personal and the collective unconscious; the immanent and transcendent Mystery). Passion without humbleness can become arrogance, and arrogance may be a sign that the person is only aware of the personal dimension of the process. Humbleness without passion can become weak and even boring and may be a sign that the person is overlooking the personal grounding of the process. An attitude of passionate humbleness honors both the personal and transpersonal dimensions of the creative process.

Before closing this section, we should stress once again the very general nature of the integral creative cycle outlined here. Although we believe that it can serve as an orientation for integral pedagogical practice, it should not be made paradigmatic in any strict sense for all individuals. There are many dispositions and associated dynamics in the unfolding of the creative process. (Incidentally, a serious consideration of the diverse individual rhythms in the gestation and maturation of creative fruits may lead to the revision of standard academic practices such as predetermined timeframes for academic accomplishment or collective deadlines for the delivery of inquiry outcomes). Furthermore, there can be an indefinite number of seasonal subcycles (Autumn–Winter–Spring–Summer) in the context of a larger creative project. Finally, and perhaps most important, our suggestion of a rough correspondence between creative stages and specific human attributes should be taken as a didactic orientation and not in rigid fashion. A human being is a multidimensional unity: Body, vital, heart, mind, and consciousness are petals of the human flower. All human attributes are present and operative to some extent at all stages of the creative cycle. This fact does not preclude, however, that as in the early stages of human development—from organic matter and vital impulse to proto-emotions and differentiated feelings to thoughts and formal cognition—certain attributes may have greater preeminence than others at certain stages. For these and other reasons, the sequence sketched here, although we believe it accurately reflects deep dynamics of the creative cycle, admits an indefinite number of possible variations and should not be viewed in a strictly linear fashion.

Integration of Feminine and Masculine Principles

In this expanded educational context, we can easily recognize that modern academia (both mainstream and alternative) focuses on the Autumn and the Summer phases—action and harvest (the more "masculine" aspects of the process)—and tends to overlook the facilitation of spaces for the Winter and the Spring: germination, gestation, and giving birth (the more "feminine" aspects of the process).[10] Students spend most of their time both inside and outside the classroom reading, studying, and discussing knowledge already elaborated by others (Autumn), after which they are usually expected to "produce" new and original contributions in their final presentations and papers (Summer). In other words, the deep structure of modern education tends to skip the more feminine, and more deeply generative, stages of the creative process (Winter and Spring). Seen in this context, the scarcity of genuinely creative developments in academia should not be surprising. There is much "second-order" creativity or smart mental permutation of already known ideas but very little "first-order" creativity or organic, multidimensional emergence of truly innovative developments. Given the innumerable "abortions" of the creative process that these dynamics cause in the Western educational process almost from day one, it is understandable (perhaps inevitable) that so many students develop a lack of confidence in their own creative potential.

We strongly suspect that this deeply masculinized pedagogical container may also be behind the intense (and also masculinized) reactivity of the feminine sensibility (of both men and women) that faculty and students often witness in the classroom, even in those courses where the "feminine" is honored and included in content and/or more superficial process (e.g., inclusion of a feminine ritual in a masculinized pedagogical process). The true feminine is understandably in a state of paralyzing despair that can easily burst into anger because it cannot understand why it still feels profoundly dishonored when it is apparently attended to and even explicitly championed. This situation parallels the current despair of the African-American community in the United States, which, as Cornell West (1999) pointed out, at least had hopes for a future genuine integration before its members gained civil rights but today faces an increasing nihilism in the wake of the unsatisfactory alternatives of either becoming "like the white folks" or remaining in the ghetto (and the jail).

In future years, it is likely that integral transformative education will gradually restructure the pedagogical process in ways that truly and deeply integrate the "masculine" and "feminine" dimensions of the inquiry process. This may involve the facilitation of spaces not only for the intellectual discussion and production of knowledge but for the vital germination and gestation of the creative seeds of the individual.

Basic Features of Integral Transformative Education

To conclude this section, what follows is a summary of some basic features of integral education:

1. Integral education fosters the cocreative participation of all human dimensions in the learning and inquiry processes. A genuine process of integral learning cannot be directed exclusively by the mind but needs to emerge from the collaborative epistemic participation of all human dimensions: body, instincts, heart, mind, and consciousness. All human dimensions need to be actively encouraged to participate creatively at all appropriate stages of the inquiry and learning process (e.g., as inquiry tools into subject matter, as evaluators of inquiry outcomes).

2. Integral education aims at the study and/or elaboration of holistic understandings, frameworks, theories, or visions. Whether disciplinary, multidisciplinary, interdisciplinary, or transdisciplinary, integral inquiry builds bridges across disciplines and searches for commonalities while honoring differences in its striving toward integrated understandings that counter the partial or fragmented current state of human knowledge.

3. Integral education fosters the activation of students' unique vital potentials and their creative development in the construction of knowledge. Each human being is a unique embodiment of the Mystery potentially able to develop a unique perspective to contribute to the transformation of his or her community or society. When learning and inquiry are grounded in one's unique vital

potentials, academic life becomes not only existentially significant but also more creative, exciting . . . and fun!

4. Integral education balances the feminine and the masculine. It combines the more masculine elements of the training of skills and analysis of already constructed knowledge with the more feminine element of creatively engendering new knowledge from within. As in life, a dialectical relationship between these fundamental principles exists in the creative process, and integral education seeks practical ways to honor and actualize this relationship.

5. Integral education fosters *inner* and *outer* epistemic diversity. Taking into account the importance of multiple perspectives for the elaboration of valid, reliable, and complete knowledge about any object of study, integral education incorporates inner or intrapersonal epistemic diversity (i.e., vital, instinctive, somatic, empathic, intellectual, imaginal, contemplative ways of knowing) and outer or interpersonal epistemic diversity (i.e., knowledge from the various human collectives, ethnic groups, cultures, classes, genders, etc., as well as from associated cross-cultural epistemological frameworks and standpoints), with these two types of diversity being intimately connected.

6. Integral education promotes the integral development and transformation of students, faculty, and the larger educational container or institution. The inclusion of all human dimensions in the learning process naturally enhances the transformative, healing, and spiritual power of education, as well as its potential to restructure academic policies and institutional practices.

Challenges and Prospects of Integral Transformative Education

In this section, we briefly discuss several challenges faced by participatory integral pedagogies and suggest that they can be seen as precious opportunities to rescue the transformative and spiritual potentials of educational practice.

From Lopsided Development to Integral Transformation

Modern Western education focuses almost exclusively on the development of the rational mind and its intellectual powers, with little attention given to the maturation of other dimensions of the person (see, e.g., Hocking et al., 2001; Miller, 1991). As a result, most individuals in our culture reach their adulthood with a somewhat mature mental functioning but with poorly or irregularly developed somatic, vital, emotional, aesthetic, intuitive, and spiritual intelligences (Gardner, 1983/1993).

Given the extreme mind-centeredness of this way of life, a continued emphasis on mental learning and inquiry seems nearly inevitable, which leads to the greatest tragedy of cognicentrism: It generates a vicious circle that justifies itself. Because modern education does not create spaces for the autonomous maturation of the body, the instincts, and the heart, these worlds cannot participate in an inquiry process unless they are mentally or externally guided. Yet, insofar as they are mentally or externally guided, these human dimensions cannot mature autonomously, and thus the need for their mental or external direction becomes permanently justified.

Complicating this situation further is the fact that, after many generations of mind-centered life and education, often combined with the gross or subtle control and inhibition of the body, instincts, sexuality, and passions, these nondiscursive worlds not only are undeveloped but are frequently wounded or distorted and may even manifest regressive tendencies. Thus, when an individual seeks knowledge in these worlds, the first thing that he or she typically encounters is a layer of conflicts, fears, or confusion that perpetuates the deep-seated belief that these worlds are epistemically barren. What is normally overlooked, however, is an essential primary intelligence that lies beneath this layer which, if accessed, can heal the root of the conflict while fostering the maturation and epistemic competence of these worlds from within. What is needed, then, is to create spaces in which these human dimensions can achieve epistemic competence according to their own developmental principles and dynamics rather than those the mind thinks are most adequate. Only when the body, instincts, sexuality, and heart are allowed to mature autonomously will they become equal partners with the mind and be capable of creative participation in cocreating a truly integral process of inquiry and learning.

Rescuing the healing and transformative dimensions of education should not be regarded as turning education into a therapeutic process. The main goal of integral education is not personal healing or group bonding (although these may naturally occur, and any genuine integral process should welcome and even foster these possibilities) but multidimensional inquiry and the collaborative construction of knowledge. Take, for example, a hypothetical situation in which the access to nonmental worlds (e.g., through guided visualization, interactive meditation, or movement) activates in some students personal material in need of healing that may interfere with the aims of the inquiry process. In the context of a pedagogical (vs. therapeutic) container, this situation can be approached as a fruitful stage of the inquiry process. In other words, a skillful facilitator can use this situation to help learners become aware of deeply seated personal dispositions that may be coloring, shaping, and probably distorting their intellectual discernment. In a way, this stage could be seen as a kind of inner "hermeneutic of suspicion" that may lead to the critical identification of distorting epistemic blinders and standpoints. After this initial stage of awareness of personal dispositions and familiarization with the experiential access to nonmental worlds, a genuine multidimensional inquiry can gradually emerge.

In sum, the challenge raised by lopsided development can be seen as a fertile opportunity to turn education into a process of integral transformation that can help learners to achieve adulthood at all levels, not only mentally. In the context of integral education, transformative healing opens the doors of human multidimensional cognition.

From Mental Pride to Spiritual Awakening

Our understanding of mental pride is not associated with what is conventionally regarded as a proud personality. By *mental pride* we mean the deep-seated disposition of the mind to believe (a) that it is the most important player or chief director of any process of knowledge, and (b) that it can attain complete understanding without the collaboration of the other human attributes. Given this definition, it is possible for a person to be psychologically humble (e.g., about his or her personal talents or achievements) but simultaneously maintain a strong mental bias in life direction and the search for knowledge and therefore fall prey to mental pride.

In an academic context, mental pride manifests in a variety of ways, including (a) confusion of global intellectual visions with genuine integral knowledge; (b) difficulties in acknowledging the partiality of all intellectual visions; (c) flagrant or subtle devaluation of the epistemic value of the other human attributes, even in those cases in which such value is intellectually accepted; (d) insistence on the already developed condition of the nonmental worlds—in oneself or one's culture—as an unconscious defense mechanism against their development that perpetuates the mind's epistemic hegemony (of course, certain exceptional individuals may actually have reached a considerable level of maturity at all levels); (e) lack of patience with the normally slower rhythm that the nonmental worlds may require to offer their contributions to an inquiry process; and (f) a compulsive need to control the inquiry process mentally—for example, through premature conceptualization or application of intellectual constructs.

As the mind gradually lets go of its pride and opens itself to learn from the other human attributes and collaborate with them as an equal in the elaboration of knowledge, it can be gradually released from the unnecessary burden of having to do most of the inquiry work. The mind becomes humble, recognizing its intrinsic limitations and realizing that it does not need to know everything because there are greater sources of knowledge to which it can be connected. Then the mind can rest and relax, attain inner peace and silence, and become porous and permeable to the immanent and transcendent energies of the Mystery—energies that vitalize and illuminate the mind with a knowing that the mind will never be able to fully encompass with its mental structures but to which it can be attuned and by which it can be inspired and guided.

In sum, the deeply seated pride of the mind can be seen as an opportunity to turn education into a process of genuine spiritual awakening in intimate contact with the immanent and transcendent dimensions of the Mystery.

Beyond Cognicentrism and Anti-Intellectualism in Integral Studies

The critique of cognicentrism and the emphasis on the nondiscursive and spiritual elements of human inquiry can easily raise the specter of anti-intellectualism. The basic concern is that the incorporation of somatic, vital, and emotional experience into the educational container may jeopardize intellectual rigor. In other words, if we make too much room for somatic, emotional, and intuitive knowing, don't we run the risk of debilitating intellectual standards of analytical rigor and rational criticism? Can we really escape the degeneration of educational practice into a fluffy, warm, but ultimately uncritical process that bypasses the meticulous elaboration and appraisal of knowledge?

Although it cannot be repeated too often that including the nondiscursive human dimensions in the teaching and learning process does not imply the rejection or devaluation of intellectual knowledge, we believe this is a valid concern that deserves serious consideration. This worry is certainly understandable if we look at the historically dominant tendency of the West to polarize mind and body, or reason and emotion. From certain trends in the Romantic revolt against the Enlightenment's enthroned Reason to the 1960s Esalen Institute's "awaken the body, turn off the mind" motto to contemporary New Age's emotionalism and uneasiness with intellectual rigor, most past and present historical challenges to cognicentrism flirt with or fall prey to anti-intellectualist tendencies. The abuses of the 1960s, as well as a plethora of unsuccessful alternative pedagogical experiments in recent decades, are still fresh in the minds of many in academia, and it is therefore natural that any proposal denouncing cognicentrism and advocating the incorporation of multidimensional knowing may create suspicion in some scholars.

As should be obvious, however, anti-intellectualism reactively labors in the same deep structure of hierarchical, polarizing thinking as cognicentrism does. In other words, anti-intellectualism is the back—and equally problematic—side of cognicentrism. As many holistic educators stress, the pressing challenge today is to break away from dichotomizing tendencies and explore integrative approaches that will allow intellectual knowing and conscious awareness to be grounded in and enriched by somatic, vital, emotional, aesthetic, intuitive, and spiritual knowing without losing their powers of clarity and discrimination. In other words, the contemporary challenge is to forge a middle path that avoids the pitfalls of both cognicentrism and anti-intellectualism.

But even with this recognition, the practical challenge remains. In our pedagogical practice, for example, we have repeatedly observed how difficult it is for an overwhelming majority of students to flow between discursive reason and nondiscursive experience and to engage in an integrated inquiry that incorporates both epistemic modes harmoniously. In practical terms, this means that most students are at first incapable of elaborating intellectual knowledge from emotional/somatic experience and of remaining in mindful contact with their hearts and bodies while engaged in intellectual discussion. We interpret this difficulty as a sign of the prevalent state of dissociation between these worlds in the modern Western self. (In some individuals, these worlds are not dissociated but undifferentiated, which creates a similar difficulty but may require a different pedagogical intervention.) In our view, this predicament calls for the exploration of methodological structures that systematically bridge those different worlds, foster their collaborative epistemic competence, and lead to creative academic fruits and sound shared knowledge.[11]

Even considering this potential risk, what is really the alternative? Is it sufficient to continue offering an educational practice that exclusively or essentially focuses on the supposedly "safer" and "less messy" levels of the mind and consciousness and keeps the other worlds either at bay or in a state of perpetual immaturity under parameters set by the mind? Can we truly say, to ourselves and to the world, that we are offering an "integral" or "transformative" education if we do not incorporate the body, the vital, and the heart into the very substance of learning and inquiry? We placed "safer" and "less messy" in quotation marks because these nondiscursive worlds—now marginalized, often repressed, and given no or very little space in the classroom—tend to reappear eventually in class dynamics under different guises (e.g., compensatory mental rigidity; attitudes of superiority; angry outbursts at the "masculinized," "patriarchal," or "disembodied" pedagogical container; diplomatic passive aggression; or a diffuse sense of sadness, frustration, or resentment). Using a gross analogy, imagine a house that has not been cleaned for years and whose furniture is covered by thick layers of dust. If we leave the house alone, it will look less messy and cleaner than it will when we start stirring all the dust. But this is obviously a case of erroneous perception, and there is no doubt that the neatness and freshness achieved by a thorough cleaning will be more real and satisfying than if the house is left untouched because of worries about temporary disarray.

In sum, a participatory perspective denounces both extremes—anti-intellectualism and cognicentrism—as equally one-sided and problematic and proposes that head and heart, intellect, and emotion (along with body, instincts, intuition, etc.) can be equal partners in the inquiry process and elaboration of more integral understandings. Because of the widely undeveloped, undifferentiated, or dissociated state of many of those worlds in the modern self, this process may involve temporary periods of chaos and confusion, but we suggest that they be regarded as fertile steps toward the achievement of genuinely integrated cognition and higher orders of complexity in our creative apprehension of life and the world.

Conclusions

We believe that in future years integral education will gradually move toward participatory pedagogical approaches in which all human dimensions are actively encouraged to participate creatively at all stages of inquiry and learning. The explicit inclusion of all human attributes in the inquiry process will naturally reconnect education with its root meaning (edu-care: "bringing out the wholeness within") and, therefore, with transformative healing and spiritual growth, both of which involve a movement toward human wholeness. It will also promote a genuine integration of feminine and masculine principles in learning and creative inquiry. We believe that these two moves—multidimensional inquiry and masculine/feminine balance—are pivotal for the creative vitality of both integral studies and educational practice, and we are convinced that any institution that pioneers their systematic exploration will be remembered historically as epoch-making.[11]

We end this article by highlighting the spiritual or transpersonal dimension of human participatory inquiry. As we gradually open ourselves to the epistemic power of all human attributes, we can perhaps realize that through the exercise of our own creative capabilities we are fostering the unfolding of the Mystery's infinite generativity in the world. In other words, human multidimensional cognition channels the Mystery's outpouring of new meanings onto this plane of physical reality more loyally and completely than the isolated intellect does, and these meanings can radically change not only our perception of the world but the world itself. The world then stops being sensed as having an independently objective nature and becomes a relational and intersubjective reality that unfolds in a multiplicity of conceptual and transconceptual ways, partly depending on the human approaches and ways of knowing involved in the act of apprehension. In other words, the world is now recognized as a *hierophany*—a sacred process of divine self-disclosure, taking place in and through history, in which embodied human beings can creatively participate in intimate partnership with the Mystery. This is the wider spiritual context in which the cultivation of participatory approaches to integral education gains its fullest import. And this is the context, we believe, that is crucial for the future of education in the new millennium.

Notes

1. Although most of the following reflections are offered mainly in the context of adult graduate Western education, we believe they may also be relevant for other educational levels, practices, and cultures.

2. See Miller (1996, 1999) for two valuable discussions of the nature and contents of holistic and spiritual curricula.

3. In his manifesto of *transdisciplinarity*, for example, Nicolescu (2002) wrote: "Transdisciplinary education revalues the role of intuition, imagination, sensibility and the body in the transmission of knowledge" (p. 150).

4. We are using the term *cognicentrism* to refer to the privileged position that the rational-analytical mind (and its associated instrumental reason and Aristotelian logic) has in the modern Western world over other ways of knowing, for example, somatic, vital, emotional, aesthetic, imaginal, visionary, intuitive, and contemplative. By no means are we suggesting that the other human dimensions are not "cognitive" in the sense of not being able to apprehend knowledge or creatively participate in its elaboration.

5. For several enlightening discussions of assessment and validity in multidimensional inquiry, see Anderson (2000), Braud (1998), Heron (1999), and Kremer (1992a, 1992b).

6. Space does not allow us to discuss here the crucial relationship between epistemic and political participation in academia. It should suffice to say that as education moves from its current mind-centeredness to multidimensional knowing, it is likely that the traditional unilateral assessment by teachers will need to undergo a serious scrutiny and move toward a more integral approach involving not only teachers' evaluations but also self- and peer assessment. Our sense is that the attempt to implement a participatory integral education in the context of non-participatory academic politics may be not only incoherent but also ultimately self-defeating. For a provoking discussion of this fundamental issue, see Heron (2002). On the transformation of the traditional relationship between teachers and students, see Freire (1970/1996, 1998).

7. The images of the four seasons and planting a seed derive from Ramon V. Albareda and Marina T. Romero's innovative approach to integral growth and training (see Albareda & Romero, 1990; Romero & Albareda, 2001; Ferrer, 2003) and have been adapted for an academic context by Jorge N. Ferrer and Marina T. Romero in a variety of lectures, graduate courses, and pedagogical experiments at American alternative educational institutions such as the California Institute of Integral Studies in San Francisco and the Institute of Transpersonal Psychology in Palo Alto, both located in California. It is note-worthy that the image of planting a seed is also central in the novel research methodology called "organic inquiry" (Clements, Ettling, Jenett, & Shields, 1998), and the metaphor of the four seasons has been used in a pedagogical context by Parker Palmer (2000) in his wonderfully evocative essay, "There is a season."

8. By "vital seeds" we mean here the infinite life potentials (genetic dispositions, in scientific language) stored in the vital world of each human being. Although only a limited number of these potentials can be actualized in a lifetime, others can be passed on—biologi-cally and energetically—to one's progeny or embodied in a variety of creative fruits (projects, art, books, relationships, etc.) that can activate the vital seeds of others in the future.

9. For several compelling discussions about the pedagogical value of the inclusion of Eros in academic teaching, see hooks (1994), Pryer (2001), and Snowber (2005).

10. We are not suggesting, of course, an association between vital/heart and the femi-nine and body/mind and the masculine. In our view, regardless of gender, both masculine and feminine principles can manifest in and through all human dimensions in many ways: for example, as centrifugal action and receptive presence in the body, as the capability to energetically impregnate and gestate in the vital world, as the expression and reception of feelings and emotions in the heart, as speaking and listening on the mental level, and as prayer and receptive meditation in spiritual consciousness, to mention only a few possibili-ties. This apparent incoherence emerges from our working simultaneously with different symbolic systems which, although helpful in expressing fundamental features of the model presented, do not have to be in total synchrony with each other. For a lucid presentation

of the need to combine feminine and masculine qualities and to incorporate the nonmental worlds in integral education, see Rothberg (1999).

11. For a report of a cooperative inquiry that seeks to embody the participatory approach to integral education proposed here, see Osterhold, Husserl, & Nicol (2007). See also Ferrer (forthcoming) for a description of participatory pedagogical strategies used in the teaching of a graduate seminar in comparative mysticism.

References

Albareda, R. V., & Romero, M. T. (1990). *Nacidos de la tierra: Sexualidad, origen del ser humano* [Born on earth: Sexuality, origin of the human being]. Barcelona: Hogar del Libro.

Anderson, R. (2000). Intuitive inquiry: Interpreting objective and subjective data. *ReVision: A Journal of Consciousness and Transformation, 22*(4), 31–39.

Boyer, E. (1990). *Scholarship reconsidered: 1990 special report of the Carnegie foundation for the advancement of teaching*. Princeton, NJ: Carnegie Foundation for the Advancement of Teaching.

Braud, W. (1998). An extended view of validity. In W. Braud & R. Anderson (Eds.), *Transpersonal research methods for the social sciences: Honoring human experience* (pp. 213–237). Thousand Oaks, CA: Sage.

Chittick, W. C. (1994). Microcosm, macrocosm, and perfect man. In *Imaginal worlds: Ibn al-'Arabi and the problem of religious diversity* (pp. 31–38). Albany: State University of New York Press.

Clements, J., Ettling, D., Jenett, D., & Shields, L. (1998). *Organic inquiry: If research was sacred*. Palo Alto, CA: Serpentine.

Ferrer, J. N. (2002). *Revisioning transpersonal theory: A participatory vision of human spirituality*. Albany: State University of New York Press.

Ferrer, J. N. (2003). Integral transformative practice: A participatory perspective. *Journal of Transpersonal Psychology, 35*(1), 21–42.

Ferrer, J. N. (2008a). Spiritual knowing as participatory enaction: An answer to the question of religious pluralism. In J. N. Ferrer & J. Sherman (Eds.), *The participatory turn: Spirituality, mysticism, religious studies* (pp. 135–169). Albany, NY: State University of New York Press.

Ferrer, J. N. (2008b). What does it mean to live a fully embodied spiritual life? *International Journal of Transpersonal Studies, 27,* 1–11.

Ferrier, J. N. (forthcoming). Teaching the graduate seminar in comparative mysticism: A participatory integral approach. In W. B. Parsons (ed.), *Teaching mysticism*. New York: Oxford University Press.

Ferrer, J. N., Albareda, R. V., & Romero, M. T. (2004). Embodied participation in the Mystery: Implications for the individual, interpersonal relationships, and society. *ReVision: A Journal of Consciousness and Transformation, 27*(1), 10–17.

Freire, P. (1970/1996). *Pedagogy of the oppressed*. New York: Continuum.

Freire, P. (1998). *Pedagogy of freedom: Ethics, democracy, and civic courage*. Lanham, MA: Rowman & Littlefield.

Gardner, H. (1983/1993). *Frames of mind: The theory of multiple intelligences.* New York: Basic Books.

Heron, J. (1999). *The complete facilitator's handbook.* London: Kogan Page.

Heron, J. (2002, July 22–24). Our process in this place. Keynote speech at the International Conference of Organizational Spirituality, *"Living spirit: New dimensions in work and learning."* University of Surrey, UK. Retrieved February 17, 2005, from http://www.human-inquiry.com/Keynote2.htm)

Hocking, B., Haskell, J., & Linds, W. (2001). *Unfolding bodymind: Exploring possibility through education.* Rutland, VT: Foundation for Educational Renewal.

hooks, b. (1994). Eros, eroticism, and the pedagogical process. In *Teaching to transgress: Education as the practice of freedom* (pp. 191–199). New York: Routledge.

Klein, J. T. (1990). *Interdisciplinarity: History, theory, and practice.* Detroit, MI: Wayne State University Press.

Klein, J. T. (1996). *Crossing boundaries: Knowledge, disciplinarities, and interdisciplinarities.* Charlottesville: University of Virginia Press.

Kremer, J. (1992a). The dark night of the scholar. *ReVision: A Journal of Consciousness and Transformation, 14*(2), 169–178.

Kremer, J. (1992b). Whither dark night of the scholar? *ReVision: A Journal of Consciousness and Transformation, 15*(1), 4–12.

Lattuca, L. (2002). *Creating interdisciplinarity: Interdisciplinary research and teaching among college and university faculty.* Nashville, TN: Vanderbilt University Press.

Metzger, D. (1992). Writing as a spiritual practice. In *Writing for your life* (pp. 183–244). San Francisco: Harper.

Miller, J. (1996). *The holistic curriculum.* Toronto: Ontario Institute for Studies in Education.

Miller, J. (1999). *Education and the soul: Toward a spiritual curriculum.* Albany: State University of New York Press.

Miller, J. P., Karsten, S., Denton, D., Orr, D., & Coladillo Kates, I. (Eds.). (2005). *Holistic learning and spirituality in education: Breaking new ground.* Albany: State University of New York Press.

Miller, R. (Ed.). (1991). New directions in education: Selections from *Holistic Education Review.* Brandon, VT: Holistic Education Press.

Montuori, A. (2004). Communication to CIIS Integral Education Committee. California Institute of Integral Studies, San Francisco.

Nicolescu, B. (2002). *Manifesto of transdisciplinarity.* Albany: State University of New York Press.

Osterhold, H. M., Husserl R., E. & Nicol, D. (2007). Rekindling the fire of transformative education: A participatory case study. *Journal of Transformative Education 5*(3), 221–245.

O'Sullivan, E. V. (1999). *Transformative learning: Educational vision for the 21st century.* London: Zed Books.

O'Sullivan, E. V., Morrell, A., & O'Connor, M. A. (Eds.). (2002). *Expanding the boundaries of transformative learning: Essays on theory and practice.* New York: Palgrave.

Overzee, A. H. (1992). *The body divine: The symbol of the body in the works of Teilhard de Chardin and Ramanuja.* New York: Cambridge University Press.

Palmer, P. (2000). There is a season. In *Let your life speak: Listening for the voice of vocation* (pp. 95–109). San Francisco: Jossey-Bass.

Pryer, A. (2001). Breaking hearts: Towards an erotics of pedagogy. In B. Hocking, J. Haskell & W. Linds (Eds.), *Unfolding bodymind: Exploring possibility through education* (pp. 132–11). Rutland, VT: Foundation for Educational Renewal.

Romero, M. T., & Albareda, R. V. (2001). Born on Earth: Sexuality, spirituality, and human evolution. *ReVision: A Journal of Consciousness and Transformation, 24*(2), 5–14.

Rothberg, D. (1999). Transpersonal issues at the millennium. *Journal of Transpersonal Psychology, 31*(1), 41–67.

Saso, M. (1997). The Taoist body and cosmic prayer. In S. Coakley (Ed.), *Religion and the body* (pp. 230–247). New York: Cambridge University Press.

Shokek, S. (2001). *Kabbalah and the art of being.* London: Routledge.

Snowber, C. (2005). The eros of teaching. In J. P. Miller, S. Karsten, D. Denton, D. Orr, & I. Coladillo Kates (Eds.), *Holistic learning and spirituality in education: Breaking new ground* (pp. 215–21). Albany: State University of New York Press.

West, C. (1999). *The Cornell West reader.* New York: Basic Civitas Books.

Wexler, J. (2004). Communication to the CIIS Integral Education Committee. California Institute of Integral Studies, San Francisco.

A "Developmental Action Inquiry" Approach To Teaching First-, Second-, and Third-Person Action Research Methods

Erica Steckler and William R. Torbert

Introduction

In this chapter, we suggest that it is only through action and inquiry processes such as those enacted by Developmental Action Inquiry (DAI) (Torbert, 1976, 1987, 1991; Torbert & Associates, 2004) that education, work, and leisure actually become mutually transforming and thus truly integral. In support of this assertion, the introductory section offers, first, brief descriptions of three integral qualities of DAI not focused on by other developmental approaches (e.g., Kegan, 1994; Wilber 2000). Second, we suggest the sources of these three qualities by summarizing Bill (Torbert)'s career of spiritual, educational, and managerial research, teaching, consulting, and leadership. Then, in the main body of the chapter, we introduce Bill and Erica (Steckler)'s work together as teacher and student in a PhD-level course in Action Research Methods (ARM) and later as increasingly peer-like co-authors of this chapter. We offer a close description of a few events that occurred during the course that reflect how an action inquiry approach can generate individual, group, and organizational learning and transformational development toward integrity and mutuality among participants.

The three qualities of integral theorizing, personal practice, and educational organizing essential to the praxis of DAI are:

1. Playful *first-person efforts to expand and deepen one's attention to en-compass four "territories of experience" simultaneously* (Torbert, 1972) and to establish alignment or integrity among them. These four territories constitute the full aesthetic continuum of the attention:

our individual apprehension of *the outside world*, sentience of the living being's *own embodiment and performance*, discernment of one's *feeling/interpreting/strategizing*, and regardfulness for the dynamic quality and *source of attention itself*.

2. Leaderly *second-person initiatives to create communities of inquiry* where the individual members and the community as a whole are guided, not just by single-loop incremental feedback from a hierarchical superior, but also by double-loop transforming feedback (Argyris & Schon, 1974; Argyris, Putnam, & Smith, 1985) and by triple-loop presencing and re-aligning feedback (Senge et al., 2004; Scharmer, 2007) from their peers and from organizational superiors acting in a peer-like fashion.

3. Liberating *third-person disciplines* (Torbert, 1991) that foster the interweaving in everyday life of first-, second-, and third-person action inquiries.

The long-term, fundamental aims of each of these modes of DAI is to increase first-person integrity, second-person mutuality, and third-person transformational sustainability. Although DAI is based not only on the action and inquiry methods just mentioned and elaborated below, but also on developmental theory (McGuire, Palus, & Torbert, 2007), we choose not to mention the specific, sequential developmental action-logics in this chapter, in order to highlight the importance of action practices and research inquiries in generating developmental transformations.

The main body of this chapter is about the Action Research Methods (ARM) PhD course and will illustrate in detail how first-, second-, and third-person action and inquiry can interweave to generate single-, double-, and triple-loop feedback that aligns the four territories of experience in real-time to help participants increasingly develop and integrate skills, capacities, and awarenesses as both researchers and leaders. The amalgamation of this intentional, multidimensional individual and shared development can in turn transform the given organization (in this case the PhD course in ARM) beyond a typical "community of practice" (that helps members become more competent in a pre-defined arena, primarily through single-loop feedback) toward a true "community of inquiry" (that helps members develop new capacities and worldviews, as well as new competences, through single-, double-, and triple-loop feedback).

In order to give these extremely abstract concepts a little initial embodiment, we begin by briefly tracing the wide variety of organizational settings in which Bill Torbert first learned and later guided significant attempts at integrating learning, productivity, and transformational development in education and business. Starting in early adulthood, Bill's most significant learning organizations included the first-person research/practices of the Gurdjieff Work (Ouspensky, 1949) (in which he participated from 1964—1989), where he studied the interplay among his perceptions of the outside world, his bodily sensations as he acted, and his emotions and thinking, all through cultivating a trans-cognitive attention. At the same time, he engaged repeatedly in the second-person research/practices of various group dynamics approaches (Tavistock, Bethel, Esalen), where he studied how one's own speaking and timing and leadership action can help shape the vision, strategies, norms, and levels of trust and inquiry of teams with whom one is working or playing. As well, he sought mastery of third-person research/practice skills in social science at the Yale PhD program in Individual and Organizational Behavior, where he studied how quantitative, qualitative, and action research can interweave to help larger organizations and institutions transform.

Torbert's later educational experiments in generating integral education for others as well as himself included the directorship of the Yale Upward Bound War on Poverty program for high school students (1966–68) (Torbert, 1976), as well as the creation of an action-and-reflection-oriented entrepreneurship course for 400 undergraduate students at a time at the Southern Methodist University Business School (1970–72) and for 100+ graduate students at a time at the Harvard Graduate School of Education (1972–76). These experiments resulted in the gradual creation and articulation of "liberating disciplines" (Torbert, 1991), a kind of organizing that simultaneously supports and challenges participants and the organization as a whole to develop toward becoming a true community of inquiry.

Still later, as dean of the Boston College MBA program, Torbert's focus shifted to institutionalizing and sustaining a transformational program within a relatively conservative, conventional university (Torbert, 1987). Next, he took a number of long-term consulting roles aimed at generating both personal and organizational developmental transformation in business and not-for-profit settings (Fisher & Torbert, 1995; Torbert & Associates, 2004; Rooke & Torbert, 2005), in order to learn more about the developmental timing of interventions meant to influence others' first-, second-, and third-person action inquiry. Finally, he generated a core PhD course in Action Research Methods (ARM) at Boston College's (BC) Organization Studies Department for over 10 years, until his retirement in 2008. This was one of a small handful of action research courses taught in the United States, with the explicit intention of simultaneously supporting students' intellectual, experiential, and practical development through the building and ever-evolving reconstruction of liberating disciplines. The result is an existentially challenging setting in which students assume more leadership responsibility than usual and the teacher is more transparent about his or her own learning than usual, as will be illustrated below. Students and leaders stumble across learning challenges and opportunities in real time that can cross-pollinate and transform the "I," "We," "It," and "Its" quadrants referred to in integral education (Esbjörn-Hargens, 2007, current volume). We illustrate DAI in practice in this chapter by retelling and analyzing one version of this ARM course.

Erica took the ARM class as a requirement of the first year of her doctoral study. She had known very little about the course or the method prior to reading the syllabus on the first day of class. Ultimately much of the method resonated with Erica, who has appreciated the integration of multiple experiential dimensions including awareness, inquiry, integrity, reflection, action, testing, expression, effectiveness, and learning enacted in the present, individually and with others, with a transformational intention. She found herself creatively and developmentally inspired by the first-, second-, and third-person research practices that she developed over the semester, so she volunteered to co-author this chapter thereafter.

Course Overview

Because the course includes autobiographical writing, audio-recordings and selected transcriptions of class meetings, as well as individual and group-oriented study and reflection by students and leaders as it proceeds, it is possible to convey up-close what this embodiment of integral education involves in particular instances. The course experience we highlight in this chapter involves fewer than 10 participants, including BC members required to take the course and members from neighboring universities electing to take the course.

The syllabus for the ARM course is arranged in four subsections—Mission, Strategies, Practices, and Assessments—that reflect the "four territories of experience." It begins with the following statement of Mission that also reflects the four territories of experience:

I.   *Wonder-full listening*

II. *Presencing theorizing*

III. *Timely, transforming acting, and*

IV. *Mutually inquiring and empowering researching/assessing of validity, efficacy, integrity, mutuality, sustainability, and justice*

In the syllabus, Bill notes that this mission is "pre-formulated by the professor" and asks "How does it ring to you?" The class noted that this mission sounds slightly mysterious, as well as somewhat more experiential and action-oriented than a typical course mission. We discussed the unusual overarching course goal of introducing members to, and co-creating a space to practice and question together, a theory that supposedly makes each of us and the collective group more aware in the present of our attention, thinking, and action, and the integration of all of these with the world around us. Further, we talked about how the goal of developmental action inquiry is to enable us to find and enact truths in a timely fashion. Overall, we converged around accepting this pre-formulated mission (all this based on Erica's class notes).

In the next section of the syllabus, Strategies, the first strategy is entitled "Treating the class as a real-time research/practice process" and describes how every class will be recorded, with participant-leaders taking turns partially transcribing as well as leading a meeting, and writing a second-person research paper about that meeting and the ones leading up to it, to be shared and discussed with all the other participants.

The second strategy is entitled "Confidentiality, Transparency, and Accountability" and includes never identifying any other member of the course in any recounting of course events with persons who are not course members. This rule also applies to members of the course who may later choose to write about it for publication, and these members are asked to share a draft of the paper with other course members prior to publication. This strategy is in effect in this chapter—members are not identified in recounting events and are instead referred to by pseudonyms, and a draft of the paper has been shared with all of them.

The third strategy describes the regular "Activities outside class time," including the three papers to be written during the semester: an autobiographical, first-person paper about each participant's developmental evolution up to the present, with next steps; a second-person paper about the class meetings, already described; and, at the end of the semester, a potentially publishable third-person paper about this kind of research (see, for example, Hartwell & Torbert, 1999; Chandler & Torbert, 2003).

The section of the syllabus on practices gives the weekly schedule of readings, with the final weeks of assignments blank, in anticipation of co-structuring the assignments by then. The assessments section of the syllabus indicates that there will be a grade for each of the three papers given by the instructor (25% each), a participation grade developed so as to provide feedback to each participant about others' assessments (25%), and the opportunity for members to challenge and reconstruct the grading process as a whole, if they wish. Our class ultimately opted not to reconstruct the grading process, although there was brief discussion about how we might and if other classes had. Finally, a bibliography of major contemporary volumes related to action research is appended to the syllabus, including the following: Argyris, 1971; Bernstein, 1985; Habermas, 1984, 1987; Varela, Thompson, & Rosch, 1991; Wilber, 1998; Sherman & Torbert, 2000; Ogilvy, 2002; Hallward, 2003; Lundberg & Young, 2005; Shani et al., 2007; Scharmer, 2007; Reason & Bradbury, 2008.

First Person

As the syllabus is reviewed and discussed during the first meeting, course members quickly become aware that they will play a number of risk-taking, leadership roles in the class that include the following opportunities for developing first- and second-person research practices: (1) writing and analyzing their autobiographies early in the semester (to be shared only with the instructor, unless a given student later chooses to share with others); (2) leading at least one class each after the instructor leads the first two; and (3) writing second-person papers about the class they lead, to be shared with and discussed with the rest of the class the week afterward. As a starting point, the instructor suggests a 10-page minimum for the autobiography (some papers are as short as 15 or 20 pages, but most students write far longer papers, from 30 to 200 pages). The following short excerpts from one such autobiography provide a flavor of the openness and intimacy with which students write in their first-person voices. This person had tried to "charm her way out of" (her phrasing) an assignment everyone had: to lead the class for one session. So, Torbert invited her to write autobiographically on the theme of power (and she later gave her permission for the essay, or excerpts, to be used for research and educational purposes). Here is a little of what she wrote:

> *Power is a funny word. It can conjure up many different thoughts and emotions. Many people shudder over the traditional definition of power in its most unilateral sense. Others rejoice over the thought of power as a mutually transforming process. When you first said (and later repeated in different ways) that a consultant must become comfortable with the issue of power and capable of helping to transform how power is understood and exercised in organizations, I thought, "Then consulting is not the field for me."*
>
> *Through the course of this class with you Bill, I have been forced to face my own negative view of power head on. It has been a somewhat uncomfortable journey, one I have only recently felt that importance of . . .*
>
> *(After writing about the positive kinds of power her parents exercised . . .) While it sounds like an idyllic childhood, power did not always have a positive influence upon me growing up. I completely resented my brother's use of power within our family. However unconscious and not intentional it was, his actions were a great force. He unilaterally transformed our family from an almost idyllic way of life to a living hell. My parents were constantly consumed with his problems, were constantly yelling at him and changing plans to accommodate Sandy. I remember lying awake at night listening to them yell. It happened more often than I even care to mention. He even robbed me of my sleep. My brother's use of power was even more directly felt by my sister and I through repeated rounds of being hit in my stomach. As I am writing this I am feeling the*

disgust and anxiety, still, throughout my whole body. I remember, like it was yesterday, the feeling of having the wind knocked out of me due to a sharp punch.

In addition to this relationship with my brother, which has tainted my feelings towards power, I have, several times, put myself in situations where I experienced a complete loss of power. One of these was the loss of a child that I was pregnant with at a very young age. Another was an assault that happened while I was under the influence of alcohol and was powerless to defend myself . . .

So I have lived through some positive experiences of power and some quite negative ones. Where am I now? I think it depends upon the realm of my life that I am examining. One thing this organizational development class has taught me is that I am a very different person in different areas of my life.

This kind of first-person research and expression in developmental action inquiry tracks quite well to the Individual-Interior, or "I," quadrant of the Integral model of education (Esbjörn-Hargens, 2007, current volume), tapping into the self and consciousness through contemplation and critical reflection on personal and interpersonal experiences. After participants write an initial story-draft of their life, the instructor offers detailed written feedback, including questions about how different life events may suggest certain developmental action-logics or moments of transformation between action-logics (Torbert & Fisher, 1992). Understanding how a difficult time in one's life (or a difficult theme, such as inclusion or power or intimacy) may have represented a conflict between action-logics can lead to a deepening self-acceptance, as well as to more active inquiry and greater openness to whatever one's own and others' current transforming edge is. Thus, this first-person paper tends to become much more than an exercise in using case study data to test a theory. If there is sufficient trust between the instructor and the participant, and if the participant takes sufficient initiative, the participant can use the rest of the course as a primary site for experimenting toward enacting a personal double-loop transformation from one action-logic to another.

The DAI approach to teaching and action researching also embodies an integral theory of education through second- and third-person research methods. The remainder of this chapter focuses on three separate incidents of second-person research that highlight the participants' transformational processes in the "We/You" quadrant of integral education (and notice that even the particular autobiographical excerpt we have shared was influenced by a second-person event in the class). First, we will share how our group stumbled on a learning moment related to how membership commitment, inclusion, and in-group/out-group norms can develop in a community of inquiry.

Incident I—Inclusion: The Volunteers vs. the Draftees?

On the day he took the lead in generating the class agenda and guiding the class meeting, Bob (all names except our own are pseudonyms) invited us to explore ideas of membership and commitment to our evolving community of inquiry. Bob's inspiration for this focused exploration was based on an exchange in an earlier class between himself (a student at another area university who had elected the course) and Jim, a BC PhD student who was required to take the course. Bob had been "inviting" Jim to participate more fully, trying to demonstrate the advantages of engaging in a deeper inquiry together, in line with becoming "a community of inquiry." But Jim had resisted "buying in," generating a sense of tension between the two. In this class, Bob was again raising the issue, but this time with the aim of understanding "where we want to go forward as a group," when Jim enters the conversation:

> **Jim:** *First of all, just some background here. Bob and Sue, you are volunteers for this class. You are here because this is something you want to learn. You think this is something important. I am a draftee. I'm here because they will not give me a Ph.D., unless I pass this class and pass the comprehensive exam. It is not a course that I would decide to take otherwise. It's not something that I think should be a requirement, but it is. And I have this feeling that because of the nature of this action research course and how you're supposed to participate here and write your papers that I'm sort of in a position having to hand over a part of my life that I do not want to hand over in order to do well . . .*
>
> *. . . (and) I was being asked sequentially by the three people who felt the most empowered by this (Bob, Sue, and Bill T.) to justify myself. And I was the person who felt the least empowered and who was sort of being offered the role of this anti-action research guy in the class. And that bothered me a lot . . .*
>
> *. . . And so I left class and I thought about it too much and I got kind of freaked out about it. It all boils down to I felt like I was being singled out. And so I guess my question here is, and this may be my learning goal, is that given all the things I said about my connection and disconnection from the class, how am I supposed to participate in the full transparent level that everything I read in this class tells me I'm supposed to participate in? You know, not hurt the group by being withdrawn from it or anything like that.*
>
> **Bill:** *Well, one of things that struck me is that you don't affect me as the least participative person in class and in fact, you repeatedly raise significant issues. And here you are now sort of whole-heartedly entering*

into this and sharing what you actually felt between classes. So I don't feel like it's necessary to coerce you to do anything more. In fact, one of the things [that] strikes me when I think about it is, gosh, you've been present in several different ways, somewhat critically. If we cannot accept a critical voice in here, then we are really in trouble as far as creating a community of inquiry is concerned. So, I don't know. I mean, I don't myself experience you as required to do more.

> **Bob**: *On that point, first I'm really grateful that you share this. I'm asking myself why did I go back again. You said you felt irritated. And maybe I have the sense that I know better and am therefore trying to ask you what is your problem, what is it that you're not getting here. I'm questioning myself whether I have that frame. Maybe I . . . maybe I do. [Pause]*

> **Sue**: *I really appreciate this discussion, because I think a lot of what we've been talking about is the difference between our intention and the impact we are actually having on the group. We've just heard all these different perspectives. From you, Bob, on what your intention is and you are getting some feedback in various ways about the impact you're actually having. And you are just talking about a particular intention you are coming from. But it had a certain kind of impact.*

In his second-person paper, Bob offers a careful analysis of his *intended results* when he had originally been speaking with Jim and of the *actual impact* he had on Jim. Then he analyzes of his own *specific actions*, as well as the *assumptions* that generated his actions. Finally, he offers what assumptions he would like to make and what actions he would like to take in the future. At the conclusion of the paper, Bob summarizes his central insights into the *actual assumptions* he had been operating from in the original conversation:

> **[Bob]** *This session has had a profound impact on me personally. I have learned to see many blind-spots I was not aware of until now and have transcended single-loop thinking into double-loop thinking. I really appreciate that Jim put himself out to share with us how he really felt in class. Before that, I believed religiously that action inquiry must be good for all, and had no idea of the kind of coercive effect the group can have on people, (mostly generated by me), and the potential damage that comes with it. My prior single-loop thinking included believing single-mindedly in the benefits of a community of inquiry (COI) without questioning its potential harm to people. I never questioned the goal of creating a COI (the why), I was only concerned about how to create it. When I saw a member not benefiting from it as much, I mistakenly thought it must be his fault and*

that only if I can help him to see its value, will he enjoy it and learn from it as much as I do. This is typical single-loop thinking where I try to influence people's behavior in order to achieve a fixed goal.

We can see that although Bob had originally imagined that Jim required a double-loop change of perspective (or frame or assumptions), it is Bob himself who ultimately recognizes that his perspective or frame calls for a double-loop change, if he is in fact going to be an effective agent of a community of inquiry. The norms of a community of inquiry cannot be established by fiat—by implicitly hierarchical, dualistic thinking and acting, which can only result in unquestioned norms, declining trust, and unmanageable conflict—but only by a vulnerable, dia-lectical self-disclosing inquiry process that Jim is in fact the first to model in the interactions we have just reviewed, and that Bob then enacts in his second-person research paper. More generally, there is no mechanical, general way of creating a community of inquiry; it must be constructed from the materials and limitations of each distinct situation by an increasingly conscious, skillful, and, above all, truly mutual action inquiry process among the participants.

Incident II—Control: The Instructor vs. the Students?

The incident we highlight next deals with an observation of an initial power dynamic that one of the members of this evolving community of inquiry brought our attention to in a second-person research paper, informed by transcription of an audio recording of class, as well as jotted class and journal notes during the two weeks leading up to the paper. The budding researcher/practitioner tried ". . . to be aware of not just *what* people were saying, but *how* they were saying things." The particular issue of control was raised in terms of describing the actual physi-cal setting for one particular class. It was one of the first moves by a student to confront, albeit indirectly, issues of institutionalized power and control, and it opened the doors for further inquiry and mutuality-building among our members. In particular, the inquiry deals with the degree to which the instructor is genuinely sharing control of the class as a whole and to what degree he is actually exerting as much or more unilateral power than a typical professor.

Consistent with the principles of action inquiry that help cultivate single-, double-, and triple-loop feedback (Torbert, 2004), this section is structured by Erica, with opportunity for Bill to respond. This example of inquiry-in-action is also consistent with a key assumption of Integral Theory that multiple ways of knowing occur through participatory relationships and a variety of inquiry methods (Esbjörn-Hargens, 2007, current volume). The student-researcher's statement of intention at the outset of this second-person paper reads:

My goal for observing, listening, and assessing our . . . class session is to discover moments and spaces of group development and challenges, and to explore these together as we pursue our shared commitment to mutual, empowering learning and transformational growth in our group research.

The following excerpt and typical seating chart (Fig. 5) provide the basis for class consideration of (and now readers' attention to) the power and control dynamic within this potential community of inquiry.

. . . Bill typically indicates available and desirable seating positions by placing piles of handouts in particular locations. It seems like Bill's intent is to get us into a more circular and less-dispersed configuration. Although I now expect these piles of handouts that indicate a preferred seating configuration, this imposed structure has felt a little suspect to me, a little off-putting, given the relatively free-sit norms that have emerged in my other classes. I do see the value in closer seating arrangements, and any initial reaction has so far subsided immediately once discussion gets under way.

As a result of the timely sharing of this observation with the group, our awareness shifted to consider the application of status-based power, or institutionalized control, in terms of a preferred seating schema imposed by someone who arguably should be an equal-status participant. Upon reflection, the irony of the presence of a "legitimate" leader, in this case one who is institutionally appointed, in a transformationally oriented self-study group that is explicitly modeled after a peer-like community of inquiry cannot be ignored. While each member agreed, to one extent or another, to play at this task of creating a community of inquiry in which mutuality, integrity, and sustainability are expected outcomes of the process,

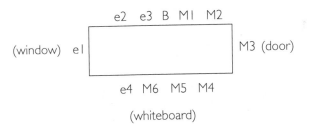

Note: B = Bill; M1 = member 1; M2 = member 2, etc.; e1–e4 = empty seats

Figure 5. Typical ARM Seating Arrangement

Bill's presence as professor-expert-evaluator—in addition to the requirement for four out of six of us to take the course—makes it easy to interpret our gatherings for learning and development as fundamentally coerced, which undermines the voluntariness, mutuality, and trust at the very core of a community of inquiry. While Bill often switched sides of the table every couple of weeks (and notably he never positioned himself at the "head" of the table), and members were free to sit in front of whatever pile of handouts we wished, our compact seating configuration, typically oriented around the door-side of the table, was strongly influenced by Bill's piles. There was no spreading out, no empty seats in between. What if one of us had resisted or refused to sit in front of one of the piles of articles that Bill placed neatly at desirable seating locations around the table? Most likely, Bill would have noticed early on in the class and asked us to move back into his ideal, tightly configured arrangement. I'm not sure that any of us would have challenged his subtle but obvious authority in the classroom, and therefore in our community, in that event.

Another facet of the challenge of power is that even when the opportunity to share power is offered, as when Bill offered the opportunity to revise the suggested grading process, it is not always accepted in whole or even in part, as when the group did not suggest or pursue changes in the assessment system. Further, no one challenged the fact that this course met for one extra hour each week than other comparable three-credit classes (and had been doing so throughout its history). In fact, despite awareness and discussion of the seating pattern generated by the instructor's initiative, the pattern did not change very much thereafter.

The important implication here is that even if Bill was not exercising control, there may be manipulative elements from the simple fact of his position of authority that ultimately have retrogressive effects. Although student-members became more empowered over the semester—manifest in more generative and collaborative development of the class-to-class agendas, with increasing numbers of the topics discussed influenced by what the student-researchers chose to focus on in their second-person research papers, and later in choosing readings for the last several class meetings—Bill's leadership of the class remained something that we all negotiated to find an appropriate, palatable balance between unilateral and mutual control.

Here begins Bill's rejoinder on this critical issue of power and control in a group that is convening to some degree because of members' pre-defined institutional roles, status, and legitimate power and to some degree because of their dedication to becoming a more mutual community of inquiry in which the very issue of what kind of power is being exercised how and by whom becomes discussable and transformable. First, as Erica's prior comments indicate, I did share power with the class in a variety of ways and offered to share power in even more ways than the class took up. Second, I did not hesitate to exercise power myself (for I wished us to become mutually empowered, not mutually unempowered), and my intent when exercising power was to create conditions for increasingly mutual exercises of power. Third and as an example of the prior point, with regard to my initiatives to influence the seating arrangement, I had only two motives that I was and am aware of: (1) I wished to model the fact that a meeting leader can influence the quality of the meeting by considering the physical arrangements as well as by planning the intellectual and emotional discussion topics and research exercises (and I hoped that the student meeting leaders, either through implicit mimicry or through explicit discussion, would gradually choose to exercise such power as well); and (2) in the early sessions, I wished to seat myself more on the edge of the group than in the center (as the seating chart shows), in order to make it easier for the conversation *not* to focus around me. Fourth, when Erica speculates that if a member of the group had contested my seating suggestions I would likely have "asked (them) to move back into (my) ideal, tightly configured arrangement," I am quite confident she is wrong, given the motives I've just described. Instead, I would want to use the contestation over my "power move" to increase our ongoing awareness of the power issues at stake and whether such exercises of power increases or diminishes trust, mutuality, and inquiry.

Returning to a joint authorial voice, we agree that, although one can offer some general answers to the question of how power is generated and used to create a community of inquiry, none of these general answers are of any use if the actors in the specific group are not awake to the "dance of power" being enacted whenever the group is meeting. In general, groups are initially constituted by a larger organization based on some taken-for-granted pre-definitions of mission, membership, roles, and power-distribution. Under such circumstances, power is likely to be hierarchically distributed and exercised in a relatively unilateral, uninquiring fashion. Subordinate members may passively accept their relatively dependent, low power roles, or may passive-aggressively express counter-dependent de-commitment while remaining official group members. The official leadership may either defend its unilateral power and punish expressions of creative, independent power, or it may use its power to support low-power members to act with increasing independence (as we believe Bill did when he supported Jim's role as an active critic of the group purpose and process). No one can unilaterally transform anyone else from dependence through counter-dependence and independence to inter-independence.

In action inquiry, an important practice is to observe when and how power is being exercised. Doing so creates a space for reflection and potential double- and triple-loop learning whereby the exercise of power becomes increasingly mutual. A full-fledged peer community of inquiry can evolve only gradually through making the difficult issues of membership, power, and intimacy discussible and transformable. Over the 10 years of the Action Research Methods course, about half the students have chosen voluntarily to create small action inquiry groups the following year, and some of these continued meeting for many years. In effect, because the course is required of some of its participants, a full-fledged community of inquiry is likely to evolve only after the formal conclusion of the course. To conclude this discussion of the exercise of power in the ARM course, we believe that second-person research in the midst of practice in the present that makes the actual power relationships in the setting discussable and transformable is a *sine qua non* of truly integral education that supports human and organizational development beyond dependence and independence to inter-independence.

Incident III—Between-Member Conflict and Transformation

The third set of incidents from the ARM class that we focus on concerns issues of feedback and intimacy among the members. Nadine, one of the "draftees," had shifted from a low participation mode after a class in which she presented a difficult conversation between her and one of her apartment-mates. She was unquestioningly clear that the difficulties were caused by the apartment-mate, until another member of the class pointed out succinctly how she was acting toward the apartment-mate in precisely the same way as she was complaining her apart-ment-mate was acting toward her. Immediately thunderstruck by the truth of this critique (perhaps the purest and most consequential piece of triple-loop feedback sent and received in the same moment in the course), Nadine reported the fol-lowing week that she had excised the tension and transformed the relationship the evening after the class session.

This experience led Nadine to experiment with more direct feedback to every other class member in her second-person research paper a few weeks later (and both experiences led her to write a third-person paper about the kind of experiences that can transform a person from feeling like a draftee to feeling like a volunteer). In particular, she shared her own personal observations and reflections about the personal learning goals for the rest of the course that other members of our com-munity had expressed in the prior session. When Sue read Nadine's comments the day before the next class, she felt negatively evaluated by Nadine's comments about the personal goals Sue had shared with the group. The following excerpts are from a series of emails that were made public in our class, and that eventually precipitated a conflict-confrontation exercise that Bill suggested and facilitated.

> "Hi Everyone,
>
> Please find my second person paper attached . . . I hope you will find it useful—I have made a lot of assumptions in my analysis of our conversation and I hope it will be taken in the spirit intended—to be helpful and constructive and to generate further discussion.
>
> Looking fwd to see you all on Wednesday!!
> Best, Nadine"

"Hey Nadine,
 Your analysis generally made me feel misunderstood and the object of unfounded assumptions/projections, which makes it less safe to share things like personal goals in the first place . . ."

Sue goes on over the course of two or so pages to identify specific problematic clauses and assumptions from Nadine's second-person paper, and responds to each of these by clarifying what the actual intentions and assumptions guiding these goals actually were. She evaluates Nadine's feedback as "unskillful," and requests that Nadine approach observation and reflection with more "curiosity and generosity" and fewer "meandering assumptions." Sue concludes this email with an invitation to discuss the issues with Nadine further. Nadine responds:

"Hi [Sue],
 I must admit I was a little surprised at your email. Honestly, I didn't mean to be overly harsh . . . If you don't feel that what I wrote was representative of your motives, then you are totally free to disregard my comments! Seriously, it's fine. But, I'm sure it would be an interesting topic to discuss in class tomorrow . . . you can surely use that forum to make yourself more understood . . . clearly what I took away from our talk is not the message you sent/intended.
 In any case, you are totally right that I could have been more curious and generous about my assumptions. Guess it's a learning process."

Sue responds:

"Hi [Nadine],
 I'm sure you didn't mean to be harsh, but what you said did come across (at least to me) as you engaged in your own private exercise of projecting motivations or assumptions onto me. And that's what I'm objecting to. Of course, as you point out, I am free to disregard your comments. But that doesn't seem to me to be a helpful way to think about this because it doesn't address the fact that your comments have an impact—both on me personally and on how you come across to me."

Sue closes this final email by agreeing that the topic would be interesting to discuss in class, and asks permission of Nadine to bring the email exchange to class the next day.

When this email interaction is presented to the class, Bill suggests a possible "liberating discipline" that he calls an "angel" exercise, whereby Nadine and Sue can talk about their conflict in the class, with two other members serving as "angels" for each. The "angels" can speak as Nadine or Sue over their shoulders, in an effort to get at underlying issues and perhaps diffuse some of the one-on-one personal tension. Bill introduces, frames, and advocates for this exercise by suggesting, "Let's just see if the class is interested by this, and it seems that it might make it a more complete challenge for [our community of inquiry]." We all agree to participate, and Nadine and Sue are each allocated two other members of class to act as their voices in dialog. This has the dual-effect of immediately depersonalizing the issues and engaging all of us in the transformational task of moving beyond where two of our members, and therefore our group as a whole, have gotten stuck. Finally, as a result of Nadine's second-person paper, the email exchanges, and the confrontation and feedback exercise we do in class, Sue uses her second-person research paper written during the following week as a forum to reflect on and inquire about her and our personal, interpersonal, and the group learning trajectory. (To give another impression of the degree of members' commitments to these research practices, the paper was 15 single-spaced pages long, with 16 singled-spaced pages of transcript as an appendix.) Here are two pages of Sue's paper (AI refers to Torbert's *Action Inquiry* text [2004]):

> *Much of the content of this exercise was the giving and receiving of feedback among members in the group. In the tables on the next pages, I summarize the feedback that was exchanged during the session. I characterize the feedback as single-, double-, or triple-loop feedback. Single-loop feedback is information that tells me whether or not my last move advanced me toward the goal. (AI, p. 16) Double-loop feedback addresses a person's strategy, structure, or goals. (AI, p. 18–19) Triple-loop feedback highlights the present relationship between our effects in the outside world and our actions, our strategies, and our attention itself (Ibid.).*
>
> *I was struck by the richness of the feedback we gave each other, and I was generally impressed by the way people gave feedback during the session, which for the most part, I experienced as caring and skillful. (I say "for the most part" because I think both Nadine and I said things in the heat of the moment that could have been said more compassionately and with less charge.) I was also struck by the breadth of the feedback, and how each person was able to see something different, and important. I very much appreciated the diversity of voices around the table, because I got to see a lot more about how I was behaving and making sense of the situation than I would have if I'd been talking just with Nadine, or even with just one or two of you there. Each person brought something important to the discussion, and I am grateful for your participation.*
>
> *I received five single-loop, seven double-loop, and two possibly triple-loop pieces of direct feedback from all six members of the group.*

The feedback to me covered several main themes:

The impact on Nadine of my evaluative comments and the way I presented my feedback, both in the emails that preceded the conversation and in the conversation itself.

Challenges to "own" my piece of the situation—it's not just Nadine's "incompetence" that's making me angry, it's something in me too!

Challenges to see the good faith efforts that Nadine made to frame her paper as her own assumptions—which is inherent in a second-person paper—and which she invited people to test and discuss.

Invitations to look for the truth in what Nadine wrote—perhaps by considering that the motivations she attributed to me might be coming from my subconscious shadow side.

Nadine received four single-loop pieces of feedback, four that were double-loop, and two that could be interpreted as either single- or double-loop feedback. Feedback to Nadine covered the following main themes:

Challenges to take more responsibility for the impact of her paper on the people she is writing about who will be reading the paper.

Challenge to the appropriateness of the attitude "it's not a situation to me" in responding to someone who has been impacted by something Nadine wrote.

Invitation to view the alter-ego exercise as an opportunity to engage in mutual inquiry and learning, rather than trying to "make Sue feel better."

Invitation to explore different ways of phrasing writing that address concerns or potential concerns of second-person paper readers.

Overall, this mini-cosmos of reflection and refraction among members of our group points to the consequences and learning we experienced around the idea of "competent" feedback, and how a mutual commitment to gifting one another with skillful feedback can generate true intimacy. A key developmental lesson to be gleaned from this series of communications, misperceptions, reactions, and interactions is the idea and evidence that we can and do get more competent at giving significant feedback as we thrash and blunder incompetently through such feedback cycles first. We begin to see that sometimes, when we are sure the only competence issue is how to give the other the precise single-loop feedback he or she clearly needs, we gradually discover that it is we ourselves who receive some even more important double-loop feedback. The ability to transform through feedback that enables, not just single-loop, but also double- and triple-loop learning is dependent on the co-occurrence of a choice and a skill set to activate and digest that feedback. As Sue noted in the second-person paper:

It is tricky to evaluate whether participants accepted and digested feedback and used it to transform themselves, test their own frames, and feel the limitations and self-contradictions inherent in their view of reality. These processes are internal ones, which may or may not be reflected in observable behavior. Moreover, they take time. To accept and digest feedback, and then transform oneself—especially in a brief encounter when emotions are running high—is an extremely challenging undertaking.

Overall, these two members of our class proved themselves to be willing and active, and eventually even competent, agents of private and public change as they (and we) struggled through the dance of their feedback loops. Indeed, Nadine later in the course delivered a piece of feedback with double- and triple-loop reverberations to the instructor, Bill, helping him to reframe a very significant (to him) relational dilemma he had been facing for a decade and to act differently than he could have imagined prior to the feedback from Nadine (in the end, he apologized to an old colleague whom he had previously imagined owed him an apology). Thus, Nadine not only moved herself (with the support and confrontation of others) from "draftee" to "volunteer" during the course, but also became a valued source of transformational feedback to other participants and even to the "sole institutional power-possessor" in the course. This third set of incidents in our action inquiry model represents another juncture where developmental learning was integrated within each "I," across at least two "You's," amidst our "We" (the group) and our collective "It" (the ARM class), and even (through this chapter) across other "Its" (the classes you, our readers, teach differently because of reading this, and perhaps also new university/societal norms of how classes ought to work, to which this chapter may make a contribution).

Conclusion

In this chapter we have detailed three sets of learning incidents from a PhD-level Action Research Methods course that demonstrate ongoing development toward a community of inquiry that encourages first-, second-, and third-person research and welcomes single-, double-, and triple-loop feedback, as community participants develop and integrate skills, capacities, and awarenesses as members, leaders, and researchers.

The first example of how we stumbled on an early learning moment regarding inclusion is enacted in a group and organizational context with themes of personal and membership commitment, in-group and out-group norms, as well as elements of coercive pressure, individual resistance, and a growing awareness of individual territories of experience as well as group dynamics. Bob's invitation to explore norms of membership resulted in his own double-loop questioning of his original operative action-logic of "knowing better" than a co-member how to engage in a community of inquiry. As a result of this in-class confrontation and discussion, followed up by Bob's second-person research paper that further analyzes the set of interactions, a personal, (certainly for Bob, and probably for several of us), interpersonal, (certainly between Bob and Jim, and probably between and among others of us), and collective, (certainly for our group as a whole), transformational double-loop learning occurred that enabled all of us to re-evaluate our implicit and enacted concepts of inclusion and voluntary versus coerced participation in a community of inquiry.

The second example of a reflection about the role of institutionally-endowed power and control in our group shows the tension inherent in growing awareness of and movement beyond centralized, unilateral, already legitimate sources of power toward more distributed, mutual, and communally-creative sources of power. In the highlighted incident, unilateral control is enacted through Bill's preference for and influence over a "tight" seating configuration. Further evidence of Bill's power in our community of inquiry is presented in terms of his institutional role as professor-expert-evaluator, enacted through grading assessments, class duration requirements, and a pre-formulated mission statement for the course. Through the process of our independently- and jointly-authored exploration of whether and how an instructor might genuinely share control of the class as a whole and to what degree Bill might actually be exerting as much or more unilateral power than a typical professor, we engage in the practice of inquiry-in-action with him, thereby reducing the mythical "unopposable" power organizational subordinates can project on superiors. The class chose not to accept some aspects of this more mutually empowered offering. We did not change the grading structure or the mission for our group, nor did we challenge Bill's control (no one sat on the outskirts of the table where no piles of paper had been placed, and no one publically questioned the requirement of an additional hour together each week). On the other hand, however, our community of inquiry embraced and invoked increasingly mutual power and leadership over the course of the semester as we individually and collectively awakened to and participated in the "dance of power" in our group, manifest in more generative and collaborative development of class-to-class agendas, the influence of second-person research papers, and the choice of readings, discussion, and exercises for the last several class meetings. In these ways, we moved from a taken-for-granted, conventional unilateral, power and control tradition in classrooms toward a not-just-talked-about-but-actually-performed mutual power dynamic.

With the third example, we explore a double-loop feedback interaction that deals with the issue of between-member conflict and intimacy and results in strategic and paradigmatic changes by different members of the group. A key transformation in this third set of incidents is the movement from draftee to volunteer in the case of Nadine, whose struggle through feedback cycles with Sue results in further third-person research and a growing personal awareness of how practices in developmental action inquiry can transform her own personal, interpersonal, and group actions and experiences. This third incident echoes similar issues of required versus voluntary participation that arose in the first example between Bob and Jim, except that in this case Nadine and Sue, with the active support of the other participants, *both* acknowledge double-loop learnings about the blind-spots in their action logics, and the instructor himself is offered a triple-loop learning opportunity. Another shared facet of this incident with the others we highlight is Bill's continued exercise of power, in this case by creating the "angels" exercise. In this case, however, Bill's influence attempt is explicit and tests whether others consider the exercise useful. Since all of the participants agreed to participate in this experiment-in-inquiry and did so actively, Bill's authority in this case seems more collaborative and less coercive. (Put differently, any other member of our group might have made a similar suggestion for addressing the issue by this mid-point in the semester, and we likely would have decided in the same way whether to accept it). Regardless, the balancing of different types of power, gradually moving toward greater dispersal of initiatives and greater mutuality and away from a single hierarchical source of power continues to play out in this example as it has in others preceding it. Finally, the experiences of conflict and feedback along with increasing intimacy among the various participants in the group, (as exemplified by this set of incidents between Nadine and Sue), highlights an essential quality of any community of inquiry—that all the members must develop increasingly strong and peer-like relationships. These must not generate or accept dependency or co-dependency, and while respecting one another's independence, must also support mutual transformation and inter-independence.

This attempt at generating a transformational community of action and inquiry was limited by the time and role constraints of the larger institutional context within which it was enacted, as well as by respect for the limited commitment to action inquiry that some of its members were willing to make. We certainly do not claim that the class became a full-fledged community of inquiry during its brief 100-day existence. Nevertheless, we hope that it illustrates how development to later individual and group action-logics can be generated in a classroom. Development, we are proposing and illustrating, is generated, not through talking about developmental theory so much as through interweaving first-, second-, and third-person actions and inquiries with increasing appreciation for sending and receiving single-, double-, and triple-loop feedback, and with increasing attentiveness to and inquiring dialogue about issues of inclusion, power, conflict, and intimacy as these present themselves.

References

Argyris, C. (1971). *Intervention theory and method.* Reading, MA: Addison-Wesley.

Argyris, C., Putnam, R., & Smith, D. (1985). *Action science: Concepts, methods and skills for research and intervention.* San Francisco: Jossey-Bass.

Argyris, C., & Schon, D. (1974). *Theory in practice: Increasing professional effectiveness.* San Francisco: Jossey-Bass.

Bernstein, R. (1985). *Beyond objectivism and relativism: Science, hermeneutics and praxis.* Philadelphia: University of Pennsylvania Press.

Chandler, D., & Torbert, W. (2003). Transforming inquiry and action: Interweaving 27 flavors of action research, *Journal of Action Research 1, 2,* 133–152.

Esbjörn-Hargens, S. (2007). Integral teacher, integral students, integral classroom: Applying integral theory to graduate education, *Journal of Integral Theory and Practice, 2*(2): 72–103.

Fisher, D., & Torbert, W. (1995). *Personal and organizational transformations: The true challenge of continual quality improvement.* London: McGraw-Hill.

Habermas, J. (1984/1987). *The theory of communicative action, Vols. I & II.* Boston: Beacon Press.

Hallward, P. (2003). *Badiou: A subject to truth.* Minneapolis: University of Minnesota Press.

Hartwell, J., & Torbert, W. (1999). A group interview with Andy Wilson, founder and CEO of Boston Duck Tours and Massachusetts entrepreneur of the year; *and* Analysis of the group interview with Andy Wilson: An illustration of interweaving first-, second-, and third-person research/practice. *Journal of Management Inquiry. 8*(2), 183–204.

Kegan, R. (1994). *In over our heads: The mental demands of modern life.* Cambridge, MA: Harvard University Press.

Lundberg, C., & Young, C. (2005). *Foundations for inquiry: Choices and tradeoffs in the organization sciences.* Stanford, CA: Stanford University Press.

McGuire, J., Palus, C., & Torbert, W. (2007). In Shani, A. et al. (Eds.) *Handbook of collaborative management research.* Thousand Oaks, CA: Sage.

Ogilvy, J. (2002). *Creating better futures: Scenario planning as a tool for a better tomorrow.* Oxford, UK: Oxford University Press.

Ouspensky, P. (1949). *In search of the miraculous: Fragments of an unknown teaching.* New York: Harcourt Brace.

Reason, P., & Bradbury, H. (Eds.) (2008). *Handbook of action research,* 2nd ed. London: Sage.

Rooke, D. & Torbert, W. (2005). Seven transformations of leadership. *Harvard Business Review.* April, 67–78.

Senge, P., Scharmer, C., Jaworski, J., & Flowers, B. (2004). *Presence: Human purpose and the field of the future.* Cambridge, MA: Society for Organizational Learning.

Shani, A. et al. (Eds.) (2007). *Handbook of collaborative management research.* Thousand Oaks, CA: Sage.

Scharmer, O. (2007). *Theory U: Leading from the future as it emerges.* Cambridge, MA: Society for Organizational Learning.

Sherman, F., & Torbert, W. (Eds.) (2000). *Transforming social inquiry, Transforming social action.* Boston: Kluwer Academic Publishers.

Torbert, W. (1972). *Learning from experience: Toward consciousness.* New York: Columbia University Press.

Torbert, W. (1976). *Creating a community of inquiry: Conflict, collaboration, transformation.* London: Wiley Interscience.

Torbert, W. (1987). *Managing the corporate dream: Restructuring for long-term success.* Homewood, IL: Dow Jones-Irwin.

Torbert, W. (1991). *The power of balance: Transforming self, society and social inquiry.* Newbury Park, CA: Sage.

Torbert, W., & Associates. (2004). *Action inquiry: The secret of timely and transforming leadership.* San Francisco: Berrett-Koehler.

Varela, F., Thompson, E., & Rosch E. (1991). *The embodied mind: Cognitive science and human experience.* Cambridge, MA: MIT Press.

Wilber, K. (1998). *The marriage of sense and soul: Integrating science and religion.* New York: Random House.

Wilber, K. (2000). *Integral psychology: Consciousness, spirit, psychology, therapy.* Boston: Shambhala.

Teaching Integratively

Five Dimensions of Transformation

Roben Torosyan

A better-informed people is not necessarily a better-educated people. [Perhaps] the twenty-first century needs a new kind of learning and a new kind of leader to help us. [We need to] focus not just on the buildup of more knowledge but also on the fashioning of new relationships to the knowledge we already have.

—Kegan & Lahey, 2000, p. 234

Introduction

I teach to transform myself, others, and the world, and to realize I cannot change things. Many educators face related paradoxes. The word comes from the Greek *para-* for "beyond" and *dokein* for "to think"—literally "beyond thinking." On one hand, for example, learners struggle with written grammar. But they also struggle to express themselves deeply, a skill which often requires deliberately ignoring errors and the internal critic.

While educational theories help educators develop such dueling competencies, it can be overwhelming for us, let alone for our learners, to reconcile these often contradictory demands. As the epigraph above suggests, everyone needs to not only *see* relationships, but to form different relationships *to* what they see. To that end, this chapter first describes big picture conceptions of knowledge, then shows five overarching patterns that cross many domains of learning. After providing a caveat about the risk of such grand narratives, I offer some pathways for classroom application, in terms of (a) our curriculum or content, and (b) our pedagogy or methods.

Background: Interdisciplinary, Integrative, and Integral Education

Big Picture Conceptions

Since my teens, I have had a fantasy of organizing all of knowledge. I also loved the arts. When I got to college, I initially wanted to pursue architecture, the mother of the arts and sciences. I started by taking civil engineering prerequisites for architecture, but soon became part of that lower half of class that fell below the class average of a C. I eventually changed majors to art history, and there found inspiration in big ideas. I saw a lecture by Kirk Varnedoe that drew on the late nineteenth century novella *Flatland* (Abbott, 1884/2002) as a metaphor for the process of "going meta," or getting above any phenomenon. In the 1900s several revolutions in perspective occurred, from art to physics to literature, denoting a zeitgeist or spirit of the times that used an especially reflexive kind of thinking.

Such big shifts, I learned, were part of larger patterns of thinking throughout the disciplines and daily life. In 1990, I came across a "Roots of Knowing" (Hussey, 1988) approach to education, proposed by Rachel M. Lauer, a former chief psychologist for the New York City schools who had founded a "thinking and learning center" at Pace University. I later worked with Lauer for five years while writing my doctoral dissertation at Teachers College on her learning-centered methods for encouraging consciousness development (Torosyan, 2000).

Lauer argued, for instance, that most thinking involves a cyclical "PEDA process" of perception, evaluation, decision-making and action (Lauer, 1971, 1983, 1996–97). Others suggested similar cycles. Schon claimed that we interpret experiences "through our repertoires of values, knowledge, theories, and practices that [we] bring to the experiences" (Zeichner & Liston, 1996, p. 16). Using such "appreciative systems," we spiral from appreciation to action to reappreciation. For learning to then be transformative, as Jack Mezirow (1991) argued, learners need to "understand more clearly the reasons for their problems and the action options open to them so that they can improve the quality of their decision making" (p. 203).

As Lauer further showed, thought and action are filtered through an epistemology or way of knowing that conveys an often unconscious set of assumptions about what is true, real, or powerful, or how things work (Lauer, 1996–97). Development in such a worldview happens (and fails to happen) in individuals as well as across society from ancient times to the modern and postmodern revolutions. As Michel Foucault (1973/1994) postulated, "In any given culture and at any given moment," things operate according to a characteristic "episteme," a mode that "defines the conditions of possibility of all knowledge, whether expressed in a theory or silently invested in a practice" (p. 168). A sequence of development of mindset (Bateson, 1972; Bois, 1970) unfolds on the part of whole cultures or epochs. In Kieran Egan's view (in Olson & Torrance, 1996), students recapitulate the discoveries that constitute their cultural history.

To surface such patterns, teachers should, in Lauer's argument, help learners focus on the underlying "universal meta-concepts" or "metacepts" (Lauer, 1996–97, p. 387) behind each worldview. After much practice applying these "meta" themes, learners gradually clarify their own thinking and free it up. Ideally, they "finally grasp the whole orientation, the grand theme of knowing implied in each episteme" (Lauer, 1996–97, p. 378). These epistemes are less empirically demonstrable than a heuristic or tool for understanding and solving problems of life.

To promote such a meta-view of the landscape of learning, some courses introduce many disciplines at once (see Fig. 6, Box A, next page). Related courses have evolved nationally, although few draw on the 70 years of scholarship streams in "integrative" learning. Work in "integrative education," called such as early as the 1940s (Reiser, 1958), has continued in research on student development and the process of personal maturation (Baxter-Magolda, 2004), explicit attention to crossing disciplines in interdisciplinary studies (Klein, 1990), and transformative learning's focus on the process of reframing problems and orientations (Mezirow, 2000). Meanwhile, outside of education, other professions have evolved related movements, from "integrative medicine" and its appreciation of complementary and alternative spiritual and emotional practices (Snyderman & Weil, 2002) to "integrated design" for sustainable development of neighborhoods (Engel-Yan, Kennedy, Saiz, & Pressnail, 2005) to an "integrative systems" approach to aircraft engine design (Sosa, Eppinger, & Rowles, 2003).

Across another broad range of work are several big picture conceptions of nature, knowledge, and events. In psychology, George Lakoff and Mark Johnson (2003) famously elucidated the main metaphors people live by, such as *argument is war* or *time is money*. In organizational development, Gareth Morgan (2007) showed images people have of the workplace, such as a well-oiled, if bureaucratic, machine, an adaptive organism, or a self-organizing brain. In the sciences and beyond, biologist Tyler Volk (1995) worked out a number of "meta-patterns" or universal principles of organization, such as "binary," "cycle," and "break," while Edward O. Wilson (1998) sought "consilience," a unity of knowledge to integrate the arts and sciences. In history, David Christian (2004) described big timelines moving from "many worlds" to "few worlds" to "one world," in both natural history and human evolution, and John Lewis Gaddis (2002) asked historians to step back and widen their view of the landscape of the past. Each such conception went "meta" or got above other theories.

According to the American Association of Colleges & Universities (AAC&U), three related "new academy reforms" are now influencing mainstream higher education in the United States: (1) intellectual skills across the curriculum, (2) social responsibility and civic engagement, and (3) "integrative learning" (Schneider, 2005, p.11). When the AAC&U published a monograph on integrative learning (Huber & Hutchings, 2004) and held its first ever conference on the subject in 2005, it marked a watershed moment—as faculty focused explicitly on integration for the first time across much of mainstream higher education. Meanwhile, others

Box A: *Classroom Application: Connecting the Disciplines*

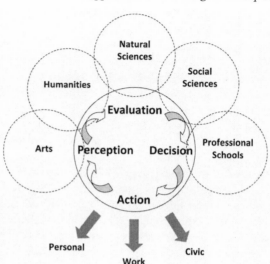

In a course called "Concepts That Unite Disciplines," Lauer and I took a "meta-concept" such as empathy, interdependence or systems thinking, and invited three guest professors each week to help students apply each concept to personal, professional and civic life. Critical thinking was conceived as a "PEDA process" (Lauer, 1996–97, p. 375) of perception, evaluation, decision and action, and channeled according to different disciplinary frameworks for knowledge. As a result of simulations, role plays, writing exercises and other active methods, students reported thinking about their interests differently, noticing overarching worldviews, and wanting to change individual behaviors, social structures and educational systems. One wondered, for instance, "How do I fit into the overall picture? Can I raise my standards of work ethic to include contributing to the overall betterment of the world?" Another added, "Most importantly, I would like to know how to take what I have learned and use it in order to create change." (See syllabus and materials at http://www.faculty.fairfield.edu/rtorosyan/).

Figure 6. Classroom Application: Connecting the Disciplines

have encouraged "integral" education (Ferrer, Romero, & Albareda, 2005, current volume; Torbert et al., 2004; Wilber, 2000), and aimed beyond mostly intellectual or emotional connections, to also link body, mind, and spirit (Awbrey, 2006; Blair & Caine, 1995), while correcting a commonly imbalanced focus on either mental life alone, or turning the mind off entirely.

Common to this work is a desire to help people "integrate their learning across contexts and over time" (Huber & Hutchings, 2004, p. 1). Intellectually, "integrative learning" comes from a collective desire, as Boyer (1990) famously suggested, to promote "discovery and creativity, integrating and interpreting knowledge from different disciplines, applying knowledge through real-world engagements, or teaching students and communicating with the public" (summarized by Huber & Hutchings, 2004, pp. 1–2). To that integrative end, psychologists and philosophers have proposed overarching frameworks with distinct parallels.

Parallels Across Frameworks

Developmental theorists propose discrete stages of complexity and sophistication—typically three to six phases, positions, orders, or ways of knowing. As one compares their stage descriptions (see Fig. 7, next page), overall parallels appear. Most schemes begin with a level of sensory knowing (Lauer, 1971; Torosyan, 2000), an impulsive order of mind (Kegan, 1994), focused on instinct, the bodily senses, or sexuality (Wilber, 2000, 2001). In this first sensory dimension, which I term "1-D," sensation and play dictate life. Infants center on orality and anality. Adults experience strong instincts and desires, including sexual impulses.

Eventually, however, development involves managing such sensations. With concrete operations (2-D categorical), children learn to use symbols and language (Piaget, 1929/1997). Moving to the right in the table, then, the second dimension steps back from and builds upon the prior one, just as a two-dimensional line extends one-dimensional points into a series. A child, for example, one day sees that a shorter beaker has as much liquid as a taller, thinner one. As Jean Piaget (1929/1997) showed, the child "assimilates" experience though an existing lens, but after enough new experience, "accommodates" or switches lenses—in this example achieving "conservation," the ability to see how things are the same despite changing physical appearances. Such skill in remembering and understanding, the first two of Benjamin Bloom's taxonomy (adapted in Richlin, 2006), are needed at all ages. For example, professors expect learners to discern basic patterns, whether to notice an artwork's contrasts and juxtapositions, create a chemical reaction that will produce a specific result, or mathematically model economic behavior given interacting variables. Across these instances, what matters are not simply sensate observations (1-D) but structures (2-D) for such observations, and the conventions valued by society (Wilber, 2000, 2001).

The liability of such thinking, however, is that one thinks only in concrete, about dualistic dichotomies of only two attributes or options at once. People often see knowledge as "received" or "mastered" (Baxter-Magolda, 1992, 2004), or as something absolute and held by external authorities. When William Perry (1968/1999) interviewed Harvard undergraduates, for instance, he found that first

Torosyan, Lauer	1-D Sensory: sense, feel, intuit	2-D Categorical: sort and standardize sensations		3-D Relational: research, theorize and test categories		4-D Meta-reflective: transform framework used to research and theorize		5-D Integrative: unify subject and object
Bloom's taxonomy		Remember: Recall terms and ideas	Understand: Grasp meaning	Apply: Use learning in new situations	Analyze: See patterns; compare and contrast	Evaluate: Assess evidence	Create: form one's own approaches or theories	
Piaget's stages	Sensorimotor: see objects	Pre-operations: use symbols and language	Concrete operations:	Formal operations: test hypotheses, think systematically		Post-formal operations: relate reasoning systems to each other		
Perry's positions		Dualism: "Just the facts, ma'am"		Multiplicity: "pick an opinion, any opinion"	Relativism: "bullshit" to play "teachers' games"	Commitment within relativism: choose and mix paradigms		
Baxter-Magolda's ways of knowing		Absolute: knowledge is received (women) or mastered (men)		Transitional: women dialogue; men debate	Independent: females gain voice but value exchange; males value own thinking	Contextual: share responsibility for constructing others		

	Impulsive: subject to impulses, perceptions	Imperial: attend to impulses, subject to individual's needs, interests, desires	Interpersonal: attend to needs, subject to interpersonal relationships and mutality	Institutional: attend to relationships, subject to individual's authorship, identity and ideology	Inter-individual: attend to authorship or ideology; subject to inter-penetrability of self-systems
Kegan's orders of consciousness					
Wilber's quadrants and levels	**Magical-animistic:** preconventional, premodern, body, instinct, sensation, "me"	**Mythic-conformist:** symbol, power, civilization, culture, self-protective, conformist	**Rational-scientific:** conventional rules; modern, formal, empirical study, mind, ethnocentric/"us"	**Pluralistic:** postconventional; postmodern; intersubjective; meta-systemic	**Integral:** spirit, global, transcendent interconnection, "all of us"

Figure 7. Parallels Across Frameworks

year students want, as Craig Nelson put it, " 'just the facts, m'am' and expect to memorize them (just) long enough to pass the exam" (Nelson, 1999, p. 170).

To get beyond seeing only right or wrong distinctions, see shades of gray, and discern *what* facts are relevant to any particular situation, people move to what Perry (1968/1999) termed "multiplicity" (3-D relational), where learners acknowledge opinion and uncertainty, and see truth as determined not just by outside authorities, but personally. As Piaget (1929/1997) showed, children eventually use abstract reasoning, the scientific method, and systematic thinking. College students apply and analyze, in Bloom's taxonomy, when they learn how, for example, an artwork's juxtapositions depend on its context, a chemical reaction may produce unforeseen or indeterminate results, or economic models shift dynamically as assumptions shift. In each example, one needs to tolerate ambiguity in interpretations, see fluid relations and consider multiple attributes at the same time. Otherwise, principles can become ossified. One classroom exercise, literally bringing fruit to the discussion, helps get beyond text alone to a felt sense of the flexibility demanded by this mindset (see Fig. 8, Box B).

In response to such a relational world, learners often conclude that nothing can be known or that all opinions are equal, retreating into relativism (Perry,

---

Box B: Classroom Application: When Is a Lime Not a Lime?

In one classroom exercise, my mentor Rachel Lauer put three objects out on a table: a fresh lime, another lime that was old and rotting, and a blackened, dried lump. She wrote on the board, "When is a lime not a lime?" Conventionally, in a categorical (2-D) view, we think we know a lime when we see one, and at some point the aging object cannot rightly be called a lime. But when we try and discern exactly what that point is, we find the object is itself always changing, just as every object and context changes. That is why general semantics, the study of how language transforms thinking, recommends we "index" people and things (Hayakawa, 1978), to say, for example, not simply "Roben thought X" but "Roben jogging at 6:35 p.m. on this day on that trail thought X." By specifying time, place and circumstance, I acknowledge that the nature of things depends on the interaction of surroundings and situations (3-D). The activity also symbolized how, at root, everything is always already in a process of evolving flux and transformation. That process is one of the cross-disciplinary "meta-concepts" (Lauer, 1996–97) that constitute 3-D relational thinking.

Figure 8. Classroom Application: When Is a Lime Not a Lime?

1968/1999). Nelson (1999) called this the "Baskin Robbins" mode where learners pick opinions the way you "pick a flavor, any flavor" of ice cream, "based on feelings or intuition, not on reasoned analysis" (p. 171). Often one does so to escape the quite understandable pain of having to decide between competing "goods"—choices that seem equally good. When one decides (from the Latin *decidere*, literally "to cut off"), one inevitably cedes something, or gives up an option. But as Bloom's taxonomy recommends, life requires that people not only recall info (2-D), and analyze it (3-D), but eventually move to make such decisions, "evaluate" them, and ultimately construct their own connections (4-D) as well.

To be truly changed by learning, then, is to treat experience not as "information" but as "transformation" (Mezirow et al., 2000). As Lev Vygotsky argued, development requires not just 2-D "accumulation of knowledge" or a 3-D "sequence of stages like Piaget's" (Egan, 1997, p. 514), but the 4-D "transformation of forms of mediation" (Wertsch, in Egan, 1997, p. 514). When Robert Kegan (Mezirow et al., 2000) asks "What form transforms?" he suggests that the vessel itself must change, creating a new 4-D framing or mindset.

Seeking such change, educators are often frustrated at learners who depend on authority (3-D) rather than self-direct their own actions (4-D). But, as Kegan argues;

> Can we fault them for feeling whole when we like their work, incomplete when we don't? It's just that the self they're directing is not the one we're hoping for at that moment. They're directing the self that seeks *alignment* not the one that *self*-authors. (Lecture, November 18, 2006)

Only when learners eventually achieve "commitment within relativism" (Perry, 1968/1999), do they assume that they share responsibility not simply for entertaining perspectives but for actively constructing knowledge. Such "capacity [of learners] to internally define their own beliefs, identity, and relationships" (Baxter-Magolda, 2001, p. xvi) amounts to what Kegan (1994) termed "self-authorship," relating ways of reasoning as the entire table above relates frameworks to each other.

Most of these frameworks, however, focus on a cognitive, an emotional, or a spiritual emphasis—rarely integrating all such dimensions. In response, integral theorist Ken Wilber describes four perspectives and their associated methodologies or areas of focus: (1) the subjective (the "I"), (2) objective or behavioral ("It"), (3) intersubjective or cultural ("We"), and (4) interobjective, social or systems ("Its") (Wilber, 2000). Others emphasize "nested world contexts" (O'Sullivan & Taylor, 2004, p. 14) or what Wilber, borrowing the term from Koestler, terms "holons." Every issue differs according to the scale of our focus, ranging from the human intrapsychic, interpersonal, or group community (Lauer, 1996–97), to empirical microscopic, macroscopic, or ecosystem levels. But in addition to *where* we focus, it matters *how* we do so—ideally using what Wilber (2000) calls magic, mythic, rational, pluralistic, and integral approaches. While may not be entirely accurate to map Wilber's levels in strict correlation with the other frameworks above, he seeks to unify all five dimensions (1-D through 5-D). Of course, such unifying attempts run the risk of being simplistic, as narratives often do.

The Problem with Grand Narratives

The final belief is to believe in a fiction, which you know to be a fiction, there being nothing else. The exquisite truth is to know that it is a fiction and that you believe in it willingly.

—Wallace Stevens, 1957/1989, p. 189

Every story smoothes over differences and forces facts to fit an overarching framework (literally to "arch over" or dominate the domain of understanding). So too with every unifying theory: Give a person a hammer, and everything can become a nail—pegged with a label. A "theory of everything" (Hawking, 2002; Torosyan, 2001; Wilber, 2001) thus necessarily essentializes—in so doing it risks telling a story that reduces the world's complexity to a deceptively monolithic simplicity. Postmodern critical theorist Jean Francois Lyotard (1984) famously endorsed a skeptical "incredulity" toward such "meta-narratives," those grand claims to reach a perspective above it all. For no attempt to transcend limits is ever total, pure, or complete.

When, for example, I label five developmental mindsets, I reduce reality to a few categories, and thus fall prey to categorical labeling, itself one of my developmental stages. Often I also find myself looking for the "right" way to either write efficiently, teach well, or achieve the most enlightened critical stance on my own view of enlightenment. Yet developmental dimensions help: They make me aware of just those kind of tendencies to act impulsively, categorize, relate or reflect, where such patterns come from, why they are understandable, and why they are not at all easy to combat—in my own mind let alone in those of others. After all, I still personally fall back to simpler developmental dimensions, all the time.

But, equally important, "higher" dimensions are not reified entities, or superior at all times, places, and circumstances. Moral theorist Lawrence Kohlberg (Kohlberg & Mayer, 1972), for example, first proposed "Development as the Aim of Education," suggesting that teaching should improve people's ability to solve problems and act morally. But if we view such progress as linear, we forget that different strengths and capacities are needed at different times.

Rather than take developmental dimensions to be a hierarchy, or see progress as strictly linear, I envision development as iterative, cyclical, and spiraling, as do integral theorists. As I grow personally, then, I always return close to where I begin, although forever different. Thus the integrative framework I propose is less an essentialized, monolithic statement of anyone's thinking, and more a heuristic reference tool (Lauer, 1996–97) for reasoning. My instrument is necessarily blunt and imprecise, for I am not observing neutrally but actively contributing to what I observe, but it helps me to uncover assumptions and diversify ways of being.

Yet even my attempt to use a framework and qualify its limits is fraught with a problem of language and reason: One can never fully get *out* of the way one frames things, even to describe that framing. As Surber (1998) puts it, "any attempt to theorize culture objectively is already informed by its own cultural prejudices and becomes destabilized and self-undermining in the very process by which it attempts to conduct its critique" (p. 183). In philosophy, such a criticism comes from post-structuralist and pos-tmodernist discourse, where the task is "not . . . to propose yet another theoretical discourse but rather to force . . . existing cultural discourses to show themselves" (Surber, 1998, p. 183). I want to similarly surface ideologies, but also organize them into a few succinct frameworks for workability and ease of recall.

Such narratives, however, also risk subsuming everything to their structures. With a debt to Foucault, Minnich (2005) shows that the way many "meaning systems deal with being disrupted" (p. 5), is to "readjust themselves to neutralize, absorb, and/or recast challenges as mere additions, thereby maintaining themselves at base just as they were" (p. 5). To avoid maintaining my assumptions just as they are, I must use such systems tentatively. As Stevens suggests in the epigram above, then, I consider my framework fictional, as it at once uses empirical data and is made up by me as I go. Yet I choose to believe in a fictional picture, remaining aware of its limits, skeptical, and nevertheless action-oriented at the same time.

Pathways and Pitfalls for What We Teach, and How

Rather than see recall of foundational content, making of conceptual connections, and developing process or skill competencies as separate, we should unite these diverse dimensions (Fink, 2003; Weimer, 2002). The very content we teach should be more than either subject matter (2-D) or connections (3-D) alone, but connected content, and content-rich connections (4-D). To teach integratively, then, is to facilitate experiences that help develop a mobility of mind along all five dimensions—sensory (1-D), categorical (2-D), relational (3-D), meta-reflexive (4-D), and integrative (5-D).

Each dimension, however, has limits, and each strength has distinct liabilities (see Fig. 9, next page). Rather than propose another hierarchy, I use Lauer's (1996–97) five stages and re-label them dimensions, using a spatial metaphor for living and learning. As physicists attest, we need 1-D lines to create a plane, 2-D planes to make 3-D space, interpenetrating dimensions to make the 4-D curvature of space-time,

	1-D Sensory	2-D Categorical	3-D Relational	4-D Meta-reflexive	5-D Integrative
Key operations	Sense, feel, intuit	Sort, standardize	Research, theorize, relate	Transform frameworks used to research and theorize	Consciously unify separation of subject & object
Pathways provided	Alive to external and inner data	Achieve order, structure	Adjust theory, notice perspective	Step back from framework behind how one changes	Integrate body, mind, spirit; transcend language
Pitfalls risked	Assume only one's own feelings are justified; seek only immediate gratification	Force facts to fit theory; presume others are wrong	Stuck in framework behind *how* one changes theory	Limited by language; create separation	Limited clarity, distinctness, or closure
One takes as an object for consideration	(Not applicable: Subject and object are undifferentiated)	Observations, impulses, intuitions	Assumptions used to achieve order	Framework behind adjusting of theory	Intervening language used to step back from framework
One is subject to	Observations, impulses, intuitions	Assumptions used to achieve order	Frameworks behind adjusting of theory	Intervening language used to step back from framework	Blurring of people, systems, boundaries

Figure 9. Five Dimensions of Thinking, Learning, and Living

and twisted dimensions to create the 5-D textures of string theory's picture of the cosmos (Greene, 2004). Each dimension adds to the picture of physical reality.

Likewise, the five dimensions of transformation build on one another, are not neatly linear, and oscillate between simple and complex. They are also not age-specific but "spiral-like" (Cranton, 2002, p. 71) in their cyclical progression, and are each inextricably dependent on the other dimensions to be used well. We need sensations to create categories, which we relate to each other to notice patterns, which are subject to the frameworks we hold, all of which is subsumed by a world beyond the language of separation. If each dimension is a lens filtering our perceptions, we can then examine those lenses and even transform them.

At every transformation, *that to which one is subject becomes object for consideration*. That is, whatever way one thinks or operates, one steps back or "goes meta" in some way from that thinking or operating. As the table above shows, I am subject to my feelings and desires (1-D) until they become object, something I can label and categorize (2-D). Likewise, every category can be blurred, and observations and categorizations can be tested empirically (3-D). That thinking can in turn become object for consideration with meta-reflection (4-D), where we step back and notice the very patterns we use in relating (3-D) our categories (2-D) of sensation (1-D). Finally, with fifth-dimension integration, we experience mystical moments of unity, where we are no longer subject to our meta-reflection, because we experience no separation between subject and object in the first place.

Rather than rely on any one dimension alone, we can build on each of the other dimensions, as a global positioning system triangulates signals in order to give the most accurate picture of what is going on. While my teaching does not program activities to rigidly conform to the five dimensions, or even explicitly address them all the time, my ultimate aim is to use them throughout both course content and teaching methods as I describe below.

Curricular Content: Topics, Problems, Sources

College classes commonly focus on a few limited kinds of content, often involving verbal-logical intelligence (Gardner, 1983) alone. To expand our practice, I suggest we not devalue such intelligence, but interweave it with a greater variety of topics. *What* we teach can vary with each dimension. In each discipline, educators can choose curricular problems that are about sensory observations, categories, and structures, finding relations, going meta, and integrating (see Fig. 10 on the next page, with examples that follow below).

In art history, for example, students learn to notice frivolity and "primitive" anthropomorphizing of forms (1-D). As in many disciplines, people also need to recall some foundational concepts to share some basic cultural literacy with others (Hirsch, 1987)—so students learn terms like contrast and juxtaposition (2-D), and take historical context and revolutions into account (3-D). Sometimes a discipline's

	1-D Sensory	2-D Categorical	3-D Relational	4-D Meta-reflective	5-D Integrative
Art History	Frivolity; "primitive" anthropomorphic forms	Contrast; juxtaposition	Historical context; modernist revolution	Dadaist break; postmodern turn	Return to beauty, participant art
Philosophy	Play as a virtue; the value of selfishness	Ideals; mind-body dualism; categorical imperative	Empiricism; fact vs. inference; ethic of care	Paradigm shift; language & power; deconstruction	Taoist paradox; Sri Aurobindo; mindfulness
Psychology	Observation; primary impulse	DSM-IV categories of disorders; variable	Data analysis; differential diagnosis	Critical psychology; positive psychology; eclecticism	Integral psychology

Figure 10. Curriculum and Content Across Disciplines

content requires another step to shift the very way things are known (4-D). In my teens, for example, modern art began to intrigue me precisely because it reframed what "art" itself could mean. Abstract expressionists showed that splashes of paint did not have to represent anything, because art was not a predefined thing but a reflexive process determined by artists and viewers alike. Most exciting to me, a urinal was declared art, simply because it could be.

In philosophy, content can highlight the virtue of play and Ayn Rand's valuing of selfishness (1-D), or mind-body dualism, ideals, and Immanuel Kant's notion of law in the categorical imperative (2-D). Philosophy also explores empiricism, and the difference between an observed fact and an inference or generalization from such an observation, and the relational ethic of care (3-D). Meta-reflexive content includes Thomas Kuhn's paradigm shift, the influence of language and power, and deconstructing the very ways we use empiricism or relational ethics (4-D). Beyond finding cognitive dissonance (3-D and 4-D), Taoism, Sri Aurobindo and work in mindfulness finds an indivisible wholeness (5-D).

In psychology and other social sciences, and even the natural sciences, people learn to make observations (1-D), categorize such facts to label disorders (2-D), and make a differential diagnosis by weighing numerous and sometimes conflicting indicators (3-D). In critical psychology, the very acts of psychologizing are questioned, just as positive psychology aims beyond pathologies to instead highlight productive life (4-D). Integral psychology further brings back a return of consciousness and spirit (5-D) to understanding human surviving and thriving (Wilber, 2001). Besides such spanning of content across dimensions, however, our methods should also employ multiple learning styles (Richlin, 2006), as follows.

Pedagogical Process: Methods of Teaching and Learning

Activities, assignments, as well as how we think about our teaching, can draw variously on play, structuring, making connections, thinking about overall thinking patterns, and bringing it all together (see Fig. 11, next page).

Of special relevance to integral educators may be the 4-D and 5-D use of various methods. I have students write haiku, for example, to capture their own insights in ways that transcend literal 3-D language or 4-D reflection, and use more indirect (5-D) communication instead. To make classroom discussion transformative, I have students "sayback" (Elbow & Belanoff, 2000) what they understand, and check whether they grasp an opposing view (4-D) to the other's satisfaction (Torosyan, 2004–05). But further, they can listen for not just words or even intent (4-D), but hidden messages and deeper meanings, and simply resonate with others (5-D). After I participated, for example, in a training program on group dynamics facilitation, I noticed patterns of my own (4-D) like needing approval and leaping to respond to triggers or painful emotions (Torosyan, 2008). I also use perceptual devices that trick the eye to have students experience (5-D) and not simply relate (3-D) or reflect upon (4-D) a change in how they actually see things.

Pedagogy/ Methods	1-D Sensory	2-D Categorical	3-D Relational	4-D Meta-reflective	5-D Integrative
Writing	Free writing	Describe a thinker or a problem's elements; compare and contrast	Write-Pair-Share; Pass the sheet; list more than one possible solution	Take a point of view opposing your own; write 100 questions and self-assess	Write haiku; capture spirituality with indirect language
Classroom discussion, group work	Play games, discuss spontaneously	Use ground rules, order ideas, give mini-lectures	Her from as many as possible; divide labor among groups; post-it ideas up on wall chart	Leverage the wildly differing styles in class; move post-its to suggest new patterns	Resonate with the group as a whole; hear not just words, or even intent, but hidden messages
Visual devices	Doodle, scribble, line, shape, to play with visuals	Draw a symbol for a concept, draw chart for contrasting movements or approaches	Illustrate inter-dependent variables with visual displays of information (Tufte, 1990)	Reframe using a different shape; extend boundaries of a chart or illustration	Find the edge of a hole; use perceptual devices that "trick" the eye
Objects and bodily-kinesthetic movement	Feel objects	Sort objects; learn foreign language using total physical response	Relate different ways of sorting objects	Reshape objects; find patterns to ways of relating sortings	Do a gallery walk; use body sculpture to express learning
Virtual reality, augmented reality	Chat freely; move avatars or objects in virtual space	Build virtual molecule	Nursing; see veins better with visual augmentation	Reorient a virtual space or site	Simulate psychedelic experiences

Figure 11. Pedagogical Methods Across the Dimensions

One writing exercise shows 4-D self-assessment in action. In my modern philosophy course, my students often arrive skeptical of the subject's relevance and why they must take the requirement. To motivate their interest, I have them write a "Hundred Questions" to begin with what most drives their own inquisitiveness (see Fig. 12, Box C).

Another way to integrate dimensions is to break assignments into steps, each appealing to different pathways and overcoming different pitfalls of the dimensions. Early on in my philosophy course, for instance, I have my students write a letter

---

Box C: Classroom Application: One Hundred Questions

Instructions: To begin, make a list of a hundred "power questions" (Gelb, 1998) that are important to you. As Gelb describes:

> Include any question as long as you deem it significant, from "How can I save money?" or "How can I have more fun?" to "What is the purpose of my existence?" and "How can I best serve the Creator?" Do the entire list in one sitting. Write quickly; ignore spelling, grammar, or redundancy (recurring questions help show emerging themes). The first 20 or so will be "off the top of your head." In the next 30 or 40, themes often begin to emerge. And, in the second half of the list you may discover unexpected but profound material (Gelb, 1998, p. 59).

Afterward, read about my experience (in Gelb, 2002), list a few common themes from your list, then rank 10 questions most significant to you, with the most important first. Describe any unexpected discoveries, and connect to at least one of the 12 big questions in the text. Post online. Then reply to a post that has no replies, saying what the post makes you think about.

Outcomes: Pushing for quantity over quality, the structure overcomes nervousness about competence in philosophy, and instead encourages playful (1-D) curiosity. Categorizing themes holds a mirror up to one's own thinking (4-D), and clarifies often unspoken philosophical values (2-D). Selecting a few top questions forces learners to link disparate interests and prioritize them (3-D). When learners share their goals and why they matter, many end up resonating (5-D) with me or other readers about deeply personal and powerful experiences. For example, one teenaged student described losing a younger brother to a terminal disease, another was surprised to realize his parents were human beings, and another struggled to manage a personal financial crisis.

Figure 12. Classroom Application: One Hundred Questions

to a novice who has never studied the subject. They do so through three to four drafts, so they can receive feedback from others before submitting the last one to me (see Fig. 13, Box D).

The very way I (and my students) do reflection depends on the dimensions used. In one course I taught, for example, an initially resistant student used 4-D reflection on his own behaviors by creating a personal project to improve his time management skills. But in the process, I likewise had 4-D realizations about how I unintentionally invited mimicry from him, making it unclear how much he was really transformed (Torosyan, 2007–2008). When my student reported sympathizing with people, for example, his awkward language revealed I may have influenced him to simply parrot back my repeated emphasis on empathy.

Box D: Classroom Application: Letter to a Novice

Instructions: First draft: Write a letter to a friend who knows nothing about modern philosophy, explaining one of our 12 big questions, with an example. Free write: No stopping, no correcting. As Joan Didion said, "First draft: Don't get it right, get it done." Bring three copies to hear what resonated with others. *Outcomes:* This draft usually gets writers excited and playing freely (1-D), just getting ideas out of the mind and into concrete words (2-D). *Second Draft: Resee and Reshape:* Reread, then list, "What haven't I said yet?" writing from your first felt sense (Fulwiler & Hayakawa, 2007; Sondra Perl in Elbow & Belanoff, 2003). Then outline after the fact, reorganize, and check it against samples and comments I posted. This draft should look very different from your first. *Outcomes:* Students get to see early writing not as a static product (2-D) but instead as a fluid process of reorganization (3-D) and reflection on their own points of view (4-D). Finally, it moves the student to commit to some order and sequence (2-D). *Third Draft: Edit & Self-Assess.* Cut to 350 words max. and self-assess the following: (a) Clarity (1/3 of grade): Uses action verbs, cuts unneeded words, uses correct grammar, and uses logical organization (2-D). (b) Fundamentals (1/3): Uses a primary source, and addresses an actual friend's interest. (c) Analysis (1/3): Questions assumptions (yours and others), and clarifies your own personal philosophy and values. *Outcomes:* This stage practically forces healthy conformity to high standards (2-D). At the same time, the self-rating helps internalize a sense of one's own strengths and weaknesses (4-D). Students found the assignment "more personal" and said things like, "it forced me to cut out the b.s. I was surprised to see how much other students could rip apart my paper, but it was very helpful in the end."

Figure 13. Classroom Application: Letter to a Novice

Teaching integratively also means attending to the rhythms of learning. For instance, I build trust in early sessions, need to rejuvenate their energies at mid-term and later, and provide closure towards the end. To punctuate two reflective moments, at midterm and at final, I have students look back at all their work and specify what they learned (see Fig. 14, Box E).

Each dimension, then, includes pathways of simpler ones, and discards pitfalls—in both curriculum and instruction. And yet, to use a simpler dimension well often requires abandoning aspects of more complex dimensions. So, for instance, if I want to play one of Bach's Goldberg Variations and simply enjoy the pianistic process, I do well to rid myself of reflexive self-consciousness. To improve, however, I need to slow down and examine sections meticulously. Similarly, actors often say of a performance that they were truly "*in* it" at precisely those times where they lost sense of performing and were simply *being* another person. Yet developing that presence and self-possession usually takes years of acting lessons and disciplined practice to make conscious efforts eventually unconscious and simply habit or informed intuition.

In sum, I find the use of five dimensions helpful to tell what it means for our learners to do well—whether at knowing things, doing things like critical thinking or problem solving, or valuing and caring about the world differently. Such a rich diversity of modalities can not only help my students learn but inform how I teach and how I live outside of professional life. Just as our daily lives involve a whole range of capacities, then, our teaching can range from impulsive fun, to orderly structures and reliance on ethical principles, to adapting plans to where students are, to critical self-reflection on our actions, to experiencing an integrative oneness—of learning and not learning, transforming and failing to transform, even of love.

Box E: Classroom Application: Midterm/Final Integrative Portfolio Reflection

Instructions: Review your own progress (on goals from start of term or midterm) and show: How your philosophical thinking has **changed since the start of term**; How you make connections to **other subjects** and to personal, professional, and **civic life;** and What you want to remember to be thinking about philosophically a **year from now.** Quote your own writing, and peer feedback, to demonstrate how you learned. Limit to **250 words max.**, excluding quotes of self or others. **Self-rate** against: (a) Reflectiveness with which you ask big questions, seek answers, and analyze and critically evaluate assumptions, and (b) Specificity with which you **apply insights to improve your thinking, problem solving or decisions,** learn from mistakes, and change behavior to reach your goals.

Figure 14. Classroom Application: Midterm/Final Integrative Portfolio Reflection

If we integrate dimensions, we use all three modes Fink (2003) described as vital to significant learning: experiences (doing, observing; simulated), information and ideas (primary/secondary, accessing them in-class, out-of-class, online), and reflecting (on *what* and *how* one is learning, alone and with others) (p. 107). Finally, by shifting dimensions ever more freely, I hope other educators find too that together we can not only help our students live lives of meaning and examined thought, but renew and revitalize our own practices, to integrate thinking and feeling, heart and soul, while accepting with grace whatever it is that we cannot change.

References

Abbott, E. A., & Stewart, I. (2002). *The annotated flatland: A romance of many dimensions.* Cambridge, MA: Perseus.

Awbrey, S. M. (2006). *Integrative learning and action: A call to wholeness.* New York: Peter Lang.

Bateson, G. (1972). *Steps to an ecology of mind: Collected essays in anthropology, psychiatry, evolution, and epistemology.* San Francisco: Chandler.

Baxter-Magolda, M. B., & King, P. M. (2004). *Learning partnerships: Theory and models of practice to educate for self-authorship.* Sterling, VA: Stylus.

Blair, B. G., & Caine, R. N. (1995). *Integrative learning as the pathway to teaching holism, complexity, and interconnectedness.* Lewiston, NY: EmText.

Bois, J. S. (1970). *Breeds of men; toward the adulthood of humankind.* New York: Harper & Row.

Brookfield, S. (1995). *Becoming a critically reflective teacher* (1st ed.). San Francisco: Jossey-Bass.

Christian, D. (2004). *Maps of time: An introduction to big history.* Berkeley: University of California.

Cirillo, J. M., & Artiz, C. S. (2005). A module approach to online integrative teaching and learning. *MountainRise: A Journal of Scholarship of Teaching and Learning, 2*(1).

Cranton, P. (2002). Teaching for transformation. *New Directions for Adult and Continuing Education, 93,* 63–71.

Engel-Yan, J., Kennedy, C., Saiz, S., & Pressnail, K. (2005). Toward sustainable neighbourhoods: the need to consider infrastructure interactions. *Canadian Journal of Civil Engineering, 32*(1), 45–57.

Egan, K. (1997). *The educated mind: How cognitive tools shape our understanding.* Chicago: University of Chicago.

Elbow, P., & Belanoff, P. (2000). *Sharing and responding* (3rd ed.). Boston: McGraw-Hill.

Elbow, P., & Belanoff, P. (2003). *Being a writer: A community of writers revisited.* Boston: McGraw-Hill.

Ferrer, J. N., Romero, M. T., & Albareda, R. V. (2005). Integral transformative education: A participatory proposal. *Journal of Transformative Education, 3*(4), 306–330.

Fink, L. D. (2003). *Creating significant learning experiences: An integrated approach to designing college courses.* San Francisco: Jossey-Bass.

Fulwiler, T., & Hayakawa, A. R. (2007). *The Blair handbook* (5th ed.). Upper Saddle River, NJ: Pearson/Prentice Hall.

Gaddis, J. L. (2002). *The landscape of history: How historians map the past.* Oxford; New York: Oxford University.

Gardner, H. (1983). *Frames of mind: The theory of multiple intelligences.* New York: Basic Books.

Gelb, M. (1998). *How to think like Leonardo da Vinci: Seven steps to genius every day.* New York, NY: Delacorte.

Gelb, M. J. (2002). *Discover your inner genius: How to think like history's ten most revolutionary minds.* New York: Harper Collins.

Gross, R. (2002). *Socrates' way: Seven master keys to using your mind to the utmost.* New York: Tarcher/Putnam.

Hirsch, E. D., Jr. (1987). *Cultural literacy: What every American should know.* Boston, MA: Houghton Mifflin.

Huber, M. T., & Hutchings, P. (2004). *Integrative learning: Mapping the terrain.* Washington, DC: American Association of Colleges & Universities.

Hussey, M. (1988). Education in the quantum field. *Central Park, 13.*

Kegan, R. (1994). *In over our heads: The mental demands of modern life.* Cambridge, MA: Harvard University.

Kegan, R. (2000). What "form" transforms? A constructive-developmental approach to transformative learning. *Learning as transformation: Critical perspectives on a theory in progress.* San Francisco: Jossey-Bass.

Kegan, R. (2006). Teaching for development: Joining the undergraduate as a maker of meaning. Keynote address. *Lilly Conference on College Teaching,* Miami University of Ohio.

Klein, J. T. (1990). *Interdisciplinarity: History, theory, and practice.* Detroit: Wayne State University.

Koestler, A. (1967). *The ghost in the machine.* London: Hutchinson.

Kohlberg, L., & Mayer, R. (1972, November). Development as the aim of education. *Harvard Educational Review, 42*(4).

Lakoff, G., & Johnson, M. (2003). *Metaphors we live by.* Chicago: University of Chicago.

Lauer, R. M. (1996–97). A meta curriculum based upon critical thinking. *ETC., 53*(4), 374–387.

Lyotard, J. (1984). *The postmodern condition: A report on knowledge.* Minneapolis: University of Minnesota.

Mezirow, J. (Ed.) (2000). *Learning as transformation: Critical perspectives on a theory in progress.* San Francisco: Jossey-Bass.

Minnich, E. K. (2005). *Transforming knowledge* (2nd ed.). Philadelphia: Temple University.

Morgan, G. (2007). *Images of organization* (Updated ed.). Thousand Oaks: Sage Publications.

Nelson, C. E. (1999). On the persistence of unicorns: The trade-off between content and critical thinking revisited. In B. A. Pescosolido, & R. Aminzade (Eds.), *The social worlds of higher education: Handbook for teaching in a new century* (pp. 168–184). Thousand Oaks, CA: Pine Forge.

Olson, D. R., & Torrance, N. (1996). *The handbook of education and human development: New models of learning, teaching, and schooling.* Cambridge, MA: Blackwell.

O'Sullivan, E., & Taylor, M. M. (2004). *Learning toward an ecological consciousness: Selected transformative practices.* New York: Palgrave Macmillan.

Perry, W. G. (1968/1999). *Forms of ethical and intellectual development in the college years: A scheme* (Orig. published 1968 ed.). San Francisco: Jossey-Bass.

Piaget, J. (1997). *The child's conception of the world.* New York: Routledge.

Regan, T. (2007). *Commencement address, Fairfield University, May 20, 2007.* Retrieved 122007, from http://www.fairfield.edu/press/pr_index.html?id = 2107

Reiser, O. L. (1958). *The integration of human knowledge: A study of the formal foundations and the social implications of unified science.* Boston: Sargent.

Schneider, C. G. (2005). Making excellence inclusive: Liberal education & America's promise. *Liberal Education, 91*(2), 6–17.

Snyderman, R., & Weil, A. (2002). Integrative medicine. *Archives of Internal Medicine, 162,* 395–397.

Sosa, M. E., Eppinger, S. D., & Rowles, C. M. (2003). Identifying modular and integrative systems and their impact on design team interactions, *ASME Journal of Mechanical Design,* Vol. 125, pp. 240–252.

Surber, J. P. (1998). *Culture and critique: An introduction to the critical discourses of cultural studies.* Boulder, CO: Westview.

Torbert, W. R., et al. (2004). *Action inquiry: The secret of timely and transforming leadership.* San Francisco: Berrett-Koehler.

Torosyan, R. (2000). *Encouraging consciousness development in the college classroom through student-centered transformative teaching and learning.* Unpublished doctoral dissertation, Teachers College–Columbia University, NY.

Torosyan, R. (2001). A system for everything: Book review of *Brief history of everything* by Ken Wilber. *New Ideas in Psychology, 19*(3).

Torosyan, R. (2004–2005). Listening: Beyond telling to being the teaching message. *Journal of the Assembly for Expanded Perspectives on Learning, 10*(Winter), 27–36.

Torosyan, R. (Winter, 2007–2008). Teaching self-authorship and self-regulation: A story of resistance to transformation. *MountainRise: A Journal of Scholarship of Teaching and Learning, 4*(2), 1–21.

Torosyan, R. (2008). Self-reflections on group dynamics. *Journal of Creativity in Mental Health, 3*(1), 1–15.

Tufte, E. R. (1990). *Envisioning information.* Cheshire, CT: Graphics.

Volk, T. (1995). *Metapatterns across space, time, and mind.* New York: Columbia University.

Weimer, M. (2002). *Learner-centered teaching: Five key changes to practice.* San Francisco: Jossey-Bass.

Wilber, K. (2000). *Sex, ecology, spirituality: The spirit of evolution* (2nd, rev. ed.). Boston: Shambhala.

Wilber, K. (2001). *A theory of everything: An integral vision for business, politics, science, and spirituality.* Boston: Shambhala.

Wilson, E. O. (1998). *Consilience: The unity of knowledge.* New York: Knopf.

Zeichner, K. M., & Liston, D. P. (1996). *Reflective teaching: An introduction.* Mahwah, NJ: Erlbaum.

Encountering the (W)hole

Integral Education as
Deep Dialogue and Cultural Medicine

Matthew C. Bronson and Ashok Gangadean

Preface

The crisis of our times, as we see it, is at root a failure of the human imagination and chronically entrenched hermeneutical patterns. Progressive educators feel the current call to relevance in their practice, to claim in the classroom and curriculum the power of human communities to forge a better, more sustainable, and just world. Yet all too easily, the project of connection and integration glossed under "integral education" ends up putting "old *mind* in new bottles." Without new thinking based on deep dialogue, the integral project can generate new dogmas, new taxonomies, new ideological schisms that merely replicate, rather than intervene in the turf wars and real wars that embody the cultural pathologies of late modernity.

We note that despite millennial efforts to leave the older dysfunctional patterns of minding behind and mature into truly integral patterns of life, these chronically entrenched ego-mental patterns continue to dominate all aspects of our lives—including our institutions and the educational practices of cultural reproduction that occur within them. So one focal theme is to bring this impasse out into the open—to articulate and disclose the extent to which such ego-mental patterns of minding continue to dominate our lives today and impede, repress, block, and marginalize genuine attempts to enter Holistic Rational Space for the advancement of our human condition at all levels.

In this chapter, a philosopher and a linguist explore integral education as the confluence of the rivers of reason and grace. They present in dialogic form a notation for indicating the deeper integral logic that underlies and makes possible the intelligible universe as revealed in sacred texts and everyday conversation. Models and exercises for enacting this approach are provided for courses in philosophy and introductory linguistics. The authors address the political and practical challenges of enacting integral education as an intervention in the status quo practice of "dichotomosis," toxic either/or thinking, in the Academy and society. Issues of assessment and accountability are critical for integral educators who wish to maintain credibility and rapport with a mainstream that is increasingly streaming over a cliff. Deep dialogue across difference points the way to re-channel the force of the collective consciousness toward an ancient future worthy of our evolutionary potential and critical role as citizens of the planet.

Dialogue of 5/17/08
(MB = Matthew C. Bronson; AG = Ashok Gangadean)

Introduction: Opening the Door to Integral Dialogue

MB: Here we are. I guess we can begin where we've begun before, which is here in this present moment, this time in 2008. The world continues to move along in its various paths. Many people believe, indeed, a consensus exists among progressive elements of society that we are passing through a moment of multiple crises where the survival and sustainability of the human and more-than-human worlds is quite literally at stake. Lots of wonderful groups and people are grappling with these crises productively, trying to think about what their part is to play and making some of the shifts that need to happen (Hawken, 2008).

One has the feeling that time is short and, yet, certainly there is enough time for whatever important work one can do. And in the area of education, many people are responding by seeking sources of new thinking and ideas, paths of action that will intervene in the endless conflicts that seem to characterize our time. People are coming to the doors of the universities and to the research institutions and saying: "What do you have for us? What knowledge and models of being together can you contribute to the public sphere since you folks have the time and luxury to take a step back from the hullabaloo of everyday life and actually reflect? What is it that you can bring to the table, to the collective conversation?"

I'd like to highlight by way of entering our dialogue the accountability and the responsibility that we have as educators to provide real solutions to the root issues of our day. A great deal of the educational enterprise is designed to stifle imagination, to pigeon-hole people and put them in the right occupational slots (Montuori, 2006; Freire, 1970; hooks, 1994, 2003). And certainly you as a professor in a liberally-oriented college (Haverford College) and myself also from a progressive institution (California Institute of Integral Studies or CIIS), have a big stake in these issues. Our institutions have committed to somehow educating the whole person.

But that's also a commitment of the Jesuits and many other groups with a particular agenda and vision of what "wholeness" is. They, as do our institutions, strive to educate "body, mind, and spirit." I wonder if we can articulate together a vision of wholeness, of integral education, that speaks to these concerns without advocating a particular school of thought or tradition to the exclusion of others. The aim would be to frame integral education as a "big tent" where experimentation, inquiry, and respectful dialogue can occur aligned with certain core values and a trajectory toward transformation and expansion of human capacity.

So here I am right at the door of our respective institutions and practices. I knock at that door as the world in crisis. The world really is looking for different ways of being together, and we have learned something about how to do that in our work in integral education. You and I want to share some of what we have learned with the caveat that we don't want to be just adding another dogma, another grid to overlay experience. We are aware that the notation system we introduce in this chapter runs the risk of such an "overlay" though as you will see our intention is to actually use the notation to enhance experience. We want to frame the discussion within the larger project of being human, a project of meaning-making in which people from many different camps can recognize themselves. We invite them to draw meaningful connections between our experiences as educators and their own unique institutional settings and personal journeys.

So I just greet you and thank you for this precious time that we have together to do this work and invite you to think about this question: *What's knocking on your door today?*

AG: Well, thank you Matthew. This is a wonderful way to frame it, starting out with the theme that we face all kinds of intensified crises as we enter the global age of the twenty-first century. It is global in many senses but, most importantly for our discussion, in the sense that starts with culture as worldview (Bennett, 1993, 2003). The ideologies and forms of life that emerge from diverse worldviews are increasingly, through technology and other means, entering a common marketplace of interaction which results in increasing clashes and collisions. And it's clear from global wisdom of the ages that the crises that we face in the human condition are a net result of how we are using our consciousness.

The great wisdom traditions as you know concur that if we are more in egocentric patterns, monocentric patterns, or objectifying patterns and using our consciousness as a technology that makes our world and our reality, then we're going to have a world that shows up as an ego-mental world, that is one with fractures, fragments, polarizations, and all kinds of crises across metaphorical and literal borders. Ego-mental thinking is a particular form of dichotomous either/or thinking, a closed system of reasoning that dissects the world into hard categories by rote, without imagining alternative schemes or approaches. It is the logic that leads to fundamentalism, conflict, domination, war, and the hegemonic control of one group by another (Gangadean, 1997).

A real alternative exists and has always existed: The wisdom traditions have taught for millennia that there are more integral patterns, holistic patterns, meditative intelligence, however you word it (Chaudhuri, 1965). As a cautionary note we want to avoid postulating this integral alternative in binary opposition with ego-mental thought and avoid making the former good and the later bad. As I see it, integral intelligence includes the insights of ego-mental thought but is free from its constraints. I am speaking of integral ways of using our intelligence and technologies of consciousness to surf the domain of reality, ways that have emphasized a unified theme of deep interconnectivity as objective reality. This deep interconnectivity gets dislodged and alienated through ego-mental patterns that continually re-emerge in human consciousness.

So I think it is important just to start off, as you beautifully frame it, that we are at this crossing into the twenty-first century in a period of unprecedented globalization (Inda & Renato, 2002). We face enormous challenges in the crises that surround us that could do us in if we do not individually and collectively somehow manage to live the wisdom and move into an integral way of being wholly human. And I agree with the way you stated it that it's natural to look to our educational system and higher education where we reproduce our culture most transparently and deliberately. The purpose of education in this context seems to be to cultivate the citizens of the future, to be a counsel to society-at-large and to ask deep and searching questions. How well are we in education providing critical modes of thinking that bring us in touch with these patterns of consciousness? Or to what extent are we simply reflecting that culture of dominance, of the ego-mental pattern, rather than intervening? I think the questions of critical thinking, the standards of literacy, and how we conduct our consciousness are all on the table before us. And I'd love to be able to explore that with you at this time.

MB: I think that's a really critical piece because it brings home the fact that we are always already recreating the world. And certainly in education, that's transparent where in each class, in a sense, we have an opportunity to re-think the world (Freire, 1974; hooks, 1998). Yet we as educators continually disappoint ourselves or disappoint our institutions in some measure, at least with respect to achieving this ideal. There are pockets of excellence, beauty, and power, of course (Palmer, 1997). What we want to do today is to foreground what is working and appreciate the ways in which that is not separate from the true spirit of the university and the academy.

This means getting "back to roots," which is the most "radical" approach when we consider the etymology of the word from the Latin "radica" or root. It is a way of reclaiming the best of the Enlightenment and the various other traditions without fetishizing them, without putting them in a museum, to think from history critically back to the present so that we can have it be different. This is distinct from simply putting the great masters and the great books, the Vedic and philosophical texts, for example, which you work with, putting them in a diorama behind thick glass and teaching people to be in awe of them. And so it really is about breaking down that glass, isn't it? And letting people touch and connect directly with these ancient traditions and currents of thought that have always been present but are too easily, back-grounded or forgotten; easily regained, but somehow easily forgotten as well.

Liberating the ((Text)) from Behind the /Glass/[1]

AG: Well said. I would like to pick up on that theme of the text behind the glass windows in the museum, the objectification. When I finished my training in logic and analytic philosophy at Brandeis and was looking into the depths of logic and the European tradition from Aristotle to the post-Fregean mathematical logical model and from there to integral logic, I found a deep polarization. It was only after that, arriving at Haverford in '68, 40 years ago, I began asking searching questions such as: How do you cross worlds? How do you enter different mental ecologies? Is it possible? Can you actually communicate? Is it a rational discourse? How do you think critically across alternative widely divergent worldviews? I didn't see any clear charting of those waters by prior research.

That's when I went to India for the first time, after three years at Haverford, in 1971 to 1972, and I didn't intend to study Indian philosophy. I was going to learn Sanskrit, play the sitar, and tabla, learn the music, and immerse myself in the culture. I was lecturing at the University of Poona on my logic from the West and started to study Vedic and Buddhist thinking. It blew me away because for the first time in my life, even though I'm of Indian origin growing up in the West, I discovered that everything is rooted in meditative intelligence. I found a critique of ego-mental logic in the integral forms of meditative thinking that are evident in critical moments in the sacred texts. For example, at one point in the *Bhagavad Gita*, Arjuna breaks down on the battlefield during a polarized war, a fratricidal war, and his life implodes on him. He drops his weapon and says to Krishna, "Help me."

Then the dialogue between Krishna and Arjuna begins, taking Arjuna into deeper and deeper alternative yogas, moving him out of the ego-mental state that was at the heart of his breakdown and making him literate in ways of conducting the mind that shift him into the Aumic stage of the higher self. When I discovered that, it blew me away because no one in my European heritage and training of the most highly rigorous analytic thinking prepared me for the meditative, integral intelligence. Furthermore, I wasn't trained to recognize that ego-mental thinking fragments, polarizes, and, in the absence of conscious alignment with a more integral order of being, ultimately leads to degeneration and breakdown. That gave me a hint as to why I did not find a coherent integral logic, why logic itself and its rationality were polarized (Gangadean, 2006a).

The meditative opening that I find in Buddha's awakening, it's the same point. You find that the egomind is the root cause of existential suffering. We have a choice. We don't have to cling to that mental pattern. We're addicted to it, and we can rehabilitate our minds to the path of mindfulness. These kinds of opening give us a whole new horizon in the search for integral rationality and answer the questions of critical thinking across worlds, they put you "out of the box." So when I returned to Haverford I was clear I was going to start teaching in these areas. I literally had to reinvent teaching and pedagogy to bring these texts into the classroom. Essentially, you couldn't put it behind our glass windows and make it into the objectified forms of narrative that you just talked about.

MB: You could, but not given your breakthrough and where you were standing now. You saw that these sacred texts were portals to new ways of being and thinking but only if they were held in a way that allowed that fullness to come through. In other words, one could easily look at the *Gita* and analyze the use of the future subjunctive in the Sanskrit original in a traditional grammatical analysis, a wonderful exercise and potentially worthy scholarship if it were tethered to a particular task of exegesis. But that would be beside the point in the context of the present discussion. It's also about using the text to actually activate this shift in consciousness, and in that sense, connecting up with the *sangha*, with the spiritual community, with all those who have come to read these texts before and to be standing in that alternate stream of intelligence. I mean that's certainly what I experience in my own classroom at times. And I wonder if that's what you feel as well, that you are in a sense bringing these texts alive and in turn raising the level of aliveness in your students?

Representing ((Logic)) and the Living ((Spirit)) of the Text

AG: That's exactly right. But it took me a year or two of fumbling to realize I had to step back and, as I said, reinvent pedagogy to bring authentically and rigorously the hermeneutic of these alternate texts and methods of thinking into the classroom. Of course, when I returned, my department and I agreed that I would start teaching Hindu thought and Buddhist thought, along with my work in logical theory and philosophy of language. And then even in my courses on metaphysics and ontology, I naturally started to talk about the *Gita* and who is Krishna and about Hinduism, the way it typically happens in the academic ways of presenting it. Then I felt upset. I was getting sickened by it because I realized I was violating the traditional text. And by the end of the first year, I realized, "No, I can't teach it and objectify the content." I had to find an alternative way authentically to help the students bring the text to life, offering a critique of the egomental patterns rather than buying into the ego-mental patterns that so deeply structure our education (Gangadean, 2008).

MB: So didn't that require a disruption or intervention in the normal way of reading? What affordances did you provide students so they could be reading from that deeper level?

AG: Well, since I was concerned about moving across worlds and I realized that the Aumic space of Krishna was one that bridged worlds, I started there. When Krishna speaks, it's clear that Krishna is the incarnation of Vishnu teaching from the grammar of Aum and attempting to help Arjuna recognize his ego-mental patterns of consciousness and the predicament of the existential situation. One first set of questions is: What is the nature of this dialogue across those two dimensions? How can Arjuna really understand? Can Arjuna understand what Krishna is saying to him from the Yogic voice? And how is Krishna going to communicate to Arjuna who is so much lodged in this ego-mental pattern?

MB: Yes, it's kind of like, "How does the butterfly speak to the caterpillar?"

AG: Yes, something like that, exactly. So that thematized the question, and after a year or two of struggling with the thematizing of the deep dialogue of the text itself as problematic, calling into question our entrenched habits of education and information processing, a new horizon opened in the classroom for me. It took two or three tries, to answer your question, until we began to see how to open deeper space in the classroom, to enact a pedagogy that would lead students reliably to an authentic encounter with Buddha's text. The challenge was to do this without begging all of the questions and reifying the content as one would do in traditional critique in an ego-mental mode.

MB: Well, also in a sense bringing forward the good senses of somebody who knows how to think about text rigorously but also being willing to bracket that so that one is encountering it for the first time, with the beginner's mind. So it's an interesting juxtaposition of, on the one hand, the newness, the originality of this encounter, and on the other hand, giving students the background knowledge, the context. One must be careful to not prepare them in a way that is going to prefigure their encounter, but in a way that will rather enhance it, which is different.

The value of the old way of thinking, or a more traditional humanities approach, is that you get to understand what it is that the masters have thought about this text (Fish, 1980). This is like the setting for a beautiful jewel, necessary but background to the main act. And the students' own experience of the text is the real jewel of the ring. I think this is what you're talking about. The real gem or the jewel is the shift in awareness that emerges in the classroom. And, continuing with the metaphor, the hermeneutic training, critical theory, and background knowledge become merely the setting for the actual experience of the text in vivo. Am I on track with this?

AG: Very much so. In terms of beginner's mind, for example, one of the first things I would say to students in the opening class was that they were coming into a wisdom laboratory—an alive thinking intensive laboratory—where we would be encountering the voice and text of Buddha. I told them that they had to be willing to, as you said, "bracket," take a look at, their deeply entrenched patterns of education and consciousness at this point; they had to be willing to be critical and courageous and stand back. I would tell them that they would be asked to experiment with seeking to enter the integral state, the source of transpersonal wisdom from which Krishna or Buddha are speaking in these classical texts, for example. And students would flock to this; they had such a hunger for this kind of alternative way of being educated as the word got through in the community, so they were excited at the idea of a philosophical laboratory of thought experiments that, as you say, worked hermeneutically. The hermeneutic issues became essential and heightened, so that they had to see that which lens they were using to read the text and listen to Krishna or to Buddha made all the difference.

MB: And that is a point I'm wondering about in terms of my own work. I've just written something called the *Grammar of Transformation* (Bronson, 2009). The piece is looking at what the steps are that are necessary for people to be able to step into a new worldview and how they incrementally test the waters and try on new behaviors, and then get the feedback necessary to be able to assimilate the new behavior and worldview.

I wonder in this case, then, if we could be quite concrete about what you put in front of people and what you ask them to do. How do they begin to experience the degrees of freedom that we would hope for and to let go of the everyday ego-mental way of relating to the world? Are there specific exercises and then models for how to proceed? Then is there an intersubjective testing where they come back with each other in small groups or in dyads and talk things through and then come back to it again? What exactly are the steps that you ask your students to go through so that those shifts more reliably occur?

AG: That's well said. And I'll give you some examples. Once the theme opens up that Krishna or Buddha or the meditative voice is speaking from a linguistic rational space distinct from our ordinary ego or ego-mental objectifying pattern; they seem to get that. But they don't yet fully understand; well, what is this other dimension? Krishna speaks to Arjuna, "How do I understand it?" Then Buddha alleges that the ego is destined to suffer, indeed, the source of suffering, and we have a choice. How do we profit from that? In a moment we could talk about how after a decade of experimentation, this led to finding a way to encode these two dimensions, trying to bring them out in their diversity and relations by using single brackets, / /, and double brackets, (( )), to mark them as we explored these in our two earlier essays (Gangadean & Bronson, 2004; Bronson & Gangadean, 2006).

The basic idea is that the everyday logic of ego-mentalism, of subjects and objects, dichotomies and polarities, could be designated with the use of /single brackets/. The deeper, encompassing integral logic of Krishna and Buddha's teachings was designated by placing the statement in question in ((double brackets)). This way of distinguishing the everyday versus integral-holistic logical modes turns out to be very useful by way of cultivating discernment among the two modes in teaching: learning and living.

It took a while to reliably activate the integral awareness I was after in students and, at first, the exalted state of the awakened masters would seem inaccessible to them. They began to see the limits of their own thinking right away, "Oh, I never realized I was egoing or that there was even such a thing, and that objectifying in content might have consequences for my life. I'm beginning to get it. But I'm having trouble crossing into this other awakened state or integral state that the teacher is pointing to." So at first it seems so far away.

Everyday /Logic/ Is a Form of ((Logic))

I then discovered one particular experiment that electrifies that issue. I would suggest that, alright, if you draw a diagram with a single-bracket ego-consciousness below, and then you draw a chasm and a line, and above that is the AUM space, or the Buddha space, or the God space, or the Allah space, however you name that fundamental field, then it seems so transcendent, so far away, so out of reach, that students almost implode and become demoralized. "I'll never get there. I see it. I acknowledge that I need to get there. I don't know how." So a breakthrough for me pedagogically was to draw the double brackets all around the single-bracket space signifying a classical axiom of diverse integral philosophies, as, for example, in the Vedic and Aurobindan traditions (Chaudhuri, 1965) that we're always surrounded and situated in the ((primal field)). That it has a tremendous pull on us every moment of our lives. It's quite possible, even natural, to go into the ((zone)), enter into "flow," (Csikszentmihalyi, 1988) into these peak moments of performance, to get out of the ego spontaneously. A runner who has been running for three years, suddenly she finds herself ((RUNNING)). And she is not thinking, "I am running." It's "((running am I))." She ((is)) the ((running)) itself.

MB: Yes, that experience of flow is something that I think everybody can identify with at one time or another. High-functioning people often have experiences of flow where they are working at their highest or best capacity, often in a social setting but also alone in nature. So that is a pointer to students that this is not so alien from their experience. It is somewhere in the direction of what they know as "flow." Then what sort of coaching do you offer them? They get the diagram showing that everyday reason is a subset of an encompassing integral logic. Do you then point out that, in fact, our capacity to function in an ego-mental state is itself dependent on that integral logic? That the integral ground of being makes all meaning possible and, thus, all meanings, even ego-mentally construed meanings, are dipping their cup in the same well? Isn't that the case?

AG: That's beautifully said. Yes, it is along those lines. Each student now picks up from that kind of moment when they say, "I recognize that I've had those magic moments." "It's all pure alchemy." "It is peak performance." I've had people say those things. Or "I've been jiving with my friends and suddenly the music takes over."

One can employ the double brackets to interrupt the usual meaning of words and to indicate that they should be read from the deeper source, from the trans-/rational/ point of view. I call this ((Meditative Reason)) (Gangadean, 1993). My students had many different moments of ((flow)) in their lives and they can relate to the concept of connected reasoning that does not begin with the a priori separation of subject and object. By the way, I get a number of very articulate high-level athletes in my classes now because they know that Professor Gangadean would invite them to become literate and find ways to communicate about being in the realm of peak performance and to articulate the phenomenology of that ((experience)), of ((being-in-the-zone)) as athletes say.

How Do We Know the ((Shift)) Has Occurred?

MB: What a wonderful connection. I think that would be one of the criteria that we would want to apply in our integral education interventions: Are they accessible to people with different intelligences (Gardner, 1999)? Are they couched in a way that's general enough to be applicable to people with wide ranges of needs but specific enough to really touch them where they live? Picking up on your terms, will it be the case that whatever single-bracket propositions they come with, that they will still be able to find the way to the double-bracket?

If we look at that shift in awareness that you were talking about, which really is thoroughly grounded in the perennial philosophy and in the study of the sacred texts and masters, that's a much firmer grounding than the particular fad of the day, isn't it? It will be good to prioritize the shift and to know reliably how and when we are achieving it in our modes of assessment. If we focus on the shift as the key outcome, then we're never going to get too tied up in our own right way of achieving it as educators, never get too far afield. Do you follow me?

AG: Absolutely, I think what you just said is so important in terms of alternative learning abilities and capacities in universities. I find evidence of this shift in the final projects I collect at the end of the semester. For example, I have had fine students of the highest order in physics attempting through physics to go into the unified field of nature and consciousness and to understand non-locality and the butterfly effect. They have asked what it would mean to look at causation in the holistic integral model rather than the ego-linear modes of /space/ and /time/.

In other examples, I get brilliant explorations in biology, in psychology, working toward alternative models of understanding psychic life. In economics, students have inquired into other ways of understanding economies and money, and the flow of ((money)), and the ((soul of money)) and so forth.

I find similar depth in the work of athletes, artists of all kinds. They find a connection from this root inquiry to their individual area of interest, whether it is music, the fine arts, architecture, or the nature of ((sacred spaces)). It's boundless really, the range of areas, the inter-religious dialogue that is possible when these ((connections)) are made by students.

MB: Let me see if I've understood part of the genius of what's so powerful for your students. Is it that you are giving them in, for example, the double-bracket, single-bracket notation and in the orientation that we've been talking about, a language, a terminology, for meaning that would have otherwise been implicit in their lives? Are you helping them to discern the footprint of the whole in the ways in which they're always already being entangled with something that is more than just ego-mental thinking? So in other words have you given them a place to name what has otherwise gone unnamed? Like the "dark matter" of meaning, the gravity that is holding it together? It seems that is why they are able to take it out in such diverse directions. I'm very impressed with what you were just going through with that list. It really suggests that you're working at a level of connection that goes much deeper than what we think of as the usual disciplines.

AG: Yes, that's actually very well put. It does indeed help them. The notation captures how all of us, all human beings, we do have our peak moments. Often we feel that they fall upon us. "I didn't know what happened when I fell in love and had this communion with this other person in an ((I-Thou)) moment. It was magic. I wish I knew how to do it again!" Because, falling in love is a kind of divine ((madness)). "It's out of my control," one feels. You know, those moments, we recognize them. But we don't have the ((technology)) to express what is happening because we are always situated in that powerful ((force field)) and it can overwhelm our ability to express it. We go into dreams, and we dream and we let go. It's the ego boxes that open up and relax and allow the more fluid flow of the unified ((seeing)) and our psyche to come up. When we dream, we don't know how to process the dream. We don't have the technology.

So the conflation of these two dimensions is in the egosphere and our ego-objectified technology and language dominates and deforms the source. It represses the ever-present possibilities of articulating and actually cultivating on a cultural level a lifetime of ((integral)), whole being living, quality living, that all of the great teachers are trying to teach us. And so, naming these two dimensions, artificial though it may be at first, disentangles these fields, allowing the /single bracket/ to be contra-distinguished from the ((double bracket)) dimension.

MB: The notation itself is a reminder, a means to bootstrap, to bring up this other perspective. Then I think that's what allows it to gain its own force so that the notation itself becomes not so important as the ability to actually effect those shifts and then to be able to recognize it as a difference that makes a difference. I would hope this to be the case with all such proposed integral ((technologies)) such as Wilber's AQAL model. The critical question is whether a given set of strategies can themselves be transcended at a certain point, put aside like a ladder that has helped you to climb a wall and, once you are atop the wall, becomes superfluous.

AG: We wouldn't need the single-bracket, double-bracket distinction, were it the case that our culture, higher education, and parenting somehow helped our kids to gain the literacy of ((integrated intelligence)) from early years and to know the grammatology of what we're calling the double-bracket integral state. If we collectively helped our children to gain bicultural literacy as to when they are ego-languaging and thinking and using that mental or mind operating system and taught them how to upgrade and develop ((skills)), intelligence, capacities, and ((literacies)) in the integral holistic dialogic patterns of using their intelligence, it would not be necessary. It is an intervention required because that is not the case (Gangadean, 2009, 2010).

Passing Through the Zero Point: Meta-Cognition as Gateway to
Integral Consciousness

MB: Well, you remind me, I was visiting a fifth grade classroom a few years ago. I was supervising some teachers. The teacher said, "OK, children I want you to reach back and turn on your brains." She would do this routinely before any activity requiring mental activity. It turned out to be very effective for her. You could see the kids literally reaching behind and sort of turning a little switch and rolling their eyes and feeling their brains coming on. What you're talking about is actually the next switch, which is, "OK, kids, turn on your integral mind."

So I think there is an understanding of these issues implicitly, even here with the fifth grade teacher; yet she wouldn't necessarily have known about the fact that it doesn't have to stop there. I think what we're talking about is that, actually, a very, very high level of rationality is not dogmatic. It is capable of questioning its own assumptions in real time. It is meta-cognitive. So I think when rationality becomes meta-cognitive, we're starting to pass through what I call the "zero point," which is sort of that in-between place between the single- and double-bracket worlds that we need to pass through. Meta-cognition is apparent in all the examples that you were talking about; there were critical moments where the students themselves recognized in themselves, in their own bodies, these patterns of ego-mentalism. And for such awareness to occur, one must already be standing somewhere outside of that stream of ego-mental consciousness. Then once one has recognized that, one can say, "Oh, if I'm not that, what am I, and where am I standing?" And it seems as though that becomes the teachable moment, if you will, and our job as teachers then becomes to cultivate the incipient meta-awareness. Does that make sense?

AG: Absolutely, in fact, it's a critical point because the integral intelligence is the maturation of rationality. Meta-cognition arises from ((integral interconnectivity)) and leads to an awareness wherein the mind sees itself surfing the deepest layer of the field of reality itself, that all the things that ((co-arise)) with mind are in dynamic interplay and that even language itself is working in that way. Students become familiar with the holistic fractal structure of ((reality)) and we begin to get integral ((literacy)). This is when rationality begins to mature and come to the fullness. That is the essence of ((moral)) consciousness.

MB: This is one of the important nexuses where the humanities approach that you're talking about could be really instrumental. I'm also struck by how diverse the wide range of folks that come to your classes are, which also speaks to the fact that even though you're teaching these "spiritual texts" you're doing it in a way that's honoring the scientific, the artistic, the thematic implications of those texts rather than seeing them, again as something behind glass.

In my linguistics courses, students tape a conversation in which they themselves participate. They transcribe it carefully and perform discourse, pragmatic and phonetic/phonological analyses. They end up learning the basics of linguistic analysis while at the same time cultivating a profound "linguistic mindfulness" that extends to all areas of their lives. This is a kind of meta-linguistic, meta-cognitive awareness of the power of language to create and sustain power dynamics and social and personal realities (akin to "critical language awareness;" Fairclough, 1992). It gives them a chance to cultivate their agency as communicators and knowers as well as helping them relate better to the people around them. In a way, I am asking them to treat their own everyday way of languaging as a sacred or philosophical text, subjecting it to the same scrutiny and attention that you devote to other texts.

Cultivating Global Citizenship

AG: It's remarkable because what you outlined in linguistic mindfulness is directly parallel to the kind of hermeneutical mindfulness, of the critical awareness about one's own mind-lens, the critical thinking faculties. I think you say it very well that this is really a more integral form of rational life and critical thinking.

You gestured to how this kind of linguistic mindfulness can even affect relationships. That's a very key point because in this day and age we are hopefully educating global citizens to go out into life, with critically awakened inner life, in the quality of their inner dialogue and the dialogue between persons in relationships. The aim is to build respectful relations in the workplace, in families, in the civic space of citizenship, as one would hope for in a true democracy. These skills of mindful discourse are cultivated through ((deep dialogue)) with awakened critical thinking between worlds. I think what we're both agreeing is that there is a dimensional shift into this integral awareness, seeing the big ship, the "mother ship" as you call it. This ((whole picture)) is not a mere footnote, not on the margins. It's not an aside. It's at the very heart of liberal arts education and the art of ((being human)) (Gangadean, 2006a).

Our present times call upon us to educate global citizens, competent and rationally literate persons who are capable, empowered with cultural literacy, inter-cultural literacy, and skills of being able to negotiate alternative mental ecologies or lenses, worldviews, ideologies, disciplines, forms of understanding. And to gain that kind of specific competence, skills, and literacy in negotiating diverse worlds is a hallmark of a well-educated liberal arts student and citizen in the twenty-first century (Gagadean, 2006b, 2006c).

Deep Dialogue: The Main Act

MB: I wonder if we can close by reflecting on the central place of deep dialogue in integral education. What has happened by default or unmindfully before in the way of dialogue needs to be fore-grounded and articulated more explicitly. I think one of our main points to the reader here will be that respectful, deep dialogue among diverse people is, in fact, the main act. It's essential for ((integral education)) if it is to resist being turned into another dogma competing in an intellectual marketplace. A kind of intellectual reification can happen with any ideas. For example, when as integral educators we put up the four quadrants of Integral Theory to guide our planning of a class, where we have one subjective experience and one intersubjective experience and one interobjective experience and so forth, it might seem that we have covered the material in an integral way. But simply having something from each quadrant in the curriculum by itself does not make for integral education. It may, in fact, be beside the point in that it makes us feel that we've done something "integralish" when we may simply be putting an old mind in a new bottle.

AG: That's what I find often. Quite often I get rather disappointed when "integral themes" are raised. I'm watchful to see if it's "integral" in the "/box/"? Is it "integral" in the bottle? Is it "integral" in the objectified content? And the presenter seeks to integrate the content within the ego-mental rational space. Or, by contrast, is "it" integral where it really ultimately matters—in the technology of consciousness? Or depending on whether we're using our minds in the ((integral calculus)) of holistic reason? Because if we're using the older /ego-mental calculus/ and we're talking the "integral" talk it's going to remain in the. It's going to remain dis-((integral.)) It's going to lay there in the quadrant of /integral/ thought.

To bring it to ((life)) is to move into the ((Integral Dimension))—into the living open space of deep dialogue. One of the geniuses of Socrates and Plato is to have linked rationality and dialogue. There is no accident that Plato was a genius in writing dialogues, bringing Socrates to life in the life of inquiry—through the "alchemy" of really open creative dialogue. It's the space of critical inquiry, rational growth, and becoming a whole human being. I've experienced this at the Language of Spirit Dialogues too, where you and I met (Bronson, 2004).

MB: Let's dedicate this chapter to a renaissance of such dialogues. We have attempted to embody our commitment to this model by having written it together through a dialogue process. And we offer it as a model for new ways of constructing text, new ways of constructing knowledge, new ways that are old ways. The idea has been to point the way in the format of the chapter itself toward what integral education looks like in practice.

AG: And I would just add by reconnecting with the theme you opened this conversation with—having a sense of responsibility in higher education. It is time to take responsibility for our discourse, for where we are on this road, and the importance of addressing the crises on the planet and cultivating and facilitating the growth of integral global citizens. These citizens must be equipped with the literacy and the rational skills and capacities to go into the world as whole beings, as mindful global citizens who will help bring forth sustainable global cultures through which the entire human family may flourish together with our Sacred Earth across all borders.

MB: And the good news is the pieces are already there in front of us. And it really is just about making a simple shift, albeit one that must be enacted in particular contexts—teaching philosophy and linguistics in our case—with as much patience, mindfulness, subtlety, and wisdom as we can muster. Therein lies the whole story.

AG: Well, it's been a pleasure dancing with you.

MB: Thank you for answering the door. And for leaving it open.

Note

1. For a more detailed presentation of this notation system and its logic, see Gangadean, A. (2008). *Meditations of Global First Philosophy*. Albany, NY: State University of New York Press.

References

Bennett, M. (2003). *Developing intercultural competence: A reader*. Portland, OR: Intercultural Communication Institute.

Bennett, M. (1993). Towards ethnorelativism: A developmental model of intercultural sensitivity. In M. Paige (Ed.), *Education for the intercultural experience* (pp. 21–71). Yarmouth, ME: Intercultural Press.

Bronson, M. C. (2009). The grammar of transformation: What ESL graduate students can teach the anthropology of consciousness. In M. C. Bronson, & T. Fields (Eds.), *So what? Now what?: The anthropology of consciousness responds to a world in crisis* (pp. 232–253). Newcastle-upon-Tyne, UK: Cambridge Scholars Publishing.

Bronson, M. C. (Ed.). (2005–2006). [Special double issue, Revisioning Higher Education], *ReVision 28*(3–4).

Bronson, M. C. (Ed.). (2004). *ReVision* [Special double issue, Language of Spirituality], *26*(3–4).

Bronson, M. C., & Gangadean, A. (2006). ((Circling)) the /square/: Reframing integral education discourse through deep dialogue, *ReVision, 28*(3), 36–47.

Chaudhuri, H. (1965). *Integral yoga: The concept of harmonious and creative living.* Wheaton, IL: The Theosophical Publishing House.

Csikszentmihalyi, M. (1988). *Flow: The psychology of optimal experience.* New York: Harper & Row.

Fish, S. (1988). *Is there a text in this class? The authority of interpretive communities.* Cambridge, MA: Harvard University Press.

Freire, P. (1970). *The pedagogy of the oppressed.* New York: Continuum Press.

Fairclough, N. (Ed.). (1992). *Critical language awareness.* London: Longman.

Gangadean, A., & Bronson, M. C. (2004). The quest for a global grammar, mythos and cosmology, *ReVision, 26*(3), 39–48.

Gangadean, A. (1993). *Meditative reason: Toward universal grammar.* Revisioning Philosophy Series. New York: Peter Lang

Gangadean A. (1997). *Between worlds: The emergence of global reason.* Revisioning Philosophy Series. New York: Peter Lang.

Gangadean, A. (2006a). A planetary crisis of consciousness: From ego-based cultures to a sustainable global world. *Kosmos: An Integral Approach to Global Awakening, 5*(2), 37–39.

Gangadean, A. (2006b). The awakening of global reason: The logical and ontological foundation of integral science. *World Futures,* January 2006, 56–74.

Gangadean, A. (2006c). Spiritual transformation as the awakening of global consciousness: A dimensional shift in the technology of mind. *Zygon (A Journal on Science and Religion),* June 2006, 381–392.

Gangadean, A. (2008). *Meditations of global first philosophy: Quest for the missing grammar of logos.* SUNY Series in Western Esoteric Philosophy. New York: SUNY Press.

Gangadean, A. (2009). *The awakening of the global mind: A new philosophy for healing ourselves and our world.* (Audio CD). Sounds True: Louisville, CO.

Gangadean, A. (2010). *Time, truth and logos: Quest for an integral global logic.* University Press of America.

Gardner, H. (1999). *Intelligence reframed.* New York: Basic Books.

Hawken, P. (2008). *Blessed unrest: How the largest social movement in history is restoring grace, justice and beauty to the world.* New York: Penguin Books

hooks, b. (1994). *Teaching to transgress.* New York: Routledge.

hooks, b. (2003). *Teaching community: A pedagogy of hope.* New York: Routledge.

Inda, J. X., & Renato, R. (Eds.). 2002. *The anthropology of globalization: A reader.* Malden, MA: Blackwell.

Montuori, A. (2006). The quest for a new education: From oppositional identities to creative inquiry. *ReVision, 28*(3), 4–20.

Palmer, P. (1997). *The courage to teach: Exploring the inner landscape of a teacher's life.* San Francisco: Jossey-Bass.

III

Case Studies

Jazz, Creativity, and Consciousness

A Blueprint for Integral Education

Ed Sarath

Introduction

In the Winter 2000 semester, I proposed a Bachelor of Fine Arts curriculum in Jazz and Contemplative Studies (BFAJCS) at The University of Michigan School of Music, Theatre, and Dance. The curriculum was designed to combine a full slate of coursework in jazz and overall musical training with about 25 credits of coursework that included meditation and other contemplative practices and studies.[1] It seemed like a perfect fit: Jazz's improvisatory core brings the field into close proximity with the heightened presence that is commonly associated with meditation practices, and the jazz tradition boasts a long legacy of artists—e.g., John Coltrane, John McLaughlin, Don Cherry, Wayne Shorter, Yusef Lateef, Sonny Rollins, and Herbie Hancock—who have deeply engaged with meditation and related spiritual pursuits in order to harness the synergistic interplay between these areas and their work and lives (Lewis, 2008; Berliner, 1994; Boyd, 1992). Improvisation, in fact, might be thought of as a kind of meditation in action; and meditation as improvisation in silence. Thus, while there would be no denying that this curriculum would venture into new academic terrain, it could also be seen as directly rooted in the creative and transpersonal richness of the jazz heritage in particular as well as contribute to explorations of the intersection between contemplation and creativity in general.

Despite this reasoning, the curriculum stirred a debate of epic proportions that essentially riveted this major school of music for a period of two months. Some colleagues argued that there was no place for meditation in an academic setting. Others asserted that meditation was a valuable tool from which students could benefit, but wondered how it might be taught and evaluated for course credit.

169

Still others viewed this curriculum as a pioneering venture that signified an effort to chart new educational terrain, and thus should be supported.

When the dust settled and the votes were tallied, the curriculum was approved by a solid two-thirds majority of the faculty. In this chapter I will attempt to illuminate the salient principles in which this curriculum is based, which I believe may be applied to wide-ranging areas and are key to advocacy of this work.

Overview of a Broader Educational Shift

In my view, the significance of the BFAJCS curriculum extends beyond its impact on the students and faculty directly involved. In fact, this curriculum may serve as a prototype for a new educational paradigm whose expanded terrain can be applied in a wide range of fields. I will refer to this emergent model as an "integral" approach, a heading that is inspired by an increasing body of cross-disciplinary work that is oriented toward an expanded vision of human development. Three central aspects of integral thought—ontological, developmental, and epistemological—may be cited as definitive of this perspective, with the work of the philosopher Ken Wilber (1999, 2006) regarded by many as a primary reference. The three aspects are represented in Wilber's (1999) four-quadrant model of the human being and cosmos—or to use, as Wilber does, the Pythagorean "Kosmos." The Upper-Left quadrant refers to individual subjective experience, the Lower Left to collective intersubjective experience. The Upper Right refers to individual objective experience, the Lower Right to the exterior physical world.

A developmental perspective applies equally to Left-Hand quadrants and Right-Hand quadrants with the former having levels of depth and the latter having levels of complexity. Regarding the individual, development entails growth along a number of parameters or "lines"—spiritual, cognitive, physical, emotional, relational, sexual, etc.—and proceeds through various "stages" (Wilber, 1999, pp. 50–59). An important aspect of integral thought is the possibility of consciousness development through states that Wilber (2006) categorizes as gross, subtle, causal, and non-dual—in which a widening awareness can occur along any of the lines of development.

Of particular significance to an integral education paradigm is the epistemological dimension, where transformational methodologies ranging from silent meditation to contemplative approaches to movement, creative arts, writing, reading, and interpersonal interaction are central. This rich process-continuum also includes conventional modes of learning as well. What is important is that all inquiry is informed by contact with the interior dimensions of consciousness. Wilber is outspoken in his advocacy of the arts as vehicles for this contact.

> This is art in its original and highest meaning: the subjective revelation of Spirit. When an artist is alive to the spiritual domains, he or she can

depict and convey those domains in artistic rendering, which wrestles Spirit into matter and attempts to speak through that medium. When great artists do so, the artwork then reminds us of our own higher possibilities, our own deepest nature, our own most profound ground, which we all are invited to rediscover. (1999, p. 394)

While integral values and approaches are explicitly evident in some "alternative" educational institutions—e.g., California Institute for Integral Studies, Naropa University, Maharishi University, JFK University (i.e., the School of Holistic Studies)—they represent significant departures from what typically constitutes learning in mainstream academe. Indeed, Michigan's BFA in Jazz and Contemplative Studies curriculum may be one of the very first initiatives at a mainstream university to notably incorporate integral principles. This curriculum will be explored below.

It is interesting to note that Wilber does not appear to venture significantly into any sort of mechanics of creativity and its relationship to the transformational results he ascribes to art. I believe that exploration of this dimension may illuminate important aspects of integral thought and will provide a brief overview of what this inquiry might look like. Let us consider education in terms of three components: subject, process, and object of knowledge. In other words, education involves a knower, a process of knowing, and an object of knowing, or in Esbjörn-Hargens' (2005) terms; the "who," "how," and "what" of integral learning. Conventional education has largely focused on the objective domain, which might be categorized as a third-person paradigm (Roth 2006, Sarath 2003, 2006), where what Gardner (1993) calls "logical mathematical" intelligence prevails. Integral education also spans process (i.e., epistemology—ways of knowing reality) and subjective dimensions, thus uniting third-person engagement with second- and first-person dimensions. Jazz study with a contemplative component exemplifies the rich objective, process, and interior/subjective dimensions of the integral paradigm. And due to jazz's capacity to not only juxtapose these aspects but to achieve a genuine synthesis, an integral jazz studies model may lay groundwork for new conceptions of the integral paradigm itself.

Let us briefly examine each category, beginning with the third-person approaches that conventionally prevail, to get a clearer sense of the scope of integral learning. We are so accustomed to coursework where the primary modes of study are lectures and readings centered around third-person content that we scarcely consider alternative modalities or goals. Third-person education is an important part of the emergent model, but as the dominant and exclusive orientation it is limited in both its assimilative mechanisms and the sense of meaning and purpose it promotes in the educational enterprise. Carl Rogers (1980) sums it up with his "mug-and-jug" analogy: "The instructor is the jug and pours information into the passive receptacle which is the mug, which is the student" (p. 189). Third-person education may be correlated with the distanced mode of inquiry that characterizes scientific method as it is conventionally construed, and while this subject-object divide has been challenged through scientific (e.g., quantum theory) and philosophical (postmodern critical theory) developments, it continues to prevail in the classroom.

Past decades have seen increased emphasis on the need for education to place greater emphasis on creativity (Rogers, 1980; Maslow, 1971; Smith, 1990; Palmer, 1998; Gardner,1993), which in its interactive aspects brings into play a second-person component. Here is where jazz, an idiom in which musicians improvise, perform, compose, and arrange as well as delve into ancillary theoretical, historical, and aesthetic concerns may excel; few other genres engage musicians in this kind of creative expanse. Literature on creativity, moreover, increasingly acknowledges the interior dimensions of the creative process (Richards, 2007; Senge et al., 2004; Nach-manovitch, 1990; Csikzsentmihaly, 1990; Maslow, 1971; Baruss, 2007; Montouri, 2003, 1994), at which point we begin to broach the first-person realm. Episodes of what is variously termed "flow," "peak experience," and "transcendence," to cite a few of the many terms to describe the heightened states of awareness invoked by practitioners in many fields, may be thought of as windows into the inner dimensions of creativity. Jazz musicians provide vivid testimonies of these states, among whose characteristics are enhanced flow of ideas, mind-body coordination, communion with surroundings, and heightened well-being.

Jazz pianist-psychologist Denny Zeitlin states that "very often I get into an altered state of consciousness where I feel that I'm really part of an audience, and that we're all listening to the music. In fact, we've become the music—everything has merged. And an audience can be tremendously helpful in reaching that ecstatic state . . . it's really magical when that happens . . ." (as quoted in Milano, 1984, p. 30). Jazz trombonist Melba Liston talks about extraordinary moments when "everybody can feel what each other is thinking . . . You breathe together, you swell together, you just do everything together, and a different aura comes over the room" (Berliner, 1994, p. 392). Violinist Stephen Nachmanovitch describes this union as a type of "entrainment," which he equates to the "trance states in the sama dances of the Sufis," where "the audience, the environment, and the players link into a self-organizing whole" (1990, p. 101).

Literature on transcendent experiences (James, 1962/1902; Murphy & White, 1995; Csikszentmihalyi 1990; Stace 1970) suggests that these experiences are often fleeting and difficult to invoke at will, leading some practitioners to pursue more formal, systematic methodologies such as meditation in order to gain more consistent experiences of heightened consciousness as well as integrate this experience into life. From this standpoint, I would suggest that a more complete representation of the core of first-person education is perhaps found in the transcendent experience invoked in meditation, where the dissolution of the egoic self and merging with a more expansive or unbounded realm of consciousness—hence the self uniting with the Self, or the first-person "I"—may be more pronounced:

Then, with increased familiarity . . . the process of transcending became more and more natural. The whole physiology was by now accustomed to just slipping within, and at some point it would literally "click," and with that the awareness would become fully expanded, the breath would almost cease, the spine would become straight, and the lungs would cease to move. There would be no weight anywhere in the body, the physiology was at rest. At this point, I began to appreciate that this inner silence was not an emptiness but simply silent consciousness without content or activity, and I began to recognize in it the essence of my own self. Eventually, even the thin boundary that had previously divided individuality from this silent consciousness began to dissolve. The "I" as a separate entity just started to have no meaning. The boundary that I put on myself became like a mesh, a net, it became porous and then just dissolved, only unbroken pure consciousness or existence remained . . . The physiology after that state is incredible. (Andresen, 1990, p. 313)

To be sure, this kind of quintessentially first-person educational experience is not a common topic in curriculum committee deliberations. And indeed, significant improvements would likely result if methodologies for this kind of experience were added to conventional third-person models. But integral education involves more than juxtaposition of diverse methodologies. Integral education involves a dynamic synthesis of first-, second-, and third-person learning in order that a more complete kind of development might unfold. At which point the questions arise: What would an integral model look like, and how do we as educators at mainstream institutions get there? Let me discuss briefly why an integral approach to jazz may serve as a prototype for movement in this direction.

Weaving Integral Threads:
The Importance of Epistemological Diversity

A central feature of the resultant integral model is the weaving of what I call "integral threads"—organic connections between first-, second-, and third-person kinds of inquiry—within and between the different experiences and courses in a curriculum. To varying degrees, students will weave these threads on their own, arguably even in the fragmented, epistemologically narrow curricular models that conventionally prevail. However, these models are not nearly as conducive to substantive integration of the three dimensions as is an integral model. A jazz curriculum with a contemplative component brings two powerful new epistemologies—improvisation and meditation—that promote movement in an integral direction. As we consider how these two epistemologies are rich in integral threads that interweave the three dimensions, several principles bear emphasis.

First is that every kind of inquiry or experience contains first-, second- and third-person aspects to varying degrees; it is not that mathematics, for example, is exclusively third-person and devoid of first- and second-person features. Wilber (2006) states: "every event in the manifest world has all three dimensions" (p. 19). What differs is which aspects prevail. The exquisite, attributeless silence of nirvakalpa samadhi, in which the personal egoic self merges with—sometimes described as dissolving into—the eternal Self, may be described as a primarily first-person experience. However, located within this totality of this self-Self union is a self-referential interactive process aspect that may be seen as a core kind of second-person experience. While relativistic objects of perception are transcended, the self-Self wholeness serves as a transcendent object of perception (Dillbeck, 1988) that embodies aspects of third-person experience. Accordingly, when I ascribe first-, second-, and third-person qualities to various integral epistemologies, I identify that which prevails and in no way suggest the other two are absent.

From this perspective, improvisation can be seen as a primarily second-person modality that not only contains, but also uniquely invites connections to, first- and third-person aspects. Meditation can be seen as a primarily first-person modality with fertile second- and third-person aspects and connections that may be harnessed. And conventional objective-analytical inquiry may be seen as primarily third-person with second- and first-person aspects, even if these are more dependent upon accompanying first- and second-person epistemologies. Here a further principle may be cited as we arrange these modalities within a unified learning model; this has to do with the respective integrative capacities of the modalities. First-person epistemologies, representing a more unified experience, have the greatest integrative capacities, second-person epistemologies are next in line, and third-person epistemologies, being most differentiated, are least integrative. Put another way: meditation, particularly if approached in the framework that I outline below, is most equipped to span first-, second-, and third-person dimensions; improvisation the next most equipped; and conventional analytical-objective inquiry the least. In no way is this a values hierarchy and in no way ought it be interpreted to privilege meditation and marginalize intellectual engagement. Rather, it is a recognition of an alignment that allows the synergistic relationship of the three epistemologies to be most optimally harnessed.

Meditation

Meditation arguably represents one of the most radical departures from conventional educational practice conceivable and as such warrants considerable attention when it comes to integrating this kind of practice in the academy. A landmark development for this kind of pedagogy in the United States has arguably been the *American Council of Learned Societies Contemplative Practice* program, which was launched in

1997 and has recently been subsumed by the *Center for the Contemplative Mind in Society*, which facilitated the ACLS program from its inception (Bush, 2005). The program has supported the design of coursework involving a contemplative component at over 100 academic institutions.

Having been a fellow in that program's first year and fairly active in the subsequent contemplative studies "movement" it has spawned, I have argued for a more nuanced approach to contemplative practice in order for this work to progress. My vision recognizes a wide diversity of practices and, while respecting the need for individuals to find what works best for them, also seeks to illuminate possible benefits and limitations from different approaches to practice.

A wide variety of meditation practices exist, from the silent sitting practices of a variety of mystical traditions, to movement meditations, to contemplative approaches to art, poetry, music, and theatre.[2] By taking time to withdraw from ordinary mental, physical, emotional, or other sensory engagement, meditation practices provide not just temporary glimpses of heightened consciousness—their ultimate aim is to cultivate the capacity for heightened consciousness throughout the whole of life. By regularly allowing the conscious mind to fathom deeper levels of itself, awareness becomes more receptive to transcendent infusion in and outside of meditation. Day-to-day experience and actions become increasingly grounded in a deeper and more expansive awareness. Qualities such as inner calm, well-being, freedom from anxiety, compassion, and unboundedness that are accessed in meditation begin to gradually become present in everyday life. A mounting body of scientific research provides objective support for these kinds of claims (Austin, 1998; Davidson, 2004; Travis et al. 2004).

Following are testimonies from some of my students about their experiences in meditation and the benefits they have gained:[3]

> [In meditation] . . . I experience a kind of immense stillness . . . a light-ness and calmness in my mind and body. If I have had a stressful day, I often feel as though a weight has been lifted off my shoulders.
>
> Meditation helps me . . . to relieve stress [and] is the perfect way to start the day because I open my eyes feeling elated and energized. After meditation I am much more calm and my mind is more clear to make better decisions.
>
> Meditation has allowed me to appreciate more deeply and fully the world around me. The colors of the sky, the movement of animals, the smells of trees and flowers on my walk to class, the feel of clothing on my body.
>
> I find myself more delighted in and excited about words, their sounds, and almost infinite connotations. I become more effortlessly engrossed in the novels and poetry I read, and also absorb more of their content and meaning.

For the purposes of integrating meditation practice into the academic world, and also to gain ultimate benefits from the practice, I believe it is important to distinguish between what I propose as *formal, quasi-formal,* and *non-formal* meditation practices. At first glance, these distinctions may seem to favor certain forms of meditation and exclude others. In fact, they promote a more nuanced understanding of meditation and contemplative practice that in fact allows for the very ideals of flexibility and inclusiveness being sought.

I propose three criteria as central to formal meditation practice. One is regularity of practice. *Formal* meditation is done daily, not just on occasion, just as formal musical study involves daily, not occasional practice. Second is a systematic understanding of the mechanics of the practice; how to meditate, the wide range of experiences that might constitute proper practice, how one deals with thoughts, agitation, and other experiences that may arise and be misunderstood as impediments. In most instances, this presumes direct contact with a teacher and affiliation with a meditation tradition, as opposed to learning meditation from a book. A third aspect extends directly from the second—the inclusion of theoretical models of the structure of consciousness and its development. Access to a teacher and tradition also provides analytical understanding of the nature of consciousness and the states and stages through which consciousness develops over time.

Needless to say, much of this context will be absent in *quasi-formal* meditation, which involves learning meditation from various media—books, CDs, DVDs, etc—or other sources outside of formal contexts as I have defined them above. The procedure for meditation from these sources may closely resemble those of formal frameworks. What differs is the broader set of criteria that comprise the formal environment—community, interaction with a teacher, tradition, advanced programs, etc. In no way does this suggest that a given individual might not benefit considerably from this kind of practice. It is simply to delineate in a more nuanced way the distinctions between kinds of engagement with meditation.

Non-formal meditation includes activities that induce transcendent states as a by-product but are generally not engaged with this as the primary or sole intention. Athletes, artists, writers, and scientists may rightfully describe their work as meditative (Murphy & White, 1995; Baruss, 2007). As discussed above, jazz musicians provide vivid testimonies of these experiences. But since such activities contain no analytical models of consciousness (as related to the particular endeavor and its transformational capacities) that might shed light on the significance of what is experienced, nor systematic procedures for insuring consistency of experience, nor for dealing with obstacles that might arise, they are categorized as non-formal rather than formal. Moreover, I do not believe it is unreasonable to surmise that the reason many jazz musicians have gravitated toward formal meditation practice is that they sensed a more complete kind of development might stem from these practices—one that informed not only their music but their overall lives. Murphy and White (1995), in fact, note a similar pattern among some athletes who have had profound episodes of transcendence during sports yet turned toward the more formal practice I am talking about. In both instances, it is not a question of one approach vs. the other, but rather the possibility of gaining the best of both worlds—weaving formal and non-formal practice.

A continuum of contemplative practice that spans formal and non-formal realms uniquely spawns rich integral threads. For example, a formal meditation tradition will provide first-person grounding and third-person theoretical engagement that is intimately linked with this grounding. Now the intellect focuses its gaze on some detail that is intimately connected to a personal experience, establishing a pattern where mind and feeling or intuition can inform each other in ways that rarely transpire in the strictly third-person conventional educational paradigm. Formal practice traditions that also involve some kind of physical, creative, or interactive engagement will invite the integration of second-person inquiry into the mix. If not, students may gain second-person experience through non-formal means, which are inherent in a jazz curriculum given its improvisatory foundations. Increasing interest in cross-disciplinary applications of jazz and improvisation suggest that corresponding second-person, interactive attributes may be accessed by more than practicing musicians (Kao, 1996; Barrett, 1998; Montouri, 2003, 1994). I will shortly delve into my own approach to improvisation study and practice to illuminate its second-person qualities.

While an implicit allegiance to formal over quasi-formal practice may be inferred in the above discussion, I must emphasize that my aim is not impose on students one approach over another but rather expose them to a continuum of possibilities so that they can make informed decisions as they embark upon a contemplative pathway. I emphasize that this is a personal decision and that no one can ultimately say what is best for someone else. At the same time, I believe it is important to acknowledge the benefits of affiliation with a formal lineage, particularly given the tendencies in today's world toward push-button approaches, whereby if gratification is not instant, one is prone to move on to something else. Here a simple Zen saying is apt: "Many shallow wells do not yield water." Forman (2004) and Lesser (1999), in their insightful commentaries on the emergent spiritual renaissance of the past several decades, both recommend grounding in tradition-based meditation practices, along the lines of my above argument, before venturing into more self-styled approaches. This point is not difficult to make with jazz students, who know well the rigor required in the acquisition of the skills necessary to play this music. It is not that, as some would have it, students need to close themselves off to all other music and focus on jazz, but they do need to invest a certain amount of energy in laying tradition-specific groundwork. Indeed, I teach a very eclectic approach to jazz and improvised music that places core grounding within a rich array of creative possibilities.

Most important in relationship to the present discussion are the integral threads that extend from formal practice and that may be even more profoundly interwoven through a formal—non-formal spectrum of engagement. Let us now look at the integral threads spawned by the primarily second-person improvisation process.

Improvisation: Second-Person Integral Entryway

Improvisation embodies second-person experience through its interactive nature. It also broaches first-person experience through its heightened sense of moment-to-moment creative flow, even if occurring in the midst of turbulent physical-mental-sensory-emotional engagement and bears important similarities to the heightened presence of meditation. Elsewhere (Sarath, 1996) I have proposed a consciousness-based model of the improvisation process that illuminates these connections. The essence of the model is that improvisers invoke an inner-directed, nonlinear kind of temporal conception in which relationships between moments and their past and future are subordinated. I contrast the nonlinear conception of the improviser with the linear, expanding temporality of the composer who, because of the discontinuity of the process (composers usually fashion works over a series of creative episodes that spans weeks if not months), is able to develop large-scale temporal relationships between moments and what precedes and follows them. I suggest that both temporalities serve as pathways to transcendence, but that the inner-directed, nonlinear time conception that drives improvisation, because it is conducive to interaction, most embodies second-person experience.

In my improvisation teaching, I use what I call "silence studies" to not only enhance the nonlinear temporal experience but also open up first-person connections. Here students are asked to create music that involves significant stretches of silence; I propose that they think of silence as the backdrop against which music flows, and that notes are but interruptions in the silence. But in these studies silence is more than just the time required for wind and brass players to take a breath; moments of silence are protracted passages in which no notes sound. I will sometimes follow silence studies with meditation, inviting students to simply enter the space they had just created in their music-making.

Rich third-person connections may be drawn from these first- and second-person platforms. Within the realm of music; Kramer's (1988) and Barry's (1990) work in musical time, Clifton's (1983) appropriation of Husserl's phenomenology to musical understanding, Meyer and Narmour's implication-realization theory (Narmour, 1990) are a few of the theoretical areas that may be directly broached. Beyond music, connections to consciousness studies through the transformational windows opened up through the work of Csikszentmihalyi, 1990; Maslow, 1971; Wilber, 2006; Forman, 1990; and Wade, 1996; temporality of language as seen in Lee's (1974) notions of lineal and nonlineal temporality; and a host of other psychological, aesthetic, philosophical, and cultural connections may be harnessed. As considered above in regard to the establishment of intuition-intellect links in formal meditation practice, as or more important than what is studied is the formation of patterns in which mind and feeling are linked; once these linkages are in place, a framework is at hand that can be developed to enhance any kind of third-person study. Let us now examine some of the coursework in which these connections are established and developed.

BFA in Jazz and Contemplative Studies Coursework as Frameworks for Integral Threads

The BFAJCS curriculum can be thought of in terms of three general areas. First is coursework in jazz and overall musicianship studies, which comprises roughly two-thirds of the curriculum. Next is a slate of classes offered by various units across campus (e.g., psychology, philosophy, cultural studies, religious studies) that include a contemplative studies component of one kind or another (practice, theory, or both). Most of these classes existed before the BFAJCS curriculum was designed, but several were either explicitly created for the curriculum or altered to take on a greater contemplative aspect once the program was in place. Third are electives that students take to complete the 120 credits required by the curriculum. While in this first stage of development of the program, integral strands that interweave first-, second-, and third-person experience by no means pervade the entire curriculum, a look at the instances in which these strands are intact suggest that promising further inroads may be indeed be made in this direction, laying groundwork for integral strides not only in jazz but for a variety of fields.

Above I mentioned improvisation training approached with a contemplative orientation. This dovetails nicely with two courses taught with a more overt contemplative thrust. One is Creativity and Consciousness (CC), the other is Contemplative Practice Seminar (CPS). It should be emphasized that these classes, while listed within the Jazz Department, are open to and attended by students from across the university. Out of 25 students, perhaps a third at most will be majors in Jazz and Contemplative Studies. In Creativity and Consciousness, students are introduced to meditation and related practices (contemplative movement, writing, drawing, etc.) and basic theoretical ideas corresponding to this work. Readings are drawn from authors such as Csikszentmihalyi, Wilber, Maslow, Jung, Murphy and White, Forman, and Lesser and aim to trigger dialogue, thinking, and writing projects related to the emergent integral paradigm. Students often resonate with the idea of a "trans-traditional" spirituality, or the growing interest in a "spiritual-but-not-religious" segment of the population, even if some if not many students are affiliated with religious traditions. The majority of students report having had some fairly dramatic instance of "flow" or "peak experience" and this serves as an excellent entryway into the terrain of the course.

Contemplative Practice Seminar engages students more deeply in contemplative practice. Readings, writings, and discussions pertaining to theoretical ideas continue but now students are expected to sustain some kind of regular practice for the length of the term. They are exposed to the range of possibilities described above—formal, quasi-formal, non-formal—and encouraged to use this semester as a unique opportunity to explore ways of knowing and being that, while veering significantly from how education is generally construed, may have important transformational benefits. In addition to conventional assignments (written essays) and grading criteria (attendance, participation in discussions), students are required to keep a journal in which they log and reflect on their experiences in contemplative practice.

BFA in Jazz and Contemplative Studies majors take four terms of Contemplative Practice Seminar in order that they have available a framework for sustained engagement in practice. While multiple semesters of a single course heading may not be the norm in much of education, it is commonplace in music both in the realm of ensembles (e.g., classical music students enroll in symphony orchestra and chamber music even up to eight terms apiece) and private lessons. Just as the repertory studied in music ensembles and lessons changes, both the student rosters and the inner landscapes traversed in Contemplative Practice Seminar also may change, effectively making each semester in this course significantly different from that previous.

And it is within these classes that the first-, second-, and third-person integral threads noted above are woven together, providing a foundation from which students may then make these connections on their own to other studies. For example, a continuum of contemplative practice in CC and CPS courses that ranges from silent sitting meditation to contemplative movement and writing and interactive activities spans first- and second-person terrain. Readings, discussion, and writings around theoretical topics yield strong connections to third-person learning. Jazz students, moreover, have the advantage of robust improvisatory engagement as well as intensive craft studies (music theory, technique, history, aesthetics, etc.) that exemplify the second-to-third-person part of the continuum.

Concluding Thoughts

Perhaps one of the most compelling aspects of the integral paradigm is its capacity to unite the best of conventional, third-person education within an expanded first-, second- and third-person synthesis. Movement in an integral direction therefore need not be seen as a compromise of the "tried and true" and might even be seen as a strengthening of conventional approaches due to the connections inherent in a broader range of experiences. Esbjörn-Hargens (2007, current volume) and Gunnlaugson (2004, current volume) emphasize the capacity for integral education to bridge the long-standing divide between conventional and alternative education by acknowledging the important contributions provided by both realms. An integral model takes us beyond the either-or dichotomy and allows us to have the best of conventional and alternative worlds, if not more.

I have attempted to show how a field such as jazz, particularly when involving a contemplative component, might be particularly conducive to movement in an integral direction. While one might argue that the addition of a contemplative aspect to any field of study may steer that field in an integral direction, the improvisation-meditation continuum that is possible in jazz provides a uniquely fertile ground for integral connections to be established and developed that span the first-, second-, and third-person dimensions that are central to integral education. In weaving "integral threads" between students' inner experiences and wide-ranging intellectual areas, important inner linkages between intuition, feeling, body, and mind are made that transform education from a data-input model to one that makes possible a far more complete kind of mental-emotional-creative-spiritual development.

On our campus, a debate has begun to rekindle recently about the educational experience of student-athletes. Concerns have been expressed about athletes gravitating toward less rigorous curricular pathways and thus either graduating with an inferior education or, in many cases, not graduating at all. While these concerns are long-standing and legitimate, they overlook an important point. That is, the epistemological spectrum traversed by athletes is far closer to an integral paradigm than that of most conventional students, and that from this standpoint much more egregious deficiencies may be found in the curricular pathways pursued by most of the student body. Think about it: Student athletes—particularly those playing football, soccer, hockey, basketball—improvise. They invoke dramatic episodes of flow, often manifesting as heightened mind-body coordination and present-moment awareness (Murphy & White, 1995). It is not uncommon for athletic departments to bring in mind-body consultants who introduce student-athletes to meditation and related practices to help them invoke these experiences on a more consistent basis. Student-athletes integrate intensive analytical focus (e.g., study of game film, techniques, learning play books, etc.) with these heightened intuitive, improvisatory, and transpersonal moments, thus weaving strong integral threads that might be harnessed in entirely new kinds of coursework by an astute university. Yes, there is an educational crisis at hand, and it is to be found in the exclusively conventional, third-person education prevailing in the humanities and sciences and specialized professional schools, where the integral engagement and resultant threads found in athletics and arts are absent. Rojcewicz (1999): "Higher education as we know it is ill" (p. 2).

The arts, embodiments of what Rojcewicz (2001) calls "noetic learning," are more likely to cure academe than athletics. But if headway in this direction is to be made, an understanding of the depth to which the reigning paradigm is rooted in opposing values will be essential. Indeed, even the arts are not immune to exclusion of second-person (let alone first-person) experience. Colleagues outside of music are often surprised to learn the extent to which improvisation, central to the epistemological core I am advocating as well as most of the world's music, is marginalized in musical study (Sarath, 2002; Schuller, 1986). With jazz students (who generally form a distinct minority at most schools) being a notable exception; most music majors graduate with little or no training in this core process. Thus, even with creativity having attained buzzword status on most campuses, progress remains elusive on this front in music. One can thus imagine the even greater obstacles inherent in advocating contemplative practice, which while a first-person integral pillar is hardly a buzzword in the academy. Indeed, it is difficult to imagine a better example of paradigmatic change than the shift from conventional to integral education.

Nonetheless, I am optimistic that this kind of change will ultimately manifest. When and how remain to be seen. Undoubtedly, small inroads similar to that which I have made in my work in jazz and contemplative studies will be key. I hope my reflections on this work are helpful to colleagues across fields who seek to make similar inroads.

Notes

1. In this chapter I use the terms meditative practices and contemplative approaches interchangeably. Distinctions that do exist between them are beyond the scope of this chapter.

2. Some excellent sources for meditation practice are Goleman (1996); Shear, (2006); and DePraz, Varela, & Vermerschj (2003).

3. Testimonies from journals of students enrolled in Jazz 455 Creativity and Consciousness and Jazz 450 Contemplative Practice Seminar courses at the University of Michigan.

References

Alexander, C. & Langer, E. (Eds.). (1990). *Higher stages of human development*. New York: Oxford University Press.

Andresen, J. (2000). Meditation meets behavioral medicine. *Journal of Consciousness Studies*, 7(11), 17–74.

Austin, J. (1998). *Zen and the brain*. Cambridge, MA: MIT.

Barrett, F. (1998). Creativity and Improvisation in jazz and organizations: Implications for organizational learning. *Organization Science*, 9(5), 1–23.

Barry, B. (1990). *Musical time*. Stuyvesant, NY: Pendragon.

Baruss, I. (2007). *Science as a spiritual practice*. Charlottesville, VA: Imprint Academic.

Berliner, P. (1994), *Thinking in jazz: The infinite art of improvisation*. Chicago: The University of Chicago.

Boyd, J. (1992). *Musicians in tune*. New York: Simon and Schuster.

Bush, M. (2005). Foreword. *Teachers College Record*, 108(9), 1721–22.

Clifton, T. (1983). *Music as heard*. New Haven: Yale University Press.

Csikszentmihalyi, M. (1990). *Flow: The psychology of optimal experience.* New York: Harper and Row.

Davidson, R. (2004). Long-term meditators self-induce high amplitude gamma synchrony during mental practice. *National Academy of Sciences Review, 101*(46), 16309–16373.

Depraz, N. Varela, F., & Vermersch, P. (Eds.). (2003). *On becoming aware: advances in consciousness research.* Amsterdam: John Benjamins.

Dillbeck, M. (1988). The self-interacting dynamics of consciousness as the source of the creative process in nature and in human life. *Modern Science and Vedic Science, 2*(3), 245–279.

Esbjörn-Hargens, S. (2005). Integral ecology: The what, who, and how of environmental phenomena. *World Futures, 61*(1), 5–49.

Esbjörn-Hargens, S. (2007). Integral teacher, integral students, integral classroom: Applying integral theory to education. *AQAL: Journal of Integral Theory and Practice, 2*(2).

Forman, R. (Ed.). (1990). *The problem of pure consciousness.* New York: Oxford.

Forman, R. (2004). *Grassroots spirituality.* Charlottesville, VA: Imprint Academic.

Gardner, H. (1993). *Multiple intelligences: The theory in practice.* New York: Basic Books.

Goleman, D. (1996). *The meditative mind: Varieties of meditative experience.* New York: Penguin.

Gunnlaugson, O. (2004). Toward an integral education for the Ecozoic era: A study in transforming the global learning community of the Holma Institute for Integral Studies. *Journal of Transformative Education, 2*(4), 313–335.

James, W. (1962). *The varieties of religious experience.* New York: Penguin. (1st ed., 1902). New York: Longman, Green and Co.

Kao, J. (1996). *Jamming: The art and discipline of business creativity.* New York: Harper Collins.

Kramer, J. 1988. *The time of music.* New York: Schirmer.

Kuhn, T. (1962). *The structure of scientific revolutions.* Chicago: University of Chicago.

Lee, D. (1974). Codifications of Reality: Lineal and nonlineal, in *The Nature of Consciousness,* Robert Ornstein (Ed.), pp. 128–142. New York: Viking.

Lesser, E. (1999). *The new American spirituality: A seeker's guide.* New York: Random House

Lewis, G. (2008). *A power stronger than itself: History of the AACM and American experimental music.* Chicago: University of Chicago.

Maslow, A. (1971). *The farther reaches of human nature.* New York: Penguin.

Milano, D. (1984). The psychology of improvisation. *Keyboard Magazine, 10*(10), 30–35.

Montouri, A., & Purser, R. (1994). Miles Davis in the classroom: Using the jazz ensemble metaphor for enhancing team learning. *Journal of Management Education, 18,* 21–31.

Montouri, A. (2003). The complexity of improvisation and the improvisation of complexity: social science, art and creativity. *Human Relations, 56*(2), 237–255.

Murphy, M. and White, R. (1995). *In the zone: Transcendent experience in sports.* New York: Penguin.

Nachmanovitch, S. (1990). *Free play: The power of improvisation in life and the arts.* Los Angeles: Tarcher.

Narmour, E. (1990). *The analysis and cognition of basic melodic structures.* Chicago: The University of Chicago.

Palmer, P. (1998). *The courage to teach.* San Francisco: Jossey-Bass.

Richards, R. (Ed.). (2007). *Everyday creativity and new views of human nature: Psychological, social, and spiritual perspectives.* Washington, DC: American Psychological Association.

Rogers, C. (1980). *Dialogues.* Boston: Houghton-Mifflin.

Rojcewicz, P. (2001). *Noetic Learning through music and the arts: A view from the conservatory.* Rattapallax Press eBooks.

Rojcewicz, P. (1999). *Imagination and poetic knowing in higher education.* Rattapallax Press.

Roth, H. (2006). Contemplative studies: Prospects for a new field. *Teachers College Record, 108*(9). 1787–181.

Sarath, E. (1996). A new look at improvisation. *Journal of Music Theory, 40*(1), 1–39.

Sarath, E. (2002). Improvisation and curriculum reform. *The New Handbook of Research on Music Teaching and Learning.* New York: Oxford University Press.

Sarath, E. (2003) Meditation in higher education: the next wave? *Innovative Higher Education, 27*(4), 215–234.

Sarath, E. (2006). Meditation, creativity, and consciousness: Charting future terrain within higher education. *Teachers College Record, 108*(9), 1816–1841.

Senge, P., Scharmer, O., Jaworski, J., & Flowers, B., (2004). *Presence: An exploration of profound change in people, organizations, and society.* New York: Currency Doubleday

Schuller, G. (1986). *Musings.* New York: Oxford.

Shear, J. (Ed.). (2006). *The experience of meditation.* St. Paul, MN: Paragon House.

Smith, P. (1990). *Killing the spirit: higher education in America.* New York: Viking.

Stace, W. (1970). *Mysticism and philosophy.* London: Macmillan.

Travis, F., Alexander, C., & Dubois, D. (2004). Psychological and physiological characteristics of a proposed object-referral/self-referral continuum of self-awareness. *Consciousness and Cognition, 13,* 401–420.

Wade, J. (1996). *Changes of mind: A holonomic theory of the evolution of consciousness.* Albany: SUNY Press.

Wilber, K. (1999). *Integral psychology. Collected works,* Vol. 4. Boston: Shambhala.

Wilber, K. (1998). *The marriage of sense and soul: Integrating science and religion.* New York: Broadway Books.

Wilber, K. (2006). *Integral spirituality.* Boston: Shambala/Integral Books.

Grounding Integral Theory in the Field of Experience

Terri O'Fallon

Introduction

Inspired by the promise and potential of being able to make a difference that matters in a world full of suffering, Pacific Integral was born out of the commitment of four entrepreneurs to pursue a path of discovery. Pacific Integral is a privately run educational program for professionals interested in leadership development from a variety of backgrounds, focusing on applying integral theories as informed by our lived experience. This chapter will describe some key aspects of the learning process from our seven-year experiment. I will briefly outline how we developed our educational program, and how this experience enabled us to develop our understanding of Integral Theory. I will then describe how our experiences and research in both of these areas spawned new insights into the relationship between state/awareness stages, the structural/adult development stages, and behavior along with the models generated from these insights. This brief chapter focuses on how this model was developed within an integral educational context. However, in the conclusion I discuss three elements of our integrated educational context, which have contributed to accelerated developmental growth both vertically and horizontally. It is my hope that by sharing our discoveries with other educators we can support the ongoing effort to design new learning communities, which support human growth and development in unprecedented ways.

Developing Integral Services

Our first attempts to teach students to apply Integral Theory in practical ways were easier said than done. The first step on such a path is often to teach the

185

work didactically and/or cognitively without much of an experiential or applied component. This often follows from an assumption that students can simply go out and skillfully apply a theory once they have intellectually understood it. We aimed to avoid this pitfall with the Generating Transformative Change program we developed. The curriculum was envisioned from initial experimentation using the AQAL model of Integral Theory (Wilber, 2006), in addition to other well-respected work in the field included Kegan and Lahey's Seven Languages of Transformation (2001), Adaptive Leadership propounded by Heifetz (1994, 2002), Developmental Action Inquiry by Bill Torbert (2004), and Spiral Dynamics with Beck and Cowan (1996). The focus of our design for the 18-month long program was to engage participants in actual experiences of applying integral elements to their work and their lives, with six intensives lasting five days where participants received initial supervised practice and inter-sessions where they would apply these practices to their daily lives, returning to the next intensive for a deeper layer of learning. From this, a mode of continual adaptation and re-envisioning became a way of life very early on in the development of our services as we began our attempt to answer for ourselves, "What really is the embodiment of Integral Theory, and what is our particular expression of it?"

Applied Research in the Field

It became apparent that our co-learning would be far more potent if we had a keener understanding of the effectiveness of our program and if we could document change in our participants. Thus, we decided it was important to deepen our understanding of developmental levels in adults and began using Susanne Cook-Greuter's (2002) Leadership Development Framework (LDF) assessment process. This inventory documents nine adult levels of maturity, from earliest to latest: Impulsive, Opportunist, Diplomat, Expert, Achiever, Individualist, Strategist, Construct Aware, and Unitive. Applying these inventories to our population, which included every participant that came into our program as well as the faculty, helped us understand adult developmental maturity in ourselves, our participants, and ultimately of each cohort's collective general level. This proved to be one of the greatest revelations of our dynamic experiment. Robert Kegan (1994) asserts that generally people do not move more than one stage in less than two to five years, yet we are finding that a one- or two-stage change is a common occurrence for those who have completed our 18-month program.[1] This research has been invaluable in our understanding of program development, and our own embodied understanding of what people typify when they score at any one of these nine levels on this scale.

Learning from the Research

The initial scores immediately helped us become aware of how inadequate we were in imagining where our participants and we were in these levels of adult development. Some people who seemed incredibly wise and insightful tested at earlier levels of development than others who had remarkable capabilities but did not seem to have the same quality of awareness and wisdom. This put us into a disorienting dilemma; our expectations based on our understanding of theory were out of line with our experience. While we had used and taught models of developmental structure stages and state stages for several years, it now became clear that it was primarily from an intellectual understanding. With these results, we began to experience a far more nuanced understanding of how the development of structure stages (represented by the LDF pre- and post-testing) related to the state stages (our experience with people's capacity for awareness). Our implicit understanding related to our phenomenological experience with real human beings became more visible to us. As a result, we are developing our own theory related to the developmental structure stages tested by the LDF and the state stages (O'Fallon, 2007).[2]

Grounded Model of the Adult Development Structure Stages, State Stages, and Behaviors

What we have noticed is that the interpenetration of the state stages and the structure stages in the world of real human beings is difficult to untangle. An early level Achiever with prodigious awareness often has an equal or greater impact on the work that is being done as a second-tier Strategist whose awareness is less developed. Our participants and clients, upon receiving their LDF results, seemed to intuitively recognize this, knowing their own contributions and those of others. At first this was a puzzle to us, but as we worked with our experience our own model began to unfold. We began to look at the space of awareness each participant could hold relative to the interpenetration of his or her state stages and structure stages.

Awareness: Consciousness Roaming Space

Figure 15 (next page) shows the mapping of the developmental structure stages and the awareness state stages. It represents the relationship between the structure states (on the left) and the state stages (on the right).

If you draw a line from the structure stage of a person's adult developmental level on the left, to their mature state/awareness stage on the right, a triangle is

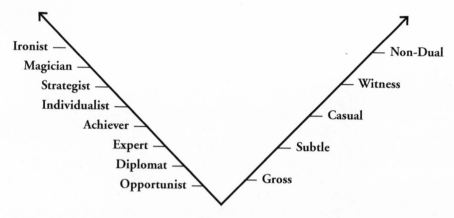

Figure 15. Map of Structure Stages and State Stages

formed which depicts a visual representation of the consciousness space within which a person has to roam (Fig. 16).

If you overlay someone else's "room to roam" designation on the same diagram, you can compare the spaces of the two triangles (Fig. 17). You can see that the space occupied by each person is different, but the size of the space is similar. In this hypothetical case, the Achiever "roaming space triangle" represents as much, or more consciousness space as the Strategist has because, in this depiction, the Achiever has attained levels in the state stages where the Strategist has not, whereas the Strategist has attained levels in the structure stages, which the Achiever has not.

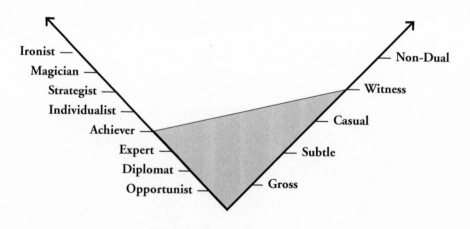

Figure 16. Consciousness Space

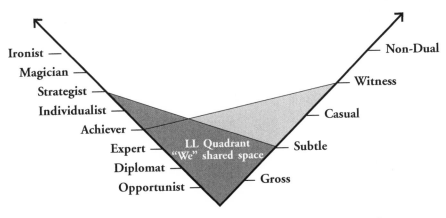

Figure 17. Comparison of Developmental Stages and State/AWARENESS STAGES

In addition, the space below the crossing lines depicts the two people's Lower-Left quadrant (LL) shared space, showing the likely "We" space the two can comfortably engage in; in this case, the Achiever would not likely be able to take a fourth-person perspective (a capacity developed at a later developmental level) and the Strategist would not likely be able to understand the later level of states (witnessing) that the Achiever seems to have.

Figure 18 adds yet another dimension we observed. The third leg of this diagram, the line down from the V, represents the behavioral skills that each

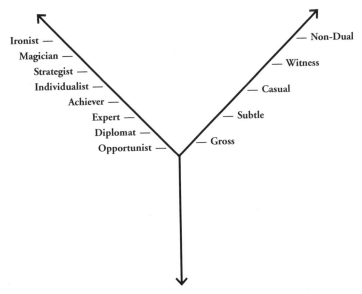

Figure 18. Behavior/Skills

person has. A person may have a later structural stage and good awareness but still not have particular skills and behaviors they need to navigate in the world successfully. In our empirical observations all three legs of this diagram are needed for balance.

Thus this simple diagram supports a more realistic and complex understanding of a person than any one of these areas would alone. In general it represents our experience of the interpenetration of state and structure stages, which corresponds to the Upper-Left quadrant in Wilber's (2006) AQAL model. The shared space corresponds to the Lower-Left quadrant and the behaviors line represents the right quadrants. This is a more robust model of real people who are learning to lead and who are working in organizations.

What Works?—Concluding Thoughts

After nearly seven years of dynamic steering and experimentation, testing, and learning from this process we are adding to our understanding of the application of Integral Theory in the real world of business and life. We have a plethora of experiences that exemplify the application of Integral Theory using a practical, seamless teaching approach that facilitates the development of applied perspectives in the world, which we are documenting with a research-based process. Through this we can adjust the teaching approach of our curriculum to the appropriate presentation methods related to the ways people are more likely to receive the material, while also designing experiences which open to the emergence of the disorienting dilemmas that occur naturally in group life. We feel that the following features of our program have been important factors in any initial successes.

1. We usually have representatives of at least four levels of development in each cohort, and through the natural exposure to people of many levels, including the faculty presence, we theorize that this creates a multilayered horizontal and vertical influence that contributes to developmental growth of the individuals. As depicted in the diagrams above, we experience that there are roaming spaces that overlap amongst people in a collective, and there are also roaming spaces that do not overlap. There appears to be a pull from the spaces that do not overlap, which may provide enough exposure to provoke a developmental change, or movement to a later structure stage. They may also receive enough exposure to states, to evoke growth into later state-stages.

2. We have designed a container of learning, which seems to remove the cultural cap to development. In these containers, others do not

impede their group members from natural personal exploration and precocious learning, an experience that is often uncommon in their usual milieu. It is our sense that people have the capacity to grow both horizontally and vertically as a result of an open environment and that interpersonal and systemic containers that we are normally embedded in may impede individual development. Thus we design a learning context that encourages exploration and actively works throughout the 18 months with individual and collective projection in the moment, insights about group paradoxes as they arise, and individual and group shadow. These and a myriad of other practices allow individuals and the collective to witness themselves explicitly rather than to live in the paralysis of non-aware engagement that many collectives embody implicitly. Developmental changes, however, occur in a context, so in addition to these internal transformations, we engage these individuals and the collective with applied integral skill sets (the third leg in the diagram above). We have real world service projects for our cohorts to work within, which begin with simple definition and recognition, then move to practice, embodiment, and finally creative adventuring related to their work in the world. These external projects combined with the internal cultural workings of the cohorts themselves seem to raise the cultural cap on their development.

3. We experience the influence of teaching awareness practices on developmental growth, and also the reciprocal effect of development on awareness, if the two previous points are in place. Each level of development has a natural awareness that arises with it. For example, the conventional Achiever is reflective or has developed awareness after the fact. Through the developmental stages this capacity for awareness seems to come closer and closer to the moment, and individuals gradually become aware of a wider range of subtle phenomena. By teaching awareness practices explicitly, there can be a possible influence toward the movement into to the later structure (and state) stages. While increased awareness itself is not enough to move to a later stage, it is a necessary component: that missing component can prevent movement forward. Likewise, when people develop structurally through the developmental stages, by nature of the stage attainment they also develop awareness. However that awareness can be more or less robust and not activated well given certain contexts, so awareness practice can bring a more full-bodied expression of one necessary component of a stage. Also the third leg of the diagram above puts both the structure stages

and the state stages in action and embodiment, so experience in
a variety of contexts also conditions these two factors.

Our empirical and grounded experience indicate that balancing these three collective elements is supportive of the development of both individuals and collectives,
of bringing wisdom to the personhood of our participants and the culture of their
cohorts, and of developing numerous skills and behaviors that can be used in a
variety of worldwide contexts.

Notes

1. I recognize that Kegan's developmental stages span slightly broader ranges than
those we are measuring using the LDF. The relevant take-away for us is that through sup-
plying an appropriately challenging and supportive environment for integrative learning,
structure stage development can be accelerated beyond what is typical in the developmental
literature.
2. This model is similar to the Wilber-Combs Lattice (Wilber, 2006), which uses
an X and Y axis to represent state stage and structure stage development.

References

Beck, D., & Cowan, C. (1996). *Spiral dynamics: Mastering values; leadership and change.*
    Malden MA: Blackwell Publishers.
Cook-Greuter, S. (2002). Ego development. 9 levels of increasing embrace. Unpublished
    manuscript.
Heifetz, R. (1994). *Leadership without easy answers;* Cambridge, MA: Belknap/Harvard
    University Press.
Heifetz, R., & Linsky, M. (2002). *Staying alive: Leadership on the line.* Cambridge, MA:
    Harvard Business School Press.
Kegan, R. (1994). *In over our heads. The mental demands of modern life.* Cambridge, MA:
    Harvard University Press.
Kegan, R., & Lahey, L. (2001). *How the way we talk can change the way we work: seven
    languages for transformation.* San Francisco: Jossey Bass.
O'Fallon, T. (2007). Leadership and the interpenetration of structure and state stages—A
    subjective exposé. *Integral Leadership Review, 7*(5) Retrieved June 1, 2008 from http://
    www.integralleadershipreview.com/archives/2007-11/2007-11-article-ofallon.html
Torbert, W. (2004). *Action inquiry: The secret of timely transforming leadership.* San Francisco.
    Berrett-Koehler Publishers Inc.
Wilber, K. (2006). *Integral spirituality: A startling new role for religion in the modern and
    postmodern world.* Boston: Shambhala.

An Open Way of Being

Integral Reconceptualization of Mathematics for Teaching

Moshe Renert and Brent Davis

Introduction

Mathematics for Teaching (MfT) is a burgeoning branch of math education research framed by the question, *What mathematics do teachers need to know in order to teach mathematics?* In this chapter, we offer a genealogy of the field by correlating the evolutions of the objective, subjective, interobjective, and intersubjective strands of MfT. In the process, we point to multiple evolutionary tensions, including stability versus novelty of mathematical knowledge, school math versus grander mathematics, mathematics as a science versus mathematics as a humanity. We argue that teachers' mathematical knowledge should be understood as an open disposition—that is, as a pedagogical readiness to recognize evolutionary tensions as they arise and to harmonize them dialectically. This open disposition infuses the teaching of mathematics with meaning and life, and promotes cultural evolution.

What is "Mathematics for Teaching?"—Four Answers

Mathematics for teaching is an area of mathematics education research that studies connections between teaching and the subject matter of mathematics. Research in this area is organized around the primary question, What *mathematics* do teachers need to know in order to teach mathematics?

For much of the twentieth century, answers were taken to be self-evident. It was assumed that knowledge of advanced mathematics was required in order to teach grade school math. This assumption is still enacted in the vast majority of teacher education programs today. Pre-service teachers are typically required to obtain college credits in post-secondary mathematics, and prospective secondary teachers are often required to complete university degrees in mathematics prior to enrolling in education. However, contrary to this line of reasoning, as Begle (1979) showed, there is little or no correlation between teachers' college math credits and the performance of their students.

Interest in MfT arose in the late 1990s in response to this worrisome finding. At that time, most researchers (e.g., Ball & Bass, 2000) framed their work in terms of Shulman's (1986) notion of Pedagogical Content Knowledge (PCK). PCK is a specialized type of teacher's knowledge that links content and pedagogy. It includes, for example, familiarity with certain forms of abstract representation that a teacher might use to help students better comprehend complex mathematical ideas. Developing this notion in the context of mathematics, Ma's (1999) study of contrasts between Chinese and American teachers provided evidence of highly specialized knowledge in elementary mathematics teaching. Ma used the name Profound Understanding of Fundamental Mathematics (PUFM) to refer to this knowledge, and described it as a broad awareness of the horizontal and longitudinal connections among the concepts that comprise grade-school mathematics curricula. This contribution triggered a revision of the orienting question of MfT among researchers, as they began to ask, What *specialized mathematics* (i.e., PCK) do teachers need to know in order to teach mathematics?

But the answers remained elusive. It was not clear what set of specialized concepts and results could constitute a body of mathematics useful for teaching. Oriented by this problematic, Ball and Bass (2003) suggested a new vantage point by pointing out that the mathematical knowledge of teachers is not static, and that it should be thought of as knowledge-in-action. In their view, mathematics teaching is a form of mathematical practice that includes interpretation and evaluation of students' work, correlation of students' mathematical results with the processes of their production, construction of meaningful explanations, and assessment of curriculum materials. Ball and Bass called for a practice-based theory of MfT that focuses on the specific knowledge that teachers use in their daily work. As might be expected, they also proposed an updated framing question for the study of MfT: What mathematical knowledge is entailed by the work of teaching mathematics?

Ball and Bass's preliminary research focused attention on a key process of teachers' mathematical practice that they called *unpacking*. For them, unpacking is the prying apart and explicating of mathematical ideas to make sense of their constituent images, analogies, and metaphors. Whereas mathematicians often convert their ideas into highly condensed representations to facilitate mathematical manipulation, teachers employ the reverse process of unpacking ideas to reveal and explain the meanings of mathematical constructs. Adler and Davis (2006) have also studied unpacking, along with other aspects of teachers' mathematical work. Their somewhat worrisome findings were that mathematical ideas addressed in teacher education courses in South Africa are predominantly compressed, not unpacked.

The three framings of MfT noted above share one key quality: They are constrained in scope to the immediate worlds of teachers and their students. Davis and Simmt (2006) critiqued this limitation. Drawing on a complexity framework, they argued that teachers' knowledge of established mathematics is inseparable from knowledge of how mathematics is established. Any distinction between the two is inherently problematic since it ignores the similar nonlinear dynamics that underlie categories of both knowledge and knowing. Davis and Simmt broadened the notion of MfT to include multiple nested systems:

> Mathematical knowing is rooted in our biological structure, framed by bodily experiences, elaborated within social interactions, enabled by cultural tools, and part of an ever-unfolding conversation of humans and the biosphere. (p. 315)

Using this expanded view of mathematics, Davis and Simmt explored various complex phenomena to reveal some essential aspects of MfT. According to their analysis, teachers must have access to the interconnected images and metaphors that underlie mathematical concepts, and must also be skilled at translating among different mathematical representations. Acquiring and enacting such skills requires a strong disciplinary background, including familiarity with the interrelationships of mathematical ideas, and the histories of their emergence. Teachers should be aware of the recursive, nonlinear processes by which mathematical concepts are elaborated, especially through a curriculum. Teachers should also recognize the crucial importance of collectivity for knowledge production, and be adept at engaging and mobilizing social groupings.

As this brief overview of MfT shows, four key answers have been offered to the question of what constitutes mathematical knowledge for teaching. They are:

1. teachers need to know more advanced math than the math they are teaching;

2. teachers need to know specialized mathematics (i.e., PCK);

3. teachers' mathematical knowledge is enacted in their daily work and must be unpacked; and

4. teachers' mathematical knowledge is embodied in multiple, nested, co-implicated systems of cultural mathematics, institutionalized education, and personal learning.

Each of the answers suggests a different research question for the field. The four are:

1. How much advanced mathematics do teachers need to know?

2. What specialized mathematics do teachers need to know?

3. What mathematics is entailed in teachers' daily work? and

4. How do complex dynamics shape teachers' mathematical knowledge?

Examination of the four answers reveals a clear pattern wherein successive answers offer increasingly expansive interpretations of mathematical knowledge. The trends are from knowledge as static to knowledge as dynamic, from knowledge as Platonic to knowledge as embodied, and from knowledge as pre-established to knowledge as emergent. These trends suggest that the answers are not random, and that the field of MfT is on an evolutionary path.

What may this evolution signal for the future MfT research? Do the four answers contradict one another, or can they perhaps be integrated into a coherent whole?

MfT, Complexity Science and Integral Philosophy

In our analysis, it appears that the work of Davis and Simmt is most readily aligned with integral philosophy. In particular, their development of principles of complexity science bridges well to integral principles. As they described, complexity science has been used to study such varied physical phenomena as anthills, brains, eco-systems, and cities. Integral philosophy seeks to extend the findings of complexity science regarding the external realm of nature, and to apply them to the internal realms of self and culture. Indeed, one of integral philosophy's main claims is that essentially the same patterns govern evolution in the three realms of self, culture, and nature (e.g., Wilber 1995, 2006; McIntosh, 2007). This claim is supported through an expansive framework of reality, an Integral map that encompasses all three realms—a construction that draws on results and insights from complexity science, developmental psychology, and Western and Eastern philosophical traditions.

The most comprehensive effort to integrate the evolutionary dimensions of self, culture, and nature into a comprehensive map of reality is Wilber's (1995) Integral Theory and its AQAL (all-quadrants, all-levels) model. It depicts development as proceeding in four parallel hierarchical strands that represent the four irreducible dimensions (quadrants) of being—the subjective, objective, intersubjective, and interobjective.

Integral Theory does more than represent existing reality. By using rich ontological language to describe the evolving structures of consciousness and culture, it
invites us to reflect on the shared mechanisms that underlie evolution in all strands
of reality. Such reflection brings forth and illumines new integral awareness, thus
contributing to the formation of the emergent integral structure of consciousness.
The AQAL model is an enactive paradigm, not a static map of reality.

Quadrants of MfT

The four quadrants of the AQAL map are four major dimensions of being in the
world, and represent the interior and exterior of individual and collective experience. They are often referred to as the subjective, objective, intersubjective, and
interobjective; or the intentional, behavioral, cultural, and social. These quadrants
provide four fundamental perspectives on every complex evolving phenomenon.
Since MfT is certainly one such phenomenon, it is open to elucidation through
the fourfold lens of the quadrants (see Fig. 19).

The common reference point that is perhaps easiest to identify is the objective dimension of mathematics as a representational system. There is little question
that MfT includes the objects of mathematic—numbers, fractions, quadratic equations, triangles, Pythagoras' theorem, logarithms, formal proofs, and the like. These
objects populate the long lists of prescribed learning outcomes. Indeed, mathematics
education as it is practiced today is focused to a large extent on training students'
proficiencies in manipulating mathematical objects.

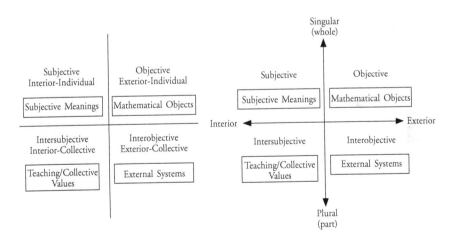

Figure 19. Quadrants of MfT: AQAL and Process Views

Since teachers are entrusted with promoting and assessing their students' mathematical proficiencies, it seems reasonable to require them to be proficient in manipulating mathematical objects. In other words, a teacher should be able to do well on a trigonometry test as a qualification for teaching trigonometry to his or her students. It may well follow from this that the more adept math teachers are in manipulating mathematical objects, the better equipped they will be to teach math in their classrooms. But Shulman's (1986) notion of pedagogical content knowledge revealed that effective teaching is dependent not only on *how much mathematics* teachers know, but also on *how they know mathematics*. The subjective meanings that teachers assign to mathematics play an important role in their teaching.

An examination of the subjective dimension of MfT highlights the importance of the subjective meanings that both teachers and learners access while engaging with mathematics. Learners of mathematics often appear to be guided by the goal of sufficiency; that is, they access only as many representations as are needed to make sense of a mathematical object in order to meet the desired learning outcomes. Skilled teachers, on the other hand, are guided by the goals of depth and inclusivity. They employ multiple representations, images, and metaphors to maneuver among the numerous diverse meanings that arise in pedagogical encounters. The difference between teachers' and learners' modes of access to networks of mathematical meanings may provide a clue as to why, as Begle (1979) discovered, proficiency in advanced mathematics does not necessarily contribute to better teaching. When future teachers study advanced mathematical topics, such as calculus and linear algebra, they approach them as first-time learners, and are likely guided by sufficiency considerations (i.e., the upcoming college test). Perhaps incoming teachers stand to benefit more from re-learning elementary mathematics from an advanced standpoint. Such a study would allow these teachers to re-examine familiar mathematical topics, such as arithmetic and algebra, and to become acquainted with the multiplicities of meanings that inhere in even the most rudimentary mathematical object.

The subjective dimension of MfT includes not only mathematical meanings, but also attitudes and affect in both teachers and learners. So we may ask: What emotions does mathematics evoke in teachers and learners? What aspects of mathematics enliven the learning process and pique learners' interests, and what aspects lead to boredom and disengagement? Why do so many children, and later many adults, fear mathematics as they seem to do? Lastly, what might teachers do to mitigate the distress experienced by some students when they try to learn mathematics? These questions are commonly asked by math teachers at all levels of instruction, and are therefore rightly considered part of MfT.

Shifting focus to the intersubjective dimension of MfT, we note that most teaching and learning of mathematics take place in communal settings. That is, the notion of collectivity is central to the practice of math education—a detail that has been recognized in a large literature developed around social, socio-cultural, and actor-network theories.

Intersubjectivity refers to the shared meanings and values of the learning collective. It is the cultural substrate that underlies the teaching and learning of mathematics. Intersubjectivity is realized when a group of students comes to a shared agreement that degrees are easier to manipulate than radians, and when students believe that "doing math is good for you because it makes you think," and when someone is considered "smart" because he can solve math problems. Easy to overlook, intersubjectivity is the often-transparent "the way things are."

Sidorkin (2002) suggested that community and fellowship are the strongest attractors that schools offer to children. If that is the case, then teachers of mathematics should take great interest in the ways that the subject matter of mathematics promotes the formation of communities. A teacher who can deconstruct collective meanings and effect changes in shared values has the potential to have a profound influence on students. In what ways can mathematics contribute to intersubjective relationality? Conversely, how can human relationality in the classroom be channeled to bring about lively engagement with mathematics? These questions belong to the epistemological field of MfT.

If values and shared meanings represent the interiority of collectives, then systems and institutions represent their exteriority. Every culture finds external expression in the social systems it creates. We shift our focus to the interobjective dimension of MfT.

When students ask, "but when will I ever use this?" they are referring to a mathematical object's external utility. The value of the object is seen to derive from its usefulness to larger systems. Textbooks often use applications of mathematics to broaden the scope of mathematical concepts. Indeed, external utility can act as a powerful motivator when students take interest in the external applications in which the mathematics is embedded. As teachers, we have yet to meet a student who wasn't at least a bit interested in the mathematics of personal wealth creation. This monetary motive for learning math illustrates how interwoven mathematics and its teaching are with a host of different social systems, including those of science, technology, and economics.

Of all such external systems, schooling systems appear to exert the most profound influence on MfT. One can hardly think about arithmetic, algebra, and geometry without simultaneously conjuring images of drills, textbooks, tests, and marks. A teacher who navigates the interobjective dimension of MfT skillfully, and who possesses a healthy critical awareness of the institutional dimensions of school mathematics would be able to utilize external systems to stimulate student interest in mathematics.

Our four-quadrant survey revealed four fundamental dimensions of MfT. The objective (exterior-singular) dimension deals primarily with the objects of mathematics. The subjective (interior-singular) dimension deals with personal meanings, emotions, and attitudes associated with the teaching of mathematics. The intersubjective (interior-plural) dimension deals with shared meanings and values. And the interobjective (exterior-plural) dimension deals with external systems that enfold and are enfolded in mathematics and teaching.

Awareness of the four quadrants and their underlying dynamics can greatly broaden a teacher's field of vision. When a class is struggling with quadratic equations, for example, the teacher might study the underlying algebra to identify different types of equations and suitable methods for solving each type. She might also explore individual and collective meanings that students attach to the equations in an effort to better anticipate potential sources of difficulty. When she inquires about how students feel about the subject matter, she may well find that they are not much interested in it. Moreover, she may realize that the quiz scheduled for the following day is causing the students a great deal of anxiety. She may then consider ways in which to engage the network of intersubjective relationships in the classroom to create a collective ethos that is more conducive to the study of algebra. She may also choose to bring in an interesting optimization problem from the area of personal finance.

The important point in this example is that the mathematical knowledge required by the teacher is not limited to understanding of quadratic equations. Educators who choose to privilege one quadrant to the exclusion of all others may be thought of as quadrant absolutists. For instance, a teacher who believes that good learning hinges on proficiency in solving algebraic equations absolutizes the exterior-singular quadrant. This teacher's view may be too narrow to notice or include personal meanings and shared values. When a researcher asserts that all knowledge is socially constructed, he likewise absolutizes the interior-plural quadrant and may fail to take notice of objective realities or personal constructions of mathematical meanings.

This is not to say that educators should feel compelled to examine every occasion of MfT painstakingly from all four perspectives. Clearly each event requires its own balance of emphases, and each teacher brings her own strengths and preferences. Still, a quick check of all four bases is likely to promote more creative paths to engaging with it.

Waves of MfT: Correlating the Evolutionary Strands

A process view of the four quadrants (Roy, 2006) reveals them to be non-dualistic. As shown in Figure 19, every occasion is governed by a tension along the interior/exterior axis, and by a tension along the singular/plural (whole/part) axis. These dynamic tensions combine to produce the primary structures that are the quadrants of MfT.

The quadrants themselves are not static but rather evolving complex structures. In the context of MfT we discern four interrelated strands of evolution:

1. the evolution of mathematics;

2. the evolution of subjective cognition;

3. the evolution of collective values and conceptions of teaching; and

4. the evolution of systems in which mathematics and teaching are embedded.

Integral philosophy adds that these evolutions move through increasingly complex structure-stages. Each successive structure-stage both transcends and includes the patterns of its predecessors. Our goal in this section is thus to identify a series of structure-stages that reflects the evolution of MfT, by examining some of the evolutionary strands of MfT—mathematics, teaching, and cognition—in greater detail.

In his examination of the evolution of mathematics, Davis (1996) outlined five stages: oral, pre-formalist, formalist, hyper-formalist, and post-formalist. In the pre-formalist stage, mathematics attains independent existence through abstract objects (e.g., number) and a distinct mode of reasoning. At this stage mathematics is seen as describing essential, unchanging forms in the natural world. In the formalist stage, mathematics becomes a distinct discipline with a rigorous methodology for knowledge production. This methodology, embodied in the "formal proof," begins with axioms that are believed to represent unshakeable truths (e.g., 2 parallel lines will never meet), and derives new truths through deductive reasoning. The hyper-formalist stage does away with the need for truths to correspond to the material world, seeking only internal coherence among propositions. Finally, the post-formalist stage conceives of mathematics as a socio-cultural interpretive system that is rooted in human construction of reality.

In another study, Davis (2004) traced a genealogy of teaching. He identified eight principal stages in the history of teaching: mystical, religious, rationalist, empiricist, structuralist, poststructuralist, complex, and ecological. Each of these has a distinct conception of knowledge, and hence assigns different meanings and purposes to the activity of teaching. For instance, the religious stage conceives of the universe as complete and unchanging, and of divine knowledge as being revealed by a higher authority. It follows that teaching at the religious stage seeks to induct the learner into revealed truths. The structuralist stage, on the other hand, regards the universe as emergent and continuously changing. Personal learning and collective knowledge are framed in terms of embodiment and social agreement. It follows that structuralist teaching seeks to enculturate the learner by facilitating personal interpretation and construction of meaning.

When it comes to cognitive development, the early stages are very familiar. They are Piaget's stages of cognitive development in children: sensorimotor, preoperational, concrete operational, and formal operational. The formal operational mind's capacity to take third-person perspectives enables the emergence of perspectival rationality, scientific objectivity, and worldcentric judgments of fairness and care. Subsequent research in developmental psychology (e.g., Commons, Richards, & Armon, 1984; Cook-Greuter, 2005; Kegan 1982, 1994) has pointed to the existence of post-formal stages of development in adults. Since the postformal mind is able to take even more perspectives (fourth- and fifth-person perspectives) than the formal operational mind, it is open to what Gebser called integral-aperspectival awareness—the bringing together of multiple perspectives and contexts without unduly privileging the monological perspective of the subject. Wilber (2000b) used the term *vision-logic* to refer to post-formal cognition, and distinguished at least two stages of post-formal development. In the early vision-logic stage, the learner moves into a cognition of dynamic relativism and plurality. In the mid- and late vision-logic stages, the learner enacts a cognition of dynamic dialecticism and holism.

We next proceed to elucidate stages in the evolution of MfT by correlating the stages of MfT's evolutionary strands. Our synthesis is summarized in Figure 20.

Integral philosophy offers an instructive perspective on possible interrelations of these disparate evolutions. Gebser (1949/1984) posited that the stages of development in human consciousness mirror epochal stages in human history. Each stage of consciousness is a coherent system for sense-making, a natural epistemology that

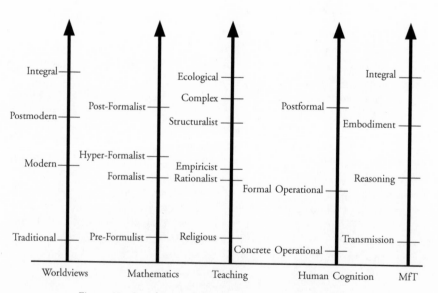

Figure 20. Correlation of the Evolutionary Strands of MfT

arises from the need of societies and individuals to respond to external life conditions in a specific period. Each stage of consciousness brings forth a value-based worldview that organizes individuals' perceptions and interpretations of reality. Graves (1970) referred to the dialectic pattern of the emergence of worldviews as the spiral of development. McIntosh (2007) following Spiral Dynamics developed this notion through a list of eight stages of consciousness development: *archaic, tribal, warrior, traditional, modernist, postmodern, integral,* and *postintegral.* Some of the stages are historical, some are current, and some can only be anticipated. The three stages most commonly found in the developed world are *traditional, modernist,* and *postmodern.* We examine some of their characteristics, and consider how the stages of MfT may be conceptualized through them.

It bears mention that our discussion of the stages of consciousness is necessarily broad and framed in general terms. The stages of consciousness mentioned thus far do not correspond to types of people or to particular individuals. The reference is to categories of consciousness within people that manifest through groups of people, entire societies, or phases of history. Since consciousness is comprised of numerous developmental lines (e.g., cognition, ego, needs, morals, values), its stages are never entirely fixed or rigid in their scope and application. Wilber (2000b) used the term *waves of consciousness* to point out that the stages of consciousness are fluid and overlap one another, much as bands of color coincide in the visible spectrum. Keeping in mind this understanding of the terms used in this discussion, we may proceed to look at MfT as seen through the traditional, modern, and postmodern waves of consciousness.

TRADITIONAL MATHEMATICS

The traditional wave of consciousness is ethnocentric and conformist. Individuals operating within its pattern seek belonging in a reference group and are willing to submit to the group's centralized authority. This wave usually draws on foundational scriptures for truth validation. In the traditional wave, mathematics is seen as an ideal form within creation. Its definite structures and unquestionable truths appeal to traditional consciousness. Teaching in this frame seeks to induct students into a set of authorized texts, be they religious scriptures or texts of mathematics. Success is measured according to conformity with pre-determined results. Traditional teaching correlates primarily with Davis's religious stage of teaching, and its control structures persist into Davis's rationalist and empiricist stages. Mathematics lends itself to traditional teaching practices more readily than do some other school subjects, as evidenced, for example, in blind acceptance of recondite rules (e.g., "invert and multiply").

MfT, as viewed by traditional consciousness, is primarily concerned with teachers' proficiency in transmitting incontrovertible truths. Guardians of the discipline, teachers are to be faithful conduits of established knowledge. They must be masters of the subject matter. The more mathematics teachers know, the readier they are to indoctrinate others.

How teachers know mathematics is of little interest in the traditional wave because there is only one mathematics to know in the first place. According to this way of thinking, individuals who have the university credentials to prove their proficiency in mathematics should make fine teachers. Indeed, the best mathematics teachers should be expert mathematicians. For many years, this view of MfT afforded mathematicians the status of ultimate authorities on matters of mathematics education. Different versions of this view still prevail in higher education, where a PhD in mathematics is often the sole credential for instructing university-level courses.

Modern Mathematics

The modernist wave of consciousness is characterized by individuality and rationality. Individuals operating within its pattern seek to achieve personal autonomy, status, and material wealth, usually through competition with peers. Since this wave appeals to the scientific method and to objective reasoning for truth validation, mathematics has become its quintessential technology. Its tools are critical for physics, computers, and stock markets. Correspondingly, its methods of formal proof and rigorous logic are prevalent in the discourses of the exact and social sciences. Correlating with formalist and hyper-formalist stages of mathematics evolution, the modernist view of mathematics promotes the discipline to top-tier status among school subjects. Every child is required to study mathematics in each grade of K-12.

Teaching in the modernist wave seeks to help learners construct logically coherent understandings. It offers systematic progress through the subject matter by employing linear curricular structures. In fact, modernist schooling practices draw explicitly on efficiency-oriented industrial processes, treating students and curricula as inputs and final grades as outputs. Hence frequent assessments (i.e., quality controls) play a key role in the process of learning. Examinations and grade promotion create a meritocratic environment in which learners often compete for preferred standings along a bell-curve of achievement. Mathematics fits well in the project of assessing and ranking students for placement in a stratified society, serving as both milieu and means of sorting. Its apparent neutrality appeals to the modernist sense of objective fairness. Modernist teaching thus correlates with rationalist and empiricist stages of teaching.

MfT, as viewed by modernist consciousness, is primarily concerned with teachers' proficiency in providing clear instruction. Since learners are regarded as rational beings, subjective sense-making is a central focus of the modernist wave of MfT. Not only must teachers be well versed in results of arithmetic, algebra, and geometry, they must also be aware of the multiple ways in which learners make, connect, and apply multiple meanings of mathematics. Moreover, since teachers are expected to train students to "think mathematically" and to "problem solve," teachers also need to be able to analyze learners' thinking patterns, distinguish valid thought processes from erroneous ones, and understand the sources of students' errors.

Postmodern Mathematics

The postmodern wave of consciousness is pluralistic and inclusive. It is characterized by sensitivity to others, especially those marginalized by dominant discourses. Appealing to local and subjective determinations of truth, postmodernity deconstructs Western mathematics to reveal the ways in which it has been used to dominate other ways of knowing. It also deconstructs school mathematics to reveal that, far from being an objective medium of pure rationality, mathematical discourse has a part in producing the disparities of power that prevail in modern societies. This view correlates with the post-formalist stage of mathematics development.

The postmodern wave of teaching regards learning as an ongoing construction of meanings that give shape to learners' subjective worlds. Here teachers provide suitable contexts for students' constructions, facilitating the complex, nonlinear, recursively elaborative process of learning. Postmodern educators prefer formative assessments that help guide the learning process to summative assessments that are used to compare and rank.

Of all school subjects, mathematics is the least open to the advances of postmodern ideas. Of all the school subjects, mathematics often serves as the exemplar of stable and universal truths: "*2+2 equals 4. It always has been and always will be.*" The postmodern view of mathematical results is that they are dependent on human subjects who construct their meanings, and thus mathematical results are regarded as collective internal constructions. Mathematical symbols are afforded meaning by people who interpret and enact them. So, in the postmodern view, what matters most is not whether *2+2 equals 4*, but rather the constellation of contexts, uses, and discursive conventions that bring forth and perpetuate such "truths." As non-Euclidean geometries and abstract grammars show, mathematical boundaries are subject to the rules of the discourses in which they are situated.

MfT, as viewed by postmodern consciousness, is primarily concerned with the multiple co-implicated networks that embody mathematics. This wave sees mathematical knowledge as enabled by biology, conditioned by culture, and situated in social experience. Thus it extends MfT's reach to include psychology, sociology, cultural studies, history, philosophy, and other co-evolving spheres of human activity. The postmodern wave of MfT also highlights the collective dimension of mathematical knowledge production. Postmodernist viewpoints tend to promote an egalitarian attitude that seeks to include all learners in the production of diverse interpretations and multiple meanings. When a learner claims "2+2 equals

5," traditional and modernist consciousness would call this an error. Postmodern consciousness would frame it as an issue of relative fit that provides an opportunity for deepening of meaning and for the emergence of mathematical novelty—for all participants in the mathematical conversation.

Our examination of MfT through traditional, modernist, and postmodern lenses reveals three distinct waves of MfT: *transmission, reasoning,* and *embodiment.* The first wave, transmission, is concerned with perpetuation of established mathematical truths. It focuses on the extent and depth of teachers' formal disciplinary knowledge. The second wave, reasoning, is concerned with learners' rational engagement with mathematics. It focuses on the ways in which teachers know the mathematics entailed in their work. And the third wave, embodiment, is concerned with the collective networks that embody and enact mathematics. Its focus on the network dynamics that enable the emergence of mathematical knowledge in the classroom reflects a recognition of the emergent nature of mathematical knowledge. Recall that these are the same foci that we encountered in our survey of the history of MfT. We can now see that this history represents movement along the spiral of development: from the traditional, to the modernist, and on to the postmodern wave of consciousness.

It may seem a little surprising that the field of MfT has experienced such rapid evolution in its short history. But since it is situated at the intersection of mathematics and teaching, two fields which already possess rich evolutionary histories of their own, it is not surprising that researchers drew on existing insights from these fields to conceptualize MfT. In the process, MfT's evolutionary timeline was abbreviated.

The history of MfT also represents a step-wise movement among the quadrants. The first stage, transmission, focuses primarily on the exterior-singular quadrant of mathematical objects. The second stage, reasoning, focuses primarily on the interior-singular quadrant of subjective meanings. The third stage, embodiment, focuses primarily on the interior-plural quadrant of intersubjective networks and the exterior-plural quadrant of interobjective systems. Sfard (2005) detected a similar pattern in her survey of mathematics education research. She noted that the 1960s and 1970s were the era of the curriculum, the 1980s and 1990s were almost exclusively the era of the learner, and the first years of the 2000s were the era of the teacher. It appears that each new wave of consciousness dialectically opens up and draws attention to a new quadrant.

Integral MfT

So far we have referred to the spiral of development in tracing the past and present of MfT. We can also use it to anticipate what might lie ahead—and so we turn now to the next wave of consciousness in the spiral, the integral wave.

Before proceeding, a qualification is in order. We are not attempting to predict the future of MfT with any degree of certainty. The waves of consciousness are dynamically evolving patterns of organization that arise from human activity in response to lived conditions. And so there is no telling what emergent forms MfT may take during the integral wave. However, the contours of the integral wave that are manifest in other areas of human activity might help to anticipate what eventual directions MfT might take.

The integral wave of consciousness is an emergent wave that succeeds the postmodern. As such it responds dialectically to the apparent failings of postmodern thinking: its inability to solve current global crises, its value relativism, and its uncompromising rejection of the traditional and modernist worldviews. The integral wave also responds to the culture wars that divide the traditional, modernist, and postmodern worldviews, as each tends to discount the contributions and values of the others. The integral worldview recognizes the importance of the evolution of consciousness and culture to global well-being. It is therefore committed to the health of the entire evolutionary spiral. Integral consciousness acknowledges the contributions of every significant historical worldview. At the same time, it recognizes and rejects pathological aspects of these worldviews.

Just as the modernist wave gave rise to the epistemological capacity of reason, as noted above the integral wave employs a new emergent capacity, called *vision-logic*. Vision-logic is the ability to see how different elements of an evolutionary system work together dialectically, to experience their different perspectives from within, and to harmonize them by valuing each element for its contribution to the entire system (see Karpiak, this volume). Wilber (2000a) described it as follows:

> The point is to place each proposition alongside numerous others, so as to be able to see, or "to vision," how the truth or falsity of any one proposition would affect the truth or falsity of all the others. Such panoramic or vision-logic apprehends a mass network of ideas, how they influence each other, what their relationships are. (p. 249)

Vision-logic is network logic. It is aperspectival and stands in contrast to the commitment of earlier waves to monological perspectives. Kegan (1994) defined vision-logic as "the capacity to see conflict as a signal of our overidentification with a single system" (p. 351).

Math education is a field marked by academic turf battles that result from the attempts of traditional, modernist, and postmodern consciousnesses to impose their monological perspectives on education. The math wars (Schoenfeld, 2004) that raged in the United States in the 1990s have left the field divided and polarized. While educators (e.g., Ball et al., 2005) agree that these disputes within the discipline do not serve the needs of students, there is little agreement on how to reconcile the seemingly opposed claims of different camps.

The three waves of MfT—transmission, reasoning, and embodiment—also represent seemingly irreconcilable perspectives on the relationship between mathematics and teaching. Is school mathematics pre-established or emergent? Should teachers be committed to the curriculum, to rationality, or to the creativity of students? Should students be assessed on the basis of the final answer, the logic of its derivation, or their committed engagement? These questions divide math education practice and research. This is where integral awareness may offer a starting point for reconciliation. It can promote cultural evolution by valuing the three waves of MfT for the contributions that they make in various contexts, and by disposing of their respective weaknesses. Doing so requires the open attitude enabled by vision-logic.

Between Agency and Communion: Evolutionary Tensions of MfT

What are the main points of disagreement among the transmission, reasoning, and embodiment waves? We argue the three perspectives diverge over these questions:

1. Is mathematical knowledge stable or emergent?

2. Is mathematical knowledge Platonic or embodied? In other words, does mathematics manifest in mathematical objects or in enacted subjective meanings?

3. Who is the learner—an individual or the collective?

4. What is the subject matter—school math or accumulated cultural mathematics?

5. Should mathematics be taught as a science or as humanity?

These questions seem to represent a set of irreconcilable dualities. However, the integral wave casts them as necessary, inescapable, and dynamic tensions, which are necessary for the evolution of MfT. Theorists have argued that evolution proceeds through the complimentary processes of differentiation and integration (e.g., Laszlo, 1996; Wilber, 1995). Differentiation is the tendency of every complex system to push outwards and participate in a level of organization more complex than its own. Integration points to the competing tendency of every organizational level to pull inwards toward self-unity and wholeness. Each of the five questions cited above is a particular instance of the interplay between agency and communion within the field of MfT.

Mathematical knowledge for teaching, as viewed by the integral wave, entails an awareness by teachers of the tensions that shape cultural evolution in their field, and the capability to harmonize these tensions dialogically in pedagogical contexts. We will now examine the five types of tensions more closely, in order to see how teachers might translate them into practice.

Two of the tensions are already familiar: the interior-exterior tension between mathematics as Platonic and mathematics as embodied, and the singular-plural tension between mathematics as individual and mathematics as collective. As discussed, these tensions combine to form the axes of the epistemological field that we call the quadrants of MfT. We have already seen how awareness of the four quadrants can enhance teachers' ability to respond to pedagogical situations skillfully. Next, we will examine the remaining tensions: stability versus novelty, math versus mathematics, and mathematics as science versus mathematics as humanity.

Stability versus Novelty of Mathematical Knowledge

One of the main tensions among the transmission, reasoning, and embodiment stages of MfT revolves around conceptualizations of mathematical knowledge. The first sees mathematics as inherent in nature and transcendent; the second sees it as manifest in rational structures; the third sees it as emergent and socially constructed. In an integral perspective, all are partially correct.

Mathematical truths are emergent, as shown by the fact that there was a time in human history when "2" carried no meaning. Of course, pairs of objects existed, but encounters with quantities were not interpreted numerically. At some point, humans began to notice the "twoness" of different sets of objects, and found ways to signal, retain, and generalize their experiences of "two." Lodged in collective situations, the initial meaning of "two" was constituted in social action. But once 2 was formalized through shared signs, it began an inexorable evolution from a situation-dependent adjective (two *somethings*) to an objective and independent noun (a *two*). With every new generation that signified the number two, the reality of "two" became more entrenched and transcendent.

Wilber (2006) refers to significations that have such transcendent status as Kosmic habits. The older the habit, the more self-evident and secure its rehearsed meanings come to be for those who participate in it. Many concepts of school mathematics have been in use for so long that school mathematics often appears to embody unitary meanings. Yet teaching and learning of mathematics are in fact heavily dependent on multiple meanings that emerge through interpretation. As fixed as "two" may seem to us, as determiners of its metaphysical status, every pedagogical encounter enhances the collective meaning of "two" by occasioning unique subjective meanings.

This brings us to the question of radical novelty. How realistic is it to expect brand new results of formal mathematics to emerge in the classroom? It is doubtful that something as momentous as a new conceptual representation of the number two might come from any given elementary school classroom. But provided the right environment, students can take unorthodox approaches to mathematical problems, and do produce unexpected results. From our own experiences as teachers, we have noticed that when we open up the environment to discussion that allows novelty, our students often surprise us with new mathematical insights. They arrive at insights by intuition, or through pictures, or by thinking about video games. They rarely arrive at them by strict application of logical rules to initial axioms. It frequently seems that we are learning new math from our students as they build their understandings.

The integral wave of MfT recognizes that school mathematics is both stable and emergent. Once teachers become conscious of the constant dynamic interplay between stability and novelty in the mathematics classroom, they can derive much interest and satisfaction from it. Sensing and responding to the degree of stability of each mathematical context is part of a teacher's daily work, and so it is essential for selecting an appropriate pedagogical methodology.

"math" versus Mathematics

Not many people use the phrase "school mathematics." For most, it is simply "math" (with a small "m"). From the standpoint of most children, math is likely to be identical with invert-and-multiply, quizzes, sohcahtoa, and the myriad of other situation-specific fragments of math education. When a child protests that she "hates math," her aversion often stems from some central aspect of math education practice, such as rote memorization, repetitive exercises, or high-stakes testing. Yet the same child might use different forms of mathematics outside of the classroom without being particularly aware that she is doing mathematics, nor resenting it in the least. She may enjoy solving Sudoku puzzles, playing card games, or following the standings in a tennis tournament, for example. It is likely that she would not resent these mathematical engagements because she would not identify them with small-m math.

Many teachers choose mathematics as their discipline because they see themselves as mathematical. Yet once they enter their practice in the classroom, many switch perforce to teaching the orthodoxies of school math. They direct their instruction to prescribed outcomes, teaching to tests, meeting grade-level expectations, and insisting that students "show all their work." The integral wave recognizes that the practice of math teaching is provided with coherence as a discipline, and gains a uniform professional identity, by enforcing these orthodoxies. However, the profession's general adherence to such practices robs math education of life and dynamism, and disconnects school mathematics from children's lived experience. What's more, this tendency can dilute the mathematical interests of teachers to the point that they forget what it was that made them choose teaching math as their vocation.

Integral teachers are conscious of the interplay between "math" and mathematics. They continuously strive to find ways to enliven curriculum by connecting it to what we term "grander mathematics." This may be as simple as starting the lesson with an intriguing puzzle, or making a reference to an interesting statistical item from the news, or talking to the students about what the exchange rate of the dollar actually means to their buying power. Such little sidetracks are part of teachers' tools of the trade, and they serve to broaden mathematics and keep it meaningful for both the students and themselves.

Mathematics as a Science versus Mathematics as a Humanity

The practices of mathematics education not only distance school math from informal mathematics used outside of the classroom, they also determine which human engagements are considered to be properly mathematical. These early determinations carry through to the perceptions of adults, setting up rather rigid distinctions between mathematical and non-mathematical engagements. For example, many people would agree that a Sudoku puzzle is a mathematical activity, since it involves numbers. But fewer people are liable to view a cryptic crossword as a mathematical activity. Yet the thinking processes of solving cryptic crosswords—the decomposition of words, methodical analysis of clues—are akin to mathematical thinking. While it does not much matter if people see cryptic crosswords as mathematical, the common inability to perceive mathematical aspects of serious issues of public concern can be very consequential.

Consider the question of what mathematics might have to do with the debate on global warming. Some people may see little connection between the melting of the polar ice caps and small-m math. Issues of global warming may be discussed in social studies or science classes, but typically not in math classes, which focus on procedures that isolate mathematics as a formal, abstract and value-neutral form of knowledge. As a result, mathematical meanings are often absent from discussions of pressing issues such as global warming, except perhaps when the citation of statistics is called upon to support a given interpretation of the problem.

Yet our collective understandings of global warming have everything to do with mathematics. Comprehending the magnitude of the problem requires that vast orders of magnitude be reduced to the scale of individual experience. Logarithms, for example, provide a mathematical way to understand very large and very small numbers. Unfortunately, formal instruction of logarithms in schools focuses on manipulations of abstract expressions, and essentially achieves the opposite of providing students with the tools for active sense-making when they are confronted with the possible causes and consequences of global warming.

Davis and Hersh (1988) cautioned against the loss of meaning that results from this manner of mathematical abstraction: "The spirit of abstraction and the spirit of compassion are often antithetical" (p. 290). MfT, as seen by the integral wave, includes an awareness of the unseen ways in which mathematics is implicated in the human sphere, and is mindful of the consequences of excessive abstraction.

Conclusion: MfT as an Open Way of Being

In this chapter, we used the complexity science and integral philosophy to trace the evolution of MfT. In the process, we identified three waves of MfT: transmission, reasoning, and embodiment. We then sought to anticipate what the future of MfT may hold at the integral wave.

We find that mathematical knowledge for teaching is not a fixed set of mathematical results and processes, but rather an open way of being with mathematics in different educational contexts. What is called for is a broad awareness of the dynamic evolutionary tensions that are at play during each pedagogical encounter with mathematics. MfT at the integral wave must include a willingness to "live in" these tensions dialogically, not privileging either one of their dual ends. Living in dynamic evolutionary tensions also requires teachers to be open to the many perspectives through which pedagogical occasions may be engaged and interpreted. The best pedagogical responses, according to our evolutionary understanding of MfT, are those that promote cultural evolution and life in the classroom.

How can this open attitude be cultivated among teachers? The short answer is to increase awareness. Being aware of the manifold evolutions that underlie mathematics education can empower teachers to participate in them in a very thoughtful way. Recognizing that apparently irreconcilable dualities in mathematics education are in fact productive evolutionary tensions can encourage teachers to become less committed to monological perspectives. For example, once a teacher recognizes that mathematics is simultaneously stable and emergent, she no longer needs to commit to a single perspective. By taking this step, she would be freer to explore the lively interplay between stability and novelty in her mathematics classroom.

In order to live in the evolutionary tensions, teachers of mathematics should know about and live through the opposing perspectives in their discipline. Each of the four historical answers to the question "What mathematics do teachers need to know in order to teach mathematics?" addresses certain perspectives in this opposition, but not others. Studies in advanced mathematics, for example, deepen teachers' perspectives on established mathematics, while pedagogical content knowledge enhances teachers' awareness of how subjective meaning-making takes place. Since there will always be new perspectives to know and to harmonize, no closed, static body of knowledge can ever be the whole of a teacher's mathematical knowledge.

MfT, when understood as an open way of being, asks teachers to always remain curious about mathematics and the ways in which it connects to human experience. The career of a mathematics teacher offers a path of growth and deepening through encounters with new perspectives and the ongoing process of harmonizing evolutionary tensions. Being skilled at negotiating the tensions of MfT in the moment is the teacher's true wisdom of practice.

References

Adler, J., & Davis, Z. (2006). Opening another black box: Research mathematics for teaching in mathematics teacher education. *Journal for Research in Mathematics Education*, *37*(4), 270–296.

Ball, D. L., & Bass, H. (2000). Interweaving content and pedagogy in teaching and learning to teach: Knowing and using mathematics. In J. Boaler (Ed.), *Multiple perspectives on the teaching and learning of mathematics* (pp. 83–104). Westport, CT: Ablex.

Ball, D. L., & Bass, H. (2003). Toward a practice-based theory of mathematical knowledge for teaching. In B. Davis & E. Simmt (Eds.), *Proceedings of the 2002 Annual Meeting of the Canadian Mathematics Education Study Group* (pp. 3–14). Edmonton, AB: CMESG/GCEDM.

Ball, D. L., Ferrini-Mundy, J., Kilpatrick, J., Milgram, J., Schmid, W., & Schaar, R. (2005). Reaching for common ground in K-12 mathematics education [Electronic version]. *Notices of the American Mathematical Society, 52*(9), 1055–1058.

Begle, E. G. (1979). *Critical variables in mathematics education: Findings from a survey of the empirical literature*. Washington, DC: Mathematical Association of American and National Council of Teachers of Mathematics.

Commons, M. L., Richards, F.A., & Armon, C. (Eds.) (1984). *Beyond formal operations: late adolescent and adult cognitive development*. New York: Praeger.

Cook-Greuter, S. (2005). Ego development: Nine levels of increasing embrace. Unpublished manuscript. Retrieved June 25, 2008, from http://www.cook-greuter.com

Davis, B. (1996). *Teaching mathematics: Toward a sound alternative*. New York: Garland.

Davis, B. (2004). *Inventions of teaching: A genealogy*. Mahwah, NJ: Erlbaum.

Davis, B., & Simmt, E. (2006). Mathematics-for-teaching: An ongoing investigation of the mathematics that teachers (need to) know. *Educational Studies in Mathematics, 61*, 293–319.

Davis, P. J., & Hersh, R. (1986). *Descartes' dream: The world according to mathematics*. Mineola, NY: Dover.

Gebser, J. (1984). *The ever-present origin* (N. Barstad, & A. Mikunas, Trans.). Athens, OH: Ohio University Press. (Original work published 1949.)

Graves, C. W. (1970) Levels of existence: An open system theory of values. *Journal of Humanistic Psychology, 10*(2), 131–155.

Kegan, R. (1982). *The evolving self: Problem and process in human development*. Cambridge, MA: Harvard University Press.

Kegan, R. (1994). *In over our heads: The mental demands of modern life*. Cambridge, MA: Harvard University Press.

Laszlo, E. (1996). *The systems view of the world*. Crestkill, NJ: Hampton Press.

Ma, L. (1999). *Knowing and teaching elementary mathematics: Teachers' understanding of fundamental mathematics in China and the United States*. Mahwah, NJ: Erlbaum.

Maturana, H. T., & Varela, H. (1972). *The tree of life: The biological roots of human understanding*. Boston: Shambala.

McIntosh, S. (2007). *Integral consciousness and the future of evolution: How the integral worldview is transforming politics, culture and spirituality*. St. Paul, MN: Paragon House.

Roy, B. (2006). A process model of integral theory. *Integral Review, 3*, 118–152.

Schoenfeld, A. H. (2004). The math wars. *Educational Policy, 18*(1), 253–286.

Sfard, A. (2005). What could be more practical than good research? On mutual relations between research and practice of mathematics education. *Educational Studies in Mathematics, 58*(3), 393–413.

Shulman, L. S. (1986). Those who understand: Knowledge growth in teaching. *Educational Researcher, 15*(2), 4–14.

Sidorkin, S. (2002). *Learning relations: Impure education, deschooled schools, & dialogue with evil.* New York: Peter Lang.

Wilber, K. (1995). *Sex, ecology, spirituality: The spirit of evolution.* Boston: Shambala.

Wilber, K. (2000a) *Eye to eye: The quest for the new paradigm* (3rd ed.). Boston: Shambala.

Wilber, K. (2000b). *Integral psychology: Consciousness, spirit, psychology, therapy.* Boston: Shambala.

Wilber, K. (2006). *Integral spirituality: A startling new role for religion in the modern and postmodern world.* Boston: Integral Books.

Written in "Three Voices"

A Turn Toward Integral Higher Education

Irene E. Karpiak

The Voice of the "Scientist:" Introduction and Rationale

Scholarly academic writing has traditionally identified with standards of objectivity, logic, and rationality, aptly depicted by the white lab coat of the researcher. Most course syllabi and course assignments similarly affirm the perspective of the objective, rational, and analytical approach. And, student works are generally assessed on the basis of evidence from scholarly references, typically avoiding comments about personal points of view, biases, and ways of knowing. As students become socialized into academe, they come to accept and emulate this orientation as consonant with its culture. They have become participants in what Wilber (1996, 1997, 2000a,b) has described as the reduction of the personal and the philosophical mode of knowing into that of the scientific—the paradigm of the empirical-natural sciences, and its "cornering the market on truth" (1997, p. 23).

Yet, growing interest in integral consciousness is making inroads into adult and higher education, as educators incorporate personal, social, cultural, philosophical, and spiritual ways of knowing, that, in turn, are charting avenues for the emergence of an integral focus in adult and higher education. For example, Esbjörn-Hargens (2006, current volume), Gunnlaugson (2005), and Astin (2000), have explored various dimensions of integral consciousness as possible frameworks for curriculum theorizing and pedagogical practice. These and other educators are reaching beyond the impersonal/objective to include the personal/subjective and the collective/intersubjective, and asserting that it is problematic to separate the knower from the known and ignore the process of knowing.

For the purpose of exploring the pedagogical significance of integrating the objective, subjective, and intersubjective dimensions for integral education and development, I reflect on my work of incorporating features of Wilber's (2000) Integral model in my graduate teaching in adult and higher education. I describe my practice of having students approach their inquiry, in accordance with Wilber's model, through various "voices" and ways of knowing, structured through an assignment of course-related writing in "three voices." Finally, I analyze the online postings of students' written work from a recent semester, with respect to their significant features according to Wilber's Integral framework.

The Voice of the "Artist:" My Discovery of Wilber

My association with integral education and the "three voices" began as a doctoral student of adult education, when my advisor, Dr. Howard Williams (whose own work centered on "the ways of knowing and curriculum"), introduced me to the works of integral philosopher, Ken Wilber. On reading Wilber's (1977) *The Spectrum of Consciousness,* I had the experience not unlike that once described by playwright, Arthur Miller, on reading Henri Bergson's *Creative Evolution*—"moving day for the soul." Wilber's work had a profound influence on my own orientation and development as an adult educator. It represented for me, as a student of adult education, an evolutionary, transformative perspective and framework that spoke to my own life and growth. My subsequent dissertation dealt with the life changes and psychological development of professionals at midlife and drew abundantly on Wilber's (1977) "full-spectrum" model of consciousness development to distinguish development's complementary processes.

The Voice of the "Scientist:" A Rationale for Writing in "Three Voices"

Since the publication of his initial volume over 30 years ago, Wilber has continued to explore, develop, and articulate his Integral Theory. In building a rationale for the more recent version of his theory, Wilber (1996) presents an historical account of the evolution of knowledge in Western society. He heralds the initial success of the Enlightenment period to differentiate what had previously been the "embedded" disciplines of Science, Art, and Morals or the "Big Three," noting also the substantial discoveries in each domain that arose from this differentiation. He also points to the less desirable consequences arising from the dissociation or separation of these three domains into distinct domains, each pursuing its own logic and standard of validity in isolation from the other. A further consequence was the diminution of the subjective and moral domains of art and philosophy, and their subsequent "collapse" or reduction into the domains of science.

As a way to challenge this incorporation and to provide new ways to meet and resolve the complex demands and problems of postmodernity, Wilber (1996) argues for the integration of these three disciplines—drawing together the span and logic of *science*, the depth and aesthetics of *art*, and the community and morals of *philosophy*. In sum, the task of the postmodern world is to integrate what had previously been torn apart.

Vision-Logic and the "Big Three"

Wilber (2000a) goes further to note that the interior aspects of knowledge are what need to catch up; the real problems of our world are not so much *exterior* as *interior*—a matter of human consciousness, of the mind looking not only objectively at external objects, but also, the mind looking at itself. The challenge now, "is how to get people to *internally transform* from egocentric to sociocentric to worldcentric consciousness . . . the *only* stance that can freely even eagerly embrace global solutions" (2000a, p. 541). The more we can go *within*, and the more we can reflect on that self, the more detached from that self we can become. He urges us to explore those depths, as well as our own personal depths, and to explore the breadth, the connection of one event or issue with another, and finally, to integrate both of these perspectives of depth and breadth into a larger, more comprehensive whole. Wilber sums up, "In short, the more one goes *within* the more one goes *beyond*, and the more one can thus embrace a *deeper identity* with a *wider perspective*" (2000a, p. 265). For this task, he looks to the integrative capacity of "vision-logic" (2000b), the "integral vision" (2000b), and "second-tier thinking" (2000b).

Vision-logic represents this integrated way of knowing, its distinguishing feature being its wider and deeper perspective on the world, one not afforded at previous stages. Vision-logic's integrative power is to unite male and female, center and margin, and biosphere and noosphere. Wilber clarifies:

> . . . vision-logic is a high holon that operates upon (and thus transcends) its junior holons, such as simple rationality itself. As such, vision-logic can hold in mind contradictions, it can unify opposites, it is dialectical and nonlinear, and it weaves together what otherwise appear to be incompatible notions. (2000, p. 191)

Each of the "Big Three," that is, Science, Art, and Morals, can be distinguished, respectively, through the "voices" of the scientist, artist, and philosopher. Wilber offers the suggestion that even in the case of programs directed toward consciousness purposes, the application of the "Big Three" could yield a more comprehensive approach than is presently the case in many such programs. More specifically, he suggests that in the case of consciousness studies, the "It" could deal with its scientific dimensions, the "I" could address the personal accounts of consciousness, and the "We" could approach the associated collective structures. Wilber's ideas provide both a rationale and framework for the "Three Voices" project that follows, in this case applied not to a consciousness studies program but to graduate adult and higher education.

A Project: Students Write and Post in "Three Voices"

Wilber's work, in particular his explication of the "Big Three," science, art, and morals, inspired me to reflect on the relevance of this premise for education and on a possible strategy of having students prepare their written assignments in "three voices"—the scientist "It," the artist "I," and the philosopher "We." The project began with a graduate seminar, *The Critical Literature of Adult & Higher Education*, where I introduced the practice of having students write sizeable portions of their class assignments in three voices—those of the scientist, artist, and philosopher. Since then I have expanded the use of the "three voices" to writing in other classes, including *Adult Learning and Development, Human Relations*, and, most recently in the solely online courses, *The Uses of Narrative in Teaching and Research*, and *Autobiography and Lifewriting*.

For the purposes of this chapter, I draw on the experience of the course in which this work was initiated—*The Critical Literature of Adult & Higher Education*, a core or required semester-long course for students pursuing a Master's degree in adult and higher education. Its aim is to introduce students to the "critical" authors and ideas that have shaped the field and to develop students' critical thinking abilities. It also examines the way in which authors and students alike come to address the *central questions* of education, including education's purposes, processes, content, learners, and outcomes. The course materials include readings by key authors in the field, among them Paulo Freire, bell hooks, John Dewey, Jose Ortega y Gassett, Johnetta Cole, Derek Bok, Parker Palmer, Eduard Lindeman, and David Kolb. Its format entails a primary in-class component and an online supplement. Students are directed to prepare their critiques (in approximately 400 words) of each respective reading in three voices, that is, to identify these three voices (The Scientist, The Artist, and The Philosopher) and to take the stance of each respective voice as they prepare their critiques.

The course syllabus of *The Critical Literature of Adult & Higher Education* includes the following objective: "To promote an integrative perspective that includes scientific, artistic, and philosophical dimensions of knowing." This feature of writing is also indicated in the process description of the course syllabus, followed by the guidelines for preparing the critiques:

> An "integrative" response to each article draws upon the scientist, artist, and philosopher in each of us (and gives each one balanced attention).

The action of bringing the *outside* and the *inside* views, the "I," "It," and "We" together is intended to promote integration within the writer and to develop a perspective that is more inclusive and complex.

The Scientist: This voice represents the "It," the objective, theorizing, *outside* view. As the scientist, you should introduce the topic, define it, and outline or highlight its main features according to the text, making clear what the text and authors attempted.

The Artist: The qualities distinguishing the artist, the "I," include interiority, subjectivity, sincerity, and truthfulness. Interiority includes reference to one's personal experience and impressions in relation to the topic. Bring in your personal comments, reflections, experiences, and observations.

The Philosopher: The criteria for the philosopher, the "We," include goodness, justness, care, and concern. The question to ask is what personal viewpoint has emerged? How has this reading affected you, as the reader, concerning what is worth doing? What does it suggest to you for possible implications, or for doing things differently?

A second feature of the course assignments concerns the expectation that these critiques in "three voices" are to be posted on the University's Web-based Course Management System's "Discussion Board" *prior* to each weekly class meeting. Accordingly, students contribute to each weekly reading through the online posting of their critiques (in the three voices), through their subsequent responses to the critiques and comments of their class peers, and finally, to the weekly, in-class discussion centering on that particular reading.

Students Post Their Critiques in "Three Voices"

Students generally begin with the voice of the Scientist, and then move to the Artist, and finally to the Philosopher (although this order has not been prescribed in the syllabus). This exercise begins with the initial awkwardness and reticence to using this new format and analytical perspective. Initially, their Scientist voice is infused with the Artist (personal response to the reading) and carries hints of the Philosopher (their opinion about the issue). Their Artist portion tends to extend the formal tone of the Scientist, while the Philosopher, with its more challenging function, tends to receive the least amount of space, often appearing as an afterthought. But, on the basis of my feedback and the opportunity to read the online critiques of others, their voices begin to take shape, in time becoming quite distinct, each revealing its unique language and perspective. The Scientist voice provides concrete material, summarizes the main points, highlights others, and initiates comprehension. It seems to invite the Artist voice that draws in the personal and experiential, as well as the expressive appreciation of the ideas. The Artist, in turn, appears to serve as a bridge to the Philosopher.

One Student's Critique in Three Voices

In the following excerpt from one week's critiques of an article, by educator, Parker Palmer (1997), one writer, whose critique is titled, "Up Close and Personal," illustrates the unique features of each voice and the way in which Palmer's view of "problems" become unfolded through each of the voices.

The Scientist

Parker J. Palmer explains four problems with current educational practices. First students are taught to observe, not experience the world. Often observation is not even firsthand; it comes from reports by people who experienced reality. This separation creates a rift between the known and the knower, which helps create the second problem: objectivism. . . . The third problem is the creation of a competitive and isolated spirit among learners instead of a spirit of community and cooperation. As a result, educated people "lack the capacity to enter into and help create community in the world," and "they carry the habit of competition into all their relations with life." As the learner draws away from the known, away from others, and toward objectivity, the learner has less harmony, reverence, and respect for the known. This leads to the fourth problem of manipulation: manipulation of knowledge, others, and the world.

Why do these problems persist? Palmer says the most likely reason is because it is safer to look at knowledge from afar rather than get close and let it transform us. Getting close means we become students as well and lose our power as teachers. Interaction of this nature is hard because "to learn is to face transformation."

The Artist

Palmer's comments on objectivity made me think of TV news reporters. They are so removed from the reality of what they report. I once heard a saying about news reporters that nothing is so bad that the words "And next" can't wipe it away. They take their listeners on a journey through the news without being touched by the information. We can learn about horrible explosions without getting burned or even smelling smoke. This desensitizes the listener.

I think Palmer has a good point that this is also happening in the classroom. The teachers take the students on a learning journey where they are essentially untouched and unchanged by the learning. I think we need to ask ourselves, "Are we desensitized as learners?"

The Philosopher

I believe that experience is the best teacher, and I wish that all our learning could be as firsthand experiences, but is this even feasible? In reality, we do not have time to go do it all ourselves. Perhaps we should approach each college class with a new goal. We will learn the information, and then we will decide what we will take the time to go experience for ourselves. We can't experience it all, but let's make a decided effort to choose to experience something from each class. I believe we would graduate with a deeper and more meaningful education if we experienced more, allowing those experiences to transform us.

In the above posting the student, in her Scientist voice, picks up on the central problems identified by Palmer; she explores these and makes them personal and reflective through the Artist's voice. Both seem to give rise to the Philosopher's voice that now rather boldly inclines toward a prescriptive stance directed to students and their investment in their learning.

A further illustration of this process of writing in the three voices is provided by Tess, a returning "adult" learner, who responds to the article, "Tales from the Dark Side," in which its author, Stephen Brookfield (1994) brings to light the oft-unacknowledged aspects of engaging in critical reflection. Tess' Scientist voice opens with a review of the author's rationale, followed by a summary of the various features of the dark side of higher education, described by Brookfield.

As she shifts to and identifies her Artist voice, Tess focuses her attention on Brookfield's concept of "impostorship," which she, notably, draws out of the educational arena and into her own life. From this perspective she depicts her turmoil and bewilderment on becoming a new mother, now being called upon to do what she feels to be overwhelming. Her struggle centers on the demands of this new and intimidating mothering role: "I had to read a book on how to give him a bath!" The detail of her struggle to orchestrate the various demands of meal preparation, and her attempts to shift from role of cook to mother have the effect of illuminating Brookfield's other concept of "road running," referring to the fluctuations that go on between seeming progression and regression.

Tess then assumes the voice of the Philosopher, and with it, she shifts her perspective from the personal to the social, in her case to the educational, at which time her tone becomes more thoughtful and reflective. She imagines now the possible occurrences of impostorship and road running among students, and this thought brings her to pose the question of what might be the best means for preparing students for the student role—perhaps through student services, she wonders. Finally, she turns her focus beyond both the personal and the educational arenas, to those of health care, career, and family, observing that the dark sides are to be found there, too. She closes with a commentary on the imperative of timely and appropriate supports to carry one through these dark times in whatever context these may occur.

Students in the Voice of the Scientist

As students become familiar with this writing project, their article critiques in the voice of the Scientist generally conform to the convention of more formal, objective, *outside* view of scholarly writing, wherein the main points of the article are outlined and particular themes or issues highlighted. Students identify salient points and matters of interest. Some provide their own critical comments concerning the article and some challenge the assumptions of the author. Yet, overall, these critiques may be said to be characterized by uniformity, perhaps in part due to the effects of the online postings that allow students to read existing postings prior to preparing and submitting their own. This latter feature is also one much valued by students who may be having a problem understanding a particular article. Some jokingly confess that when they are struggling with a particular reading, they look to the first posting for ideas and direction.

Students in the Voice of the Artist

With the shift from the Scientist to the Artist—from the "It" to the "I" voice—the writing seems to come to life. The tone of the postings changes from one of objective to subjective and from impersonal to personal. Now come the individual comments, associations, and responses arising from that reading. Students offer unique observations regarding the connections of the readings to other course readings, to their own circumstances, or to the postings of their class peers. Students remark on having gained new insights regarding their role as future educators, as well as lifelong learners. One student notes that the reading has been an inspiring force for her to become an adult educator, who would "make a difference." Some express their view personally and provocatively, as if a challenge to the present system; in the words of one: "Where is the learning: Where is the education?" Reading John Dewey (1964) brings many to recall and describe, from their own past, the moments and episodes of "having *an* experience." And, upon reading a chapter by educator, Johnetta Cole (1993), one student is moved to write, "Stand up and cheer for Ms. Cole. I want to ask her to encompass me in her circle of learning."

As Artists, they frequently reflect on their own past experiences. Learning takes on a broader, even historical quality, as they recall lessons learned from their parents and inspiring teachers. Some students move into an autobiographical mode that draws connections between past events and present behaviors. They consider, from a developmental perspective, their life as learners and as growing individuals; they note the differences between what they were like in their earlier schooling and undergraduate years, and how, since then, they have altered their understanding of and regard for education. At times their writing takes on a seemingly confessional tone, in recognition of their own tendencies to distance themselves from others, as was noted when reading Parker Palmer's (1997) mention of the tendency in education toward personal distancing.

It is important to emphasize that these postings are shared via the online discussion board, creating a dialogical, participative process, wherein writers post and respond to one another, and in the process engage in further reflection. Carly, in her Artist's voice, reflects upon and engages with another student, Bret, concerning her experience of being a "returning adult" to graduate school.

Carly: I returned to college after being a stay-at-home mom for several years. My personal experience caused nervousness, lack of confidence in my academic ability and fear of failure, which affected my behavior in my first class. I was a quiet listener, somewhat of a "fish out of water." The environmental experience of being in class began to affect my personal experience. I began to reflect on theories I was learning and how those theories applied to me. That change in my personal experience began to affect my behavior with my family, as well as my behavior in class. I have seen the cyclical effects that internal and external experiences have on each other.

Bret: I remember your nervousness and I can identify because I felt the same way. Did sharing your experiences help you feel more comfortable?

Carly: Yes, I think it did. Listening to others share their experiences also helped.

This exchange is not at all atypical of the nature of the postings. Students respond to their peers' postings with warmth, good humor, and support, mentioning their own and related experiences, tuning in to the feelings, offering hope and possibilities. In simple terms, the Artist appears to promote this interest and concern. As one student commented in a personal note to me, she found herself going to this online course more frequently than to other courses, being drawn to read the Artist postings.

Students in Voice of the Philosopher

As students articulate their new perspectives on learning and education, they look to the future. The Artist's voice seems naturally to have prepared and invited the more prescriptive voice of the Philosopher. Having addressed the feelings, experiences and recollections in the Artist voice, students seem disposed to theorize and philosophize about a given issue or theme, and to shift their perspective from the personal to the wider socio-cultural arena. As Philosophers, some students take on a critical stance in relation to these authors and their society. They challenge the authors with alternative views or with the prospects of unacknowledged problems arising from the views presented. In response to one author's assertion of the dysfunctional effects of competition, one student offers a challenge to this assumption, citing instances when competition *can* serve education. Several others consider the possible resistance of the learning public to adopt the ideas presented; and one student encourages author and former president of Spelman College, Johnetta Cole (1993), to consider possibilities even wider than those she had outlined—that her approaches should service not only education, but society as a whole.

As students wrestle with the content and concepts presented in the articles, they begin to distinguish between concepts, such as that of power versus empowerment. Pursuant to reading Freire (1973), one student suggests that educators should trade power *over* students with the power *from* the knowledge of having changed and shaped lives. Johnette Cole (1993) prompts them to consider how the concept of "worldcentric education" might be fostered through undertakings such as world travel and cultural interaction; or what benefits might arise from offering curricula of studies in higher education that are culturally diverse. Finally, they envision a better world, as one writer expresses, "free of ignorance, superiority, and inferiority; [while maintaining] awareness of own ignorance."

Concerning the process of learning, students reflect on the role of experience in creating knowledge, contemplating opportunities for them to experience life's conditions rather than be *told* about them. One writer, in reflecting on the implications of Kolb's (1984) model of experiential learning, concludes: "The challenge with experiential learning comes not in our ability to pull back the blinds and take a look, it is in our ability to look within ourselves and engage in active and *critical* reflection upon our own and others' experiences." Powerfully drawn to authors, such as Eduard Lindeman (1961) and Parker Palmer (1997), these students imagine the kind of education that could result, if both learners and educators drew on their ideas. In addressing the needs of learners, they imagine an alternative—they ask "what if?" As one student wrote about learners, "these vessels are not empty; they are filled with personal experiences that color the students' perceptions of themselves and the world around them."

Curiously, despite the focus of this graduate course on adult and higher education, students frequently turn their attention to grade school problems and solutions. They emphasize how important it is for children to have their experiences acknowledged and affirmed; and they consider what possible improvements to education might follow were adult education principles applied in the course of student learning, both at the K-12 and post-secondary levels. Finally, they reflect on the concept of lifelong learning and consider ways to promote this essential ideal in children.

Turning to the subject of teachers and faculty, these students wonder: How can we teach the teachers? They respond with ideas: make efforts to reach learners, respect learners' perspectives and expertise, empower adults to engage in learning, and share personal experiences and wisdom with the class to prepare learners to face the "harsh realities of the world." In response to Parker Palmer's (1997) plea for greater engagement between teacher and learner, one writer agrees, noting that words are merely ink on paper that gain their power through being understood.

It is notable that the language, tone, and engaged quality that has been established in the online postings carries into the online dialogue that transpires as students' responses and conversation build. The language is at times powerful and evocative, with expressions of gratitude to others for their comments of challenge or support, or for helping them to clarify a point. As for the theories (of life and learning) that student may offer, at times their peers affirm these through their mention of own experiences; at other times they refine them; often times they build upon them; and frequently they reflect on emerging, yet remaining questions. At times, the tone becomes a chatty one, as the dialogue brings up associations with previous ideas or experiences. Finally, this forum opens up further lines of discussion that continue throughout the postings of that week. As an example, when Tess (mentioned earlier) shared her own sense of impostorship, as a young mother of a newborn, her narrative prompted others throughout the course of that week to relate their own sense of impostorship in a variety of settings, including the classroom, family, and work.

My Artist: Learning from Student Postings

As I read the students' initial postings and their responses to those of others, I am learning about the *inside* of my students—their fears, concerns, experiences, and personal backgrounds—in ways that few other class projects would permit. I find myself drawn in to their feelings and expressions, looking into the ways in which connections are made between the reading materials, their associations of the present, and memories of their past. I am equally drawn to their perspectives, now understanding more about the bases of their responses and the sources of their stance; I am grateful for their willingness to share who they are with others, thereby enriching the quality and depth of the conversation. Finally, I am humbled by their struggles and reminded once again that my educational experience is unique to me and so unlike many of theirs; that the many advantages I have had as a student, the feeling of being "in my element," bears no resemblance to the alienation and sense of marginality known by some.

My Scientist: Integral Features of the "Three Voices"

Several features emerge from the substance and tone of the students' writings, and which are associated with the spheres of Wilber's Integral model of the "Big Three." Concerning Wilber's description of the "I" language as "your presence, your consciousness, your subjective awareness" (1999, p. 121), these students' Artist voice echoes this mode, as one of self-expression, subjectivity, and sincerity (albeit to varying degrees). The notable features of their postings in the Artist voice, prepared in such a personal, self-expressive way, are that they allow their personal experiences to intersect with the readings and other peer postings, permitting conscious connections and meaning making. The Artist also provides windows into the lives of others, permitting an *inside* view that allows writers to see how others construct meanings and understandings from events and experiences. As students read the postings of others, they gain a sense of how another has experienced learning, community, relationships, or other significant happenings.

The voice and language of the Artist appears also to enable these students to interpret past events in light of new understanding. For instance, Tess' narrative enabled her to articulate her experience of becoming a mother and to interpret that experience as one of impostorship and road-running. Further, through sharing this episode with others, she encouraged them to engage with her struggle, and perhaps even to acknowledge their own. This is the kind of knowing that has been the subject of those who have researched narrative in our lives, such as Polkinghorne (1996), who has remarked on the power of narrative to contribute to the "cognitive restructuring process" (p. 82), a mode of understanding by which people come to make sense of their own and others' experiences and life events. Through their forthrightness, these students provide a window into their feelings and experiences, and subsequently further growth of understanding, not only on their own part, but also of others.

With regard to the Philosopher, Wilber (2000) clarified earlier that the Philosopher's language, being distinct from the "I," concerns itself with the "We"—a collective and evolving worldview that aligns itself with justice and goodness. As was revealed in the previous section, the students' Philosopher takes on the tone not of functional strategies, but of cultural change of the sort that arises through alterations in attitude, values, orientation, or understanding. A further observation concerns how these students articulate their values and attitude as an educator. Week by week, as students prepare and post their critiques, attend to the postings of others, and dialogue and respond to these, they participate in the development of their own professional and philosophical stance. Week by week, they have had the opportunity to comment on each of the central questions concerning the purposes of education, how we come to know, what is worth knowing, what motivates and concerns the learner, and what outcomes can arise from participation in higher education. As the course progresses, built through the three voices, their attitudes begin to take shape. By course ending, they have gained a formed, if incomplete, sense of where they stand as future educators. In their final class meeting, they prepare a multi-media presentation that lays out their best up-until-now philosophy concerning the central education questions.

A final significant feature of the online discussion board concerns the closeness and community that develops as the students proceed with their semester-long postings. This feature is especially significant, given the growth of Web-based instruction, where the creation of community represents a major obstacle as well as challenge. Postings in the Scientist voice appear to assist students in understanding the readings, since students range widely in what articles they find to be accessible or difficult, and in these cases they can clarify or draw clarity from the various contributions of others. Postings in the Artist voice, on the other hand, appear to promote appreciation of the concepts and of their application in life. Through their inclination to reveal aspects of themselves, their own struggles with the reading, or their experiences relevant to the readings, they reach out to others. The postings become rich not only with the "three voices" postings, but also with the replies by others, as in, "Your experience was exactly as my own." If it is true, as said, that our deepest human need is to be understood, then the communication that happens and the tone of recognition that follows would surely, in this regard, serve these learners.

My Philosopher: Toward an Integral Education

> The fact that both of these approaches—the exterior and the interior, the objectivist and the subjectivist—have aggressively and persistently existed in virtually all fields of knowledge ought to tell us something—ought to tell us, that is, that both of these approaches are profoundly significant. They both have something of incalculable importance to tell us. And the integral vision is, beginning to end, dedicated to honoring and incorporating both of these profound approaches in the human knowledge quest. (Wilber, 1997, p. 9)

In this passage Wilber affirms the significance of both the exterior and the interior approaches to knowing and understanding. He speaks to the value of the exercise of students' writing in "three voices," thereby giving attention and distinction to both the exterior and the interior domains. Through their focus on the unique language and focus of each of the voices these students come to appreciate the respective place of each of these voices in the quest for knowledge.

The "three voices" approach to academic writing engages students in an exploration of the exterior/objective dimensions of their inquiry, the interior/subjective of their lived experience, and interior/intersubjective dimensions of their presence as members of the citizenry. In this regard, it holds the promise of supporting students in their process of acquiring a worldview that encompasses the integral vision. Significantly, given Wilber's (2000a) earlier observation that acquiring an integrative perspective can lead to the development *toward* an integral stage, it would follow that promoting "I," "It" and "We" perspectives can hold at least the potential to further the processes of development toward the more complex and integrated.

References

Astin, A. W. (2000). Conceptualizing service-learning research using Ken Wilber's integral framework. *Michigan Journal of Service Learning*, Special Issue, pp. 98–104.

Brookfield, S. (1994). Tales from the dark side: a phenomenography of adult critical reflection. *International Journal of Lifelong Education, 15*(30), 203–216.

Cole, J. B. (1993). *Conversations*. New York: Double Day Publishing Group, Inc.

Dewey, J. (1964). Having an experience. In A. Hofstadter. & R. Kuhns (Eds.), *Philosophies of art & beauty*. Chicago: University of Chicago Press.

Esbjörn-Hargens, S. (2006). Integral education by design: How integral theory informs teaching, learning and curriculum in a graduate program. *ReVision 28*(3), 21–29.

Freire, P. (1973). *Education for critical consciousness*. New York: The Seabury Press.

Gunnlaugson, O. (2005). Toward integrally informed theories of transformative learning. *Journal of Transformative Education, 3*(4), 331–353.

Kolb, D. (1984). *Experiential learning: Experience as the source of learning and development*. Englewood Cliffs, NJ: Prentice-Hall, Inc.

Lindeman, E. (1961). *The meaning of adult education*. Montreal, Canada: Harvest House.

Palmer, P. (1997). *The courage to teach*. San Francisco: Jossey Bass.

Polkinghorne, D. E. (1996). Narrative knowing and the study of lives. In J. E. Birren et al. (Eds.), *Aging and biography: Explorations in adult development* (pp. 77–99). New York: Springer Publishing.

Wilber, K. (1977). *The spectrum of consciousness*. Wheaton, IL: The Theosophical Publishing House.

Wilber, K. (1996). *A brief history of everything*. Boston: Shambhala.

Wilber, K. (1997). *Eye of spirit: An integral vision for a world gone slightly mad*. Boston: Shambhala.

Wilber, K. (2000a). *Sex, ecology, spirituality: The spirit of evolution*, Second Edition. Boston: Shambhala.

Wilber, K., (2000b). *A theory of everything: An integral vision for business, politics, science, and spirituality*. Boston: Shambhala.

Wilber, K. (2006). *Integral spirituality: A Startling new role for religion in the modern and postmodern world*. Boston: Integral Books.

Integral Education, Integral Transformation, and the Teaching of Mind-Body Medicine

Joel Kreisberg

Mind-Body Medicine offers a unique opportunity for transformative education in medicine and health. Through the use of Integral Theory, Mind-Body Medicine (MBM) has the potential to act as a lightning rod for personal transformation. In teaching Mind-Body Medicine in John F. Kennedy University's Master of Arts in Holistic Health Education, Integral Theory facilitates the integration of conventional, post-conventional and integrative classroom approaches. This integration brings about a degree of personal and collective transformation seldom found in traditional institutions of higher learning. Using the four quadrant system, known as AQAL, developed by Ken Wilber (1995), students and teachers explore aspects of self, community, and the world using the experiential and academic materials of Mind-Body Medicine. The journey is complex, requiring commitment, vision, and will, but the rewards are great. I am proud and excited to share the work we have done in this course.

The following discussion begins with a brief history of Mind-Body Medicine. Since its inception within the context of the contemporary field of biomedicine, it is no surprise that Mind-Body Medicine is often taught using conventional classroom pedagogy. In order to move beyond this traditional model, a review of Integral Transformative Practice and how this practice is used as action learning in a class I teach in Mind-Body Medicine follows. This class also utilized a relatively new tool called Integral Health to identify and assess health from a multi-quadrant perspective. The use of Integral Health and how it facilitated an integrative classroom methodology will then be discussed. After a brief introduction to Integral Life Practice, a description of how the students synthesized the lessons of the classroom by creating their own Integral Mind-Body Medicine Program will be presented. This activity offered students an opportunity to individualize their programs while reflecting on the purpose and value of their design. The conclusion of this article offers a review of lessons and opportunities learned by the integration of Integral Theory and Mind-Body Medicine in an integrally informed classroom.

What Is Mind-Body Medicine and How Is It Taught?

According to the National Center for Complementary and Alternative Medicine (NCCAM), Mind-Body Medicine "focuses on the interactions among the brain, mind, body, and behavior, and on the powerful ways in which emotional, mental, social, spiritual, and behavioral aspects, can directly affect health" (National Institute of Health, 2007). As a clinical practice, Mind-Body Medicine uses a variety of interventions, including, but not limited to meditation, affirmations, prayer, biofeedback, ritual, body-mind centering, expressive movement, and expressive arts. While, in many respects, Mind-Body Medicine is a recent addition to the clinical and academic field of medicine, evidence for mind-body interactions has been mounting for almost a century.

In the early twentieth century, evidence began to accumulate about the connection between mental or mind-states and body reactions. Walter Canon's MD seminal research in the 1920s revealed a primitive sympathetic reflex with adrenal adaptation in response to perceived danger—Canon (1932) coined the term "fight or flight response." In 1929, Dr. Edmund Jacobsen (1938) published his landmark book, *Progressive Relaxation*, in which he demonstrated physiological homeostasis with his practical technique of focused systematic muscle contraction and relaxation. He demonstrated that 80% of patients with "psychosomatic illness" were cured with this approach. In 1932, Dr. J. H. Schultz, of Germany, published his first book detailing a specific form of self-hypnosis called "autogenic training." By 1969, six volumes on autogenic training had been published by Schultz and Luthe (1969), including some 2,800 scientific references.

In 1970, Dr. Elmer Green and his wife, Alyce (Green & Green, 1977), introduced the concept of autogenic feedback training into American medicine; this became known as biofeedback. Their earliest work proved that 84% of patients with migraines and 80% of patients with hypertension were remarkably improved and symptoms were adequately controlled with temperature biofeedback training. Since that time, it has been demonstrated that every physiological response that can be measured and fed back to the patient visually or audibly is capable of being brought under voluntary control.

In the early 1980s, George Solomon's research introduced the field of psychoneuroimmunology (PNI), which has provided significant evidence for the interconnectedness of body, mind, and attitude. Most remarkable is the finding that virtually every neurochemical produced in the brain is also produced in white blood cells and usually in the intestines. To some extent, the field of Psychoneuroimmunology suggests that the "mind" is in every cell. Dr. Candice

Pert's (1999) discovery of beta endorphins, natural opiods, was the first major step in demonstrating that the mind can produce a wide variety of mind-altering chemicals, ranging from anandamide to neurotensin. These neurochemicals have analgesic, neuroleptic, and hallucinogenic effects. Psychoneuroimmunology is the research providing the foundation for the clinical practice of Mind-Body Medicine as well as much of the human potential movement.

Psychoneuroimmunology is a young science that offers integration of perspectives from several fields including psychology, neurophysiology, and immunology. Modern medical sciences find this field of study progressive in that it blends first-person (subjective) perspectives with third-person (objective) perspectives. As a clinical tool, psychoneuroimmunology must be considered beyond conventional, because it integrates interior and exterior perspectives by advancing experiential activities with behavioral outcomes. Yet, psychoneuroimmunology is dominated by a third-person research perspective providing objective measures of validity supporting the integration of Mind-Body Medicine into modern clinical practice.

Mind-Body Medicine, as an integrative field of study, has grown up in the conventional medical context, requiring evidence-based rational understanding of causality as well objective measures of validity for both understanding and efficacy.[1] Due to this environment, the field of Mind-Body Medicine has been dominated by objective third-person perspectives of the Upper-Right quadrant (UR). However, revisiting the definition offered at the outset of this article from the NCCAM, it is apparent that Mind-Body Medicine has aspects in all four quadrants of Integral Theory's AQAL model. Mind-Body Medicine "focuses on the interactions among the brain [UR], mind [UL/UR], body [UL/UR], and behavior [UR], and on the powerful ways in which emotional [UL/UR], mental [UL/UR], social [LL/LR], spiritual [UL], and behavior [UR], can directly affect health" (NIH 2007).[2] Because of this combination, Mind-Body Medicine has emerged as a signature field for the holistic and integrative medical movement.

There has been considerable investigation of Mind-Body Medicine using Wilber's AQAL system. The most notable examples include the works of John Astin (2002), Marilyn Schlitz (2005), and Elliot Dacher (2006). A review of the Mind-Body Medicine literature suggests that, while much of the Mind-Body Medicine perspective can potentially be associated in all four quadrants, the predominant approaches, to date, remain in the upper or individual quadrants. One significant reason is that the science of psychoneuroimmunology is more easily done with an orientation toward individuals. Psychoneuroimmunology and Mind-Body Medicine do not lend themselves readily to collective perspectives, due to the complexity of measuring outcomes on groups and the overall emphasis of contemporary bio-medicine on outcomes for individuals.[3]

Interestingly, Mind-Body Medicine is typically taught from a third-person perspective because it emerges as clinical science useful in a modern setting, inheriting the dominant objective perspective of contemporary biomedicine. In other words, Mind-Body Medicine includes both experience (UL) and behavior (UR); however, it is often taught looking at each of these from the an objective viewpoint (a third-person perspective of a first-person experience or a third-person perspective of a third-person perspective) (Esbjörn-Hargens & Wilber, 2006). Thus, Mind-Body Medicine, while including the experiences of meditation, autogenic training, movement, or expressive arts, emphasizes third-person outcomes more than first-person experiences when taught in medical settings. Physicians and graduate students discuss meditation and what studies show about its impacts, rather than practice meditation to consider its impact on the self. This is a typical example of classroom pedagogy in much of medical education, and for our purposes, this is a conventional teaching paradigm.

Many practitioners and teachers of integrative medicine, who consider themselves modern and, possibly, postmodern, often utilize educational methodologies that are strictly conventional, without any commitment to reflective approaches of postmodern or integrative pedagogy. While reasons for this are beyond the scope of this discussion, the most common reason is lack of training in educational pedagogy. Integrative medicine relies on "subject as object of study" pedagogy, often blending experiential learning practices based in the empirical methodology of John Dewey (1963) with conventional and modern classroom style, most commonly the lecture.

Mind-Body Medicine, because of its natural integration of interior and exterior perspectives can easily be taught using post-modern and integrative approaches, unlike more complex systems of alternative medicines, which are far more deterministic, such as Traditional Chinese Medicine, Ayurvedic Medicine, Chiropractic, and Osteopathy. Thus, Mind-Body Medicine offers not only a blend of experience and information, but also an opportunity to consider reflective cultural critique essential to a postmodern perspective. Interestingly, in clinical settings Mind-Body Medicine relies on experiential interaction with objective studies as a support tool to reinforce the value of the transformational experiences.

An Integral Approach to Mind-Body Medicine

I teach a class in Mind-Body Medicine, which is, as noted in the introduction, part of a Master of Arts Program in Holistic Health Education at the John F. Kennedy University's School of Holistic Studies. The program design is integrally informed due to the vision of the department Chair Michele Chase, PhD and her colleagues: Vernice Solimar, PhD, the department Chair of Integral Psychology and Sean Esbjörn-Hargens, PhD, the department Chair of Integral Theory. The overall program design provides students with a variety of experiences that facilitate perspectives from all four quadrants of Integral Theory—offering a unique opportunity for students and faculty to further engage integral transformation—both vertically (psychological stage development) and horizontally (psychological integration at any developmental stage). Yet, for a variety of reasons, aspects of the curriculum are conventional, just as aspects of the program are integrative. As with most post-secondary institutions, the curriculum is evolving as is the faculty. The integration of material, at times, comes from students having to juxtapose contrasting perspectives at the programmatic level without a clear structure from which to consider these contradictions. Still, I consider myself lucky to have such an opportunity to develop curriculum in an educational setting that clearly embraces the weaving together of the strengths of conventional, postmodern, and integrative perspectives.

Due to the orientation of the JFK program, an opportunity existed for the development of an integrally informed course that included Mind-Body Medicine. Essential to an integral vision, this would require using integral approaches to classroom design. Upon closer examination, I found no examples of Mind-Body Medicine taught using an Integral approach. Three integral practices utilizing principles of Mind-Body Medicine are actively taught throughout the United States, though not in medical education institutions. These three are Integral Transformative Practice (Leonard & Murphy, 1995), Integral Health (Dacher, 2006) and Integral Life Practice (Wilber, Patten, Leonard, & Morelli, 2008). The essential difference between these practices and Mind-Body Medicine is one of orientation. Mind-Body Medicine places the emphasis on how certain practices can influence disease while with these three integral practices the emphasis is on extending human potential, fostering personal growth, and personal health.

In classroom design, I began with a commitment to one of the three integral practices, since integral practice offers a unique opportunity for our inquiry. Attention is placed on experiencing the practices (UL), reflecting on those experiences (UL), discussing these experiences within the class (LL) as well as charting behavioral changes that occur through the practices (UR). In this way, students are committed to first-person experience and reflection, second-person sharing and discussion, and third-person evaluation. The first experiential practice students of the class committed to is Integral Transformative Practice, created by George Leonard and Michael Murphy (1995).

Integral Transformative Practice

Integral Transformative Practice (ITP) is an ongoing collective training experience developed by Michael Murphy, the founder of Esalen Institute, and George Leonard, a noted author and Martial Arts teacher, using the works of Ken Wilber, Sri Aurobindo, and other integral theorists. The initial form was published in the book *The Life We are Given* (Leonard & Murphy, 1995). ITP groups continue to practice throughout the world to this day.

Integral Transformative Practice involves eight commitments. These eight commitments include: to practice the Kata (i.e., a series of movements) five times a week; to take responsibility for oneself; to eat mindfully; to exercise for two hours a week; to engage in cognitive growth through a commitment to study; to stay current with ones feelings by being honest and truthful to one's self and one's peers; to practice in a group with a commitment to maintain the practice; and to make three affirmations or stretches—one easy to achieve, one more difficult, and one completely beyond what one might expect to achieve. All this commitments are continued for six months in the original practice.

The Mind-Body Medicine class is an eight-week course and the practices are introduced in week one. After students create three affirmations, and learn the Kata (the movement form), in week two, each student begin to fulfill their commitment to practice the entire form for the following six weeks of the course.

In terms of classroom design, about a third of each class was taken up each week by practices of the ITP. The Kata is a four-part form that includes movement, relaxation, affirmations, and meditation. Completing the Kata takes typically 45 minutes, but can take up to an hour. Given the restrictions of class time, only one or two sections of the Kata were practiced each week.

An essential requirement of the ITP is honest reflection and an assessment of aspects of each person that might be improved. Students envisioned their potential, before creating the three affirmations, which offered a vision of the person they would more like to be. These affirmations were essential to the practice of the Kata five times a week because each student spent 10 minutes of the Kata visualizing and embodying their affirmations. Weekly subjective numerical assessment allowed students to mark their progress toward achieving what they were affirming. After six weeks, students completed a final assessment. These affirmations were shared with the group, fostering a culture of support, potential and mutuality of purpose for the entire class, while recognizing that each individual had chosen his or her own path.

The strength of the ITP program is that most people experience significant personal growth from the practice, even in only six weeks. A few samples of student responses will provide a sense of how ITP can effect change.

> The ITP practice was a very transformative experience for me. It helped shift my attitude, increased my energy level, and opened my heart to the amazing opportunities that arise when we connect to our soul on a daily basis. I found myself doing the Kata more than was required because of the difference I felt throughout the day if I didn't start my day with the practice.[4]

> Overall I found the ITP to be very helpful in my life. It opened my mind up to see the bigger picture and not be so consumed with daily activities and responsibilities. The affirmations have played a significant role in my broader outlook and have really impacted my life in such a positive way that I look forward to saying them every day on my

morning walk with my dog and carry that wonderful feeling I get with me throughout the day.[5]

I think the biggest change for me has been around attitude and mind-set. I have been less anxious and stressed and more cheerful. This has been particularly remarkable because this has been one of the busiest quarters I have had at JFK. Usually at this point I would have had some sort of stress meltdown, but this quarter has been busy yet smooth. It feels like I have built up my energy and ability to take things on and be more gentle when dealing with them as opposed to forcefully powering through.[6]

These are just a sample of the experiences of the students in this class. Yet not everyone has these types of experiences. I also have examples of students from each class who felt that practicing ITP was not of benefit. The biggest challenge resulting from the ITP practice is that for some people the program is too rigid or it asks for too much of a time commitment. Especially in an academic setting, some individuals resent being assigned specific practices with a large time commitment.

Overall, more than 90% of students (more than 75 students over four years) have had significant positive experiences from the ITP process. For many, the experience is transformative—they are able to experience how much they can effect change and grow personally. This awareness occurs experientially, behaviorally, and culturally.

I learned several things from introducing ITP in my Mind-Body Medicine class. First, because of the regular assessment using objectified measures (UR), participants have a third-person record (UR) of the changes they have experienced. This coupled with their own personal experience and reflections (UL) of change, provides an impressive support of personal growth. Second, since ITP offers a system that requires students to create their own goals at three different levels of transformation, many students not only have a successful experience of growth, they also have experiences of transformation.

Finally, because the practice is done in a group and a classroom, experiences of growth and, more importantly, transformation are culturally (LL) supported through interpersonal shared experiences (second-person experiences), which have the potential to shift the classroom conversation from conventional to post-conventional and even into an integral pedagogy.

Initially, I required students to make three phone calls (LR) each week to check in with fellow students. This year, we used online technology (LR) in which students posted their reflections of the ITP process at least once each week. Each student was further required to read all posts and respond to two before the beginning of next class. This social technology, with its facilitation of continual reflection and sharing, supports a pluralistic perspective (postmodern) and rapidly becomes integrative (post-postmodern).[7] Individuals not only experience their own personal transformative process, they simultaneously experience different perspectives of the ITP program in the other students they are communicating with. Some students felt no shift; others grew quite a bit, becoming healthier within their developmental level (horizontal growth) and improving aspects of self. Still other students had significant transformational realizations that allowed for transcending and including previous developmental levels (vertical shifts).[8] All participants shared equally in the rich participatory pluralistic experience of multiple experiences, while each participant had a valid, though different, perspective.

Classroom discussions shifted in that individuals were using multiple perspectives of personal experiences. Being able to hold these differences is essential to emerging integral perspective. Needless to say, the conversation changed significantly from the usual first- and second-person dialogue as can be seen in this student's comments:

> I think one of the most valuable things for me was the community aspect. I've struggled to find a community that offers the support and encouragement I think I need to progress. Online works exceptionally well for me, though I know this isn't the case for everyone.[9]

Integral Health Assessment

Having incorporated the ITP program into my course for four years, and teaching Integral Theory in several other courses, I am interested in how to better facilitate emerging second-tier dynamics, offering a more integrally informed classroom. ITP offers an integrally informed perspective, but developmentally, the dynamics are still emerging integrative or second tier (a holonic systems view) rather than fully integral (a holonic systems of systems view). I replaced traditional texts with more integral informed texts, including Elliot Dacher's *Integral Health* (2006). Dacher adapted Wilber's four quadrants and developmental lines into a functioning clinical tool. Dacher renames the emphasis of the four quadrants—psychospiritual (Upper Left), biological (Upper Right), interpersonal (Lower Left), and worldly (Lower Right).

Utilizing Wilber's developmental lines, Dacher places three developmental lines in each quadrant, observing (as Wilber does) that these lines are representative but not exclusive (there could be many different developmental lines). The 12 lines of Dacher's Integral Health assessment are: Upper Left—cognitive, emotional, and connative;[10] Upper Right—fitness, nutrition, and self-regulation; Lower Left—personal, family, and community; and Lower Right—work, social activism, and generativity (see Fig. 21).

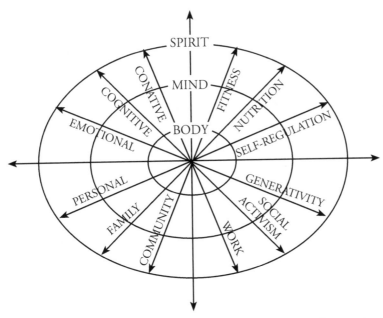

Figure 21. Dacher's Full Spectrum of Aspects, Lines, and Levels in All Four Quadrants from Integral Health.

Dacher's lines are not consistent with Wilber's because he does not hold true to Wilber's principles of nested holons, however, his concepts are certainly grounded in Integral Theory.[11] Dacher's quadrant assessment is a reasonably well-tuned clinical tool for assessing growth and transformation. Individuals are able to evaluate their personal health using a four-quadrant approach including interiors/exteriors and individual/collective perspectives. A sample student response is instructive:

> It seems to me that an integral, personal evaluation, and developing my own integral practice is where the rubber meets the integral road so to speak. This is an actual application for all the Integral Theory we learn so much about at JFK. I did find it a little daunting to evaluate myself so thoroughly. With that said, I tried to follow Dacher's advice to do this assessment in a meditative way. This type of introspection is something that I really benefit from. It is helpful to have a structure like the integral assessment to facilitate my self-appraisal process . . . I don't see myself getting to a certain line and staying there for long. I constantly move up and down from lower to higher lines and back

again. The quadrants and lines are so interrelated that, of course, to be balanced I have to work on all of them. This is a big challenge, but when I try to pay some attention to all or most of the quadrants this much it is becoming more and more clear, I feel healthier and more centered.[12]

Dacher discusses three levels of development—body, mind, and spirit—arguing that, as individuals evolve, each developmental line is centered on one of these three levels. Let us consider the nutritional line as an example. Nutrition from a physical center of gravity is focused on eating for strictly physical needs, such as hunger or energy, or to correct a deficiency. A nutritional center of gravity in the mind is eating for more mental reasons, such as knowledge of proper nutrition, or perhaps emotional eating such as eating because one is depressed or celebrating a success. A center of gravity at the spiritual level in this line is eating with a spiritual awareness, such as mindful eating, or eating with an appreciation of the circle of life, sacrifices the plants, animals, and farmers have given for this food to be offered. Dacher's Integral Health assessment asks individuals to evaluate each of 12 lines of inquiry as to the level or the center of gravity—body, mind, or spirit. Thus, Integral Health assessment is the evaluation of 12 lines, three in each of the four quadrants.

Using this Integral Health assessment, students reflectively examined strengths, weaknesses, and overall center of gravity as well as potential opportunities for inquiry in each line. I have several observations from using this integral tool in a classroom setting. First, as the above student noted, this tool is easy to use and students had a much easier time grasping the four quadrants using this model, even though all students had previous knowledge of Integral Theory. The three-level hierarchy for each developmental line is easily grasped with some requisite explanation in certain developmental lines. Overall, students (even postmodern students who tend to be suspicious of such arrangements) had little difficulty accepting this particular hierarchy.

The second observation is that students grasp the difference between the upper quadrants versus the lower quadrants far more easily using Dacher's system than Wilber's system. I believe this is because Dacher includes personal, family, and community in his model. In this Lower-Left quadrant, personal is the line of development that considers the self in relationship to other Lower-Left considerations such as community and culture. It asks one to evaluate the self as essentially egocentric to ethnocentric to worldcentric overall (but not in those terms).[13] The personal line requires consideration of how an individual interrelates with others in general, overall. The other two lines, the interrelationship between self and family and self and community are variations of this primary general line. In Wilber's system, these are three levels of complexity. Dacher's system stays away from distinguishing between social holons versus individual holons.

Dacher's articulation of the lower quadrants—interpersonal (LL) and worldly (LR)—while less broad then Wilber's use of the quadrants, facilitate meaningful assessments by the students. The activity, while experiential, requires a cognitive understanding of the three developmental stages of flourishing,[14] as well a reflective capacity utilizing self-examination of the 12 lenses that loosely correlate with the four quadrants. Unlike the ITP, which focuses on personal growth, Integral Health also assesses the lower half of the quadrants or plural aspects of self in the world. It opens up an entirely new awareness for many students in the course.

In terms of Mind-Body Medicine, Dacher's Integral Health model successfully integrates plural perspectives, such as family, community, work, social activism, and generativity, that are perspectives not yet considered by current clinical Mind-Body research. Yet, in the context of this course, they seemed appropriate and natural to the notion of connections between the mind and the body.

As a classroom methodology, Dacher's assessment uses postmodern and integrative perspectives that offer individuals an opportunity to deconstruct the self into component parts that can fit together in novel ways. It asks students to relate the personal self (upper quadrants) and the communal self in community and out in the world. Overall, the focus is on self-understanding rather than knowledge.

In terms of our class' understanding of Integral Transformative Practice, the Integral Health assessment shifted the discussion from the way in which each person was achieving their goals in the ITP process to a contemplation of a more deconstructed self with many facets that can be considered individually and, yet, still fit together into a whole or integrative perspective.[15]

Because Dacher cleverly articulates egocentric, ethnocentric, and worldcentric as the developmental levels of body, mind, and spirit, students were less stuck than they were with other explanations of psychological development such as the vMemes of Spiral Dynamics or the altitudes of Integral Theory. I observed the opportunity for reflection and growth, which had much to do with the contrast between the upper, or individual, quadrants, and the lower, or collective, quadrants. The contrast between personal goals in the ITP and the interrelational elements of the Integral Health assessment drew the class into a complex discussion about personal versus community perspectives with regard to health and transformation. Because of this discussion, I was able to introduce two second-tier perspectives offered by Spiral Dynamics—the Yellow Integrative vMeme and the Turquoise Integral vMeme (Beck & Cowan, 1996).

In Spiral Dynamics, the being tier (or second tier) emerges into the Yellow Integrative vMeme, which is characterized by: An acceptance of nature's flows and forms; A focus on functionality, competence, flexibility and spontaneity; A natural mix of conflicting "truths" and "uncertainties;" A discovery of personal freedom without harm to others or excesses in self-interest; An experience of the fullness of living on an Earth of such diversity in multiple dimensions; and a demand for integrative and open systems (Beck & Cowan, 1996).

Students' reflection on these core conditions of Yellow/second-tier perspectives found that our work in this class had fulfilled many of the above criteria. Flow, flexibility, conflicting truths, personal discovery, integration, and fullness were all aspects and outcomes of our work this term.

In contrast, the Turquoise Integral vMeme, "the Holistic Meme" or Global View is characterized by: Blending and harmonizing a strong collective of individuals; A focus on the good of all living entities as integrated systems; Expanded use of the human brain/mind tools and competencies; A concept of Self which is part of a larger, conscious, spiritual whole that also serves Self; and a global networking which is seen as routine and acts for minimalist living so less is actually more.

Interestingly, the class members noticed how few of these aspects our work had touched. Only the third criteria, "expanded use of mind tools and competencies," was addressed. This evaluation allowed for further discussion about the differences between the upper quadrants and the lower quadrants, as well as the difference between the Yellow and Turquoise vMeme, with a goal of finding balance in the AQAL system.

Returning to our previous discussions, the contrasts between these two vMemes facilitated a reflection as to the emphasis in each of the three basic forms considered so far: Mind-Body Medicine, Integral Transformative Practice, and Integral Health. The question that emerged in the class was about how to develop a practice that facilitates not only personal transformation but also interpersonal or community transformation.

In only eight weeks of this course, it would be unwise to say that we solved this riddle. However, as an offering in an integral setting, we were able to approach the question in a short time. Many students offered suggestions for how to create community transformation. For most, it became clear that we had reached a new vantage point, one in which we could begin the process over again, with a new quest, a new goal, or Integral Transformative Practice that seeks personal as well as interpersonal transformation.

As the Mind-Body Medicine class was nearing its completion I asked the students to briefly explore the Integral Life Practice (ILP). I asked students (after the ITP was done) to choose several of the "one minute" modules used in Integral Life Practice and explore them for one week. Many of the students found the practices complicated and "intellectual."

> The ILP is a little overwhelming to me. Maybe if I had a big chart on my wall I would consider each column more regularly. It's easy to see, at first glance, though, which items are at the forefront and which ones are not. Mind and Body are at the forefront of my life. Spirit and Shadow, not so much. While I work with these aspects, it's not a daily basis for me really, except for what goes on in my sub- and un-conscious.[16]

Practicing ILP did introduce even more aspects of self, that both ITP and Integral Health had not covered, for example, the three major states (gross, subtle, and causal), and shadow. Due to the focus on ITP, I believe it would be unwise to draw any conclusion about ILP as a classroom practice or classroom design from this limited inquiry. However, it is interesting to note that neither ITP nor Integral Health have any practice that considers states or shadow.

Returning to the classroom methodologies, approximately one-third of class time was dedicated to conducting the Integral Transformative Practice, online posts, and self-assessments. Another third of the class time was dedicated to student presentations of eight different forms of Mind-Body Medicine—meditation, movement therapy, ritual, biofeedback, guided imagery, prayer, autogenics, journaling, and hypnosis. This core content of Mind-Body Medicine was taught by the students themselves. The last third of the class time was devoted to general principles of Mind-Body Medicine, which were presented by lecture followed by small group discussions.

Creating an Integral Mind-Body Program

The final assignment asked students to develop an Integral Mind-Body program specifically for the individual, the student. The program must contain at least one practice for each quadrant. It should cover physical, mental-emotional, and spiritual. After experiencing ITP, Integral Health and ILP, students had an opportunity to create their own Integral Mind-Body Program. From a methodological perspective, this required a personal integration of the material covered throughout the semester. The points of contact and differences between these three models of practice served students in their own creative process. AQAL assessment facilitated a framework from which students could maintain a clear cognitive structure in creating their programs. As well, the final assignment offered a creative opening. Rather than simply an evaluation, a critique, or a discourse, this assignment asked for a truly first-person perspective of transformative practice, requiring also a clear third-person understanding of the subject of Mind-Body Medicine. Part of the assignment required the explanation of the purpose of each aspect of the program.

Mind-Body Medicine and the Integral Classroom

Due to the introduction of Integral Health, Spiral Dynamics, and Integral Life Practice, this last year's final papers were clearly of a different quality then previous years. More than any other class, students' work reflected a commitment to personal transformation and to the health of an integral community. For the first time, our work together offered a creative moment for us individually and collectively. One student wrote:

I visualize the image of cyclical spirals to guide my practice. My experience reveals the necessity to explore interconnected nodes of development instead of individual modules of practice. The concept of the spiral indicates the importance of doing inner work in preparation for the work that I am called to do out in the world. As I comprehend my own psychosomatic composition, I intend to help relieve the suffering of the individuals that I teach. My practice enables me to take care of myself so that my energy and mental clarity are available in service of my clients. With this greater clarity, I hone my intuitive and conscious healing abilities.[17]

Traditionally, Mind-Body Medicine is taught as a balance of objective and subjective perspectives. Scientific evidence is mixed with experiential pedagogy and, while often thought of as an interior approach, the experiential learning aspects often focus on empirical elements of learning. An integral pedagogy for Mind-Body Medicine includes all four of Integral Theory's quadrants in both intent and classroom design. Heuristic experiential inquiry is balanced with behavioral practices. Collective experiences offer a culture of transformation that facilitates personal growth, as well as a culture of change. An integral pedagogy honors the academic field while gracefully providing teacher and students ample room for transformative growth. Spiraling through different aspects of Integral Theory, while holding to an integrally informed experiential practice honors the potential for personal growth as well as cultural transformation. Using varied and appropriate technologies and social systems to balance didactic learning provides ample room for cognitive mastery.

For me, Integral Mind-Body Medicine offers a unique opportunity for capturing the divine creative spirit of my students as well as for myself. The richness of experience deepens as we practice together, gaining strength from learning just how much we can inform each moment with our will and our complete being. I continue to marvel at the variety and depth of experiences we have achieved as a collective, seeking healing and growth. Balancing personal with collective perspectives, using all three voices—"I," "We," and "It/s"—offers a diverse fabric of opportunities for any teacher, I can only share my awe at the potential for personal fulfillment that occurs with these explorations. I am grateful to have shared the journey with my students as well as the opportunity to reflect on the tapestry of potential that the integral classroom offers.

Notes

1. Conventional medicine in the twentieth century is centered in an Orange, modern, rational woldview. For simplicity, references to developmental levels will use the color scheme of Spiral Dynamics reference in Beck & Cowan, (1996).

2. Quadrant locations my addition based on the four quadrants of Wilber. The quadrant notations reflect the traditional focus of each perspective, in reality, all perspectives are always present—each perspective is tetra-arising.

3. Mind-Body Medicine research focuses almost exclusively on individual experiences and behaviors.

4. J. M. personal communication.

5. J. B. personal communication.

6. M. N. personal communication.

7. In the course I often use the Spiral Dynamics model to explore these distinctions. In this model the Green vMeme is pluralistic, with a values emphasis on exploring the inner beings of self and other, promoting community, sharing, consensus, and harmony. The next stage of development is the Yellow vMeme, which is an emerging 'Integrative' perspective that accepts nature's flows and focuses on competence, flexibility, and integrative open systems.

8. Vertical shifts occur when individuals are able to transcend and include previously conflicting perspectives.

9. T. S. personal communication.

10. Connative refers to the source and character of motivations (Dacher, 2006).

11. Wilber's four quadrants are based on a hierarchy of nested holons or holoarchy, meaning that each level transcends and includes the previous level, e.g., an atom, then a molecule, etc. Dacher's Integral Health Assessment does not adhere strictly to Wilber's nested holoarchy, thus the 12 assessment lines do not fit together into one whole metatheory, which is essential to Wilber's Integral Theory.

12. M. N. personal communication.

13. Dacher's assessment uses the terms, I, you, us, all of us, as the consideration for the personal Lower-Left quadrant. These match up to egocentric (I), ethnocentric (you), worldcentric (us and all of us).

14. To flourishing is the overall goal of the program. Body, mind, and spirit are the levels of development.

15. In Integral Theory, this is found in the concept of the Integral Psychograph.

16. T. S. personal communication.

17. S. C-A. personal communication.

References

Astin, J., & Astin. A. (2002). An integral approach to medicine. *Alternative Therapies, 8*(2), 70–75.

Beck, D., & Cowan, C. (1996). *Spiral dynamics.* Boston: Blackwell.

Benson, H. (1976). *The relaxation response.* Boston: G.K. Hall.

Cannon, W. B. (1932). *The wisdom of the body.* New York: Norton.

Dacher, E. (2006). *Integral health.* Laguna Beach: CA: Basic Health Publications.

Dewy, J. (1963). *Experience and education.* New York: Collier Books.

Esbjörn-Hargens, S., & Wilber, K. (2006). Towards a comprehensive integration of science and religion: A post-metaphysical approach. In *The Oxford Handbook of Science and Religion* (pp. 523–546). Oxford: Oxford University Press.

Leonard, G., & Murphy, M. (1995). *The life we are given.* New York: Jeremy Tarcher.

Green, E., & Green, A. (1977). *Beyond biofeedback.* S. Lawrence: Delacorte Press.

Jacobson, E. (1938). *Progessive relaxation.* Chicago: Univ. of Chicago Press.

Luthe W., & Schultz. J. H. (1969). *Autogenic therapies.* Volumes 1–6. New York: Grune and Stratton.

National Institute of Health, National Center for Complementary and Alternative Medicine (2007). *Mind-body medicine: An overview.* Retrieved October 1, 2008 from http://nccam.nih.gov/health/backgrounds/mindbody.htm#scope

Pert, C. (1999). *Molecules of emotion.* New York: Simon and Shuster.

Schlitz, M., Amorok, T., & Micoaai, M. (2005). *Consciousness & healing: Integral approaches to mind-body medicine.* St. Louis, MO: Elsevier.

Selye, H. (1978). *The stress of life.* New York: McGraw-Hill.

Wilber, K. (1995). *Sex, ecology, spirituality: The spirit of evolution.* Boston: Shambala.

Wilber, K., Patten, T., Leonard, A., & Morelli, M. (2008). *Integral life practice.* Boston: Integral Books.

Matching Educational Intentions with Assessment

Using an Integral Map

Nancy T. Davis

Assessment Etymology: Origin Late Middle English. From Old French assesser, based on Latin assidere 'sit by' from ad-'to, at' +sedere 'sit.'

Introduction

An institution's assessment practices are a reflection of its values. In other words, the values of an institution are revealed in the information about itself that it gathers and pays attention to. A second, and perhaps more fundamental, premise is that assessment practices should further the basic aims and purposes of our higher education institutions. (Astin, 2002, p. 3)

Looking more closely at what and how we assess is a critical component to consider when creating a class and building the container in which learning occurs. Assessment provides feedback to both those inside (teachers and students) and outside (parents, administrators, politicians, and the general public) about what is happening in the learning process. The importance of assessment is reflected in the human resources and time that are invested in assessment processes, tools, and strategies each year in education.

To understand assessment's role in education we must first consider the intents and purposes of education. Colleges and universities are institutions of society, created to reproduce the values and traditions of the dominant culture

(Pinar, Reynolds, Slattery, & Taubman, 1995). Culture acts as a norming force on the individuals within the culture (Wilber, 2000; 2004) thus those who deviate from the culture, either from less sophisticated or more sophisticated perspectives, are constrained toward the norm. Thus, in thinking about education we should also think about what kind of culture we want to create. In our educational institutions do we want to duplicate the past, or do we want to create a better world? Through education an opportunity for culture and society to "re-form" is presented. Through educational experiences, participants in society can discover images of the possible. If we want a society that values diversity, then educational institutions should reflect that valuing. If we want a democratic society, then our educational institutions should model the democracy that we wish to create. If we want students to be critical thinkers, responsible for their own learning, value their own and others' contributions, to continue to improve, then our practices should reflect those goals. If education can provide experiences for students that assist them in developing sophistication beyond the current cultural level, then education becomes transformational. It is through such a transformational process that society itself, transforms. Since what we assess indicates what is valued within the learning environment, then aligning our assessment practices with our intentions is of particular importance.

As a university teacher educator, I find my focus on aligning practices with intentions particularly salient because my role is to prepare future educators to teach in schools, colleges, and universities. One of my goals is to assist prospective and practicing teachers to realize how their practices impact the formation of culture. Thus, many of my practices focus on helping learners to develop awareness of their own values and how their practices align with those values. I have worked with teachers from kindergarten through post-secondary. Much of my academic research focuses on teachers' thinking and practices and strategies to assist teacher development. My research evolved throughout my tenure as a science educator at Florida State University. Early in my career I focused on constructivist learning as applied to teachers as I studied teacher beliefs and processes of change (Davis & Helly, 1995). Studying teaching change led me to focus on teacher autobiography and action research as a tool for professional development (Davis, 1996). I worked with several university professors to redesign their curriculum and teaching to be more consistent with their goals. Research from a five-year project with a university statistics professor (Davis & Blanchard, 2004) led me to realize how critical assessment practices are in reforming the learning environment within the university. My involvement with teachers in schools also focused on assessment as a critical leverage point in educational reform (Davis, Kumpete, & Aydeniz, 2007).

Throughout my career I struggled with notions of assessment as I wrestled with understanding my own roles in the teaching/learning process. I have scored according to objective tests, used performance assessments, allowed students to grade themselves, structured peer assessments, provided rubrics for grading, and used portfolio assessment. I have attempted to go the route of not grading students' work—after all, who was I to assess another's learning? I learned from each of these experiences, but it was not until I used an Integral framework (Wilber, 2000; 2002) that I began to clarify my understanding of my experiences with assessment. Each of the multiple purposes of assessment has important uses as long as they are applied appropriately by consciously fitting them with the educational intentions. Dilemmas such as confounding achievement with learning arise when we use data and methods with one intention to serve another. This chapter is an exploration into using Integral Theory to develop a map that connects educational intentions with appropriate assessment strategies and methods.

Since assessment provides a focal point for determining what is valued in the learning process, it is through assessment data that individuals within the learning context (and those outside it) can develop clearer understandings of what is happening. There are as many ways of assessing as there are learning contexts. So how is one to determine which is the most appropriate to use? There is not one answer, but rather a map of answers and if one can locate their intentions on the map, he or she can better align assessment with their educational intentions. In this chapter, the purposes of assessment will be aligned with practices using an Integral framework to inform and guide the process.

Why Assess? Looking at Assessment through Quadrants

Drawing from recent research on teachers' views of assessment, (Davis et al., 2007) four very different but equally valid purposes of assessment were elicited: (1) accountability; (2) comparison within and between populations; (3) building communities of learners; and (4) individual learning.

The first two purposes most readily come to mind when assessment is discussed (Davis et al., 2007). While writing this chapter, the university's newspaper arrived in my mailbox with the headlines of "Class act: Student performance raises FSU's prominence" (Seay, 2008). The focus on the prominence and reputation of the university is in part based on the scores of incoming students. Astin (2002) laments this focus of institutions of higher education on achieving excellence through "reputation" rather than on "talent development." Excellence depends upon comparing the students and faculty against students and faculty of other institutions. Individual accountability and comparison between and within populations are intended to describe to others what is happening within the educational context and are exterior uses of assessment because the methods allow individuals to look at measures and descriptions from an objective perspective.

In contrast, the last two perspectives, focusing on individual learning or development (Astin, 2002) and building communities of learners (Bruffee, 1998) are interior perspectives. While volumes have been written on learning, in spite of differing perspectives there is agreement that learning occurs in the interior of the individual. Similarly, the notion of community deals with relationships between individuals and what is accepted within the group as the norms, mores, and conversation styles (Bruffee, 1998). These interactions between individuals are an interior function of the collective community. Interior functions are subjective and depend upon differing criteria to establish goodness of the data.

In the following sections, Wilber's (1997, 2000, 2006) notions of integral knowing are applied to assessment as a way of constructing assessment to account for the various purposes (see Fig. 22). Examples of methods of assessment within each are provided. Within each intention different criteria are used to determine the goodness or appropriateness of the assessment methods.

Right-Hand Side (Exterior): Accountability

Accountability focuses on objective, standardized, measurable criteria that can be used to make judgments about how an individual is performing or where an individual fits within a population. Issues of reliability and validity come to the fore as tests are used to make value judgments about individuals and collectives in a process of evaluation. From an intention of accountability, these judgments should accurately describe the performance of individuals or groups (reliability) and the assessment instrument should measure what it claims to measure (validity).

Upper-Right quadrant. Traditional assessment practices are based upon a technical rationale (Habermas, 1973) in which judgments are made about how well the learner has reproduced knowledge and skills determined by some author-

	Interior Assessment for Learning	Exterior Assessment for Accountability
Individual	Self-Assessment (How is an individual making sense and what do they need to do to continue to develop?)	Criterion Referenced Tests Standards (How does this individual measure against standards for achievement?)
Collective	Peer Assessment (Using the group's established criteria for quality what can be done to help the individual and the community improve?)	Norm Referenced Test (How does the individual fit within the population?)

Figure 22. Intentions for Assessment

ity as important. In assessment from this perspective, individuals are compared to standards or benchmarks. These are the external measures that much of society and political entities use to gauge the effectiveness of educational institutions. Currently, most states have performance or content standards that focus on assessment as accountability, and institutions of higher education are facing the possibility of having standardized exit tests for graduates. Nationally developed tests such as the Iowa Test of Basic Skills, California Achievement Test, and state-developed achievement tests use developed criteria to determine how a student is performing. Grading done in schools is used as a value judgment rating individuals against a "standard," the knowledge or skills that the tests are designed to measure.

In my own teaching, I find that these accountability measures are useful in helping me and my students see how they are performing in the content goals (objectives or standards) of the course. To demonstrate they know which statistical formula to use to answer specific research questions, an objective test may be used. I have found that while these objective tests may increase the pressure on students within courses, they also show the student that they are able to match the content with the test maker, who is usually representative of the discipline in which the student is learning, in this case statistics. High scores on such tests may provide learners with the confidence to continue in other more sophisticated courses in statistics as they value their own performance.

Teachers in most states must demonstrate they have content knowledge by taking a standardized exam on the content of the discipline for which they are seeking certification. This exam acts as a "gatekeeper" to indicate that teachers have sufficient content knowledge to perform in teaching classrooms. These are valuable uses of such accountability measures. I work on the construction of such tests, and believe that they have a value for quality control of those seeking to enter teaching science.

Lower-Right quadrant. Assessments from the lower-right perspective describe how individuals fit within a population. How do others perform on similar tests, how many scored better or worse? In this norming process statistical measures are appropriate tools to better develop descriptions of the population and where specific students fit within populations. Universities have measures such as Grade Point Averages (GPAs), student standardized test scores (GRE, LSAT, and MCAT), graduation rates, etc., that are used to indicate the quality of their students in comparison to other institutions. Institutions of higher education use these performance measures to determine their own excellence as they compare their students' scores to those of other institutions (Astin, 2002).

In schools, norm referenced tests are used to determine which schools are more or less "effective" in terms of achievement. The move toward schools and states being rated or even given grades as suggested by The No Child Left Behind Act (U.S. Dept of Education, 2001) looks at assessment from this perspective and, while this narrow perspective is important, it is also partial. Much of the public has little data to gauge the effectiveness of schools other than through such norm-referenced measures. Parents want to know how the schools their children attend compare with other schools. If the desired outcome of schools is what is measured on achievement tests, then these norm-referenced measures are appropriate tools for comparison.

Left-Hand Side (Interior): Learning

Learning is not so easily determined since it is an interior process. Individuals make sense of information and make connections between experiences in idiosyncratic ways. Advocates of reform in education call for learning to become a way of life as educational institutions develop communities of learners who are creative, autonomous, and empowered (Habermas, 1973). To determine the quality of interpretation of interior meaning-making, trustworthiness, fairness, and authenticity are criteria that are applied, primarily in qualitative research.

Upper-Left quadrant. Educational reformers argue for a reformulation of assessment so that it can seen as an integral part of the learning process and for students to be active in their own assessment with opportunities to picture their own learning in light of understanding what it means to get better (Black & William, 1998; Pringle, 2000). This perspective involves the individual's assessment of his or her sense-making processes. What does he or she know, and how does he or she know? A concern is that the individual is aware of his or her sense-making processes and what may be inconsistent or problematic. Thus, an individual using the feedback from others looks at how he or she is measured against criteria or a population and what she or he needs to do to improve and show learning. The focus of the individual's reflection is on bringing the unconscious to consciousness so that it can be reflected upon and actions may be taken to improve. One goal of assessment as part of the learning process is to assist the learners to develop the capacity to recognize and appraise gaps in their understanding and to accept the responsibility for carrying out any actions needed to help them to continuously improve (Pringle, 2000).

Rubrics can be designed to guide learners to reflect on their own learning and to achieve the goals of the learning community (see appendix). Learners become involved in the process of assessment and can determine the gap between what they are learning and producing and the established learning goals. This focuses the learner on the understanding the goals in the educational environment, and how they are meeting these goals, which leads to internalized learning and a change of understanding (Sadler, 1989). A primary method of using assessment to enhance individual learning and responsibility is the use of portfolios in which the student makes and argument about his or her learning using data that illustrates their learning. In the Masters program in science education, we use portfolios as the final product of the program. The goals of the program are reflected in the criteria established for the portfolio. You might also note that this rubric is based on an Integral framework.

Lower-Left quadrant. The purpose of assessment in this quadrant is continuous improvement based on consensus of what determines quality. Assessment from this perspective focuses on quality criteria established and judged by the group. The ratings completed by peers provide feedback to the individual on how she or he can improve. From this perspective the focus is on communities of learners or disciplines. For example, a community of scientists determines what is considered appropriate and valid knowledge and skills within the community, how the community thinks about the discipline, and how further knowledge is appropriately generated. The peer review process reflects the intentions from this perspective, and thus for any community of learners it is a critical defining aspect of the community.

In my own teaching I modeled peer assessment on the review process of academic journals. The intent is to assist improvement, while maintaining standards of quality. My intentions are to establish a community of learners who are continually improving and maintaining a conversation about the topics being learned. The criteria are negotiated from a rubric designed to reflect goals of the course of critique (Eisner, 1997), community, and improvement. As the community establishes the quality criteria used in the rubric, they participate in a hermeneutic-dialectic process (Guba and Lincoln, 1989) that informs the community. [See appendix for a sample rubric]. I then use a rubric that I have established in my intentions for the course that focuses on improvement and continued conversation. Part of the criteria used also reflects learners providing evidence for the rating they give peers, focusing on the notions of critique (Eisner, 1997). I use a four-point scale in my rubrics with a "3" indicating that criteria have been met. I have found that the limits imposed by grading criteria often inhibit student learning. Thus, I provide a way for students to go above and beyond expectations and when they give a score of "4" they must provide an explanation with evidence to support that score.

Discussion of Purposes for Assessment

These four purposes for assessment are often confused in conversations and documents because the purposes often contradict each other. For example, accountability includes value judgments as an individual is measured against a standard or a population. Students who are focused on accountability interpret suggestions for improvement as personal judgments about themselves. The prospective teachers who I teach are initially reluctant to "grade" their peers because they don't want to hurt their friends' feelings. Only when they realize that their peer assessment grades depend on providing suggestions for improvement do they begin to speak more honestly with their peers. Most teachers can relate stories of frustration as students focus more on the grades than on the concepts being taught. The focus on value judgment sometimes results in the learner developing such a level of fear that the grades get in the way of learning (Pringle, 2000).

Separating out the purposes and the methods to achieve the goals of assessment develops a more viable way of thinking about assessment that accomplishes all the purposes. The perspective from each quadrant is important. Through the use of an Integral framework the various purposes of assessment can be differentiated. Classrooms can be created to be places where individuals come to learn and include all the purposes for assessment. The use of this Integral model of assessment can enhance the learning environment and assist in reframing the notion of assessment to include continuous improvement as an integral part. The external measures would continue to be taken and the information would become part of the community. Individual students could move through the school system with an electronic portfolio that would include all of the assessments from the various quadrants. Current developments in e-portfolios (also called Webfolios) using Web 2.0 technologies make these manageable and widely accessible to learners (Waters, 2008). Assessment could be integrated back into the whole with the focus of the classrooms to enhance learning and focus of the individuals to be able to demonstrate learning.

Conclusions

Teaching is a complex endeavor involving not only knowledge of subject matter, but also knowledge of pedagogy, content pedagogy, the learners, and the teaching context (Gallard, 2008; Shulman, 1986). Understanding underlying issues of power and authority is an important endeavor for policymakers and teacher practitioners, particularly those using Integral frameworks to inform their decisions and attempts to reform education. Being aware of potential tensions that arise when individuals narrowly define purposes of assessment can assist reformers in broadening their perspectives.

In this chapter the focus is use of the quadrants aspect of Integral Theory and to further work that can be done to focus on levels of development using anticipated responses at the differing levels of knowing. Additionally, within each stream of development, differing measures and qualities can be addressed. By using an Integral model of assessment formed by looking at and valuing various perspectives of assessment, a more sophisticated and integral perspective can be developed. External measures continue to be taken and the information becomes part of the culture of education. Providing an avenue to also value individual and group learning through assessment enhances purposes of assessment and provides an avenue for development of further sophistication. Individual students move through the school system with an electronic portfolio (Waters, 2008) that would include assessments from the each of the quadrants and show development in differing lines with increasing levels of sophistication. Assessment could be integrated back into the whole with the focus of the classrooms on enhancing individual development and the focus of the individuals on demonstrating learning.

Appendix

This is a sample rubric taken from a graduate level class on research methods.

Critical Reviews: Explanation and Tentative Assessment Rubrics

The areas for assessing critical reviews include criticalness, scholarship, connections to experience, and professionalism (organization, spelling, and grammar).

Criticalness involves looking at the underlying assumptions in the reading and posting a critique that makes explicit these assumptions. Questions to help focus the assessment of this component include:

1. Is the text examined critically looking at the implication of what is written and discussing both positive and negative contributions?

2. Is the discussion provocative? Does it raise questions in the reader's mind?

Scholarship involves showing that one is a member of a learning community (the professional community of the course content and the learning community of the class). Questions to help focus the assessment of this component include:

1. Does the writer show membership in the professional, text-writing, community through connections to other readings?

2. Does the writer show membership in the class community by referencing the contributions of other class participants?

Connections to experience involves contributing experiences as a teacher or as a learner that illustrate ideas discussed in the readings. Questions to help focus the assessment of this component include:

1. Does the writer connect to his or her teaching/learning experiences?

2. Does the writer connect to his or her research experiences?

Professionalism is the category that deals with technical issues such as organization and readability, appropriate grammar, spelling, and timeliness. Timeliness is particularly important because the participation of peers in writing peer commentaries depends upon the critical review being available in a timely manner.

The final assessment of a critical review is based upon the four-point rubric shown in Figure 23:

Category	1 point	2 points	3 points	4 points
Criticalness	Little or no critical discussion.	Some discussion of implications. Some questions are raised.	Implications richly presented. Discussion is provocative.	Implications richly presented with extensive background material. Discussion is provocative and inviting.
Scholarship	Little or no references used.	A few professional references used, but not all are relevant.	Relevant professional and classmate references used.	Exceptional number of relevant professional and classmate references used. References connected in a compelling manner.
Connections Experience	Little or no connections to personal experience.	Connections to teaching/learning experiences are superficial or lack authenticity.	Substantial connections made which enriched conversation.	Exceptional number of connections made; vivid descriptions, particularly appropriate and insightful.
Professionalism	Vague or unclear; a difficult read. Numerous spelling, grammar, and/or typing errors. And not posted by deadline.	Some focus, but not enough; an easy read. Few spelling, grammar, and/or typing errors **or** not posted by deadline and no explanation provided.	Clear and focused; a good read. Very few errors. Posted on time.	Exceptionally clear and focused; an enjoyable read **and** posted on time.

Figure 23. Scoring Rubric

Timeliness: If a posting is late and there is no explanation as to when the posting will be made, then a rating of 0 should be posted to the Discussion Board.

Absence of a posting results in a score of zero.

Total possible score per Critical Review = 16. (Note: all criteria met = 12.)

References

Astin, A. W. (2002). *Assessment for excellence: The philosophy and practice of assessment and evaluation in higher education.* Westport, CN: American Council on Education.

Aydeniz. M. (2006). Understanding the challenges of enacting assessment reform in public high school science classrooms. Unpublished doctoral dissertation, Florida State University.

Black, P., & William, D. (1998). Assessment and classroom learning. *Assessment in Education, 5*(1).

Bruffee, K. A. (1998). *Collaborative learning: Higher education, interdependence and the authority of knowledge* (2nd ed.). Baltimore: Johns Hopkins University.

Davis, B., Sumara, D., & Luce-Kaplar, R. (2007). *Engaging minds: Changing teaching in complex times* (2nd ed.). New York: Routledge.

Davis, N. T., Kumpete, E., & Aydeniz, M. (2007). Fostering continuous improvement and learning through peer assessment: Part of an integral model of assessment. *Educational Assessment, 12*(2), 1–23.

Davis, N. T., & Blanchard, M. (2004). Collaborative teams in a university statistics course: A case study of how differing value structures inhibit change. *School Science and Mathematics, 104*(6).

Davis, N. T. (1996). Looking in the mirror: Teachers' use of autobiography and action research to improve practice. *Research in Science Education, 26*(1), 23–32.

Davis, N. T., & Helly, M. (1995). Conflicting beliefs: A high school chemistry teacher's struggle with change. *School Science and Mathematics, 95*(7), 345–350.

Eisner, E. W. (1997). *The enlightened eye: Qualitative inquiry and the enhancement of educational practice.* Upper Saddle River, NJ: Merrill.

Gallard, A. (2008). *The development of an education research model framed by complexity theory.* Paper presented at the Oxford Roundtable. Oxford, England.

Guba, E. G., & Lincoln, Y. S. (1989). *Fourth generation evaluation.* Newbury Park, CA: Sage.

Habermas, J. (1973). *Theory and practice.* (Translated by John Viertel.) Boston: Beacon.

Novak, J. D., & Gowin, D. B. (1996). *Learning how to learn.* New York: Cambridge University.

Pinar, W. F., Reynolds, W. M., Slattery, P., & Taubman, P. M. (2005). *Understanding curriculum: An introduction to the study of historical and contemporary curriculum discourses.* New York: Peter Lang.

Pringle, R. (2001). *Using peer and self assessment as tools towards re-framing assessment.* Unpublished doctoral dissertation, Florida State University.

Sadler, R. (1989). Formative assessment and the design of instructional systems. *Instructional Science, 18*, 119–144.

Shulman, L. S. (1986). Those who understand: Knowledge growth in teaching. *Educational Researcher, 15*(2), 4–14.

Waters, J. K. (2008). In the driver's seat. *T.H.E. Journal, 35*(6), 43–50.

U.S. Department of Education. 2002. "Executive Summary: The No Child Left Behind Act of 2001." Washington, DC: U.S. Department of Education.

Wilber, K. (2000). *Sex, ecology, spirituality: The spirit of evolution*. Boston: Shambhala.

Wilber, K. (2002). *Integral psychology: Consciousness, spirit, psychology, therapy*. Boston: Shambhala.

Wilber, K. (2006). *Integral spirituality*. Boston: Shambhala.

Expanding Our Vision in the Teaching and Design of University Science— Coming to Know Our Students

Sue Stack

Preface

In this chapter I focus on two moments in a collaborative university action research project which aimed to improve teaching and learning within a physics faculty. I unravel some of the issues that lecturers grapple with: changing teaching cultures and beginnning a process of coming to know their students better. I juxtapose this with reflections on my own movement toward an integral/holistic teaching practice and my relationships with my own students as they move into self-authoring developmental stages.

I write this article using epistemologies drawn from auto-ethnography (Ellis & Bochner, 2000), writing as inquiry (Richardson, 2000), impressionistic writing (van Maanen, 1988), and transpersonal research methods (Braud & Anderson, 1998), which aim to make explicit the interiority of inquiry. This style aims to capture the moment—its emotional heart space as well as its physical and theoretical aspects. It aims to give the reader a sense of the "real" through fictionalising a narrative and providing a sense of story and motion forward. It also aims to model a process of "becoming" and encourages the readers to reflect on their own experiences and thinking that have the potential for transformation. It contextualises self as "self situated in culture," making apparent some of the underpinning paradigms and values which shape me as the writer, and thus asks the readers to reflect on the values that shape their own sense of what education is for.

Scene 1

It is the first week of the university year, 1999. I am sitting in a large resonant lecture theatre that might normally hold 300 students. There are 60 of us, swallowed up in the space, distant from the lecturer down at the bottom who is explaining the principle of refraction, prisms, and lenses with the aid of a slick PowerPoint presentation. Layers of information appear on each diagram with variables and formulas. Each slide builds on the others carefully, logically, beautifully, inexorably.

I am transported back 20 years to my own undergraduate physics days. The topics haven't changed; the teaching approach hasn't changed. Now we have PowerPoints and printouts, rather than scribbling down misread notes from scruffy writing on blackboards, or overhead transparencies. But we are still captive to a teaching/learning process based on particular paradigms about education, the nature of learning, the nature of our students, the nature of knowledge, and the purpose of undergraduate science. Can it change, should it change, and what might help?

I am sitting in this room as coordinator of a year-long Collaborative Action Research Project to improve the teaching of first-year university physics courses. Sitting near me are other lecturers involved in the project. I came to the project wondering how I could bring holistic and integral perspectives to the transformation of university teaching. What might it mean to be an integral/holistic teacher, or create integral science courses, or develop integral scientists? But I have to let those grand aims go and tune into this group of lecturers and their questions.

After two days of brainstorming and more days of interviewing client departments to determine their needs, we have decided on some key values and purposes to underpin the development of new teaching approaches in physics courses. In particular, we ask how we can move from *just* a dissemination of a "body of knowledge"—fixed truth claims—into a more inquiry oriented, student-centred approach? How can we induct students into the process of inquiry that a scientists might bring to their own leading-edge research to foster critical thinking and problem solving as they step into the unknown? Can we bring an inquiring mindset to the way we engage with the "body of physics knowledge?" What happens to this body of knowledge and its truth claims if we treat it as an object of inquiry?

What is this "process of scientific inquiry?" I have mulled over this for some time, bringing Integral Theory (Wilber, 1997, 1998) and other lenses to my own experiences as a scientist and science teacher (Stack, 2007). I wonder whether the glue in scientific inquiry (e.g., sense of wonder, intuitive hunches, creative insights, personal passions, corridor dialogues) is often unacknowledged because the scientific method is seen as objective, evidence-based, procedural, logical, theoretically informed, and rigorous. How can we make the interiority (Wilber's "I" and "We" quadrants) of scientific inquiry explicit? Who is the "I" that is inquiring, what processes and cultures are he or she bringing, and how can these limit/enhance what is seen?

So with this broader framework of science inquiry in mind, I asked the lecturers to unpack their own inquiry processes as scientists. They are astonished at what they value and what they have not recognised as important in their own research processes. They wonder how they can expect students to do science well if these values are not explicitly supported. We now ask: *What might a lecture or a laboratory session look like/feel like/sound like with students engaged in a broader notion of scientific inquiry: evidence gaining, pattern seeking, connecting, hypothesising, inventing, dialoguing, wondering, imagining, intuiting, theory building, critical thinking, risk taking, systems thinking, contesting, ethical reasoning, perspective taking? How can we facilitate this? What structures might support it? What are students capable of?*

While this conversation seems pivotal in helping the lecturers see beyond their own paradigm of "what science is" and "what science teaching is about" it is another matter to transform their teaching practice. During the course of the project I learn about the many barriers to such transformation—the way we perceive and make sense of another's thinking and experience, the way we think about knowledge and are captive to its solidity, the ability to see the potential within activities for deeper learning, the roles we are comfortable taking on, the ability to reflect on our own thinking, the need to develop meta-cognitive language and processes, and the need for a shared educational language about learning and development.

But I am getting ahead of myself. Dan, the lecturer who is down the front taking this lecture, has been worried that all the effort he put into making his PowerPoints over the holiday may no longer fit the aims of the project. Where does his construction of a body of knowledge leave room for students to participate in their own inquiry and meaning-making? How does it fit into a bigger picture or one that might be more relevant to the students? He tells us he has had sleepless nights worrying about it. His topic of optics is the first in Applied Physics with another three lecturers taking components of the course over the remainder of the year. I suggest to him that perhaps his prepared topic is a way for us to enter into the research project—find out how the students learn and think—in order to inform the creation of the subsequent topics, which will hopefully adopt a more inquiry oriented approach.

He is relieved and says perhaps he can ask students more questions through his presentation, to get more interactivity and encourage their participation in constructing the ideas. However, like the other lecturers, Dan is not comfortable with engaging the students at a meta-cognitive level about how they are thinking, learning, and imagining. So, one of my roles is to get student feedback about the sessions to pass onto the lecturers for discussion.

Dan is asking a question and I watch the students lean forward a little with quite a few hands up. "Another example of a prism is the . . . ?" A student says "a lens." Dan says, "No . . . well, yes, but that isn't what I was looking for . . . another example is . . . ?" A few students make suggestions but it still isn't the one Dan was seeking. He says, "Another example of a prism is . . . The EYE!" Next time

Dan asks a question only a few hands come up, most students are leaning back, disassociated.

I sigh inwardly. My first frustrated thought is "Surely this isn't rocket science!" My next calmer thought is "How can I find something in me to relate to Dan, to find compassion and understanding, to see with his eyes and to think as he does and then to find that seed within him that can lead him out of his dilemma?"

As I look down the rows of students I see one of my ex-students I taught Year 12 Physics to the year before. While the Year 12 Physics course is bound by a set syllabus with exams, criteria, standards, and moderation, I had been able to experiment considerably with my teaching approach and philosophy over a 10-year period. Perhaps this girl, Tiffany, epitomises the journey I have been on: a journey of learning to see. Perhaps I started like Dan, concerned to get across content so students could measure up to the way "learning" was perceived, valued, and measured.

Initially I was interested in ways of thinking about my students and their learning *in order to help me improve their understanding of physics*. I looked to pedagogical solutions taking into account learning styles and multiple intelligences, drawing from processes from cognitive challenge theory and constructivism. However, in aiming to improve my students' understanding of physics I also needed to understand them, to ask probing questions, to listen to their questions and conversations, and to allow myself and my understanding of the physics content to be perturbed by their perspectives. I had to open myself to their feedback and be prepared to question what I thought I "knew." And this process was transformative for me, requiring me to move from a modernist "assertive" voice into a more postmodern "speculative" voice where the content is not a fixed entity but rather *a conversation* between players, each of whom can develop rich but possibly different understandings (Doll, 1993).

This then was the beginning of the disintegration of my tightly held scientific persona into a self that could value and use a growing number of lenses and see knowledge more as a metaphor and a construct than a "truth." As I began to see my students in different ways I began to question the purpose of education, bringing in spiritual perspectives and drawing from the literature on holistic education (e.g., Palmer, 1998; Miller, 1996; Noddings, 1992; Cajete, 1994; Childs, 1996). Was it about helping students learn physics or was it much bigger . . . about helping them to develop as whole people within an expanded sense of reality? So now I wondered how physics might lend itself to an exploration of self *in the* world, rather than just an exploration of the world. How might I recruit imagination, soul passion, dialogical knowing, and playfulness to help us take on different roles, identities, and perspectives as we navigated our ways through the world of phenomena? And would this foster student growth?

As I began to explore these questions I found myself changing . . . becoming more humble, more perceptive, more able to differentiate my ego from my teaching practice. I found myself being perturbed by models or theories of learning and development—my delicate ego under threat, realising how perhaps I might be stuck in certain perspectives or developmental levels. Sometimes I wanted to reject or ignore these threatening ideas, and then when I had enough think time I would come back to them, unpacking the fear impulse and learning to be open to learning. I learned to be kind to myself and not to try to rush my own development. In the process I became more sensitive to the "other," developing strong relationships with my students, and feeling a resonance with their own journeys. I was no longer distant; rather stepping from a simple "instructor" role into multiple ones—mother, mentor, midwife, facilitator, catalyst, vulnerable learner. Like Palmer (1998), I aimed to create a spiritual space within me so I could accept my students' gifts.

In an experiment of mine I encouraged students to write in an *"I wonder"* journal where they could capture their thinking, wondering, imagination, and existential questions using a range of genres such as drawing, writing, poetry, or dialogue. I asked them: *What intrigues you, surprises you, inspires you, challenges you?* The journal then became a conversational and relational space for me and the student; one that enabled me to see deep into the interiors of my students, and be constantly surprised.

See Tiffany sitting down there in this large lecture theatre, sitting quietly, head tilted to one side. What can you see and how could you come to know her? Is she just one of many, lost on this cavernous lecture theatre, an unknowable statistic?

When I first met Tiffany I made a lot of assumptions. She appeared to be a shy motivated girl whose interior self was quite invisible to me for the first months of teaching her. However, through her journal I began to glimpse another side of her: one which astounded me, humbled me, and perturbed my thinking about how students learn, make sense of, and be in their world. Tiffany's journal, like those of her peers, is a remarkable artifact of the journey she has been on in growing into a new self. While she brings her own individual uniqueness to her journey, she is following rhythms that have been mapped by various developmental theorists.

She is someone, who, I believe, has been moving from Egan's (1986) *romantic* stage (just wanting to understand the nitty-gritty of how things work, black-and-white thinking, interest in the heroic/anti-heroic) to Egan's *philosophic* stage (needing to create her own increasingly complex generalising and integrating frameworks of the world despite being faced with competing tensions, such as trying to reconcile her belief in spirituality with physics).

I have seen indications that she is moving in perspectival levels from Kegan's (1994) *socialised mind* to *self-authoring mind*. She values the permission to question conventionally accepted knowledge and is becoming more confident in using critical thinking tools and models to do so. She doesn't need to always follow a set scientific method but is confident in creating her own rigorous processes of inquiry that suits her learning styles. She is able to reflect in sophisticated ways on her learning and ways of thinking using meta-cognitive tools with ease.

As a result of exploring the nature of paradigms, she seems to be becoming aware that her knowledge frameworks are value-laden, culturally dependent, and open to her critique and control. After some initial concern she has embraced a position of uncertainty (nothing is true) in first thinking about her science knowledge and then bringing that to her own life world. She has been in a process of reconstructing what she is prepared to consider "contingently true"—*best understanding at the time*—and wants to have an active role in the creation/modification of scientific theories rather than just learning established knowledge.

She is examining her own identity—particularly her role as daughter and her own values. She is actively seeking to re-invent herself and her ideologies—moving from a conforming Catholic into her own ideas of a more interior spirituality—but not quite yet gaining a tolerance for alternative views from her peers about spirituality. (Is she peeking into the next perspectival stage—*pluralistic mind*—and moving from Fowler's (1995) *synthetic-conventional* stage of faith to *individuative-reflective?*)

She is learning to welcome being perturbed and is becoming more aware and comfortable with the growing/transformation process. This is a process which involves discomfort; uncertainty; a dissociation from previous ideas, values, or behaviours; a trial of new roles and possibilities; and an oscillation back and forth between her old self and new self before finding her way into a new sense of self with new perspectives (Mezirow, 2000).

Her journal is an indicator to me of how my deliberate philosophical questions or perturbing activities have found their mark, how something might sit for many months before she might write about it, or equally how something I have done might have been misinterpreted. I now wonder how she will continue to grow being exposed to this university experience. To what extent should the development of her "interiors" be an aim of university courses? What happens if the teaching ignores the stages she is at and teaches at a much lower stage? Will this suppress her? If we want to develop students' inquiry skills, can we do this independent of developing the student?

How is she responding to Dan's approach? What does Dan understand about his students, and how is he aligning his teaching to their developmental needs? Would he need to know and understand each of his students, or can he get a sense of their needs by understanding development or learning models and the spectrum that his students are most likely to cover? Do these models only make sense if we are engaged in the process of coming to know another? And would having these models in mind open our view, or limit it? Am I failing to see Tiffany when I only see her with the *eye of mind* rather than through the *eye of spirit?*

And where in all this might I start a conversation with Dan? How does he see the "affordances" that physics might be able to give to assist Tiffany to continue to develop, and how are these limited by his perception of his role and his perception of the purpose of science education? What are his underpinning paradigms, and am I privileging my own? How can I honour his journey while helping him to see deeper into the potential of what he does?

It is the end of the optics lecture. Tiffany passes me with a smiling hello and I ask her how she is finding things. She tells me that she is really enjoying her pharmacy classes "We are learning real stuff that will help us when we get jobs. Its technical; it doesn't get me wondering, but I guess that is what university is about—preparing you for the workplace. I can see where it's going. I don't know why we have to learn optics though. What is the relevance?" What indeed!

I ask her if she understood what Dan had done today. "Well the stuff we had already covered last year was easy—just remembering it, but he covered the new stuff very quickly. I would have liked to have got my head around it. I am learning though that I don't have time in my lectures to make sense of things—I need to go home and puzzle over it myself, practice it. As long as I know what is going to be tested. No point spending my time on it otherwise."

"But this is so different to how you were last year in physics . . . questioning, challenging, wondering . . . totally engaged. . . ."

"Don't worry, Sue," she says, "University isn't about stimulation—that is obviously not what we are paying for. It is about getting a degree to get a job."

I wonder: "Am I expecting too much of university science education?"

*

Education ... *Educare* ... to lead out.

Science ... *scire* ... (verb) ... to know, to split apart, to separate ideas.

.... *Scienta* ... (noun) ... Knowledge.

*

Scene 2

Dan has packed up his laptop at the front of the class and I join him as we walk back to the tea room. "How do you think the lecture went?" I ask.

"Umm?" He looks at me, as if he had never considered this before.

"You have done a lot of work on that PowerPoint," I say. "The diagrams, the clear development of ideas, all the layers. Do you think the students understood it all?"

"I guess we won't know that until the test."

I pause, and take a different tack.

"I notice you asked a lot of questions throughout the lecture, though most of them were closed—just requiring one answer—rather than open ones. Did you notice how students responded to them?"

"Not really, with these glasses I can't see much beyond the front rows."

I look at Dan and notice for the first time his thick myopic glasses. "So you don't notice the body language of students, how they might lean forward when interested, or what happens when they disengage?"

"No"

I can't imagine teaching a class where I am not receiving tacit as well as explicit student feedback that helps me adjust and respond to the class. What might it be like to be shut out from this information? How can Dan come to know his students and their thinking if he doesn't physically see them? I begin to realise how he distances himself from the class even in his more intimate lab sessions—staying at the front, avoiding dialogue, letting his lab assistants work with the students as he presents lecture-like material and lock-step experiments. Are these superbly constructed PowerPoints a barrier to conversation, enabling Dan to stay in his own world? If he won't go to his students, how might I help him to begin to understand his students?

I decide to explain how closed questions can turn students, particularly this age, away from participation—students don't want to take a risk that they are wrong, particularly in front of a large lecture theatre. Questions that are open enable students to explore possibilities and determine plausibility criteria for deciding which ones might be best. It is the active discerning of criteria that helps develop rigor in their thinking. Acknowledging all contributions helps to get a range of "misconceptions" out in the open and enable them to be interrogated. By writing alternatives on the board for open discussion students feel more comfortable putting forward their views—they see that even the eventually discarded views help the whole class to better understand the concepts as well as what constitutes scientific reasoning.

Dan is looking at me horrified. "But Sue, I couldn't ask an open-ended question. I just wouldn't know which of the students' answers are right or wrong."

I look at him questioningly.

"I need to think things through myself; I can't think on my feet like the other two lecturers. I have to know exactly what it is I have to do and say."

"You have got a different learning style to the other lecturers and you need to work to your strengths," I say musingly. "What you are describing to me is a more reflective style. Probably about 20 percent of your students feel the same way and are very wary of contributing anything to the class that they haven't had time to think about. Hmmm? What if you *planned* an open-ended question, which you have already thought out ahead of time? You ask students to brainstorm possibilities, you write them on the board, and then you ask them in pairs to go through and determine which is most likely? In doing this you can model scientific thinking."

"I'll think about it," says Dan nodding.

A couple of days later Dan tells me he has designed an open-ended question for his next lab which has two possibilities. There are a number of lecturers observing the lab. Dan gives the question to the class. It is a good one and the students are engaged in thinking about it and eventually three possibilities are suggested. Dan writes two of them on the board but seems very hesitant to put up the third one. He then asks the students to use their optics equipment to test them out. For the first time in a lab session I hear students hypothesising, suggesting alternative theories, discussing different ways to collect evidence. This sounds like the beginning of scientific thinking and inquiry—a key aim of the project. The observing lecturers become actively engaged in the emerging discussions, which become a jumping-off point for deeper reflections. However, Dan is still up the front, shuffling his notes, seemingly oblivious to it all. He clears his throat and asks for the students' results. Based on their findings he eliminates all but one possibility and then gives instructions for the next arrangement of lenses.

I am feeling really positive about the session. I ask Dan at the end of the lab session how he felt it went. "I was very uncomfortable. I was completely thrown by that third possibility, but I remembered what you said and wrote it up anyway."

"I could tell you were reluctant," I say smiling, "But didn't you see how it was the highlight of the lab—it got the students involved and questioning, linking the ideas to their own experiences?"

"But it took up too much time, I had to rush to cover the rest of the lesson."

"Perhaps covering all the content is not as important as the quality of learning?"

Dan looks at me and I know that he is unconvinced. I wonder what is driving him to believe in the importance of a relatively arbitrary body of knowledge, which is not directly relevant to any of these students. How can we achieve the aims of the project (and even touch on my own wish list of integral/holistic science) when Dan seems captive to certain perceptions of science knowledge and cultures of learning despite their best intentions to change? I wonder where Dan might be positioned on a learning development chart and what cultural vMeme (Beck & Cowan, 1996) might be influencing his teaching.

At the next meeting of the project group we all share our experiences of the lectures and lab sessions of the previous two weeks. The lecturers seem surprised how each of them has observed different elements from the sessions and they discuss possibilities arising from comparing these different views. I share the feedback that I have been getting from my student interviews, handing out transcripts of student conversations and thinking. Initially there is a rejection by the lecturers of some of the student views, perhaps because they are so counter to the lecturers' own perceptions and values. However, when I offer an educational framework to examine the seemingly competing perspectives, the lecturers begin to become fascinated about what the different perspectives can tell us about the students and their learning. They move into wanting to more actively understand their students and they come up with different questions for me to ask them. I say that they can ask the students themselves, but they all say that they feel uncomfortable doing so.

It seems that I have become a mediator and an ethnographer—my role is to help them come to know the "foreign country" that is their students and their learning cultures. I wonder how I can help them to also be ethnographers.

While I might be moving into a role of helping lecturers to understand their students better, I also realize that I am beginning to see the lecturers as "people," and not just "lecturers to transform." Despite my frustration at their seemingly small movements in teaching practice, I realize that I need to celebrate something that has been very extraordinary about this project so far—the willingness of the lecturers to put themselves on the line, to be observed by their peers, to be debriefed by me and disclose things to me about themselves, which has involved considerable courage and willingness to engage in this process of self-examination and self-honesty. They appear to be moving out of their comfortable space of scientific inquiry into a community of pedagogical inquiry, which requires different ways of seeing and interpreting, different language, new referents, and a commitment to self-inquiry.

I begin to be humbled by the openness and willingness of the group and am concerned whether I might have been a little arrogant in my thinking about these very real people—evaluating them on their educational products and their stereotypes, rather than seeing them as the complex beings that they are. We are only a few weeks into this action research process and perhaps I am learning to juggle a need for reform and *doing* (projection of my own aims and expectations into visible results), with a need for understanding and *being* (tuning into to others and their invisible journey potentials). Perhaps this project is more about my own transformation and my own initiation into a more Integral practice.

So what does it mean now to continue such a journey? What reflective tools do I need? What theories or lenses do I need to challenge and let go of, and what others can help me make sense of this? What cultures of thinking and being am I embedded in, and who might help me make these more visible? As I transform myself, can I transform the world? (Stack, 2007).

References

Beck, E. D., & Cowan, C. C. (1996). *Spiral dynamics: Mastering values, leadership and challenge.* Malden, MA: Blackwell Publishing.

Braud, W., & Anderson, R. (Eds). (1998). *Transpersonal research methods for the social sciences: Honouring human experience.* Thousand Oaks, CA: Sage Publications.

Cajete, G. (1994). *Look to the mountain: An ecology of indigenous education.* Durango, CO: Kivaki Press.

Childs, G. (1996). *Education and beyond: Steiner and the problems of modern society.* Edinburgh: Floris Books.

Doll, W. E. (1993) *A postmodern perspective on curriculum.* New York: Teachers College Press.

Egan, K. (1986). *Individual development and the curriculum*. London: Hutchinson.

Ellis, C., & Bochner, A. P. (2000). Autoethnography, personal narrative, reflexivity. In N.,K. Denzin, & Y.,S. Lincoln (Eds). *Handbook of qualitative research*. (2nd ed., pp 733–768) Thousand Oaks, CA: Sage Publications.

Fowler, J. (1995). *Stages of faith: The psychology of human development and the quest for meaning*. New York: HarperCollins Paperbacks.

Kegan, R. (1994). *In over our heads. The mental demands of modern life*. Cambridge, MA: Harvard University Press.

Mezirow, J. et al. (2000). *Learning as transformation: Critical perspectives on a theory in progress*. San Francisco: Jossey-Bass

Miller, J. P. (1996). *The holistic curriculum*. Toronto: OISE Press.

Noddings, N. (1992). *The challenge to care in schools an alternative approach to education*. New York: Teachers College Press.

Palmer, P. (1998). *The courage to teach: Exploring the inner landscape of a teacher's life*. San Francisco: Jossey Bass.

Richardson, L. (2000). Writing: A method of inquiry. In N. K. Denzi, & Y. S. Lincoln (Eds). *Handbook of qualitative research* (2nd ed., pp 923–948). Thousand Oaks, CA: Sage

Stack, S. J. (2007) *Integrating science and soul: The lived experience of a science educator bringing holistic and integral perspectives to the transformation of science teaching*. Retrieved March 13, 2008, www.stack.bigpondhosting.com/thesis

Van Maanen, J. (1988) *Tales of the field: On writing ethnography*. Chicago, IL: The University of Chicago Press.

Wilber, K. (1997) *Eye of the spirit*. Boston: Shambhala Publications

Wilber, K. (1998). *The marriage of sense and soul*. Melbourne, Australia: The Hill of Content.

IV

Looking Ahead

Integral Mind, Brain, and Education

Katie Heikkinen

Introduction

A recent survey of 200 educators in an international sample revealed that the majority believed that understanding how the brain works was important "in the design and delivery of educational programs for children and adults" (Pickering & Howard-Jones, 2007, p. 111). Most educators had heard about or used so-called "brain-based" education programs and generally found them useful. At the same time, educators were concerned with the accessibility and interpretation of scientific research and its application to the real-world classroom.

Educators, it seems, yearn to learn more about the brain and the latest neuroscience and cognitive science findings. Teachers want to be more effective in their instruction, to help every student learn, and they hope that understanding the brain will provide vital insight. The fledgling field of Mind, Brain, and Education (MBE) honors this impulse and attempts to facilitate collaboration across fields and disciplines. Yet the field is new and the challenges are many. Educators need tools that will help them integrate the truths of brain and cognitive sciences in a comprehensive, transdisciplinary framework.

Ken Wilber's Integral model is one such framework. In this chapter, I demonstrate how educators can use two aspects of the Integral model—the four quadrants and the eight zones of Integral Methodological Pluralism (IMP)—to improve their teaching practice and deepen their understanding of educational research. I argue that Integral Theory brings a much-needed integrative framework to MBE, while MBE offers integral education a methodological and scientific rigor—not to mention a certain cachet. With perspectives from the Integral model and MBE, educators can create comprehensive solutions to educational problems, better assess educational research, and understand the relationship between the various research methodologies and their impact on practice in a new way.

What Is Mind, Brain, and Education?

Mind, Brain, and Education is a new field, established in part by the creation of the International Mind, Brain, and Education Society (IMBES) in 2005. Rather than merely bringing biological and cognitive sciences to bear on educational problems, the field seeks instead to build reciprocal relationships between the three disciplines of cognitive and developmental sciences, biology, and education (Fischer and Heikkinen, in press). Just as brain and mind science will improve education, the theory and practice of education will improve brain and mind science.

IMBES offers a biennial conference, occasional workshops and seminars, a biannual newsletter, and a journal. *Mind, Brain, and Education* was awarded the Best New Journal in the Social Sciences and Humanities by the Association of American Publishers in 2007 (www.imbes.org). Its articles have been mentioned in *Newsweek, The Chronicle of Higher Education, Medical News Today*, and *United Press International* (Fischer & Daniel, 2008). So while the field is in its infancy, it is in no doubt *hot*. Stories about the brain seem to capture the hearts and minds of the public. Moreover, the role of science in education has never been stronger, with many nations currently emphasizing empirically-validated instructional methods.

The founder of IMBES, Kurt Fischer, also helped to found a Master of Education program in Mind, Brain, and Education at Harvard Graduate School of Education. I received my master's degree from this program in 2007, and I have been an assistant teacher for its core course, HT-100: Cognitive Development, Education, and the Brain. It is exciting to see how students in the program are eager to integrate what they know about education from their typical position as teachers or administrators with what they are newly learning about psychology, cognitive science, development, and the brain. Yet this integration is not without struggle, particularly as students attempt to understand how to deal with the overload of information without a certain understanding of how the different disciplines relate to one another. This is where the Integral model steps in.

The AQAL Framework: Toward an *Integral* MBE

Ken Wilber, the American philosopher-writer, has done extensive work toward creating Integral Theory, which includes a comprehensive transdisciplinary framework, which he dubs the "AQAL" model. AQAL stands for All Quadrants, All Levels, All Lines, All States, and All Types. These five categories represent the primary distinctions or elements within the Integral model. Here, I will focus on the four quadrants (i.e., the interior and exterior dimensions of individuals and collectives) and how they can help educators create comprehensive solutions to educational problems and better assess educational research. For an overview of the four quadrants, see Esbjörn-Hargens (this volume).

As educators, the four quadrants can help us ensure that our understanding of a situation is as comprehensive, complete, and whole as possible. The four quadrants help us remember all of the relevant aspects of a situation that must be addressed in any case study or research agenda, if our analysis is to be as complete as possible. To demonstrate the utility of the framework, I will apply it to a simple case study of the kind that might be used in MBE research or instruction. Let us look at Gordon, a nine-year-old with a history of reading difficulties, through the four quadrants (see Fig. 24, next page).[1] Wilber (2006) calls this process of looking at something through the lens of the four quadrants a *quadrivia*.

I hope this demonstrates that the four quadrants are a quick way for teachers and researchers to make sure that "all their bases are covered" when analyzing a case study or assessing and interacting with a student, as well as an easy way to coordinate the relationship between the various bits of information. I also believe it is easy to see that most case studies—and often the reports teachers receive from disabilities specialists—lack information from at least one quadrant. In many cases, the Left-Hand quadrants are missing. The case study proceeds using a third-person, omniscient voice, as if what is reported is exactly what is happening, as opposed to one interpretation among many. But this kind of third-person reporting is not always true to the actual first-person experience. Obviously, it is a good-faith attempt to capture people's experiences, but a different kind of discourse may be a useful addition—one which captures the not only what is happening, but how the case subject feels and experiences it. In this particular case, we have quite a bit of third-person reporting about Gordon's Upper Left, but we do not have much about his Upper Left in the first-person voice. The first-person account may be more suitable to a different methodological approach like portraiture than it is to a case study; but it is important to be aware of what is present and what is absent.

Overall, this case actually focuses primarily on the upper two quadrants—the individual dimensions. We do not know as much about the collective aspects that Gordon is embedded in. Simply attempting to map the content of the case study to the four quadrants helps us see that dynamic immediately. Yet, obviously, collectives are tremendously important. The tasks that we are demanded to do determine the types of abilities and disabilities we display, and task demands are often set by the cultures and systems we are a part of.

Next, I will use the four quadrants to critique a research design. Note that this is a different application of the four quadrants. Gordon *has* all four quadrants—he has an interior with his own private feelings and thoughts. When we apply a quadrivial analysis to Gordon, we make assertions about the content of his four quadrants, which he alone has primary *access to* and can *look out from* as dimensions of his own being. A research design does not have the four quadrants. But we can still use the four quadrants as a *lens* through which we can view a research design, prompting us to ask questions about its multiple aspects.

	Inner (Felt and Experienced)	Outer (Seen and Measured)
Individual	"I" — SELF & CONSCIOUSNESS	"IT" — BIOLOGY AND BEHAVIORS
General	Gordon's inner, individual world of thoughts and feelings, meaning and interpretations, motivations.	Gordon's brain and body. Everything that happens to him as a living organism. His outer world: things he does and things others can observe.
Specific to case	Level of development in various metrics —Attitude and motivation toward school —Feeling toward and meaning made of school difficulties —Feeling anxiety and lack of confidence	—Medical and schooling history —Skills, abilities, and behaviors, such as: fine motor skills, ability to sit still, reading comprehension —IQ —Neurological assessment —Cognitive schemas/heuristics
Collective	"WE" — RELATIONSHIPS, CULTURE, WORLDVIEW	"ITS" — SOCIAL SYSTEMS & ENVIRONMENT
General	Gordon's interpersonal relationships. The ways that Gordon shares with others of describing and defining his culture and history, the shared myths and stories he uses to make sense out of things, shared language.	The outer world that Gordon belongs to: his familial and neighborhood network, his ecological, political, and economic environment, the processes and roles he participates in within these systems.
Specific to case	—Quality of relationships with family and other caregivers —Friendships and peer group; peer culture —Member of dominant white, English-speaking culture	—School system Gordon is a part of and the relevant national policy and state standards —Demands of the curriculum —Laws regulating special education —Structure of the school and the supplemental tutoring program

Figure 24. Gordon in the Four Quadrants

However, looking at an object is trickier than looking at a person. When we look at an individual that is part of the research design that we are analyzing with the four quadrants, he or she *has* the four quadrants; so to avoid infinite regress, the analyzer must make a few choices about what goes where. In this case, I am viewing the "interior" of the experiment as the interiors of all the relevant parties (i.e., the individuals involved in the research as well as the reader).

As an example, let us look at an fMRI study on dyslexia mentioned in an MBE-informed research article by Shaywitz, Lyon, and Shaywitz (2006, p. 615). I will include question marks where I discern information that would be present in a more consciously "AQAL" article, but which is actually not mentioned. See Figure 25, next page.

When educators begin to consider putting research into practice, looking at a research design through the four quadrants helps them see its potential strengths and weaknesses. Does the "all quadrant map" of the research at all match the "all quadrant map" of where I hope to apply it? Does the researcher have an agenda, any hidden biases or preferences? Do the subjects share certain characteristics that might lead to the preferred finding? Are certain subjects excluded in a way that systematically biases the findings? Are cultural and meaning-making differences ignored? What exactly happened during the research? Was it what was meant to happen? What pressures does the system put on research? What systemic pressures bear on applications? How can I use my understanding of the comprehensiveness of this research to more judiciously apply it to my classroom practice?

Looking at Mind, Brain, and Education Through the Four Quadrants

The four quadrants can help us see that the field of MBE is "more integral" than traditional educational research endeavors in several ways. It promises to cast a wider eye at what is relevant to improving education than traditional studies of classroom practice. Its paramount contribution, in integral terms, is its attention to the Upper-Right quadrant, the "It" of science. Its investigations into neuroscience, endocrinology, and genetics offer an important perspective on what is going on inside the UR bodies of our students. It also looks at the learning environment quite broadly, including not only the concrete aspects of classroom life, but also its affective elements, developmental demands, and the complex interaction between the child and his environment. The methods and tools of MBE can help integral education learn more about important aspects of the AQAL matrix. Indeed, any attempts at integral education must include the insights of this new field.

However, perhaps the most perilous risk inherent in the new field is the tendency toward committing to quadrant absolutism. Adding the perspective of brain and biology to studies of education can easily mean that the Upper Right becomes the unquestioned king, with privileged access to truth. If it cannot be seen

	Inner (Felt and Experienced)	Outer (Seen and Measured)
Individual	"I" — SELF & CONSCIOUSNESS	"IT" — BIOLOGY AND BEHAVIORS
General	*The multiple "I"s that participate in the research, from subjects to researchers. Individual differences.*	*What is observed in the research; brains and behavior; results and methods*
Specific to case	The Subjects:	The Subjects:
	Felt-sense and meaning-making of the subjects	—Behaviors and external characteristics of the subjects
	—Attitude and motivation toward reading?	—144 right-handed children, aged 7–18; 70 dyslexics and
	—Affective state?	74 "non-impaired" readers
	—Developmental level?	—Reading pseudowords and real words
		—Large sample, broad age range, boys and girls
		—What other characteristics are known? Unknown?
	The Researchers:	The Researchers:
	—Known agenda is to demonstrate the "localization of specific systems and their difference in good and poor readers" (p. 615)	—Behaviors of the researchers and characteristics of the research design
	—Third author has written a popular book on the neurological basis of dyslexia (Shaywitz, 2003)	—fMRI study
		—Examining left and right hemisphere brain sites
		—Significant difference in brain activation patterns between dyslexics and non-impaired readers
		—Compensatory systems developed in dyslexic readers
		—Used across-subject, multi-trial averaging statistics?
		Potential hidden assumptions and biases underlying choice of statistical methods
	Myself:	Myself:
	—My own personal responses as a reader of the study	—My behavior as a reader

Collective	"WE" — RELATIONSHIPS, CULTURE, WORLDVIEW	"ITS" — SOCIAL SYSTEMS & ENVIRONMENT
General	*The culture that the research is embedded in, for both subjects and researchers. Language and shared interpretations.*	*The systems that the research is embedded in, for both subjects and researchers. Economics, practicalities.*
Specific to	The Subjects: —Any relevant interpersonal issues? —What culture were they a part of? —Did they understand the instructions as intended (language and shared meaning)? The Researchers: —Any cultural biases or expectations shaping their research agenda? —The discourse of the discipline and its influence on design and interpretation Myself: —The cultural and intersubjective assumptions, biases, or expectations that I bring to my reading of the article. —My relationship to the discourse of the discipline	The Subjects: —The educational system they participate in —Compensation or payment of subjects The Researchers: —University or institution where research takes place; its pressures for publication or funding —Overall trends or fads in research in that field; —competing theoretical accounts —Laws regulating research Myself: —My position as a reader in a larger system (influencing me in known and unknown ways)

Figure 25. Research Design Viewed Through the Four Quadrants

in a brain scan, it is not a real educational outcome, blinding us as educators to any deeper, more phenomenological impacts. Although I sincerely believe that this kind of absolutism is not MBE's intent, interdisciplinary work is hard. Regardless of the intentions of the forerunners of the field, it is easy for people to slip into absolutistic thinking when they are outside of their areas of expertise or interested in a sound bite or quick fix. By applying the four quadrants to research in MBE, educators can avoid this kind of absolutistic thinking and ensure that our use of this new field is as whole, comprehensive, and integral as possible.

Comprehensive approaches to educational problems are essential. But comprehensiveness alone does not yet address the issues of *disciplinary integration*, or deeply understanding the tensions and relationships between the various disciplines. While MBE acknowledges a multiplicity of disciplinary approaches in its very name, it makes very little conscious effort to integrate these various disciplines into any overarching structure. As a consequence, it may be limited in how deeply interdisciplinary its work can be (for more on the challenges of interdisciplinarity, see for example, Stein, 2007). But an *integral* MBE—applying Integral Methodological Pluralism—has the potential to move beyond mere multidisciplinarity and find truly transdisciplinary solutions to today's most pressing educational problems.

Integral Methodological Pluralism

Just as we can use the four quadrant model to discern the various aspects of any situation as we did above, we can also apply these four perspectives to the disciplines and methodologies of research itself. The realities associated with each quadrant can be methodologically investigated from either the "inside" or the "outside," resulting in eight distinct zones. This results in a *meta-disciplinary* framework that *integrates* the truths from the various disciplines and coordinates the various strengths and weaknesses of each approach or methodology. Wilber thus expands the four quadrants into eight methodological zones of Integral Methodological Pluralism (IMP).

IMP takes a "40,000 foot" view of the disciplines and attempts to see how they all fit together through their use of injunctions or specific methods. What does science do that poetry does not do? What does poetry do that science does not? We all know intuitively that the different disciplines accomplish different things, but we know less about how they related *to each other*. Poetry and science are different, yes, but *how exactly* are they different, and how are they actually *similar?*

IMP begins to answer these questions by claiming that the various methodologies actually are different *perspectives*, looking at different aspects of reality—the *inside* and *outside* of the four quadrants. This results in what Wilber calls the *eight primordial perspectives*. The eight primordial perspectives are the eight basic ways of viewing or being in relationship with phenomena. But "you can not only take a view, you can act from it" (Wilber, 2006, p. 35), yielding eight fundamental methodologies. The eight perspectives and accompanying methodologies are summarized in Figure 26.

In *Integral Spirituality*, Wilber designates a "prototypical" methodology for each of the eight zones, and lists several other example methodologies (2006, p. 37). In Figure 26, I have listed the prototypical methodology in bold, with other examples collected from throughout the book in plain text. I have also listed Wilber's numbering of the zones for ease of reference.

Next, I will explain each of the eight perspectives in turn, using commonsense language, then the language of the methodologies or disciplines they pertain to,

Structuralism Developmental psychology "Stage" theorists	**Empiricism** Experimental/observational science Neurophysiology Genetics research Evolutionary biology Classic behaviorism
2 **OUTER** **1** **Phenomenology** Introspection Meditation Much literature/poetry Meditative cartographies States (of consciousness) training **INNER**	**Autopoiesis** "Self-creation" Cognitive science Biomedical psychiatry Evolutionary psychology Sociobiology Cognitive development **5** **6**
4 **3** **Hermeneutics** Interpretation of shared signifieds Creating fellow subjects in I-Thou relationship	**Social autopoiesis** "social self-creation" via communication Study of exchanged signifiers, interactions, and artifacts Luhmann systems **INNER** **7** **8** **OUTER**
Ethnomethodology Cultural Studies Semiotics Geneaology (Foucault) Post- and Neo-structuralism	**Systems theory** Chaos/Complexity theory Ecology Web of Life approaches von Bertalanffy systems

Figure 26. Integral Methodological Pluralism

and finally, off-set visually, examples from the field of MBE. As a tool for teachers, Integral Methodological Pluralism can help us understand how all the various types of research in the field of education fit together. By understanding the relationship between the various research methodologies, we can see their impact on practice in a new way. By taking a "virtual tour" of the eight zones, we can see where MBE has strengths to offer integral education, and where integral education can bolster MBE perspectives. My tour will begin with the individual zones, then cover the collectives. In an attempt to mirror our natural intuitions, when dealing with the interior zones, I begin with the insides, while when dealing with the exterior zones, I begin with the outsides (thus, an awkward though I hope intuitive order of 1, 2, 6, 5, 3, 4, 8, 7!).

Let us start with the Upper Left. We can view our inner-individual experience from the inside—that is a first-person story about my experience of life. Taking this approach and extending it into a methodology gives us *phenomenology:* "an approach that concentrates on the study of consciousness and the objects of direct experience" (Merriam & Webster, n.p.) This zone also includes approaches not typically thought of as "methodologies"—like meditation and consciousness training. But these too are specific injunctions taken from the individual-interior stance and are a valid way of learning more about this zone.

> As with most scientific disciplines, there are few—if any—examples of this zone in MBE. There are currently no examples of zone 1 approaches in the program I teach in, for example. Examples in teacher education could include personal reflections—about the purposes of education, reactions to case material, or relationship to the learning process. Teachers can access this zone in their practice through reflection, contemplation, or reconnection to personal values. Note that questions about the larger aims and goals of a good education are primarily accessed through this zone.

Next, we can view someone else's inner-individual experience from the outside—that is a third-person account of an individual's interior space. Note that that is not the same as a third-person account of what we *see* an individual do. That does not gain access to their interiors, how they make meaning of the world and understand it. Instead, a third-person account of a person's interior space focuses on a person's meaning-making structure, as they report it. Extend this approach into a methodology by using rigorous interviewing methods or structured self-report, plus longitudinal experimental design, yields *developmental structuralism*, the study of the patterns of interior experience seen throughout psychological development.

Zone 2 approaches are a particular strength of MBE, embracing developmental psychology ranging from Piaget to Fischer to Kohlberg. Piaget is a fixture in teacher education, although more recent research in development is often neglected. A unique contribution of integral education is an emphasis on this zone through the concept of *altitude* (Wilber, 2006).

Next, we have the Upper Right. It is easy to understand looking at an exterior-individual from the outside—that is what much of science is. Looking at an animal interact with its environment and carefully recording its behaviors is an exterior account of an exterior-individual. No attempt is made at understanding the organism's interiors. Wilber calls this approach to methodology, obviously enough, *empiricism*.

Zone 6 approaches are also a strength of MBE. These include brain research (Nelson, Goswami, Banich, Damasio), basic experimental psychology, and genetics research (Scarr and McCartney, Grigorenko, Petrill, and Justice). The empirical findings of MBE can and should be included by integral education, which in turn can situate them in a larger, transdisciplinary context.

But imagine you are that scientist, watching a rat navigate a maze—it is easy to move from descriptions like "he turned left, then right, then left again" to questions like "why did the rat take that path? Why did he learn what he learned? What's in his *mind*?" This is a motion toward taking an inside approach to an exterior-individual—we want to explain what kind of *inner structures* would account for the *observed behaviors* we see. Good-bye classic behaviorism, hello cognitive science! Wilber calls this approach *autopoiesis*, after the term coined by Maturana and Varela (1980), which means "self-creation."

Zone 5 approaches are really the core of MBE, especially since mind-based approaches to education are better entrenched in the field than brain/body-based approaches. These include classical cognitive science approaches (Pinker, Fodor, Gelman, Dehaene, etc.) and cognitive development approaches (Spelke, Carey, Gopnik). Cognitive science findings may be closer to the classroom than brain science findings, but they too typically require interpretation and translation by educators before they can be applied.

Realizing that there is an inside and outside approach to what is already divided into interior and exterior gets tricky. But let's proceed with the Lower Left, the realm of culture and shared meaning. Approaching a culture from the inside means dialoging with a culture you belong to, approaching its meanings as a participant in their negotiation. It is about making interpretations as a member of shared community of interpretation—what Wilber labels *hermeneutics*.

> Just as in Zone 1, MBE tends to lacks zone 3 approaches outside of the natural negotiation of meaning that must occur in interdisciplinary settings that include discussion or group work. Additionally emphasizing this zone in teacher education could include more explicit awareness of the conflicts of meaning between disciplines—something that Integral Theory can bring into focus—and more explicit frame-setting for group discussion norms. Zone 3 is a natural fit in the intersubjective classroom. Teachers focusing on it can build community and cultural awareness—and remind themselves that they have access to zones of truth that a scientist with an fMRI cannot see.

Leaving your own culture—whether the one you were born into or the one you have earned your membership in through scholarship—and exploring another can yield an exterior perspective on an interior-collective. What is this other culture that I am not a part of like? How can an outsider interpret it in a way that perhaps an insider could not? Extend this armchair approach with field studies, and we have *ethnomethodology*.

> MBE focuses very little on zone 4, but is not without exemplars of a more culture-based approach (e.g. Tomasello, Egan, and Gardner to a certain extent). Olsen is an excellent example of a "genealogical" approach; Lakoff and Johnson of semantics. A truly Zone 4 approach may feel more at home in an educational anthropology journal than an MBE journal. Perhaps this is entirely appropriate, leading the reader to question whether an Integral MBE must be all things to all people. I am not suggesting the blurring of disciplinary boundaries, but truly comprehensive educational research must at least have explicit awareness of each zone. The deepest understanding of mind/brain, self/body will stem from integrated approaches.

Finally, let us look at the Lower Right of systems. The exterior approach to an exterior plural neatly parallels empiricism—it is the dispassionate eye of science, only this time applied to collectives, such as ecosystems or economies. Wilber notes that the prototypical approach in this zone is *systems theory*.

A zone 8 approach is fairly common in MBE; certainly this zone's indirect influences are quite strong. Some genetics research (particularly gene by environment interactions), Fischer's dynamic development, neural network modeling (Spitzer), and neuroconstructivism (Mareschal et al.) are clearly influenced by systems theory. Much of the literature from Risk and Resilience (e.g., Bronfenbrenner) focuses not on the individual, but on the systems and structures the individual is embedded in. This is a fairly common approach in teacher education, and a somewhat familiar perspective for teachers negotiating "the system" on behalf of their students.

How do we look at a system from the inside? This is probably the trickiest distinction, since systems to do not have interiors, as organisms do. Yet groups do construct themselves (via autopoiesis) by maintaining internal coherence and boundaries. Just as organisms maintain their coherence (e.g., survival) through systems of thought and action, groups maintain their coherence through systems of communication. Approaches in Zone 7 study the signifiers, interactions, and artifacts that are exchanged within systems and groups.

Some of the cultural approaches in MBE also border on zone 7, in their focus not only on the cultural "tools" of cognition, but also on these tools as systemic and structural artifacts (see again Olsen and Tomasello). This zone is quite foreign to most educators, but using it can help remind us that the systems we are a part of "hang together" through exchanged communication and artifacts. What role do the "internal parts" (e.g., speech acts) of systems play in our classrooms?

The Implications of a Methodologically Plural Approach

Integral Methodological Pluralism can serve to facilitate research collaboration across the disciplines in several ways. First, it validates multiple perspectives by pointing out that methodologies differ because they use *different perspectives*. One methodology, say science, is not getting at *the* fundamental truth while another, say poetry, is a frivolous also-ran. Instead, each methodology makes claims *that are valid for that zone*. And those validity claims are different in different zones. Judging poetry with the lens of science gets us nowhere.

In other words, the differences between the disciplines are not insoluble tensions—which is right, nature or nurture? Genetics or experience? Cognitive science or developmental psychology?—but instead different ways of looking at the same thing. One phenomenon, many approaches, facets, and interpretations.

IMP helps education students and consumers of research reconcile these theoretical tensions by providing a framework for clarifying the arguments. In the genetics versus experience example, attempting to pick one as "most important" would be the same as asking us to pick if the Upper-Right quadrant is "true" or if the Upper-Left quadrant is true. Clearly, the answer is neither and both.

Understanding the eight zones also helps explain the significance of each methodology's rise in ascendancy through time. After behaviorism (zone 6) came cognitive science (zone 5); and as MBE much lauds, we now we are witnessing the rise of biology (zone 6). Although all of these new methods march knowledge forward, they are not *purely* forward progress or innovation. Because they are shifts from one zone to another, something is gained, but something is also lost. In other words, the rise of autopoiesis (zone 5) does not make structuralism (zone 2) go away. It may just be ignored for a while. The march of science often including shifts from one zone to the other, shifts which do not necessarily mean the "old" approach was entirely wrong—we are just seeing the same phenomenon from a new perspective. To be more precise, we are *enacting* the same phenomenon from a different methodology.

But above all, IMP can help the field of MBE avoid the quadrant absolutisms that are all too often the peril of new approaches. Two particularly common types of "quadrant absolutism" that Wilber notes are *gross* and *subtle reductionism*. To quote Wilber, "gross reductionism *first* reduces *all* quadrants to the Upper-Right quadrant, and *second*—this is the gross part—then reduces all the higher-order structures of the Upper-Right quadrant to atomic or subatomic particles" (2000, p. 135). We certainly can see the first part of this kind of reductionism in the field of neuroscience. Nothing is real unless the "spot" for it can be found in the brain. To quote Wilber again:

> The problem is that most conventional scientific approaches are locked into UR-quadrant absolutism and thus dismiss interior (UL) realities as being at best "epi-phenomena" or secondary productions of the real reality in the materialistic world (e.g., brain). This approach maintains that the brain produces thoughts the way the eye produces tears. But the brain does not produce thoughts. There is simply an occasion that, when looked at in one way [e.g., zone 1], looks like thoughts (or mind) and when looked at in another perspective [e.g., zone 6], looks like a brain. (2006, p. 164)

Using IMP helps us avoid this kind of reductionism by reminding us that for every outside, there is usually an inside. Although we certainly can and should investigate brain states, it is important to remember that this does not give us privileged access to "the truth" or "reality"—only one aspect of it.

Subtle reductionism, on the other hand, "reduce[s] everything in the Left-Hand to a Right-Hand description in the 'system'" (2000, p. 136). This is a slightly more generous form of reductionism, since it includes two Right-Hand quadrants instead of just one. But it still focuses only on the Right Hand. We see this in the field of education's current demand for "evidence-based practices." Educational interventions are measured by the results obtained in empirical studies, including individuals and collectives. But less attention is paid to the more personal, felt-experience Left-Hand impact of the educational intervention, which can only be measured through self-report (zone 1). Did any one involved actually *like* what happened? Were the students satisfied? What about the teachers? The interpersonal aspects are also left out in these "evidence" driven approaches. However, these aspects can easily be included via interviews and focus groups (zone 3).

But worse, educational research often plows ahead with empirical measures without first stopping to ask the *should*. Yes, Intervention A might work better than Intervention B according to these somewhat arbitrarily-selected metrics, but which intervention is actually the right one for our purpose, our goals, our culture? Which one is the *good* one, which one *should* we follow? Answers to these questions can only be met through the Left Hand.

Although the two inside, Left-Hand methodologies are often not considered academic methodologies by the natural sciences—though they are by the humanities and social sciences, which recognize that they are the source of meaning and purpose—following their injunctions yields deeper self-awareness and interpersonal shared meaning. They are the very source of our value judgments, the answer to the question "what OUGHT we to do?" So many educational questions have to do with the OUGHT as much as the IS. A quickness to seek the "truth" as an empirical, objective measure can mean the purposes of education are implicit, unexamined. These unexamined purposes may be inappropriate, outdated, or even marginalizing, as David Rose points out with his Universal Design for Learning (Rose & Meyer, 2002). For example, when the purposes of first grade are not made more explicit than "to learn how to read," this purpose can marginalize the blind or dyslexic. Yet a deeper apprehension of the purpose using the inside approaches of reflection upon personal and collective values can yield a something that serves more students. No amount of Right-Hand research can tell us what these purposes should be—that takes the Left Hand—but once we have consciously determined them, Right-Hand research can step in to help us best enact them.

Conclusion

Mind, Brain, and Education is an exciting new field that promises to improve educational practice and outcomes. Its contributions of biological (zone 6 and 8), psychological (zone 2), and cognitive science (zone 5) research will certain deepen our understanding of how learning takes place. Although a truly Integral approach to MBE would also include phenomenological (zone 1), hermeneutical (zone 3), cultural (zone 4), and communicative (zone 7) research, MBE offers a more comprehensive approach to educational research than ever before.

What's more, as the "age of biology" marches forward, our understanding of the brain-based or genetic-based factors that contribute to educational outcomes will become ever clearer. Exciting pictures of the "lit up" brain as it learns in an fMRI scanner are sure to become more pervasive. At the same time, demands for evidence-based practices from not only the federal government but also local institutions and parents are unlikely to go away.

These two factors combined may lead to a "perfect storm," pointing all eyes—and heightened expectations—at Mind, Brain, and Education research. This is both a promising potential and a perilous one, because the field of education is at risk of becoming utterly dominated by Right-Hand quadrant absolutism. The space for the voice of parents and philosophers, speaking of values and purposes, dreams and directions, may shrink. But the addition of an integral perspective to the already comprehensive MBE approach can avoid this peril.

By using the four quadrants and Integral Methodological Pluralism in MBE, educators are continuously reminded to ask ourselves if we have a complete picture and, if not, what perspectives are being omitted—as well as the consequences of such an omission. This questioning helps us create more comprehensive, and thus more effective, solutions to MBE problems. Being aware of the multiplicity of methodologies and disciplines also helps remind us that there is space at the proverbial table for everyone. Education should be impacted by research science, yet we should not expect science to answer all our questions. As Gardner states in *The Disciplined Mind*, "we could know what every neuron does and we would not be one step closer to knowing how to educate our children" (1999, p. 60). Some questions require different approaches, different perspectives, all of which are honored and included in Integral Theory and its AQAL model.

Note

1. Complete text available at http://billyatharvard.blogspot.com/2006_11_01_archive.html.

References

Banich, M. T. (2004). *Cognitive neuroscience and neuropsychology*. Boston: Houghton Mifflin Co.

Bronfenbrenner, U. (1977). Towards an experimental ecology of human development. *American Psychologist, 32*(7), 513–531.

Carey, S. (1990). Cognitive development. In D. N. Osherson, & E. E. Smith (Eds.). *Thinking: An invitation to cognitive science, 3*, (pp. 147–172). Cambridge, MA: MIT Press.

Carey, S., & Spelke, E. (1994). Domain-specific knowledge and conceptual change. In L. A. Hirschfeld, & S. A. Gelman (Eds.), *Mapping the mind: Domain specificity in cognition and culture* (pp. 169–200). Cambridge, UK: Cambridge University Press.

Damasio, A. R. (1999). *The feeling of what happens*. New York: Harcourt Brace.

Dehaene, S. (1997). *The number sense*. New York: Oxford University Press.

Egan, K. (2002). *Getting it wrong from the beginning: Our progressivist inheritance from Herbert Spencer, John Dewey, and Jean Piaget*. New Haven and London: Yale University Press.

Fischer, K. (1980). A theory of cognitive development: The control and construction of hierarchies of skills. *Psychological Review, 87*(6), 477–531.

Fischer, K. W., & Daniel, D. B. (2008). A good first year and an award. *Mind, Brain, and Education, 2*(1), iii.

Fischer, K. W., and Heikkinen, K. (in press). The future of educational neuroscience. In D. Sousa (Ed.) *Mind, Brain, and Education*. Bloomington, IN: Solution Tree Press.

Gardner, H. (1999). *The disciplined mind: Beyond facts and standardized tests, the K-12 education that every child deserves*. New York: Penguin.

Fodor, J. (1983). *The modularity of mind*. Cambridge, MA: MIT Press.

Gelman, R. (1990). First principles organize attention to and learning about relevant data: Number and the animate-inanimate distinction. *Cognitive Science, 14*, 79–106.

Gopnik, A., Meltzoff, A., & Kuhl, P. (1999). *The scientist in the crib*. NY: William Morrow & Co.

Grigorenko, E. L. (2003). The first candidate gene for dyslexia: Turning the page of a new chapter of research. *PNAS, 100*, 11190–11192.

Kohlberg, L. (1981). *Essays on moral development*. New York: Haper & Row.

Lakoff G., & Johnson, M. (1980). *Metaphors we live by*. Chicago: University of Chicago Press.

Mareschal, D., Johnson, M. H., Sirois, S., Spratling, M. W., Thomas, M. S. C., & Westermann, G. (2007). *Neuroconstructivism: How the brain constructs cognition*. Vol. 1. Oxford: Oxford University Press.

Maturana, H. R., and Varela, F. J. (1980). *Autopoiesis and cognition: The realization of the living*. Hingham, MA: Kluwer.

Merriam and Webster Dictionary. http://merriam-webster.com/. Accessed online April 10, 2007.

Nelson, C. A., Thomas, K. M., & De Haan, M. (2006). Neural Bases of Cognitive Development. In D. Kuhn, & R. S. Siegler (Eds.), *Handbook of Child Psychology, 6*(2), 3–19, 35–39. Hoboken, NJ: John Wiley & Sons.

Olson, D. R. (1995). Writing and the mind. In J. V. Wertsch, P. Del Rio, & A. Alvarez (Eds.), *Sociocultural studies of the mind* (pp. 95–123). New York: Cambridge University Press.

Petrill, S. A., & Justice, L. M. (2007). Bridging the gap between genomics and education. *Mind, Brain, and Education, 1*(4), 153–161.

Pickering, S. J., & Howard-Jones, P. (2007). Educators' views on the role of neuroscience in education: Findings from a study of UK and international perspectives. *Mind, Brain, and Education, 1*(3), 109–113.

Pinker, S. (1997). *How the mind works*. New York: Norton.

Rose, D. H., & Meyer, A. (2002). *Teaching every student in the digital age: Universal design for learning*. Alexandria, VA: Association for Supervision and Curriculum Development.

Scarr, S., & McCartney, K. (1983). How people make their own environments: A theory of genotype environment effects. *Child Development, 54*, 424–435.

Shaywitz, B. A., Lyon, G. R., & Shaywitz, S. E. (2006). The role of functional magnetic resonance imaging in understanding reading and dyslexia. *Developmental Neuropsychology, 30*(1), 613–632.

Spitzer, M. (1999). *The mind within the net.* Cambridge, MA: The MIT Press.

Stein, Z. (2007). Modeling the demands of interdisciplinarity: Toward a framework for evaluating interdisciplinary endeavors. *Integral Review, 4,* 91–107.

Tomasello, M. (1996). Piagetian and Vygotskian approaches to language acquisition. *Human Development, 39,* 269–276.

Tomasello, M. (1999). *The cultural origins of human cognition.* Cambridge, MA: Harvard University Press.

Wilber, K. (2000). *Sex, ecology, spirituality: The spirit of evolution.* Boston: Shambala.

Wilber, K. (2006). *Integral spirituality.* Boston: Integral Books.

Embodying Integral Education in Five Dimensions

Carissa Wieler

This Place of Immersion

Reflecting on my experience as a student while immersed in a program feels like basking in a nutrient-rich prairie lake while tracing riparian edges of the landscape. Immediate experience is coupled with objective views, near and far. And as with any study of the natural environment, what is looked at, how it is seen, and who the seer is all contribute to the art and science of understanding the natural world. In the context of reflecting on my experience as a second-year student in the Integral Psychology program at John F. Kennedy University, I begin to notice who, what, and how as I relay the sometimes intense, sometimes playful experiences I have collected during the first year in the program. My travels to El Salvador on a field course and to Istanbul for a meeting of Integral Without Borders are fodder for learning that includes and extends beyond the classroom and have become an integral part of my immersion. My background in adult learning through my first master's degree, completed in 2005, is a foundation upon which I have intuitively pieced together five dimensions of learning in an integral education context. The dimensions of intentionality, inquiry, integration, expression, and practice speak to the contours that seem to inform the richness of my immersion in integral education.

My passion for adult learning informs my thinking as I reflect on the experience of being a graduate student. I first applied adult learning informally during undergraduate work in environmental science when I designed and facilitated community participatory projects concerning relationship to place. This passion deepened during my first master's degree in natural resource management, when I designed an online adult learning program for a multi-stakeholder group in a forestry sector context. In the process, I drew from Paulo Friere's (1970) work on liberation pedagogy, Jack Mezirow's (1991) work on transformative learning, and Jürgen Habermas' (1985) work on communicative action. These works contributed to the theoretical framework and assessment of the research, centering on informed dialogue as a catalyst for critical thinking, perspective taking, and social change. I then applied this research as a manager of a community of practice for an international policy research think tank. There, I designed monthly virtual learning events, enabled by virtual technology, that brought together policy makers, non-profit and interest group representatives, and researchers to discuss common problems and solutions related to indicators of sustainable development. In that context, I worked to cultivate openness, community, and synergy. Now, as I undertake my current Integral Psychology program, my reflection naturally includes a critical dialogue lens. At the same time, I am becoming curious about the quality of critical dialogue as informed by Ken Wilber's AQAL approach, as well as the point at which critical dialogue emerges when applying the AQAL model.

I chose the Integral Psychology program at John F. Kennedy University because it offered courses that I felt could help me with my next step, i.e., a more skillful integration of interiority into applications and programs focused on sustainability. As I will touch on later, there is a growing discourse about bridging interior and systemic approaches to sustainable development, which often focuses on the pillars of social, economic, and environmental sustainability (as well as cultural/linguistic sustainability as a fourth pillar). By also incorporating human development, for example, programs intended to bolster the capacity of communities and individuals in responding to natural and social changes will have greater potential for being of service. My previous education had an interdisciplinary focus, yet little was included regarding the inner dimensions of being and likewise little to bridge the inner realm to other dimensions of sustainability. Essentially, the Integral Psychology program provides a more sophisticated meta-map, both in terms of breadth and depth, than was provided in my previous master's program. There is the freedom, here, to not only explore and link interiors and exteriors, but also to cultivate perspective taking which provides a sense of the theory looking at itself. We are encouraged to ask: What is missing, not yet seen?

This program also feels and looks different than informal learning about Integral Theory and psychology. During the past decade, I have read Ken Wilber's pioneering work on Integral Theory (Wilber, 2000, 2001), enjoyed the online offerings of www.IntegralNaked.org, and participated in the start-up of two integral community groups. Naturally, this learning has been rooted in dialogue and play, and leans toward my interests. Learning the material in the classroom (whether in-person or virtually) clarifies the biases I have as a learner and stretches me to expand my focus to include what I might otherwise miss or de-emphasize. The correctness of my understandings is then challenged by peers and teachers. The Integral Psychology program itself is structured with an inherent balance of support and challenge in a way that is more structured than the informal learning contexts. For an overview of the program and how its design is informed by Integral Theory, see the article by Sean Esbjörn-Hargens (2006). My commitment to the program, through intention and resources, creates a quality of intensity over longer periods of times, and this seems to amplify the psychoactive nature of the material. (In a mysterious way that adds to the adventure!)

Streams in this Learning Experience

Sometimes, this lake of embodied learning feels bottomless. At other times, it begins to reveal its secrets. About a semester into my studies here, I reflect on the question of what it means to be a graduate student in an integral education program and intuitively feel into the dimensions of my experience. I articulate these five dimensions as *intentionality, inquiry and reflection, integration, expression,* and *practice.* Although these dimensions seem to arise via personal reflection, in hindsight they seem generally congruent with the broader discourse in adult learning with its inclusion of inquiry, integration, and expression, as well as the Integral Institute modalities with their inclusion of intentionality and practice.

Over time, these dimensions or streams become palpable and discernable; they integrate direct experience with formal and informal adult education. It is also possible to explore each of these streams in both an experiential and an analytical way using first-, second-, and third-person perspectives. Throughout the rest of the chapter I will navigate these five streams (in order, although they often create emergent tributaries and confluences). As I explore these streams I will be drawing on a variety of integral educational contexts both formal and informal: courses in the Integral Psychology program; an Integral Theory field course; and an international gathering of integral practitioners of sustainable development. I will use poetry that I've written as a segue or portage to the next stream.

Intentionality

Why am I here? My heart is thumping as I sit facing 12 others in a circle on a grassy clearing at the residence in El Salvador. This is the first Integral Theory field course offered by John F. Kennedy University and led by integral practitioners Gail Hochachka and Vernice Solimar. We arrived the day before, and now each one is asked to speak to an intention for coming. I imagine a fire growing at the center of our circle as each person places a log. I begin to mine my depths, searching for that one phrase that says it all, searching for the inner fuel that will propel me through a journey into territory that is both unknown, through a country that is both new and well trodden, while my streams of awareness give shape to my interpretations. As soon as intention is attuned to my inner self, I experience a somatic confirmation in the belly. Others, too, sit in silence, and then begin to speak: "to open my heart . . . to be present to suffering . . . to learn . . . to do something I have never done before . . . to serve . . . to be a better person." Little do I know that this brief exercise, perhaps lasting an hour, will help motivate my growth throughout this field course.

My intention is for an embodied integral experience of El Salvador. I want to more intimately see, hear, and feel what it means to be alive in El Salvador and then to feel into the humanity behind the veils of culture and context. I want to feel my heart and mind expand and to bump up against the edges that keep me from deeper connection. This intention serves me well on the field course and is realized in multiple ways over the course of 10 days. Notably, I leave El Salvador feeling closer to my own humanity in the moment of hearing and coming to know the humanity of the El Salvadorians we encounter. In hearing and touching their stories, I also feel heard in my own life story. Interest in community resilience in face of displacement and disconnection is sparked, adding fuel to an already lit fire.

My peers are an important source of motivation and inspiration. Like me, they have arrived in El Salvador with high expectations and deep intentions. Over the course of the trip, we continuously honor our uniqueness as a group as we travel to places so raw and filled with stories that mix of sobriety and kindness. We comment again and again that it is unusual for a group living in such close quarters and for such a short time to be so highly functioning with one another and toward those we collectively encounter. Perhaps it is for this reason that the communities we visit reveal themselves to us, with perhaps unprecedented openness.

Like the experience in El Salvador, somatically experiencing and cognitively clarifying my intention for being in the Integral Psychology program helps me verify that I am internally on track. This can be important given the shifts in body, mind, heart, and spirit that take place as my inquiry deepens and I enter unchartered domains.

From my experience, intentionality seems to act like an attractor beam, it reveals what comes alive in a learning experience; the "who" clarifies an intention and shapes the "how" of the "what" that is seen. In my experience of integral education, the inquiry becomes more transparent and rich when intentionality is brought forward. Intention can also be considered a measuring tool because it can change over time, revealing shifts in thinking. The core intention may stay the same, as in my desire to bridge ecology and psychology, yet the mode of bringing this intention alive may change. Integral education tries to make space for whatever my intention might be; there is a sense of freedom in allowing my intention to evolve. At the same time I wonder, how attached am I to understanding my intention through the Integral model?

* * *

lies still
awake,
wondering if
today is the day
to sing.

Inquiry and Reflection

What am I noticing? Shifting in my seat in a class on Integral Theory, I embark on an inner inquiry, which takes me back to my youth and a desire to understand masculine and feminine forms of expression. While much of our time in this class is spent on theory, today we venture inward. The theory we are covering this day looks at four forms of feminine and masculine types from Jungian theory as discussed by Gareth Hill (2001). These types are present in both males and females. The dynamic feminine inclines toward transformation and creativity, as well as chaos and lack of focus. The static feminine tends toward wholeness and grounding, as well as restriction and limitation. The static masculine moves toward stability and benevolence, as well as rigidity and bureaucracy. The dynamic masculine tends to emphasize transformation and innovation, as well as destruction and domination. The assignment is to notice when each type shows up in our awareness and what type of pattern seems to be present. We begin by reflecting on our own lives.

Questions start to bubble up. Are each of these principles present at all times in life, albeit with varying degrees of emphasis? How do certain cultures emphasize certain forms of the masculine and feminine? Which forms of the masculine and feminine do I identify with more strongly, and how is this connected to my personality type? How possible is it to transcend the tendency toward specific types in certain ways? What are developmental factors involved? What about the confluence of nature and nurture?

I am reminded of reading about the quadrants, or dimensions of reality, for the first time (Wilber, 1996) and noticing the ones I tended to identify with. Now I notice my resonance with certain feminine and masculine expressions and not others. With continuing reflection, I notice that while my life seems to have been very dynamic, there have also been important balancing forces, enabling some form of structure and rooting. This is surprising, and I take a moment to honor these stabilizing forces.

The scene now shifts and a class discussion begins about how others have noticed masculine and feminine principles in their own lives. As classmates begin to share threads of masculine and feminine dynamics meandering through their lives, listening toggles between analysis and resonance.

As a student in this program, I feel encouraged to reflect more objectively on my motivations and biases. Integral education supports the exploration of personal perspectives and biases, as well as resonances and dissonances with peers, by grounding the inquiry with awareness and openness. The emphasis on perspective taking is a notable contribution of integral education. This emphasis seems to develop capacity for critical reflection and dialogue, as well as trust building and authentic expression. Perspective taking increases my capacity to see and hear others more fully and openly as I am less likely to be trapped by my biases and well-worn perspectives and more able to simultaneously be present to perspectives of others and with what is arising within. Within the program, there is also encouragement to reflect on the meta-view of Integral Theory itself and on consciousness, from ever-expanding perspectives.

* * *

> sunrise, fire bright,
> come, enter
> sweep this place
> with bold hues
> and subtle currents
> of Becoming.

Integration

How is my learning reflected in who I am, who I am becoming, and in what I am doing? The air is slightly cool as I slip onto the patio, positioning myself in front of the Blue Mosque in historic Istanbul. Dance music plays in the cafe nearby where a group of 50 integral practitioners from around the world have met for the past five days. This is the second annual meeting (2008) of the Integral International Development Center (Integral Without Borders). It is our last night together and the air is festive. We have explored the integral praxis of content, context, perspective, and transformation. Experiencing connection with fellow practitioners seems to energize and inform how I navigate my journey. I look out at the cobblestone street leading to the hotel, feeling the inner pilgrimage of carrying riches from far off lands to home shores. In this pilgrimage, there is feeling of fullness, wholeness, and aloneness.

During the plane ride home, I begin to review threads of our discourse. I notice how instructive it has been to learn about the various ways practitioners integrate Integral Theory in their work. I reflect on historical and recent contexts, cultural precedents and shifts, well-trodden and newly formed perspectives, and perceptions of practitioners themselves. Integral practitioners seem to be using the theory directly in the following ways:

- designing projects that incorporate quadrant/quadrivium analysis (i.e., using the quadrant lens to look both "at" and "from" four irreducible perspectives)

- using developmental levels analysis in project development, and also thematic analysis

- incorporating more than two of the five main AQAL elements in a project: i.e., quadrants, levels, lines, states, and types

- intentionally cultivating first- second- and third-person perspectives

- developing an Integral Life Practice (ILP) to work with growing edges, biases (shadow) and higher states, in order to increase health, effectiveness, and awareness

- using Integral Theory as a foundation for further theory development

- cultivating Love; Witness, Big Mind, Big Heart awareness; faith, hope, and compassion

- willingness to be in a place of "not knowing" and openness.

The application of Integral Theory in various fields is just beginning, and I notice a great thirst for it. As I discovered in my interdisciplinary programs, learning becomes more grounded and real when it is applied. At the same time, I observe that working with complexity and a need for practicality seems like a challenge for integral practitioners and students alike. I begin to wonder how much complexity a practitioner can handle. At what point has enough information been sought and processed? When does complexifying become an exercise without meaning? I wonder if some practitioners feel overwhelmed at the task of including interior domains in project research that specifically focuses on exterior social, economic, and environmental domains, given that the research for those domains is already a large and complex task. I have yet to take the Integral Methodological Pluralism (IMP) course as part of my program; even so, I sense that working with the eight zones of IMP has yet to be embedded in many project applications, which could benefit from its use.

From my perspective and background in ecology and sustainability, it seems that the integration of psychological and sociological perspectives is typically less developed in the exterior domains. I sense an opening to bridge psychology and ecology, possibly through the lenses of resilience, adaptability, and change. The practitioners who met in Istanbul seem to agree that the inclusion of interiority is a leading edge for integral applications.

At the same time, this raises another set of questions. How will this work be applied, practically, at the end of the educational tunnel? Where will the openings be for integral approaches? How might those openings be cultivated in a new type of job description, one that speaks to a broader, emerging integral consciousness while at the same time, drawing from Integral Theory, either implicitly or explicitly?

By now I have discovered that this business of integration doesn't happen in a linear fashion. I notice that what I am integrating seems to shift, or toggle, between integrating the theory itself to noticing opportunities for correlating and integrating streams across distinctions such as quadrants, levels, and lines. Yet there are moments when integration feels effortless. Looking out at the Blue Mosque in historic Istanbul, feeling full of connection and freedom to move forward, it is as though theory and practice come together for a moment. In a way, I am thinking about both theory and application and neither, just as I am feeling totally alone, yet not without connection. The path ahead is about my own steps, and is also about much more than my steps.

From the perspective of integral consciousness, it seems that there are many paths; there is a multitude of ways that Integral Theory is interpreted and translated. Some applications more explicitly reveal Integral Theory and the AQAL model while other applications are more implicit. Some applications apply Integral Theory alongside other theories, as one of many, while others make subtle departures from the theory itself. As a student in this budding field, I notice my desire to align practice with theory in more "correct" ways. At the same time, there is a deep respect for the work of fellow practitioners who risk being different and challenging or pushing the theory into new directions.

Like the interdisciplinary programs I have previously experienced, integral education feels like a pilgrim's path of shaping grooves in consciousness, cultures, processes, and systems. Similarly, integral education seeks to build bridges and cultivate integral awareness. However, the integration of interiority in integral education is the most striking divergence from other forms of interdisciplinary education. In integral education, there is a welcoming of expression of interior subjective realities on the same platform as the more exterior objective expressions. This results in both a rigor and a freedom: a rigor to meet the challenge of covering all the bases; and a freedom to more fully express one's authentic self and to be heard.

* * *

abstraction, distraction . . .
what is real?
beginnings and endings
over and over again
met with Awareness and Love

Expression

How am I giving voice to my learning? The room has been dimmed and five faces in an on-campus student-led integral discussion group look expectantly in my direction. The experiences of the Integral Theory field course in El Salvador are still fresh in my memory, having returned a week earlier. An unmistakable yearning bubbles up, a yearning to share with trusted peers that which has shaken me to the bone on this trip. On my last day in El Salvador, I promised to bring back what I had learned. Now, in the telling, I provide contexts, descriptions of physical reality, group experiences, and personal insights.

I share my perception that greater depth was possible during the field course because it held an integral lens. My peers and I witnessed both the tragedy of past and present, and the dignity of those working for change and transformation. We discussed a growing freedom to express ourselves and feel supported.

Here is a poignant story from the trip that speaks to me of openness and growth. In the first scene, we visit a river on the way to a community where we will stay for a night and a day. It is a warm day, and many of us wade into and even swim in the cool river. After a time of play, community leaders ask us to individually choose a stone and carry it with us during the time of our stay with the local community. In the second scene, we spend time with community members, softening to their histories, stories, and healing processes. We enter the caves where they hid during the recent civil war (1980–1992) and touch the artifacts that speak of a local massacre. We hold a candlelight vigil and engage in activities to connect with earth, body, and one another. It is an intense experience for many of us. In the third scene, we return to the fresh, cool river the next day, and welcome the change. Some sit quietly while others swim. Called to form a circle, we then learn that this river of life has also been a river of death—carrying the literal blood of war victims. This place of healing has also been a place of grief. With that, we are asked to hold the rocks we have chosen and say a prayer for the healing of the community and of the earth. In that stretch of time, my experience of our group shifts. There is a feeling of connecting with my peers on a much more human level than before, as if layers of identity melt away.

The story of the river seems to include at least two layers of expression. Being at the river both times is an expressive moment with nature, self, and others, and in prayer. Telling others about the experience and my interpretations is another expressive moment that deepens my connection with them and with the essence of that moment.

Feeling heard by peers at John F. Kennedy University reminds me of the way expression is connected to the receivers of that expression. As my ability to resonate with others increases, I notice that the depth of my expression changes depending, to some extent, on resonance. The same story is expressed in different ways, using different words and emphases, depending in part on who is listening and responding. Of course, it also depends on what is happening with me that day, as well as the overall reason and intention for telling the story.

To close the evening of sharing, all are invited to participate in an activity I learned during the field course. We stand in a circle, our hands interlocked. This feels like a moment of somehow embodying all that has been discussed that evening. I wonder whether the discussion group members will deepen in a felt sense of connection after this experience. I also recognize that while my experiences in El Salvador are unique to that trip, something has been woven into to a greater tapestry of life, as if beyond the experience itself and beyond the expression of it.

Expression speaks to the "miracle of we" described in Wilber's *Integral Spirituality* (2006) as it furthers embodiment of learning through modes such as storytelling, art, humor, dance, or simply engaging in a thoughtful exchange. Expression within the realm of integral education is training ground for bringing alive integral consciousness in collective spaces and perhaps also increasing span of application to work, relationships, and other places.

* * *

you have found a place to rest
feathers damp and wings held close
the tide comes in as we wait
two breathing bodies
simply being
at the cusp of unknowing.

Practice

How do I keeping the fire of learning burning? "Hello . . . hey, can anyone hear me? Helloooooooo . . ." I open my eyes slowly and peer out to a room filled with motionless bodies. For a moment, the spaciousness seems to go on forever and I am surprised to find objects in my awareness as I glance around the room. This is my first sitting with a Zen Roshi. Later that evening, I venture a question about "emptiness" and am told that instead of reaching for this place of no-thing, I can feel embraced by it. A month later, I am asking Paul Tenryu Roshi about the myriad of lineages I am drawn to: nature mysticism, Christian mysticism, Diamond Approach, Zen Buddhism. This, after he has explained the importance of studying and practicing a single lineage as a long-term commitment so that the benefits of the lineage may be fully realized. I perceive that I must cultivate a strong internal structure before multiple paths can be lived through me. Choosing a path still scares me a little as a part of me believes that there is some kind of loss associated with choosing a single lineage. Upon reflection, this belief is not congruent with the integral path: as I deepen in one path, it seems that I build capacity to access other lineages as well.

In this master's level integral education program, I am encouraged to cultivate such practices in order to widen my container for learning, stretch my limits in body, mind, and spirit, sustain my energy, and help me become a contribution. This is one of the hallmarks of integral education, which diverges from other forms of education in its emphasis on Integral Life Practice for students and teachers alike: actively transforming their own embodiment through regular personal practices in multiple domains of their life. The emphasis on practice is more than a set of recommendations: I can look to my peers and teachers for role models for what it means to become more fully human. At the same time, it is up to me to choose long-term practices that will sustain me during this time as a student, and beyond. I have found that these practices also ground the learning in tangible ways and help me identify incremental changes over time.

Learning to "sit" in more subtle states of awareness for longer times constitutes one of my budding practices. It seems important during moments when my "container" for learning feels ready to grow. Meditation creates spaciousness around that container, a way of noticing that there is an Infinite Mind that reaches beyond the confines of perception.

Besides the direct importance of meditation (for many reasons in addition to the ones I speak about), the practice of meditation (and other practices) seems important as a place of embodying the theory. In my studies, I begin to create an inner map of places that seem edgy and juicy, and then look for systems and relationships that meet me there. In my experience, practice brings about greater capacity for integral embodiment, thereby nourishing and motivating the self. Integral education may not be more difficult than other kinds of graduate-level programs, but it often feels more intense. I suspect this is because in addition to intellectual rigor, which can be found in many programs, this program also expects its students to be engaged in ongoing personal inquiry that involves our whole person. These body, mind, and spirit practices make education richer and more sustainable because they link the ideas, theories, and content our textbooks to our experienced bodies, tender hearts, and direct awareness.

I have noticed that my peers and I tend to gravitate toward certain types of practices during our studies. For students beginning an integral program, meditation and contemplation are often voiced as "shoulds" that may eventually become "wants." On the other hand, physical activity such as resistance training, martial arts, and dance seem to be big hits among students in my circles. Cultivating dialogue skills and building intentional community or places of shared resonance are motivators for participating in regular discussion groups. I have noted a longing among some of my peers to discuss the theory and application in depth with others, particularly once a common language is established. All of this feels to me like a commitment to an overall learning system, complementary to classroom learning. It takes time and energy to maintain this commitment, yet there is a payoff—a wellspring of continuous life experience to energize and nourish the learning process.

* * *

living sphere
intonations that breathe
mystery into this withered
rose, this freshly coiled
serpent
gem of the night.

A Further Shore

In this lake of embodied learning, the five streams seem to recharge and discharge it in a necessary yet also unnecessary order. The stream of *intentionality* seems to oxygenate the lake with long-term goals and fresh impulses toward wholeness and insight. In an integral education setting, intentionality shapes my gaze, what I notice and what is enlivened. My relationship with intentionality constantly shifts as my grasp on clarifying "why I am here" gives way to other questions. The stream of *reflection and inquiry* seems to heighten awareness and sharpen insight. I begin to notice what I notice and, in dialogue with peers and teachers, begin to reflect on what is being reflected in my awareness. This includes noticing what is emphasized and what is left out in the learning process. The stream of *integration* seems to move awareness into action, and action into awareness. What is learned and reflected upon becomes integrated in being and doing, and in ways of seeing out and looking in. The stream of *expression* seems to build resonance. This is the moment of turning outward and giving voice to the learning process, to reflections and unknowns. Finally, the stream of *practice* seems to sustain and amplify learning. The life practices feel essential to supplementing the learning process with other embodied and skillful practices, and they bring fullness to the experience.

Just as the lake of embodied learning begins to reveal itself, so does a further shore. There seems to be tremendous potential for inter-quadratic application: In addition to a meta-systemic focus, there is room to research and explore the relationship between individual interiority and collective exteriority. My desire to link ecology (which takes a systems perspective) with psychology (which focuses more on individual interiority) speaks to that further shore. While still immersed in the lake of student experience, it is possible to look beyond one's self, at the ecology of integral education, at the self-system embedded within that ecology, and at the important role of integral education within the larger ecosystem of integral consciousness. From my perspective as a student, this is the beauty and the burden of integral education: The lake of embodied learning has a shore, yet is also without a shore.

References

Esbjörn-Hargens, S. (2006). Integral education by design: How integral theory informs teaching, learning, and curriculum in a graduate program. *ReVision, 28*(3), 21–29.

Friere, P. (1970). *Pedagogy of the oppressed.* New York: Herder and Herder.

Habermas, J. (1985). *The theory of communicative action: reason and the rationalization of society (the theory of communicative action,* vol 1.). Boston, MA: Beacon Press.

Hill, G. (2001). *Masculine & feminine: The natural flow of opposites in the psyche.* Boston: Shambhala.

Mezirow, J. (1991). *Transformative dimensions of adult learning.* San Francisco: Jossey-Bass.

Wilber, K. (1996). *Brief history of everything.* Boston: Shambhala.

Wilber, K. (2000). *Sex, ecology, spirituality.* Boston: Shambhala.

Wilber, K. (2000). *Integral psychology.* Boston: Shambhala.

Wilber, K. (2006). *Integral spirituality.* Boston: Integral Books.

Opening Up the Path of Integral Education

Reflections on a Case Study in Changing from a Holistic to Integral College

Olen Gunnlaugson

Holma College of Holistic Studies

In the mid-nineties a small group of Scandinavian educators, social visionaries, and philanthropists gathered in rural Sweden with a provocative dream to develop an alternative college program in personal and global change studies. Inspired by social anthropologist Margaret Mead's visionary insight that the coordinated actions of small groups of concerned citizens play a central role in changing the world, Holma College of Holistic Studies (HCHS) soon emerged. Convinced of the need for viable alternatives to Western post-secondary educational models, the founding group believed that the prevailing materialistic, mechanistic, modern worldview would not be adequately outgrown without the implementation of a sustainable educational vision for global harmony and peace. In response to this challenge, the seed idea for the project was the belief that humanity needs a new holistic worldview, a new paradigm to ameliorate the mounting effects of different individual, regional and international predicaments. Consistent with Paul Ray's articulation (Anderson & Ray, 2001) of the cultural creative vision, HCHS set forth to be a part of the holistic movement by attempting to help redirect humankind's existing crash course toward a more sustainable future for all by providing a transformative learning context for idealistic young adults from around the world.[1]

During the first few years, the initial faculty members of HCHS implemented experimental varieties of holistic curriculum, which consisted mainly of a smorgasbord of weekly workshops held by visiting faculty from different cutting-edge fields of knowledge from Scandinavia and North America.[2] The program aim was to introduce students to a broad assortment of alternative spiritual and scientific frameworks and practices that would support their embodiment of the utopian ideology of the New Age movement and its "new paradigm" ideals heralding at that time what many were convinced was the beginning of a worldwide revolution of consciousness. In part, this Utopian vision gained a foothold through a growing eclectic body of New Age literature, the insular setting of the college, the annual Angsbacka *No Mind Festival*[3] and idealistic ethos of Swedish culture. It spite of initial advances gained from the college's departure from mainstream ideals of post-secondary education, a number of imbalances and problematic New Age ideals developed within the greater learning community developed over the years that followed.[4] Facilitating the change from a holistic to an integral vision and educational approach during the 2002–2003 transition year was marked by a number of challenges. Reflecting back on this ambitious program year and as a follow-up to my initial case study (Gunnlaugson, 2004), in this chapter I will revisit the holistic and integral paradigms that shaped the college over its eight-year history and share some of my more recent reflections and learning from the transition year as well as subsequent recommendations for future integral educational initiatives.

Venturing an Integral Assessment of HCHS's Holistic Paradigm

Initially, it was presumed by the founding members of HCHS that the linchpin of student transformation was a fundamental change in their worldview. Through the course of a one-year learning journey, HCHS faculty committed themselves to supporting the conditions where students could simply unlearn the "old paradigm" by adapting "new paradigm" perspectives emerging across a range of disciplines including science, religion, and the human potential movement in psychology among others. Broadly speaking, students and faculty felt an urgency to live this new paradigm Utopian vision as they approached the close of our previous century, inasmuch as it offered a generous and positive pluralistic framework to recast one's life and learning ideals. Yet in revisiting the original assumption that the transformation of the world rests upon the student's transformation of worldview, at least three critical perspectives were ignored.

First, the New Age paradigm proceeded from a simplistic binary logic and dualistic assumption in presupposing that a transformation of one's life necessarily follows from learning to embody a worldview that is in fundamental opposition to the Cartesian, mechanistic worldview. For different reasons, this dialectical view ignores the findings of psycho-social developmental frameworks (Wilber, 2000b), which claim individuals undergo *a series of transformations* in their *stages* of consciousness (with accompanying worldviews) along several key developmental lines, rather than arriving at a new and final worldview. During the transition year, we worked with Beck and Cowan's (1996) Spiral Dynamics model to convey how individuals and cultures can potentially evolve through a series of worldviews up from traditional to modern to postmodern into integral. While the old/new paradigm model initially provided an important catalyst for engaging everyone in a process of change and growth, with time this simplistic framework could not adequately account for how the diverse values and knowledge of our students, faculty, and learning community were developing.

Second, the college's new paradigm ideology was by 2001 beginning to bear a striking resemblance to the target of Wilber's criticism (1995) of New Age thought being rooted in a form of hyper-subjectivity and relativism that ignores the need for reality testing—a variation of a kind of mythic-magical thinking. Wilber (1995) elaborates, "these new age movements put a premium on self-actualization that all too often reverts to magical egotism; and this magical narcissism is worked into a mythology of world transformation that barely conceals its imperialistic thrust" (p. 581). By privileging personal development, during the holistic era of the college most students were compelled by the powerful insight that transforming oneself is the most effective way to fundamentally transform the world, however this also gave way to the problematic belief that the transformation of the world *necessarily* follows from such paths because from a non-dual intuition *we are the world*.

Third, the former educators of HCHS did not distinguish between *translative* and *transformative* educational approaches (Wilber, 2006) and often confused the two. Educational theory that offers a new language or paradigm—that is, a new translation of how the world is—will bring about horizontal or lateral shifts in our understanding. Such lateral shifts in learning typically involve introducing a new way to think and feel about the world or a subject. As Wilber (2000b) has pointed out, interpreting reality differently does not mean that the form or stage of consciousness we are interpreting reality from has necessarily changed. Prone to mistaking experiences of translative learning with transformative learning, the previous learning ethos of the college privileged feelings as the popular litmus for authentic transformation—that is, did you *feel* transformed by this class or book or relationship? While feeling is an important barometer of transformation, relying on one's emotions as the primary measure of self-assessment became commonplace and problematic in the absence of a more comprehensive and rigorous set of criteria.

Being unaware of and to a certain extent uninterested in these and other critical perspectives, the former HCHS adherents to the "new paradigm" were generally committed to a hidden reductionistic strategy of relabeling everything problematic about our Western tradition as *old paradigm*. Many of the lecturers, faculty, and students had to varying degrees internalized the deconstructive postmodern critique of modernity,[5] which often led to an unnecessary dismissal and suspicion of our modern western tradition. As Wilber has pointed out, within many postmodern circles[6] Kuhn's concept of paradigm is misinterpreted as a theory or worldview that gets employed as a weapon of deconstruction to undercut the authority of facts and claims of previous paradigms, which are brought down to the level of mere interpretations. Wilber (2003) elaborates:

> Put simply, a theory is a map of a territory, while a paradigm is a practice that brings forth a territory in the first place. The paradigm or social practice itself is called an "exemplar" or "injunction," and the theory is called, well, the theory. The point is that knowledge revolutions are generally combinations of new paradigm-practices that bring forth a new phenomenological territory plus new theories and maps that attempt to offer some sort of abstract or contoured guidance to the new territories thus disclosed and brought forth. But a new theory without a new practice is simply a new map with no real territory, or what is generally called "ideology." (p. 1)

Looking back, lacking a constructive critique of modernity as well as a coherent overarching holistic framework made it difficult for the new paradigm at HCHS to establish itself alongside other progressive models, let alone within conventional educational circles. Additionally, the eclectic set of practices and novel ideas translated through an idealistic New Age philosophy made it especially challenging to find an enduring philosophical or historical context for sustained personal and community development.

Nevertheless, the new paradigm approach fared well in its time by attracting like-minded students wanting to become the change they wish to see in the world. This shared but to a great extent unfocused commitment helped create a supportive collective context for personal and interpersonal well-being, inasmuch as the college provided an environment to explore alternative modalities of knowing, being, and living. Though HCHS rescued the healing dimension of transformative education lost to mainstream education, my core concern at that time was that the educational process did not extend far enough beyond the collective interests of students in personal development, New Age spirituality, and group processes as their core educational agenda. As an example, overlooking the perspectives of more contemporary holistic educators in North America such as Parker Palmer, Ron Miller, or Jack Miller brought about an insular approach to their education, which was reinforced by a growing bias against critical inquiry (which new students including myself increasingly demanded). This eventually produced an anti-intellectual sentiment among the previous cohort of educators and workshop leaders, in turn devaluing intellectual standards of critical thinking and fostering a learning ethos chiefly characterized by feminine, somatic, emotional, intuitive, and relational forms of knowing. Harboring the tendency to escape into a soothing Jacuzzi bath of well-being in and outside classroom interactions, at HCHS students increasingly lost interest in cultivating wakeful clarity and critical discernment in their learning, bolstered by a form of New Age "elevationism"[7] (Visser,

2003) that was prone to promoting nonrational (and at times irrational) ways of knowing as spiritual. Again, during the new paradigm phase, students tended to value a personal and collective felt-sense of harmony above all educational ideals, effectively creating the ripe conditions for the "sensitive self" and "Green vMeme" (Beck & Cowan, 1996) culture to flourish.

As I reflect back on what initially attracted me about HCHS, it was this very pluralistic, reconstructive postmodern embrace—centered in participatory sharing and the promise of a global microcosm of young adults gathered together in the interests of becoming the change they wish to see for our world. Following the initial honeymoon phase early in the first semester of the transition year, imbalances with the sentiments of our egalitarian spiritual idealism became more strikingly apparent. Inspired by the verve and promise of Wilber's comprehensive vision for humanity and research into his critical theory gave way to questioning Holma College's holistic orientation and eventually making the change to becoming an integral college.[8]

HCIS Approach to Integral Studies

During the implementation phase of integral studies at HCIS in the fall of 2003, our educational mandate was to introduce students to Wilber's Integral Theory and practice by inviting lecturers and workshop leaders who were familiar with or utilizing Wilber's Integral approach. Through the lens of Wilber's (1995, 2000a, 2001) Integral frameworks, Brian Swimme's *Canticle to the Cosmos* video series, O'Sullivan's (1999) integral vision for transformative education and Beck & Cowan's (1996) Spiral Dynamics, our leadership team made an effort to depart from the college's previous new paradigm approach and inspire student's interest in fashioning an integral historical narrative. The bi-weekly college-wide Integral Study Circles program played a role in introducing students to Wilber's Integral frameworks.[9] Learnings from the study circles gradually spilled over into the daily curriculum of the learning community. In terms of Wilber's main contributions to integral studies at HCIS, the following three aspects were most prominent during the transition year.

- First, because we focused primarily on how Wilber's work can be applied educationally, it was easier to introduce a shared language and discourse that in turn helped establish a more coherent basis for shared meaning and communication with students than previous years.

- Second, Wilber's work cultivated a useful comprehensive framework for interpreting our lives that aspired to avoid reducing, isolating, or fragmenting our understanding of the world and ourselves.

- Third, Wilber and Beck & Cowan's writings offered helpful developmental frameworks for students and faculty to engage our journeys of transformation.

Regarding the first contribution, studying Wilber's Integral frameworks helped promote a shared discourse with new distinctions in contrast to previous years that lacked coherent meta-frameworks to gauge, contextualize, and advance student's learning. This newly achieved coherency became a double-edged sword. While a number of students were highly engaged with the processes of learning Wilber's frameworks, others felt his writings were overly generalized, disembodied, and flying at too high of a conceptual altitude to satisfy their practical learning needs. As an example, when introducing the "Integral Learning Portfolios,"[10] over the course of the term a number of students found this framework very helpful in documenting and self-assessing a greater breadth of their learning accomplishments. Yet with the study circles, many students complained that the ongoing "weight" and "frequency" of the Wilber readings[11] interfered with their motivation to transform themselves in more somatic, relational, ecological, and spiritual ways that were not well accounted for by Wilber's conceptual frameworks and heuristics.

Throughout the year there were numerous struggles to address different forms of resistance from students and faculty toward Wilber's work. Part of this struggle was a byproduct of the recent changeover in the vision and espoused integral ideals (in contrast to previous holistic ideals) that we were working toward in addition to the pressures to deliver a transformative educational program. Consequently, at times it became difficult to offer a fair hearing to the relative merits of holistic educational thought in relation to the integral discourse we were introducing. As an example of one of several attempts to remedy this discrepancy, the Integral Study Circles facilitators promoted exercises in perspective taking. By investigating issues specific to our learning community as well as different subjects of inquiry through the "perspectives" and categories of Wilber's frameworks, we were able to shed new light on some of the deeper dilemmas and issues students struggled with. Looking back on this specific practice, while this exercise was beneficial in helping students *retranslate* their lives according to Wilber's integral discourse, future integrally-informed educational initiatives will greatly benefit from expanding their scope and horizons of what constitutes *integral*—something this book contributes to and that I will address at more length later on in this chapter.

Different intersubjective practices including listening circles, the world café, and generative dialogue (Scharmer, 2000) offered our learning community creative possibilities for advancing both our collective learning processes and our shared integral language. At the time a number of us speculated that these and other methods explored within the Holma Dialogue Project offered an important context for integral practice by stimulating various cognitive, emotional, spiritual, relational, and collective intelligence *lines* of development. As an example, both the listening circles and generative dialogue circles offered an experience of social meditation (Gunnlaugson, 2004) where we practiced witnessing, suspending, and sharing our thoughts instead of being exclusively identified with advocating or opposing them. These and other exercises evolved an intersubjective yoga of communication for our learning community that enabled participants to explore alternative processes of listening and speaking together.

With the second contribution of integral studies, generally speaking students and faculty aspired to cultivate an ethic of comprehensiveness in our learning and day-to-day lifestyles—again, a prominent feature of Wilber's integral ideal. In addition to the Integral Study Circles, the Holma Dialogue Project, and a broad assortment of classroom exercises with different guest lecturers, we implemented the Integral Transformative Practice (ITP)[12] (Wilber, 2000a) to support student's interests in cultivating different intelligences and more consciously engage the elusive processes of transformative learning. Introduced as an integral framework, most students gravitated to the ITP as a practical means to direct and integrate their learning and development in accordance with other integral and holistic models. The basic idea of the ITP was to help students foster an overall current of transformation through the activation of "multiple catalysts" (Swimme, 2003) on different levels of one's body, mind, soul, spirit in self, culture, and nature. Because few if any modern Western traditions of higher education offer a comprehensive approach in cultivating our myriad capacities, the ITP helped students move away from narcissistically interpreting or translating their learning experiences in personal terms alone. This helped students more effectively connect with different multiple intelligences along different developmental lines, as well as collective dimensions of their experience in the learning community, the greater region, other cultures, and ultimately our planet. Students and faculty also found that the ITP helped shift our lifestyles toward a more balanced approach to daily life. A common reflection by students was that, before arriving at Holma College, most noticed that they privileged activity in one or two of the four quadrants.

Of course the ITP was not helpful for everyone. A number of students struggled with holding to a minimum commitment of integral practices. Trying to integrate new tools and approaches introduced with the new lecturers each week made it challenging for some students to maintain a commitment to consistent practice. Within the context of each student's weekly integral coaching module, I addressed individual strategies to work with the challenges and difficulties involved with the ITP and to not simply commit to existing practices, but also foster "an approach that will permit all human dimensions to co-creatively participate in the unfolding of integral growth" (Ferrer, 2002, p. 1). In advocating for exercising and strengthening the student's broad array of potentials, qualities, and capacities, we struggled to move through our initial mind-centered approach to embrace more authentic and balanced forms of integral practice.

Regarding the third contribution of integral studies at HCIS, we introduced Spiral Dynamics[13] as a framework for students and faculty to engage their personal journeys of transformation and awakening. Most students entered the college unconsciously embedded in a *unique combination* of traditional (Blue), modernist (Orange) or postmodernist (Green) worldviews and values (i.e., value memes or vMemes).[14] Through lectures on Spiral Dynamics and personal coaching sessions, we explored the significance of our self-structures being shaped by a complex array of cultural values and worldviews that more or less inform how we make meaning and interpret our experiences in daily life. At the time, Beck & Cowan's (1996) framework offered a new broad set of color-coded distinctions that were generally helpful to students' learning about their ways of making meaning and how they translate their experience in and outside the classroom.

Exploring students' "disorienting dilemmas" (Mezirow, 2000) and "negentropic experiences"[15] (Kegan, 1994) of transformative learning within a Spiral Dynamics context provided important scaffolding for students to engage their transformative processes. During the integral coaching sessions, students and I also experimented with awareness, behavioral, and social practices to help relax our identification with our existing vMemes's *center of gravity* in order to create a space of receptivity and possibility for embodying our next memeic stage. One of the main benefits of this distinction for students was facilitating a translative shift in their basic identity from a fixed to a more fluid and changing process with important developmental milestones. In shifting from the mindset of identifying with static representations of our selves, we explored possibilities for a more dynamic integral process—characteristic of the early Yellow vMemes. While it is questionable the extent to which learning Spiral Dynamics helped students make the proverbial leap to "second tier,"[16] Beck & Cowan's (1996) work was helpful in introducing everyone to the significance of being an evolving self with the possibility of embodying more complex and nuanced worldviews (i.e., embracing the dignity and limiting the disasters of each), in contrast to the previous binary orientation of setting out to simply adapt the new paradigm.

Reflections on the HCIS Transition Year to Integral Studies

Looking back over this period, Wilber, Beck, and other integral visionaries call for vertical transformation played an influential role in characterizing the telos and ethos of our learning community. Wilber's (2000a) initial oversimplified use of the Spiral Dynamics model as a tool to gauge the *overall* development of individuals and society eventually led to his recontextualizing the model as strictly representing the worldview and values *line* of development within individuals and collectives. Retrospectively, our initial prescriptive application and interpretation of Spiral Dynamics was also problematic to the extent that we were, like Wilber at that time, routinely overextending the framework's scope of validity by conflating the distinction of moving from the *level* of green to the second tier of the values and worldview *line* with student's overall altitude or *level* of development. Given that a key guiding image within our learning community during the transition year was the heroic leap from first to second tier in the Spiral Dynamics model, we found that the model provided a more compelling narrative than the former vague shift from the old to new paradigm of our previous holistic approach. Promoted in both Wilber's book *A Theory of Everything* and the Fall/Winter 2002 issue of *What is Enlightenment* magazine, both (and other) integral sources framed the move to integral consciousness as the next evolutionary leap awaiting humanity. Naturally we were excited to be offering an education aligned with this new leading-edge current of learning and growth, a timely update and filling out of our previous new paradigm philosophy. While the heroic leap from first- to second-tier consciousness is no longer serving as the guiding narrative within current integral discourse, the drive for transcendence and evolutionary ascent continues to stand out as a significant point of emphasis within Wilber's work and integral culture. Interestingly at the time, our tendency was to either overlook or undervalue the archetypal path of descent and involution—also addressed in Wilber's writings, though to a much lesser extent.

Yet if integral development is marked by increased capacities to care for, speak the language of, and constructively work with the intelligences of previous stages of development along different developmental lines, how might integral education benefit from integrating the path of descent and in certain cases regarding it as the heroic leap forward for integral education? At the very least, tempering the path of ascent with the path of descent helps ensure that the *overall* development of students and the learning communities becomes the focal transformative ideal. From more recent conversations with colleagues and personal reflection, I am persuaded of the necessity for future integral education projects to unearth more stable and comprehensive integral transformative ideals. Particularly ones that are not simply striving for the proverbial leading edge, but are also grounding their educational concerns in service of overall development through the particular details, historical situatedness, and particular unique contexts that comprise our paths of learning in daily life.

Recommendations for Future Integral Educational Ventures

Reflecting on the strengths and shortcomings of the HCIS transition year has surfaced three key directions that I believe future integral education projects would benefit from considering. First, the pervasive tendency to interpret, assess, and compartmentalize experience *structurally* through developmental and other meta-frameworks needs to be reexamined. I am no longer convinced that every integral framework need be an expression of a *developmental* way of making meaning within a *universal* meta-map complete with a "comprehensive" set of generalizations. If our habits of mind when approaching a particular subject, a conversation or one another are continually being translated through an evolving interpretive lens that emphasizes the structural and generalizable features of our experience, we can be assured that the particular and unique facets of experience are slipping through.

To return to a previous example, positing a chasm to be leapt over between first and second tier during our transition year provided a deeper shared directionality and purpose for students and faculty—a way out of the anything goes muddy terrain of the "new paradigm" ideal. Yet, at the time there were also students who called this proverbial leap into question or doubted this form of shift altogether. How will we support those learners who hear the call to transform in their bones but are for different reasons, skeptical about leaps to second tier, third tier, or the next developmental level? As such, I believe there is a need to compel and motivate students to explore alternative pathways outside and alongside the constructs of developmental thinking as a strategy for renewing how we understand and interpret our daily experience both inside and outside an integral context.

Second, for integral studies to continue to grow into a viable knowledge enterprise continued efforts are needed to critically and compassionately recontextualize Wilber's work alongside the growing eclectic contributions of other past, present, and emerging integral thinkers. To the extent that integral studies continues to be chiefly influenced by Wilber's frameworks, I believe this growing transdisciplinary field of knowledge will be unnecessarily burdened, however to the extent that our critiques overlook, subvert, or deny the important contributions of Wilber is equally problematic. As a passionate advocate for Wilber's integral paradigm during the transition year to HCIS, I was initially drawn to his visionary sketches, captivated by his generative conceptual work, and generally optimistic about the educational possibilities of learning from an integrally-informed perspective. Yet there was also an enthusiasm for learning from other educational research approaches that are by nature integral, but do not necessarily fall under Wilber's designations. Through a growing appreciation of the merits of diverse expressions of integral thought, at the time we were hopeful that our college could emerge as one of a cluster of sites for integral consciousness to develop and evolve.[17] But alas, this was not meant to be.

Third, during the transition year we discovered the importance of exploring different "integral" capacities (i.e., meta-paradigmatical awareness, vision-logic, etc.) along different developmental lines (i.e., cognitive, emotional, relational, spiritual, etc). By striving toward not only learning how to integrate different domains and fields of knowledge, but also to integrate multiple ways of knowing, we moved out of the territory of working with integral maps as tools for study, situating, critiquing, interpreting, and understanding the world and began to gravitate toward the territory of authentic integral experience arising moment to moment. There was also an initial focus on reclaiming the gifts of our Western educational lineage during our transition year, which included a resurgence of critical thinking and the importance of developing our cognitive capacities. In experimenting with Wilber's (2000) injunction to lead with the cognitive line (i.e., capacity to take more complex perspectives) did not always lead to desired outcomes. In fact, students and faculty interpreted this invitation as a pattern that reinforces the tendency to use cognition to control and manage our experience and to taking a perspective strictly within Wilber's system of thought.

What might it mean for future integral students to aspire to meet their life experiences from locations other than from within Wilber's AQAL system or higher stages of awareness? If leading from higher stages of cognition translates in practice to internalizing Wilber's frameworks for the purposes of re-translating the world according to his categories (or any other integral thinker's model for that matter), how can future integral approaches to education interrupt this well-worn approach? How to discern other vitalizing ways of learning integrally in such a manner that the different intelligences along different developmental lines can rise to prominence without always being overseen by one's internalized integral categories or meta-cognition? How might educators stimulate and integrate the somatic, emotional, intuitive, aesthetic, and spiritual modalities of experience (dimensions of experience that were prized by the former HCHS lineage) within educational contexts without abandoning intellectual rigor and critical reflective awareness?

In revisiting a number of the challenges our learning community faced during the transition year from HCHS to HCIS, it is my hope that emerging integral education ventures will find these questions and reflections useful. By endeavoring to open up integral educational paths that build on the territory illuminated by Wilber's frameworks and the work of his critics and advocates, it is my hope that the various points addressed in this chapter will inspire conversations to further explore new routes for transformation, divergence, and reconciliation among a growing eclectic diversity of approaches to integral education.

Notes

1. According to social scientist Paul Ray (Anderson & Ray, 2001), since the 1960s, 26% of the adults in the U.S. (50 million people) have made a comprehensive shift in their worldview, values, and way of life. Ray described this amorphous group as the "cultural creatives" and claims that though they lack a common language and set of beliefs, they are the fastest growing subculture in North America.

2. The initial HCHS semester included 15-week courses on the following: World View Philosophy, Holistic Science, Non-Violent Communication, Human Ecology, Quantum Physics and Consciousness, Yoga Psychology, Liberating Dance, Eco-Philosophy, Integration of Heart and Mind in Learning, Holistic Health, Science and Spirituality, Meditation, Creativity, and Artistic Expression.

3. The No Mind festival is an annual summer event of celebration and spiritual exploration. Typically the festival features spiritual teachers, musicians, and people from around the world. Initially the event was New Age in its approach, however, in recent years it has grown to become what some have referred to as Northern Scandinavia's counterpart event to The Burning Man festival held in the Black Rock desert of Nevada each year.

4. From 2001 to 2003, I served a multitude of roles including program coordinator, lecturer, learning coach, and student.

5. As Wilber (1999, pp. 44–58) points out, *modernity* loosely refers to the period of the Renaissance and the liberal Western enlightenment paradigm. According to Wilber the critique of deconstructive postmodernism is that modernity abided by a strict adherence to the patriarchal ideals of critical reason; believed in the inevitability of progress; carried a dogmatic faith in the objectivity of science; believed in an unquestionable universal moral code and the existence of a singular, autonomous self.

6. I will add that in my experience integral circles are also subject to misinterpreting Kuhn's notion of paradigm. At least inasmuch as there is a tendency to adopt and learn Wilber's models cognitively and to either ignore or cut corners experientially with the practices or injunctions, which are necessary to bring forth new types of experiences and phenomena in one's spiritual or integral practice.

7. Unlike Wilber's "flatland" where the Right-Hand quadrants (i.e., objectivity and interobjectivity) are true and the Left-Hand quadrants are denied (i.e., subjectivity and intersubjectivity), at HCHS, the learning community assumed the reverse scenario. This created a kind of "wonderland," the equivalent to a surrealistic landscape with confused interpretations of depth, because all empirical surfaces are simply perspectives and offer no substantial commentary on reality.

8. Working as the 2002–2003 program coordinator of our leadership team, I initiated and implemented changes in the college name and visionary direction to more optimally situate our vision in the emerging field of integral studies.

9. Students and faculty focused primarily on Wilber's work up until phase four, which includes an integration of developmental frameworks, the AQAL model and his other published writings up until *A Theory of Everything*. Aside from only a few serious students and myself, most did not cover his post-metaphysical writings as they appeared on the Shambhala website: http://Wilber.shambhala.com.

10. During the autumn semester of 2002, we introduced the Integral Learning Portfolio as one of our experimental learning tools at HCIS for students to further develop and mature their understanding of integral practice. Each portfolio included five sections: (1) Autobiographical sketch outlining students values, vision, and life story; (2) Lecture Learning Journal with class notes, questions, ideas, shifts in perspective, moments of insight; (3) Personal Project in cooperation with Lulea University; (4) Integral Transformative Practice as a method for engaging an integral lifestyle; and (5) Resume.

11. While Wilber's writings are often guilty of this, I agree with the observation Sean Esbjörn-Hargen's provided, while reviewing an earlier version of this chapter, that over recent years integral theorists and Wilberians have addressed this criticism in more substantial ways.

12. Wilber now refers to Integral Transformative Practice (ITP) as Integral Life Practice (ILP) in order to differentiate it from the ITP of George Leonard and Michael Murphy.

13. According to Don Beck, Spiral Dynamics traces our development of values and worldviews back to 100,000 years ago with the first appearance of the "Beige vMeme" up

to the emergence of early "second-tier vMemes" of our present day. The first-tier vMemes (Beige, Purple, Red, Blue, Orange, and Green) cluster together our subsistence or survival level concerns. Second-tier vMemes (Yellow and Turquoise) are characterized by the new capacity of human consciousness to work from multiple perspectives that retain a non-exclusive identification with the vital concerns and values of the first-tier vMemes.

14. It is important to note the problematic interpretations of Spiral Dynamics as a taxonomy for classifying individuals according to color schemes. This becomes especially problematic when the theory is used as an overarching system of development or in matters of conflict where individuals abuse the framework as a system of judgment upon others.

15. Negentropy broadly characterizes those experiences that lead an individual or organization to develop increasing orders of complexity. Unlike entropy, which is the tendency for systems to run down, the general tendency of negentropic experience is for systems to "run up."

16. Second-tier or integral consciousness is endowed with the capacities of multiple-perspective taking, flexibility in understanding the necessary role that all the first-tier vMemes play, thinking in terms of the overall spiral of existence (not merely in terms of any one level) and making it possible to move from pluralism to integralism (Wilber, 2003).

17. Primarily due to funding issues and extensive debt accumulated since the inception of the college, we were unable to continue offering our HCIS one-year program in 2004.

References

Anderson, S., & Ray, P. (2001). *The cultural creatives: How 50 million people are changing the world.* New York: Three Rivers Press.

Beck, D., & Cowan, C. (1996). *Spiral dynamics: Mastering values, leadership and change.* Malden, MA: Blackwell Publishers.

Bohm, D. (1996). *On dialogue.* London: Routledge Publishers.

Ferrer, J. (2002). *Revisioning transpersonal theory: A participatory vision of human spirituality.* Albany, NY: SUNY Press.

Gunnlaugson, O. (2004). Towards an integral education for the ecozoic era. *Journal of Transformative Education, 2*(4), 313–335.

Jordan, T. (2000). *Dimensions of consciousness development: A preliminary framework.* Retrieved 0207 from http://www.lightmind.com/library/essays/Jordan-01.html

Kegan, R. (1994). *In over our heads: The mental demands of modern life.* Cambridge, MA: Harvard University Press.

Mezirow, J. & associates (2000). *Learning as transformation: Critical perspectives on a theory in progress.* San Francisco: Jossey Bass.

O'Sullivan, E. (1999). *Transformative learning: Educational vision for the 21ˢᵗ century.* Toronto: OISE Press.

Scharmer, C. O. (2000). *Presencing: Learning from the future as it emerges.* Paper presented at the Conference on Knowledge and Innovation May 25–26, 2000, Helsinki School of Economics, Finland, and the MIT Sloan School of Management. Retrieved 0208 from http://www.dialogonleadership.org/Presencing00.pdf

Swimme, B. (2003). The challenge of our moment. *What is Enlightenment?* Issue 23, Spring/Summer 2003, 42–55.

Visser, F. (2003). *Ken Wilber: Thought as passion.* New York: SUNY Press.

Welwood, J. (2000). *Toward a psychology of awakening: Buddhism, psychotherapy and the path of personal and spiritual transformation.* Boston: Shambhala.

Wilber, K. (1995). *Sex, ecology, spirituality.* Boston: Shambhala.

Wilber, K. (2000a). *A theory of everything.* Boston: Shambhala.

Wilber, K. (2000b). *Integral psychology: Consciousness, spirit, psychology, therapy.* Boston: Shambhala.

Wilber, K. (2002). *Boomeritis: A novel that will set you free.* Boston: Shambhala.

Wilber, K. (2003). Excerpt B: The many ways we touch three principles helpful for any integrative approach from. Retrieved 0209 from http://wilber.shambhala.combooks/kosmos/excerptB/intro.cfm/

Wilber, K. (2006). *A sociable god.* Boston: Shambhala

Contemporary Integral Education Research

A Transnational and Transparadigmatic Overview

Markus Molz

Introduction

This chapter is a tentative, condensed overview (with an appendix listing associations and programs with urls) of contemporary academic-level research and development within and on integral and likeminded educational approaches. Such an overview has to cope with serious tensions: between the requirement to give a global account across streams and schools of thought, the reality of an unbalanced geopolitics of knowledge, the question of the relationship between research and practice, and the editorial constraint of necessary brevity. As a way to surf on the waves of these tensions the following principles have guided the elaboration of this chapter.

- *First principle:* A focus on formalized transnational networks of researchers—these networks are more likely than national networks or local research teams to be major driving forces in the emerging field of educational research and development conducted in an integral or likeminded spirit.

- *Second principle:* An emphasis on activities beyond the Anglo-Saxon world to counterbalance the dominant visibility of Anglo-Saxon literature on the international level.

- *Third principle:* A limitation to referencing highly selected authors inside each network without expanding on the complexity of their respective thinking nor on the ecology of collaboration and sources of inspiration. Such a limitation is unavoidable in a short contribution,

317

and hopefully compensated by the reference section opening up to this ecology.

- *Fourth principle:* The selection of contemporary streams or networks based on the shared features listed at the end of the chapter in this volume on historical streams of integral education (Molz & Hampson), while adding the requirement of an explicit account of spirituality. This is in order to overcome artificial limitations of considering only those streams labeling themselves explicitly as integral education.

- *Fifth principle:* A broad understanding of research encompassing the whole spectrum of the theory-practice continuum in research. This is because a normative understanding of acceptable scientific research would reduce the understanding of this emerging field.

While the following compilation is based on these principles, it is certainly far from being complete. It should be considered as a base to be expanded on by collective effort. Thus there is an emphasis on the reference section in order to facilitate the actualisation of cross-connections between researchers and their projects.

Anthroposophical Educational Research

Rudolf Steiner emphasized repeatedly that theory and practice should not be separated. This attitude has set the tone for research in the Anthroposophical tradition. Steiner founded and inspired the Goetheanum in Dornach, Switzerland as the center of the Anthroposophical society. The School of Spiritual Science is the research and advanced training branch of the Goetheanum, with sections covering a variety of fields, among them a pedagogical section, steered by an international advisory board and currently directed by Christof Wiechert. The purpose of this section is to realize practice-enhancing educational research, support, and development projects.

There are at least two more international networks conducting and disseminating research on Waldorf education, informally linked to the pedagogical section but constituted and acting independently from it. First, there is the Research Institute for Waldorf Education, founded in 1996, issuing a research bulletin, collecting and compiling existing research in a transnational perspective (Nordwall, 2006), and translating major programmatic and research texts from the non-Anglo-Saxon world into English (see appendix for the Waldorf journal project).

Second, the initiative for practice-based research, has been particularly successful in building Integrated Master Programmes for professionals (Hauenstein,

Taylor, & Stöckli, 2007) as a collaborative endeavour together with the University of Plymouth (UK)—the first of which was a Waldorf education masters degree for practicing teachers. The very core of these blended-learning higher education programs are student-led action research projects.

Holistic Education

Holistic education has a complex, multi-local genesis which cannot be presented here (see Forbes, 2003; Miller, 2006; Miller, 1997; Stack, 2006). It is more of an umbrella term covering several streams than a clearly defined approach to education. It suffices to state that parts of the different holistic education communities share a number of tenets with proponents of one or the other streams of integral education. A clear-cut distinction between integral and holistic education is not possible on the basis of historical references, worldview, pursued goals, or applied methods (Stack, 2006). Nevertheless, there are genuine networks of holistic education distinct from those of integral education. They are often organized on a local, regional, or national scale.[1]

However, there is at least one international community of holistic educationalists, coordinated by Jack Miller, one of the key researchers in this field (Miller, 2007): the "Holistic Learning and Spirituality in Education Network." This network gathers and presents its work at the conferences of the Association for Supervision and Curriculum Development, which has an extremely large and international membership base. Independently, there is an international moderated list for the discussion of the principles and practice of holistic education coordinated by the Tasmanian Holistic Education Network. A compilation of recent research projects in North America on holistic education can be found in Martin (2004), and the results of a survey on actual orientations of holistic schools in Forbes & Martin (2004).

In Mexico, Ramón Gallegos Nava, author of a dozen of books on holistic education (one of which was translated into English in 2001) has established his Fundación Internacional para la Educación Holista (International Foundation for Holistic Education) in 1992, offering training programs for educators and organizing national and international conferences on holistic education.

Neohumanist Education

Prabhat Ranjan Sarkar (1921–1990) was an Indian polymath, social and political reformer, composer, and spiritual leader, prolifically writing and teaching about all aspects of life from a perspective of individual emancipation and collective welfare. He covered cosmology and cultural macrohistory (social cycle theory) to spiritual practice (a yoga blending and adapting vedic and tantric traditions) and socioeconomic theory (progressive utilization theory (PROUT)), without leaving out education (neohumanist education, see Sarkar, 1998). Sarkar founded a socio-spiritual movement, Ananda Marga, which spread worldwide and continued working after his passing away. Its educational branch, the Ananda Marga Gurukul network, runs more than thousand kindergartens, schools, and colleges in more than 50 countries, East and West. Within this network an attempt is undertaken to set up a neohumanist education research institute. Sarkar's educational vision and practice has recently been built on by academic researchers (e.g., Bussey, 2007; Inayatullah et al., 2006; Kesson, 1989).

Transdisciplinary Education

Transdisciplinarity as a concept was coined on the OECD conference in 1970 on the challenges of interdisciplinarity for teaching and research at the university. Leo Apostel, Jean Piaget, and Erich Jantsch substantially contributed to this conference (Apostel, 1972). The transdisciplinary approach has been further developed by Edgar Morin and Basarab Nicolescu (2002), with support coming from the UNESCO. Today there is an ecology of researchers, mostly in Southern Europe and Southern America, working in various criss-crossing networks on the perspectives of transdisciplinarity and complexity paradigms in education. First and foremost there are the extended networks around Morin, sociologist, emeritus director of a transdisciplinary research group at the French national research institute (CNRS). Morin has left his imprint on the intellectual landscape through uncountable publications spanning 60 years and including education (e.g., Morin, 1999, 2008).[2] Morin founded and directed the "association pour la pensée complexe" (association for complex thought), which has several thematic working groups, the sixth of which is focusing on "educational sciences and complexity."

Nicolescu and Morin together with Lima de Freitas drafted the charter of transdisciplinarity (1994). Nicolescu is nuclear physicist at the French national research institute, and instigator and coordinator of the International Centre for Transdisciplinary Research (CIRET) and its network since 1987. A special issue of the journal of the CIRET "Rencontres Transdisciplinaires" (Transdisciplinary Encounters) was devoted to the "experiences of transdisciplinary education" (Bot, 2005). Nicolescu (1997, 1999, 2002, 2005) has applied his take on transdisciplinarity to education, and he inspired several educational researchers to expand on his foundational work (e.g., Harvey & Lemire, 2001, Paul & Pineau, 2005).

The "centro da educação transdisciplinario" CETRANS (center for transdisciplinary education) was created in 1998 as an independent network organization supported by the university of São Paulo. Members and associates are from a wide range of disciplines and professions coming mainly from all over Brazil and other South American countries, but also some from Northern America and

Europe, e.g., besides Nicolescu himself, Gaston Pineau, professor of educational sciences at the University of Tours (Paul & Pineau, 2005). Humberto Maturana is another associate of CETRANS. The Center has trained dozens of educators, translated foundational texts on transdisciplinarity into Portuguese, organized and documented research workshops called "catalytic meetings" (Barros, 2000, 2002; Friaça, 2007), and issued the journal Revista Companhia. Its members facilitated dozens of pilot projects implementing a transdisciplinary approach to education or disseminating knowledge about transdisciplinarity in contexts of learning and work. In addition, they substantially contributed to various scientific conferences (e.g., the series of international congresses on transdisciplinarity, complexity, and environmental education organized by a network of Latin American and Spanish universities, see e.g., Torres, 2007).

Educational Research According to Critical Realism

The original version of Roy Bhaskar's critical realism is a philosophy of science transcending the respective shortcomings of its modernist and postmodernist alternatives. Adding several layers to his original framework, Bhaskar moved on to the philosophy of meta-Reality (Bhaskar 2002a, 2002b), an engaged philosophy of universal emancipation in face of global crisis. During this process a well-established network of researchers unfolded through the Centre of Critical Realism, the International Association of Critical Realism and its annual conferences, the *Journal of Critical Realism*, and the book series *Routledge Studies in Critical Realism*. The different stages of unfoldment of Bhaskar's work have been received, commented on, and made use of in a large range of academic and applied fields, among them in education (e.g., Corson, 1991; Egbo, 2005; Hockey, 2007; Scott, 2000, 2005; Shipway, 2002; Warner, 1993; Wilmott, 2002, Zembylas, 2006).

Since 2007 Bhaskar has been World Scholar at the Institute of Education, University of London—this position bringing along a new emphasis his own pursuits on the educational implications of critical realism (Bhaskar, 2002c). On these grounds an international conference series on "education and critical realism" has been started, the launch of a master's degree program is being prepared, and several publications are on the way in this field (e.g., Scott, 2010). Accordingly, a new wave of educational research in the critical realism tradition can be expected in the near future, taking into account the spiritual turn in Bhaskar's theorizing.

Integral Education According to Wilber's AQAL model

Wilber's AQAL model doesn't need any extra introduction in this book. Wilber himself has not focused on education in his own writings. However, there are two masters programs dedicated to the AQAL approach offered by the Integral Institute in collaboration with JFK University and Fielding Graduate University. Esbjörn-Hargens (2006a, 2006b, current volume) announced a program of methodologically integral educational research on the participants in the integral education program at JFKU. The recently launched biannual Integral Theory Conference series invited the submission of contributions related to integral education.

There is some educational theorizing being inspired by the AQAL model in recent years (see an initial compilation of respective English-language publications by Fisher, 2007). The *Journal of Integral Theory and Practice* had the summer 2007 issue entirely dedicated to education. The independent Canadian initiative, Next Step Integral, is sustaining dialogue on integral education with reference to the AQAL model while being open to contributions from other streams by means of an online discussion forum.

The above-mentioned activities predominantly involve Northern American educationalists. However, uptake of the AQAL model can as well be found in German-language academic educational discourse, generally by isolated voices connecting it to the concerns of a specific subfield, e.g., education for conscious evolution (Brehmer, 1992), educational practice development (Fuhr & Dauber, 2002), education for democracy (Langemann, 2006), human resource development (Geilenbrügge, 2004), organizational learning (Küpers, 2006a), and leadership in higher education institutions (Küpers, 2006b).

The Commission of Humanistic Psychology and Pedagogy

The Commission of Humanistic Psychology and Pedagogy was established in the early 1990s as one of a dozen of commissions constituting the German Society for Educational Research. It welcomes all German-language educational researchers and interested practitioners identifying with one or several streams of the humanistic tradition (from early alternative pedagogies to gestalt pedagogy and other educational inheritors of humanistic and transpersonal psychologies to the variants of integral education). This commission has initiated a book series at Klinckhardt Verlag. Over the years a unique community of educational researchers has built up, reflecting on alternatives to the usual fragmentation of the educational process and refusing the pervasive harsh separation between educational, therapeutic, social, political, and spiritual activity systems. Several participants in this unique nexus can be considered major proponents of an integral approach to (higher) education in Western Europe. They will be briefly introduced.

Heinrich Dauber, professor of educational sciences and teacher educator at the University of Kassel, personally acquainted with Ivan Illich—and for many years coordinator of the commission—was one of the first to introduce integral approaches to education in his courses, to publish in an integrally informed way (together with the deceased Reinhard Fuhr, co-founder of *Integral Review*, see Fuhr

& Dauber, 2002), and to supervise a couple of PhD dissertations focusing on integral (e.g., the very early thesis of Brehmer, 1992), transformative (Gremmler-Fuhr, 2005), and transpersonal (Weiss, 2008) approaches to learning.

Wolfgang Roth, professor emeritus of psychology, teacher education college in Freiburg/Germany, was the organizer of the academic conference "Science and spirituality—new perspectives for education" inspired by the Dalai Lama in 2007, and its ongoing follow-up activities (Hüther, Roth, & von Brück, 2008). Josef Keuffer, professor of educational sciences at Bielefeld University, started his academic career with a PhD dissertation on Buddhism and education in a comparative perspective (Keuffer, 1991).[3] Today Keuffer is the head of an educational research center associated with the internationally renowned experimental secondary school built up by Hartmut von Hentig.

Traugott Elsässer, former collaborator of Fritz Oser (Oser, Scarlett, & Bucher, 2006), after involvement in a research project on choreographies of teaching and learning (Oser & Baeriswyl, 2001) and a project on integral education for sustainable development, is now professor at the teacher education college in St. Gallen, Switzerland and coordinator of the educational programmatic of the integral political party, which is being founded in Switzerland. Ralf Girg, initiator of the integral science group at the University of Regensburg, brings his unique Integralpädagogik (integral-pedagogy) (Girg, 2007) to teacher education.

Other members of the commission pushing the limits of integral education are Hagen Kordes, professor of educational sciences at the University of Münster (supervisor of Langemann, 2006); Regina Mikula and Daniela Michaelis, teacher educators at the University of Graz Austria (devising a feminist introduction to integral education, see Michaelis & Mikula, 2007); Nils Altner (2006 PhD dissertation on mindful and healthy pedagogy); Jürgen Elsholz (2009, PhD dissertation on a Gebserian theory of education); and myself.

Singular Voices

The above compilation should not lead us to underscore the importance and the impact of integrally-minded educationalists not associated to one of these international networks. Some of them are singular forerunners, which could best be considered as being a sort of an international stream on their own. The following selection is necessarily arbitrary and biased through personal preference, but to make the point let me quote, among many others, Parker Palmer (2007) and Sally Goerner (2006, 2007) from the United States, Claudio Naranjo (2004)[4] from Chile, René Barbier (1997) from France, and outstanding non-academic voices like Steven Harrison (2002).

Others synthesize influences from different streams (e.g., Girg, 2007 from Aurobindo, Krishnamurti, Gebser, and others; Hübner, 2008 from Steiner and Gebser and others) to arrive at their own integral approach to education. And still others take a meta-perspective on streams (Adams, 2006; Gidley, 2007, 2008, and in this volume; Giri, 2009; Molz & Hampson, in this volume; Murray, 2009). In this case integral education and likeminded streams are flipping from the paradigm and context for research to the object and content of research, opening up the yet very little explored horizon of integral meta-studies (Edwards, 2008; Edwards & Molz, 2009) in and of education.

Conclusion

In the field of integral education and likeminded approaches we can witness today a variety of international networks of educational researchers. Besides their yet very little explored resonances, these networks have one structural point in common: Most of them have their organizational roots in the 1990s. Their output in terms of publications seems to have accelerated in the new millennium, especially in the last three years. Accordingly, they must be considered parallel developments. They differ, however, in a couple of respects. Some are the educational thread of a cross-domain movement, which can be traced back to a founder and his work. This is the case for the followers of Rudolf Steiner, Prabhat Sarkar, Roy Bhaskar, and Ken Wilber. Others seem to invite and deal with a plurality of approaches at the same time, under umbrella headings like holistic, transdisciplinary, and humanistic education.

Furthermore, there is a bewildering variety of labels. Only one of the contemporary streams brought together in this chapter self-describes as integral education (referring to Wilber's AQAL model), and it appears to be the most recent and least formally constituted one in terms of an international network of academic educational researchers. Hence, top-level terminology is a first barrier to discovering the possible resonances between likeminded educational researchers. A second barrier seems to be language, compounded with the geopolitics of knowledge. In the field of integral educational research no exception can be stated to the usual asymmetry between English- and non-English-speaking countries. Output from educational research originally written in other languages is generally not translated into English and by this very fact lacks "international" uptake more or less completely. Translation from English in other languages is barely more frequent in the educational sciences. Education is, much more than many other research fields, rooted in national systems, and so are large parts of educational research.

Besides a sphere of international exchange in English, there are different coexistent "internationalities" in educational research in general, reflected in an unaltered manner in the above compilation of networks of educational researchers working on integral or likeminded versions of education. The geographical areas in which these streams spread internationally are not necessarily the same. No single educational research network involving an integral approach has achieved truly global coverage so far. For example, transdisciplinary education has developed basically in Southern Europe and South America. The part of the critical realism community interested in education seems currently to be more concentrated in the UK, Australia, and the Scandinavian countries. Holistic and (AQAL) integral education clearly have their home base in Northern America. From the networks outlined here very little can be said about Africa and Asia.

A third barrier lies in the identification with one stream in a researchers' life. To become well grounded in one of the guiding meta-frameworks is practically a lifetime investment. A network gives a home, a social and intellectual platform, enhanced access to resources and opportunities, etc. To dis-identify sufficiently from all this is even more demanding. Accordingly, if we want to build bridges toward a truly global (transnational and transparadigmatic) community of integral and likeminded educational researchers, we need to take these three barriers very seriously.

In summary, it can be said that the integral consciousness emerging worldwide manifests itself in different cultural-linguistic educational and research contexts in ways, which are contingent while potentially resonating with each other. Integral and likeminded educational research networks today appear like computers before the dawn of the Internet: They are already powerful in themselves. However, as they are still largely disconnected from each other the incredible potential of together-ness remains largely untapped until intentional connections are established across research streams and their contingent cultural-linguistic spread.

Appendix

List of Associations and Programs with urls. (Some urls may change over time).

Pedagogical section of the Goetheanum (in German): www.paedagogik-goetheanum.ch
Research institute for Waldorf education: www.waldorfresearchinstitute.org
Waldorf journal Project: www.waldorflibrary.org/waldorfjournalproj.htm
Initiative for practice-based research IPF (mainly in German): www.ipf.ch
Holistic Learning and Spirituality in Education Network: www.oise.utoronto.ca/field-cen-tres/miller-ascd.html
Association for supervision and curriculum development: www.ascd.org
Holistic education network Tasmania discussion list: www.hent.org
International foundation for holistic education (mainly in Spanish): www.ramongallegos.com
Ánanda Márga Gurukula: www.gurukul.edu
Educational sciences and complexity working group of the association of complex thought, France (in French): www.mcxapc.org/atelier.php?a=display&ID=6
Charter of transdisciplinarity—basarab.nicolescu.perso.sfr.fr/ciret/english/charten.htm
International Center for Transdisciplinary Research CIRET: basarab.nicolescu.perso.sfr.fr/ciret/indexen.html

Center for transdisciplinary education CETRANS, Brazil (in Portuguese): www.cetrans. com.br

Integral education forum of Next Step Integral: www.integral-ed.org

Integral education seminar series of Next Step Integral: www.i-edu.org

Commission for Humanistic Psychology and Pedagogy of the German Society of Educational Sciences (in German): www.humanistische-paedagogik.de

Book series on humanistic pedagogy (in German): www.klinkhardt.de/gruppe/9/

Science and spirituality: new perspectives in therapy and education (in German): www. erziehungs-perspektiven.de

Holistic Education SIG in the American Educational Research Association: http://www.aera. net/Default.aspx?menu_id=174&id=403

International Observatory of University Reforms: www.orus-int.org

Multiversidad Mundo Real—Edgar Morin (in Spanish): www.multiversidadreal.org

Claudio Naranjo Foundation (in Spanish): http://fundacionclaudionaranjo.com

Notes

1. For instance, see the special interest group on holistic education within the American Educational Research Association. www.aera.net/Default.aspx?menu_id = 174&id = 403

2. Morin stimulated the creation of the "international observatory of university reforms" ORUS (see www.orus-int.org), and he was honoured by the creation of a university based on his educational approach, the Multiversidad Mundo Real—Edgar Morin in Mexico (see www.multiversidadreal.org).

3. See also the subsequent PhD dissertation by Paetow (2004) putting non-identity instead of identity at center stage of the educational process.

4. The subtitle of the Claudio Naranjo Foundation is "For an integral education." See http://fundacionclaudionaranjo.com.

References

Adams, A. (2006). *Education: from conception to graduation—A systemic integral approach.* PhD dissertation, California Institute for Integral Studies.

Altner, N. (2006). *Achtsamkeit und Gesundheit. Auf dem Weg zu einer achtsamen Pädagogik.* Immenhausen: Prolog Verlag.

Apostel, L. et al. (Eds.). (1972). *Interdisciplinarity—problems of teaching and research in universities.* Paris: Centre for Educational Research and Innovation (CERI), OECD Publications.

Barbier, R. (1997). *L'approche transversale. L'écoute sensible en sciences humaines.* Paris: Anthropos.

Barros, V.M. et al. (Eds.). (2000). *Educação e transdisciplinaridade I.* Brasília: UNESCO.

Barros, V.M. et al. (Eds.). (2002). *Educação e transdisciplinaridade II.* São Paulo: Triom.

Bhaskar, R. (2002a). *meta-Reality: The philosophy of meta-reality, Vol. 1: Creativity, love and freedom.* London: Sage.

Bhaskar, R. (2002b). *The philosophy of meta-reality. Vol. 1 A philosophy for the present.* London: Sage.

Bhaskar, R. (2002c). Educating the educators—Or, empowering teachers. In R. Bhaskar, *From science to emancipation. Journeys towards meta-reality—a philosophy of the present.* New Dehli: Sage.

Bot, L. (Ed.). (2005). *Expériences d'éducation transdisciplinaires. Rencontres Transdiscplinaires,* 18. Accessed 2010/2/18 from http://basarab.nicolescu.perso.sfr.fr/ciret/bulletin/b18/b18.htm

Brehmer, C. (1992). *Die Evolution des Bewußtseins und die Möglichkeit der Erforschung ihres zukünftigen Verlaufes im Rahmen eines erweiterten Wissenschaftsverständnisses.* Frankfurt: Peter Lang.

Bussey, M. (2007). Global education from a neohumanist perspective: A musical exposition *Journal of Futures Studies, 12*(1), 25–40.

Corson, D. (1991). Bhaskar's critical realism and educational knowledge. *British Journal of Sociology of Education, 12*(2), 223–241.

Edwards, M. (2008). Where is the method to our integral madness? An outline of integral meta-studies. *Journal of Integral Theory and Practice, 3*(2), 165–194.

Edwards, M., & Molz, M. (2010). Crossing boundaries, stimulating creativity: The horizon of integral meta-studies. In A. K. Giri (Ed.), *Pathways of creative research: Towards a festival of dialogues.* Delhi: Shipra Publications.

Elsholz, J. (2009). *Hermeneutik des Gespürs. Grundlagen einer integralen Bildungskonzeption.* PhD dissertation, University of Bielefeld.

Egbo, B. (2005). Emergent paradigm: critical realism and transformative research in educational administration. *McGill Journal of Education, 40*(2), 267–284.

Esbjörn-Hargens, S. (2006a). Integral research: a multi-method approach to investigating phenomena. *Constructivism in the Human Sciences, 11*(1–2), 79–107.

Esbjörn-Hargens, S. (2006b). Integral education by design: How integral theory informs teaching, learning and curriculum in a graduate program. *ReVision, 28*(3), 21–29.

Harvey, P.-L., & Lemire, G. (2001). *La nouvelle éducation. NTIC, transdisciplinarité et communautique.* Paris: L'Harmattan.

Fisher, M. (2007). *Ken Wilber and the education literature: Abridged annotated bibliography.* Accessed 2008/10/20 from www.pathsoflearning.net/resources_writings_Ken_Wilber.pdf

Forbes, S. H. (2003). *Holistic education: An analysis of its ideas and nature.* Brandon, VT: Foundation for educational renewal.

Forbes, S. H., & Martin, A. (2004). *What holistic education claims about itself: An analysis of holistic schools' literature.* Presentation at the American Education Research Association Annual Conference. Accessed 2008/10/20 from www.holistic-education.net/articles/research04.pdf

Friaça, A. et al. (Eds.). (2007). *Educação e transdisciplinaridade III (2nd edition).* São Paulo: Triom.

Fuhr, R., & Dauber, H. (2002). *Praxisentwicklung im Bildungsbereich—ein integraler Forschungsansatz.* Bad Heilbrunn: Klinkhardt.

Gallegos Nava, R. (2001). *Holistic education: Pedagogy of universal love.* Brandon, VT: Foundation for Educational Renewal.

Geilenbrügge, M. (2004). *Der integrale Ansatz nach Ken Wilber und seine Umsetzung im Bereich Organisations—und Personalentwicklung.* Master's thesis in educational sciences, University of Dortmund.

Gidley, J. (2007). The evolution of consciousness as a planetary imperative: An integration of integral views. *Integral Review, 5,* 4–226.

Gidley, J. (2008). *Evolving education: A postformal-integral-planetary gaze at the evolution of consciousness and the educational imperatives.* PhD dissertation, Southern Cross University.

Giri, A. K. (2009). *Learning the art of wholeness. Integral education and beyond.* Report submitted to the Indian Council of Social Science Research. Chennai: Madras Institute of Development Studies.

Girg, R. (2007). *Die integrale Schule des Menschen. Praxis und Horizonte der Integralpädagogik.* Regensburg: Roderer.

Goerner, S. (2006). *The coming age of change in education.* Federal Way, WA: Books for Educators.

Goerner, S. (2007). Today's Copernican flip: how putting collaborative learning at the hub of human evolution improves our chances of survival. *Systems Research and Behavioral Science, 24*(5), 481–491.

Gremmler-Fuhr, M. (2005). *Transformative Lernprozesse im Erwachsenenalter—Entwicklung eines Orientierungskonzepts für die Anleitung und Unterstützung relationaler Lernprozesse.* PhD dissertation, University of Kassel.

Harrison, S. (2002). *The happy child: Changing the heart of education.* Boulder, CO: Sentient Publications.

Hauenstein, U., Taylor, G., & Stöckli, T. (2007). *Perspektiven für zeitgemässe Masterstudiengänge.* Norderstedt: Books on Demand.

Hockey, N. (2007). *Learning for liberation. Values, actions and structures for social transformation through Aboriginal communities.* PhD dissertation. Queensland University of Technology.

Hübner, E. (2008). *Individualität und Bildungskunst. Menschwerdung in technischen Räumen.* Professorial dissertation, Technical University of Darmstadt.

Hüther, G., Roth, W., & Brück, Michael von (Eds.). (2008). *Damit das Denken Sinn bekommt. Spiritualität, Vernunft und Selbsterkenntnis.* Freiburg: Herder.

Inayatullah, S., Bussey, M., & Milojevic, I. (Eds.). (2006). *Neohumanist educational futures: liberating the pedagogical intellect.* Taipei, Taiwan: Tamkang University Press.

Keuffer, J. (1991). *Buddhismus und Erziehung. Eine interkulturelle Studie zu Tibet aus erziehungswissenschaftlicher Sicht.* Münster: Waxmann.

Kesson, K. (1989). A neo-humanist model of education. *Holistic Education Review, 1*(3), 12–18.

Küpers, W. (2006a). Integrales Lernen in und von Organisationen (Integral organizational learning—extended English summary). *Integral Review, 2,* 43–77.

Küpers, W. (2006b). Integrale Führung in Bildungsorganisationen. In S. Laske, C. Meister-Scheytt, & W. Küpers (Eds.), *Führung und Organisation.* Münster: Waxmann, pp. 118–150.

Langemann, B. (2006*). Eine integrale Perspektive auf Demokratie in der Bildung.* Masters thesis in psychology, Free University of Berlin.

Martin, R. A. (2004). *Holistic education: Research that is beginning to delineate the field.* Presentation at the American Education Research Association Annual Meeting. Wholistic Education SIG, San Diego, CA.

Michaelis, D., & Mikula, R. (2007). *Integrale Pädagogik. Die Babuschkas tanzen in die Pädagogik hinein.* Stuttgart: Ibidem.

Miller, J. P. (2007). *The holistic curriculum (revised and expanded edition).* Toronto: University of Toronto Press.

Miller, J. P. (2006). Ancient roots of holistic education. *Encounter, 19,* 55–59.

Miller, R. (1997). *What are schools for? Holistic education in American culture* (3rd. ed). Brandon, VT: Holistic Education Press.

Morin, E. (1999). *Seven complex lessons in education for the future.* Paris: UNESCO.

Morin, E. (2008) The reform of thought, transdisciplinarity, and reform of the university. In B. Nicolescu (Ed.), *Transdisciplinarity: theory and practice.* Cresskill, NJ: Hampton Press.

Murray, T. (2009). What is integral in integral education? From progressive pedagogy to integral pedagogy. *Integral Review, 5*(1), 96–134.

Naranjo, C. (2004). *Cambiar la educación para cambiar el mundo.* Vitoria: Ediciones La Llave.

Nicolescu, B. (1997). *The transdisciplinary evolution of the university. Condition for sustainable development.* Accessed 2008/10/20 from http://basarab.nicolescu.perso.sfr.fr/ciret/bulletin/b12/b12c8.htm

Nicolescu, B. (1999). *The transdisciplinary evolution of learning.* Accessed 2008/10/20 from http://www.learndev.org/dl/nicolescu_f.pdf

Nicolescu, B. (2002). *Manifesto of Transdisciplinarity.* Albany, NY: State University of New York Press.

Nicolescu, B. (2005). Towards transdisciplinary education and learning. Presented at the Metanexus Conference "Science and Religion: Global Perspectives," Philadelphia, PA. Accessed 2010/2/18 from www.metanexus.net/conference2005/pdf/nicolescu.pdf

Nordwall, S. (2006). *What studies have been published on Waldorf education?* Accessed 2008/10/20 from www.waldorfresearchinstitute.org/pdf/RCWaldorfRes.pdf

Oser, F., Scarlett, G., & Bucher, A. (2006). Religious and spiritual development throughout the life span. In W. Damon, & R. M. Lerner (Eds.) *Handbook of Child Psychology Vol. 1* (6th ed.), Hoboken, NJ: Wiley, pp. 942–998.

Oser, F., & Baeriswyl, F. (2001). Choreographies of teaching: Bridging instruction to learning. In V. Richardson (Ed.), *Handbook of research on teaching* (4th ed.). Washington: American Educational Research Association, pp. 1031–1065.

Paetow, B.-P. (2004). *Nicht-Identität als Bezugspunkt von Bildungsprozessen. Eine interkulturelle Studie zum (Mahayana-)Buddhismus aus erziehungswissenschaftlicher Sicht.* Ph.D. dissertation, University of Bielefeld.

Palmer, P.J. (2007). *The courage to teach: Exploring the inner landscape of a teacher's life* (10th ed.). San Francicso: Jossey-Bass.

Paul, P., & Pineau, G. (Eds.). (2005). *Transdisciplinarité et formation.* Paris: L'Harmattan.

Sarkar, P. R. (1998). *Discourses on neohumanist education.* Calcutta: Ananda Marga Publications.

Scott, D. (2000). *Realism and educational research. New perspectives and possibilities.* London: Routledge.

Scott, D. (2005). Critical realism and empirical research methods in education. *Journal of Philosophy of Education, 39*(4), 633–646.

Scott, D. (2010). *Education, epistemology and critical realism.* London: Routledge.

Shipway, B. (2002). *Implications of a critical realist perspective in education.* PhD dissertation, Southern Cross University.

Stack, S. (2006). *Integrating science and soul in education. The lived experience of a science educator bringing holistic and integral perspectives to the transformation of science teaching.* PhD dissertation, Curtin University of Technology.

Torre, S. D. L. (Ed.). (2007). *Transdisciplinariedad y ecoformación : una nueva mirada sobre la educación.* Madrid: Editorial Universitas.

Warner, M. M. (1993). Objectivity and emancipation in learning disabilities: Holism from the perspective of critical realism. *Journal of Learning Disabilities, 26*(5), 311–328.

Weiss, C. (2008). *Transpersonale Dimensionen in der Pädagogik.* PhD dissertation, University of Kassel.

Wilmott, R. (2002). *Education policy and realist social theory. Primary teachers, child-centred philosophy and the new managerialism.* London: Routledge.

Zembylas, M. (2006). Science education as emancipatory: The case of Roy Bhaskar's philosophy of meta-reality. *Educational Philosophy and Theory, 38*(5), 665–676.

Spirituality and Integral Thought in Higher Education

Alexander Astin in Conversation with Jonathan Reams

Alexander (Sandy) Astin is the Allan M. Cartter Professor of Higher Education Emeritus at the University of California, Los Angeles. He is also Founding Director of the Higher Education Research Institute (HERI) at UCLA. He has served as Director of Research for both the American Council on Education and the National Merit Scholarship Corporation. He is also the Founding Director of the Cooperative Institutional Research Program, an ongoing study of some 12 million students, 250,000 faculty and staff, and 1,800 higher education institutions.

Dr. Astin has authored 20 books and more than 300 other publications on higher education, and has received awards for outstanding research from more than a dozen national associations and professional societies. A 1990 study in the Journal of Higher Education *identified Dr. Astin as the most frequently cited author in the field of higher education.*

In 2002 I heard Dr. Astin speak at a Western Association of Schools and Colleges (WASC) conference. In the space of 20 minutes, he introduced the work of Ken Wilber and gave a comprehensive yet succinct overview of Integral Theory that wove seamlessly into the main thread of his talk. Reflecting on this experience, I felt that Dr. Astin would be able to provide a perspective on higher education that would illuminate the trajectory of existing trends in an integral direction.

JR: I would like to begin by thanking you for taking this time to reflect on your experience and share perspectives on some of the trends and forces that are moving higher education toward an integral approach. Your extensive history in researching higher education, especially around issues of spirituality will hopefully shed some new light in these areas. Could you begin with a brief overview of your research within HERI?

SA: Well, for the last 40 years I have been studying the development of college students during the undergraduate years and in some cases post-college

331

years. These are large scale national studies involving usually several hundred institutions and anywhere from 10,000 to 25,000 students at a time. We collect longitudinal data so we can study student growth and development, and one of the things that we have been doing for years is to try to cover the entire spectrum of student development qualities. We have a little four-cell matrix that we have been using, not entirely unlike Wilber's 2 x 2 matrix (although it was developed many years before he started publishing). One of the dimensions of student development outcomes has to do with the inner (Left-Hand quadrants) or what we call psychological measures as opposed to the outer (Right-Hand quadrants) or sociological measures.

For instance, the range of student developmental qualities we assess includes values. Now it is interesting that when we first started doing this people said, "Well, what do student values have to do with higher education?" We plowed ahead with our studies anyway, insisting that if you interpret the stated goals of liberal education broadly it covers a pretty wide range of human qualities. It isn't just simply the 3Rs or something like that, which higher education is focusing on.

But I don't think that too many scholars have paid much attention to what we claim we are doing. If you take seriously the claims and more formal descriptions of liberal education, which are embraced by almost all the colleges and universities in the U.S. and less so in Europe (it depends on the country), we are much more integral in what we are trying to do than perhaps the average layperson is inclined to believe. We are not just preparing people to fill slots in the labor force, which is what a lot of laypeople believe. We are educating the whole person. I think it's too bad we haven't had more public discussion of this because our sense about it is: Even if you don't care about the development of student values, the fact is that the experience of higher education is having an impact in some way or another on students' values. From this it behooves us to take a look at what kind of impact the experience is having.

JR: Not to mention issues like how these values impact the conditions for learning.

SA: Exactly. We don't presume to know all the relevant conditions for learning and so part of this search is open-ended. We are looking at anything that might plausibly make a difference in students' lives. A lot of that doesn't have much to do with the classroom, particularly in the residential experience, which is kind of the prototypical model for American undergraduate education. So basically what we are searching for is a deeper understanding of how and why students develop along all these different dimensions. I guess this is what Wilber would call lines—What experiences and environments are associated with different kinds of developmental patterns?

JR: So having done this kind of research longitudinally and with large groups of students at many institutions, what do you see as relevant to learning?

SA: If you try to bring the different kinds of findings together and make a kind of holistic sense out of it, I think it is helpful to look more at the independent variables—that is, the experiential aspects. That helps you to understand the lines of development and how they are affected. The overarching conclusion from all this work is almost absurdly simply: The more the student invests in the process, in the form of time as well as psychological and physical energy, the more favorable the developmental outcome. What the students get out of the experience is directly proportional to what they invest in it. I am not a fan of Milton Freidman by any means, but he entitled one of his little books *There is no Such Thing as a Free Lunch* and I think that pretty much summarizes the overall overarching conclusion that you could draw from our work. What happens developmentally is directly proportional to what the student is willing to invest in that process itself. What that means is that our job as educators would seem to be to find creative and ingenious ways of encouraging the students to become engaged in the process.

JR: I can see this having real implications pedagogically. In my own experience, giving students tasks that bring the learning into a relevant situation for them has been quite successful. Certainly the area of service learning has been quite popular in higher education in recent years because it does bring that sort of relevance and motivation more to the foreground for students.

SA: Yes, it is a very powerful experience. I would say of all of the specific kinds of experiences, service learning is at the top of the list in terms of its potency. And we have only begun to exploit its possibilities. It is still something that most students don't experience in college, although it's growing.

JR: I went to a Jesuit university for my graduate work and when I was teaching there they had a lot of service learning, so all my students went through that experience. It was exciting because they were able to see the things we were talking about in the class happening out in the world. It also helped them see the value of engaging the learning that was available to them in the classroom. What I wonder about though is how this looks from a model of education primarily being a didactic transmission of intellectual knowledge? That view might say, "What's going out and volunteering in the community have to do with higher education?"

SA: The folks who have written in this field, and we've done a fair amount of work ourselves on service learning, have been able to articulate the relevance of all this pretty well. When I am speaking to a group of faculty members, particularly if they are hard scientists, I like to use the analogy of the lab experience. Anybody who teaches science or any student who studies it will tell you that the lab experience can be the most important part of their formal scientific training. So in a sense the service learning portion of the course is like a lab experience where you get a chance to test the theoretical material in the real world. It is interesting that some of the most interesting service learning courses are in the sciences, and I think that's in part because the sciences have taken for granted the lab experience. Also the fine arts—we could learn a whole lot in academia if we would pick the brains of our friends in the fine arts, because I think they in some way have explored the more active behavioral components of their subject matter and it's not just strictly Upper-Left quadrant stuff.

JR: I know one of the things I have been interested in and reading about lately is the distinction between intellectual theory knowledge and tacit knowledge of people working professionally within a field who know how to do things, but don't always know how to describe how they know how to do them.

SA: Yes, putting it into words is the trick. I remember when I wrote a book on assessment a number of years ago I really got intrigued with this very issue, and so I had a whole chapter devoted to the piano lesson as a metaphor for this kind of behaviorally oriented pedagogy, looking at what actually takes place in a well-delivered piano lesson between the student and the teacher. All the notion of feedback and behavioral performance, then more feedback, and so on.

We had this movement that began back in the sixties of so-called experiential education and it has always remained on the margins. Those folks had a lot of great ideas but the mainstream departments in the universities are basically completely unaware of this whole movement. It took the service learning folks, who had the wisdom to realize that you had to do this out of a formal academic class, and in that way you can bring the experiential part of this into the pedagogy in a way that the ordinary faculty members can see the point. I think one of the things that limited the experiential education folks is the terminology that they used and the pitches that they tried to make. They struck academics as being very vocational and, of course, that is the kiss of death. Nobody has tried to sell service learning on the basis of its vocational value.

JR: So they learned that lesson. I know you have also done some recent work on spirituality in higher education. What can you say about that?

SA: Well, that has turned out to be very exciting and the reason why is that for years we flirted with that area, with that line of development if you will, but didn't really take a serious look at it. I think we were perhaps intimidated by the prevailing mentality in academia that says that religion and that sort of thing should be off limits in a secular institution—leave it to the department of religious studies or to the sectarian institutions.

What prompted us to get involved in this were some personal experiences that we had back in the late nineties when we went to some retreats sponsored by the Fetzer Institute in Michigan. I was a little dubious about these retreats, but after a few hours at the first one we attended I became convinced there really was something to this whole spirituality issue as far as higher education was concerned. It had to do with the inauthenticity of so much of what we do in academia. I mean, there is so much posturing and posing and lack of authenticity in the way we conduct ourselves and we encourage the same thing in our students. The most obvious case is: If the student doesn't understand the material in the class, we encourage them to make us think they understand, even when they don't, and that of course is what the exam process is all about. Or even in a sense Socratic teaching in many ways. It isn't that you really want the student to understand as much as you want the student to give you the right answer and so it becomes kind of a little contest.

So authenticity struck me as something that really needed to be looked at, as well as wholeness, so that your life as an academic or as a student is integrated. I mean this is where the term *integral* comes in—where your most deeply felt values are being acknowledged and honored and in a process where you are able to make meaning out of what you are doing. The meaning-making part of this really began to emerge as a key thing. So as we begin to talk about wholeness, authenticity, fragmentation, inauthenticity, and meaning—well, we are talking about the spiritual life. So let's call it what it is. We still debate the terminology we use, and I always say if I have 30 seconds or a minute to explain what we are doing to somebody I will use the term spirituality. If not, I might talk about meaning and purpose depending on who the audience is.

In any case, these retreats got us thinking that we ought to look at this. We got a small grant from Fetzer to study meaning, purpose, and spirituality in the lives of college faculty. This was a qualitative study where we interviewed faculty from diverse institutions and wrote a little monograph about it. We found that this is a huge issue for faculty members. The fact that they lead fragmented lives causes them a lot of discomfort. We were also surprised that quite a number of our faculty members could relate to the notion of spirituality. Sometimes they would say,"Well what do you mean by spirituality," and then we would have to finesse it and use terms like "how do you make meaning out of your life?" and "how do you see your purpose as a faculty member and a parent and a spouse and a member of the community—do you lead an integrated life or are these parts of your life fragmented?" Get them there and they will take off and tell you a lot. We were very surprised and pleased that the faculty, given a safe interview space to talk about these things, were quite eloquent and were able talk about their spiritual life and how they made meaning out of the events of the day and this sort of thing.

So this convinced us that we were onto something and we held some sessions at national conferences, which were very well attended. People came and got very engaged talking about these issues in their institutions—college presidents, faculty, students affairs folks all would come to the sessions. So just then, serendipitously the Templeton folks approached us. They had known some of our faculty work in spirituality and asked if we would be interested in doing a study with students. So we negotiated with them and we were able to get them to support a longitudinal study. That's how we got involved in this.

Religion really turns out to be just one mode of expression of spirituality and for some students it's the primary mode, but for many it is not. So we are looking at religion as one manifestation of the spiritual person.

JR: What kind of distinctions did you find between notions of religion and spirituality for faculty and for students?

SA: A lot of this has to so with whether or not the person is an active practitioner of some religious faith. Obviously, if they are then often the religion provides the framework with which they try to guide their lives and make meaning out of their experiences. But the number of people who do this religiously, so to speak, is a minority. I think it is 30 percent of the students who say they try to pattern their life according to their religious beliefs, even though 80 percent of the students say they believe in God and 70 percent of the faculty say they perceive themselves as spiritual beings. But those who pattern their lives on the basis of their religious faith are in a minority. It depends on how you frame the religious question as to what conclusion you draw in terms of its importance in the life of a student or the faculty member.

JR: So how far along is the study with the students that Templeton is supporting?

SA: We're just collected our longitudinal data and are deeply into the analysis now. We have found some fascinating things. First, a little background. One of the questions we had six years ago when we started this project was whether it is even possible with self-administered questionnaires to get the kind of material we were after as far as developmental lines are concerned. So we did a pilot study initially with about 3,700 students in 46 institutions just to see if the project was feasible. Could we actually measure important aspects of the students' spiritual and religious lives? In designing this pilot survey we spent a long time getting a sense about this as being multi-dimensional lines. They are probably related to each other, but they are worthy of our looking at them independently.

The preparatory work was very extensive: literature searching, brain storming, and so forth. We came up with about 175 questions that constituted the core of this pilot survey. We were very pleased that the students took it very seriously. We had all kinds of checks applied to see if they were actually giving us consistent responses, and they took it very seriously. It was interesting that the believers and the non-believers were equally likely to respond to the survey. We were afraid that non-believers were not willing to get involved in it. (When I say non-believers I mean people who say they have no religion).

Then we began the analyses and we were able to find some very interesting patterns. We developed three sets of measures out of this: one set having to do with their religiousness, another set with their spirituality, and a final set having to do with what we call related qualities. As you might guess, the religious and spiritual measures tend to be positively associated, but not that strongly. That partly has to do with the semantics of what we were dealing with where many people tend to equate the term *spiritual* with the term *religious*—this forces a positive association between the two sets of measures. But what we found when we finally began the longitudinal study (we surveyed entering freshmen three years ago and then followed them up this past spring), we found that religiousness, particularly the behavioral measures of religiousness such as attendance of religious services, showed a decline during the undergraduate years; whereas most of our measures of spirituality and related qualities showed significant growth during this same period of time. That was quite fascinating: Even though the two sets of measures were positively associated, they were changing in different directions during the undergraduate years.

Some of our associated measures are quite interesting and in some ways they capture many of the qualities of what people normally consider to being spiritual beings. One is called Equanimity, another measure we call Ethic of Caring, and then we have one we call Ecumenical Worldview. This last one very much captures the beginning of the critical third stage in the great chain from the personal to the transpersonal, or the ego to the transcendent level. That's a very key developmental transition and the Ecumenical Worldview we think captures that quite well.

We have actually developed a new measure that we are just playing around with which combines the Ethic of Caring and the Ecumenical Worldview. We call it Global Awareness and it is an interesting measure we are playing with. That kind of language is probably more accessible to the typical academic than the caring and ecumenism.

JR: But it sounds like through this research project you are being able to bring some rigor to those terms and what they mean for the students, rather than them just being kind of vague New Age or fluffy concepts.

SA: Exactly. That's also part of the realization that we've developed in presenting some of these early findings to people. In particular academics, who see me as a kind of a number crunching, hard-headed researcher, are more open to research on this particular subject matter.

JR: This brings us back to the notion of "How do you see these elements of spirituality, service learning and the other kinds of things you talked about—the conditions to support learning that are beyond the theoretical/intellectual—how do you see those contributing to an integral perspective within higher education?"

SA: The best way to answer that is to look back at the particular kinds of educational experiences that seem to facilitate the growth of these spiritual qualities. The panoply of experiences is quite interesting. This is very early stuff and is subject to some revision, but I think the pattern is forming now as we dig into the data in more depth. Here is a sampling of some of the kinds of experiences we have identified so far that seem to facilitate the development of these qualities: service learning being probably at the top of the list, then interdisciplinary studies, study abroad, foreign language study, participation in group organizations, participation in team athletics, group projects in class.

JR: All the things that would normally be considered to be peripheral to the real education.

SA: Right.

JR: That gives a pretty clear picture of the wide spectrum of things that are supportive of this development, but are not normally focused on.

SA: No, and that's why I think the banking model of teaching and learning—you withdraw the information from the head of the professor and deposit it in the head of the student—I just don't think it holds any water any more. I don't think this is how learning and development take place. What's interesting is that many of these items that I just listed also facilitate the development of more traditional cognitive learning. If you want to look at this thing very holistically and say, "Well what kinds of qualities do we want to promote in our young people as they prepare to go out into the world of work and family and community?" then you would really hope that you could promote this ecumenical world view, caring, charitable involvement, and other such measures. So, why not consider redesigning our educational experiences to provide more of this kind of stimulus and engagement for students on behalf of our long term concerns as they might apply to the human race? The more of these kinds of qualities that we are able to foster, well—we might lose the third world war as a result—but on the other hand we might avoid starting a third world war.

JR: This is interesting for me because I have just begun teaching at a university in Norway and I redesigned the main course they hired me for and just started delivering it this semester. The students were shocked at first by the pedagogical strategies I employ and the way I have them engaging in different kinds of learning. They say they are terrified because I am really asking them to participate and engage, (they have a concrete learning project out in the world involved in the course). But they also say they are very excited and enthused. There seems to be an openness, and they are able to recognize the value of these kinds of pedagogical strategies; they are just not used to them.

SA: Yes, it is going to take some transition in the beliefs and the mindsets of some of the students and the faculty. Another item from our findings, which kind of personifies these experiences, is interactions with people of different racial and ethnic background during the undergraduate years.

JR: One of the things we are looking at in this book and have for ourselves, is a sense that there are a number of trends like those you have been studying and researching. We see people promoting service learning, or various kinds of holistic and integral education. I think of the Jesuit school I went to and their motto of head, heart, and hands—that was how they would say to people, this is what we are about—not just intellectual pursuits but your heart and your hands are concerned too. So do you feel that these things are bubbling up as precursors to a more explicitly integral perspective in higher education, that if they all came together and were really incorporated they would actually take it to that level?

SA: I believe so, because, in a way, seeing education as not lecture and discussion, but in terms of this wide range of experiences, is much more integral, just in terms of the range of experiences we are talking about. If you were to think of pedagogy in these terms, what full range of experiences can we provide for students to bring out this whole person and foster the development of these across the board qualities? This, rather than what's some clever tactic can you use during a lecture to get students to learn a particular item of material. It's a very different approach to pedagogy.

JR: It sounds like what you are describing is in pretty stark contrast to faculty using such clever strategies for getting students to learn particular things. It is asking them to rethink assumptions about what learning is, who students are, and what education is about.

SA: I think that is well said.

JR: I think that part of the goal we have for this book is to lay out a number of these views, because there hasn't been an academic book that tries to pull these perspectives together and offer faculty and/or administrators a comprehensive overview of how these things are coming together. They are out there and people are trying to apply them in specific kinds of ways in small pockets, and there are larger forces and trends at work too. If there can be some conscious attention to moving that work forward, hopefully, good things will happen.

SA: Yes, I totally agree.

JR: Here's another question then relating to the integral world. How has your understanding of these issues in higher education been influenced by what you read of Wilber's work and his AQAL model?

SA: I think, in a way, the influence on us personally and in this research has been less profound than the influence on those students who we've exposed to the AQAL approach. Because, in a sense, the way we had designed our matrix for outcome measures way back in the sixties was motivated by the same concern: How do we create a holistic framework for looking at student development where we cover the waterfront. I think the one area where Wilber's quadrants have helped is the bottom quadrants, what Wilber calls society and culture. Culture is hidden in much the same way that one's private thoughts are hidden. One of the big challenges, it seems to me, in higher education is to begin to surface this hidden culture and address it in some way. I see that culture as representing a huge obstacle to significant change. We completed a large project a few years ago on what we called institutional transformation and found the Wilber framework very helpful particularly in identifying and pinpointing this Lower-Left aspect of higher education, which remains largely hidden from view and unexamined. I think that's the worst part of it, that it is unexamined.

In fact, I was inspired to write an editorial for the *Chronicle of Higher Education* a few years ago about this very issue. It was on the importance of "being smart" in academia and how that value distorts our lives. Working all these years in this field I have become convinced that one of our hidden shared values, which to me is what culture is, is how important it is to be smart and to appear smart. So smartness has a very high valence. So that explains some of the crazy stuff we do in academia like valuing the intelligence of the student at the point of entry much more than at the exit point. Why do we put so much emphasis on how smart the student is at the point of entry? Because it reflects on us to have smart students wanting to come to our university. Every culture in the world that has a university system does this, Japan being perhaps the most extreme and China now has really gone overboard on its recruitment of smart students. This is why faculty meetings become so unpleasant for most people because the faculty meeting is a theater where some faculty like to display their smartness and critical thinking skills and so forth, and this is what the essay was about.

But what I was really talking about was how this very profoundly important part of our belief system never surfaces, never gets talked about, and yet it affects everything we do. So if we are going to change academia we have to reach a point where we are able to identify and talk about our culture, our shared beliefs. Some of them we're willing to talk about such as academic freedom—that's part of our culture too—but some of these other deeper beliefs I think are potential obstacles to any kinds of reforms we might want to make. Because if we just take the "being smart" part of our culture, if you or I propose we want to change our pedagogy in some significant way, the fear that we might not look as smart is going to get in the way.

JR: That's why I very much appreciated the title of Parker Palmers book *The Courage to Teach*. When I taught honors students in their freshman colloquium, one of the things that I began telling them as we started the class was that because they were honors students they were at a distinct disadvantage in this class, because they were smart at the educational system the way it was designed and this class wasn't about that kind of being smart. It's very clear that it's not safe to say you don't know—there is a great fear of being vulnerable or losing your credibility or whatever it is that's tied up in that smartness.

SA: Yes, exactly. So that's been very helpful to be able to pinpoint in my own thinking what the difficulty is. I think this distinction between the individual and the community in Wilber's framework is very keen one. I think my stand on the Lower Left is that it's the shared beliefs and assumptions of a community. We tend to think of culture as costumes and art work and dances and stuff like that and that's really not what I see as the essence of culture.

JR: Those are the displays of culture, the artifacts of culture.

SA: Exactly.

JR: That was good, because what you just named, the whole culture of smartness, answered the next question I had, which was around obstacles or limitations for trying to move an integral perspective forward in higher education. This culture of smartness is like an elephant in the room no one is willing to speak about. I am wondering if you see other things, as well, which are real challenges in trying to move an integral perspective more into the public discourse in higher education?

SA: I think it's attending far too much to the Lower Right in our reform attempts. I think in a sense that is the flip side of what we have just been discussing. Whereas, the common thought is that the key lies in changing programs and practices and not to change both lower quadrants. So we say, "OK we will implement a new program to fix things." Well you know if the culture doesn't change . . .

JR: Then we will restructure again and that will fix it!

SA: Right. So we think in terms of structures. Because what happens then is the system will, by fiat or getting a big donor or whatever device, change a structure or add a new structure, but then the culture will drag it down. So, in a sense, that discourages us from thinking that we can really implement significant change. Then we hesitate, after that experience, to try it again. In a crazy kind of way focusing on the changes in structures makes us more reluctant to try to change structures in the future because the attempt often doesn't succeed.

JR: If we are thinking in terms of quadrants, do you see a great resistance to conversations around epistemological development, thinking about Kegan's work in terms of the need for people in higher education to actually have that kind of development going on in the Upper Left.

SA: The Upper-Left, Lower-Left connection is so critical. I really believe if you're a student just entering graduate training, let's say to prepare for a career in academia, that Upper Left is much more of a tabula rasa and by the time the graduate school brainwashing is done then you have absorbed a lot of the Lower Left and taken it on yourself. It becomes very difficult then to institute change because the new graduate student wants to learn the culture, wants to know: How am I supposed to believe, how am I supposed to act? So that has a very powerful influence. So to try to move into an institution of people trained in that way and say, "Let's change some of this stuff" is really tough. So I think the influence of the Lower Left on the Upper Left is so profound.

JR: An experience I have in relation to that is WASC (Western Association of Schools and Colleges) creating a new handbook of accreditation standards in 2001. In those standards there was an attempt to set out a structure that would push institutions to move from Kegan's third-order consciousness of just reacting to a checklist, to a more fourth-order self-authoring. It says here are some principals, or standards, now tell us how you address them. Do you see that kind of attempt to change the discourse and the thinking in higher education institutions having had an impact or success in some way?

SA: I think we go back to Parker Palmer's term *courage*. I think that what we need is the courage to begin to think differently, to examine one's beliefs, to question or critically look at the culture; and I think that courage is the key thing. Where do we get that? In other words how do you sanction the individual examining and questioning the culture and examining and questioning his or her own beliefs?

I wrote a kind of maverick book[1] that came out in 2007 about all of this in a sense. It's an Upper-Left book almost exclusively; but it's got a bunch of exercises in it for how do you get in touch with your beliefs, reflect on them, and understand the connection between you beliefs and your emotions. Because, at least in writing that book, it began to become really clear that our emotional life and particularly our debilitating and negative emotions all emerge from our belief systems. That our beliefs operate, if you take a computer metaphor, like the software of our minds; and they are the means by which we make meaning out of our experience and the way we spin our experience. So if you really want to change people, you want them to be able to change themselves. They have to get in touch with their beliefs and have to get in touch with the emotions that emerge from those beliefs, mainly emotions like fear, guilt, anger, and so forth. As well, to understand the conditions that activate those beliefs and lead to those emotions, because fear is a huge part of our inability to change.

JR: I notice that WASC has been using the term *reflection* a lot and what you are talking about, to be able to reflect on beliefs is being actively promoted within higher education in California and probably elsewhere as well. The challenge appears to be that doing this kind of reflection seems to be dependent on a certain level of cognitive development to be able to take a perspective on your internal state, and that this is not necessarily accessible to everybody.

SA: No, and again, if you want to talk about integral education, shouldn't the capacity to reflect on one's own beliefs and life be something that we actively try to cultivate during the undergraduate years? If you want to look at it in terms of skill development, what better skill could you have? A sort of meta-cognition, but more than meta-cognition. That's part of it but it's also just simply awareness.

JR: Yes, and it's a lifelong skill that is transferable into any aspect of our lives.

SA: They talk about things that are relevant to the goals of the liberal education. You know liberal education is based on a lot of inductive logic. We want people to think inductively and to develop that capacity. By the way, reflection was another item in our laundry list of experiences that facilitate the development of these spiritual qualities.

JR: How would you envision taking this conversation about integral within higher education to the next level?

SA: Initially, what comes to mind in response to that question is the importance of demystifying integral. It seems to me that one of the ways of doing that is to team up with an existing organization, or an existing community, which is plugged into mainstream higher education, but which is also open to reform efforts. Immediately I think of the American Association of Colleges and Universities, which is maybe the only national organization which I think is actively pursuing reform efforts and at the same time has credibility within the higher education community. Getting some kind of a formal working relationship established with that organization could be helpful, because what they claim to represent is the role of higher education in liberally educating its students. So they are committed to the notion of liberal learning, which if you take it literally, as I have already said, can be read as holistic and integral. So in connecting with an organization that is already plugged into higher education in a substantial way but which is open to ideas of this kind would be great. They are doing a project there on moral development, for example, and they have a number of projects going that I think are compatible with an integral approach. That would be my immediate sense about it because it is sort of like the problem we have with spirituality; if you just start there OK, we are talking about integral education or an integral approach to educating undergraduates or whatever, and you know the eyes will glaze over.

JR: There is a whole lot of translation work to be done.

SA: Exactly, and you and I have a very different take on that language but that is something that has developed enough over a period of years thinking about these things. But certainly the stuff that Wilber has done trying to get programs going, I am not sure that is the way to do it because those programs will be marginalized and academia is expert at marginalizing anything it doesn't understand.

JR: True. I do know that John F. Kennedy University did get WASC accreditation for an Integral Theory program. So there has been that one step at least.

SA: A multi-pronged approach probably makes more sense. I mentioned the AAC&U thing simply because that avenue has not been explored. As I understand it, you have got the Wilberites out there trying to do stuff, but I think teaming up with an established national organization would be a great tactic, and I think AAC&U would definitely be amenable to something like this.

JR: That is great because I think it is something that is possible to be of benefit, and a win-win kind of thing. It's a matter of getting into the right field of conversation.

This has been a great conversation, and I want to thank you again for sharing your insights. Discussing these topics with you has brought out what I anticipated—an understanding that there are many trends and forces in higher education offering the possibility to enable a more integral orientation to flourish.

Note

1. Astin, A. (2007). *Mindworks: Becoming more conscious in an unconscious world.* Charlotte, NC: Information Age Publishing.

Evolving Higher Education Integrally

Delicate Mandalic Theorizing

Jennifer M. Gidley

Introduction

This chapter provides a broad theoretical contribution to integral higher education by contextualising it within an evolution of consciousness narrative. Within this narrative there are three major discourses that identify and/or enact the emergence of new patterns of thinking and being: the adult developmental psychology discourse on postformal reasoning (Commons & Richards, 2002; Cook-Greuter, 2000; Sinnott, 2005); the integral consciousness discourse;[1] and the cultural historical and eco-philosophical literature on planetary consciousness (Elgin, 1997; Gangadean, 2006; Montuori, Combs, & Richards, 2004; Morin & Kern, 1999; Russell, 2000). To represent the breadth and depth of the emerging consciousness, I coin a complex conjoined term, postformal-integral-planetary[2] to conceptually link these three theoretic threads and invite dialogue between their communities of practice (Gidley, 2008). From a macrohistorical perspective where major shifts in human consciousness may occur across thousands of years, we may be in the very early stages of what many call integral consciousness. From this perspective integral education could be still in its infancy.

There are two major approaches that are currently identified as "integral education" in North America—one inspired by Sri Aurobindo's early twentieth-century philosophy and the other based on Ken Wilber's AQAL framework. In this chapter I identify three dimensions through which integral education theory could be broadened and deepened: temporally, spatially, and pedagogically. Because of chapter length constraints the first two dimensions will be addressed only briefly (see also (Gidley, 2010). Firstly, integral education theory can be contextualised within the temporal dimensions of history and futures. I address the historical dimension by identifying Rudolf Steiner education as antecedent to contemporary integral education (see also Markus Molz and Gary Hampson in the current volume). I address the futures dimension by pointing to the evolutionary/developmental features of postformal consciousness. Secondly, integral education can be broadened spatially within planetary discourses. Thirdly, although both Aurobindian and Wilberian integral education theories are strongly grounded in evolution of consciousness theory, the pedagogical implications of this could be developed more explicitly through embracing the rich pluralism of emerging pedagogies that support the evolution of consciousness. This evolutionary pedagogical deepening is my major focus here.[3]

To enact my approach to theorizing, I borrow from Goethe's delicate empiricism (Robbins, 2006) and the notion of mandalic reasoning used by Wilber (1990). I develop the term delicate mandalic theorizing as an intimation of both the delicate subtlety and the mandalic complexity of attempting to theorize about integral education. In addition to the temporal and spatial dimensions mentioned above, the evolutionary pedagogical dimension identifies additional sub-threads for theoretic integration. Firstly, I distinguish four themes—or types of discourses—that identify and/or enact new movements of consciousness: discourses that include notions of conscious, active spiritual development and contemplation; discourses that transcend static mechanistic thinking and promote fluid, organic, life-enhancing, thinking and being; discourses based on evolutionary/developmental notions of complexification of human thinking; discourses that cross linguistic and paradigmatic barriers through reflexivity and deep dialogue. These four themes are developed in section four below.

Secondly, I identify a plethora of emergent educational approaches, which are aligned to one or more of these evolutionary discursive themes. I refer to these as evolutionary pedagogies. They include: aesthetic and artistic education; complexity in education; creativity in education; critical and postcolonial pedagogies; environmental/ecological education; futures education; holistic education; imaginative education; integral education; planetary/global education; postformality in education; postmodern and poststructuralist pedagogies; soul/spirituality in education; transformative education; poetic education; contemplative education; wisdom education.[4] These are all linked with new ways of thinking that are beginning to influence both school and college/university education as part of educational evolution. A major challenge for integral education theory development is to integrate, perhaps even cohere, this pedagogical diversity.

Thirdly, at the intersections between the four evolutionary discursive themes and the plethora of emergent educational approaches, I identify four core pedagogical values—love, life, wisdom, and voice—which enable a theoretic coherence to emerge between a unitive center and the pluralism of the periphery. Through this delicate mandalic theorizing I weave the diverse evolutionary and educational discourses together through an evolving integral educational theory that reflects unity in diversity. A visual representation of this process is exemplified in Figure 27.

Broadening Integral Education Temporally—Pasts and Futures

From a historical perspective, in addition to Aurobindian and Wilberian notions of integral education I identify a third major integral education approach: Steiner education. A critique of all three approaches is that there is insufficient engagement with the broader academic discourses and kindred pedagogies. My research seeks to address this. It is worth noting that prior to the uses of the term integral from 1914 (Aurobindo, 1914/2000), and from 1949 (Gebser, 1949/1985), and the lesser-known use from 1941, (Sorokin, 1941/1992), Steiner was already using the term integral in a similar way as early as 1906 (Gidley, 2008). As part of my integration of integral theories, I undertook an AQAL analysis of Steiner education and found that it fulfilled all the criteria of Wilber's Integral Operating System

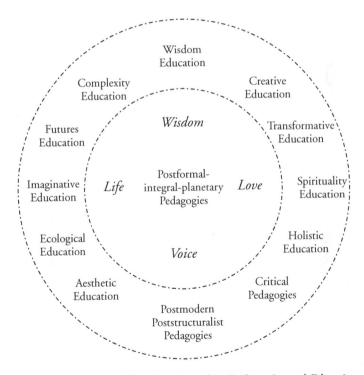

Figure 27. Delicate Mandalic Theorising of an Evolving Integral Education

(quadrants, level, lines, states, and types) (Gidley, 2007). Although this analysis was applied broadly to Steiner school education, the findings also apply to the many Steiner tertiary colleges, worldwide. Furthermore, the emphasis in Steiner pedagogy on integrating cognitive (thinking/head), affective (feeling/heart) and conative (willing/hands) dimensions is aligned to Sri Aurobindo's integration of the three yogas of knowledge, love, and action.

An underappreciated aspect of Steiner's integral educational philosophy is that he consciously carried forward the evolution of consciousness ideals of the previous century. The initial impulse for Friedrich Wilhelm von Humboldt's implementation of mass public education in Prussia was influenced by his collaboration with German idealists and romantics such as Johann Wolfgang von Goethe, Friedrich von Schiller, Georg Wilhelm Friedrich Hegel, and Friedrich Wilhelm Joseph Schelling whose work was inspired by the notion of the evolution of consciousness (Holborn, 1964). Steiner pedagogy integrated this deep understanding of human development and cultural evolution with Schiller's aesthetic educational principles, Johann Friedrich Herbart's integrative/interdisciplinary pedagogical practice, the head, heart, and hands approach of Johann Heinrich Pestalozzi, and the orientation towards the future of Novalis (pseudonym of Georg Philipp Friedrich von Hardenberg). He thus created an early twentieth-century alternative to the influence of the Industrial Revolution, through which schools had become training grounds for the factories. For other historical antecedents to contemporary integral education, see Gidley & Hampson (2008) and Hampson in this volume.

From a futures perspective, an environmental scan suggests an ongoing future flourishing of educational approaches that decry the inadequacy of the modernist industrial model of education. These evolutionary pedagogies are in a more general sense postformal in that they represent a broad movement beyond the constraints of modernist formal education. My use of the term postformal is transdisciplinary, with reference to both the postformal psychology literature (Commons & Richards, 2002; Cook-Greuter, 2000; Sinnott, 2005) and the postformal educational research (Kincheloe, Steinberg, & Hinchey, 1999). Adult developmental psychologists articulate higher stages of reasoning which include complexity, contextualisation, creativity, dialectics, dialogue, holism, imagination, construct awareness, paradox, pluralism, reflexivity, spirituality, values, and wisdom. Postformal educational researchers Joe Kincheloe and Shirley Steinberg propose four key components of postformality in education: etymology (origins of knowledge, imagination, problem detecting); pattern (deep structures, metaphoric cognition, mind-ecosystem links); process (deconstruction, logic-emotion links, nonlinear holism); and contextualisation (context, particular-general links, and power issues). If integral education theory is to fully embrace postformal cognitive development, careful consideration needs to be given to the contemporary pedagogical theories that nurture and/or enact such features as complexity (Davis & Sumara, 2006;

Morin, 2001), creativity (Montuori, 2004), construct awareness (Holmes, 1998; Peters, 1998); imagination (Egan, 1997; Nuyen, 1998), spirituality (Glazer, 1994; Miller, 2000) and wisdom (Sinnott, 2005; Sternberg, 2001).

Broadening Integral Education Spatially—Planetary Views

The use of the term planetary has been increasing within the evolution of consciousness literature and provides a socio-cultural counterbalance to the term globalization—which is often limited to the politico-economic dimensions.[5] The phrase planetary consciousness provides a supplement to the terms postformal or integral, particularly in the light of our current planetary crisis. The planetary consciousness literature emphasises the critical urgency of our planetary crisis and reflects a spacio-geographic dimension. My use of planetary is uniquely multi-layered, foregrounding critical environmental (biosphere), transcultural (anthropo-socio-sphere), philosophical (noosphere) and spiritual interests (pneumatosphere) (Gidley, 2008).

The planetary consciousness literature introduces a critical, normative element. This is lacking in much of the literature on postformal thinking, with some exceptions (Kincheloe, Steinberg, & Hinchey, 1999) and much of the integral theory literature, with some exceptions (Esbjörn-Hargens, 2005; Gangadean, 2006; Zimmerman, 2005). The planetary scale and urgency of our current crises are emphasised in my research and viewed as being in intimate relationship with the need to enable the epistemic shift in consciousness. However, although the planetary focus is on critical-ecological connections, it often omits the developmental dimension. By integrating these discourses in my term postformal-integral-planetary, these weaknesses are balanced.

The term planetary education is not common in the literature, but its critical sensibility can be found among educators whose focus is environmental ecology (Fien, 1998; Jardine, 1998); or social ecology (Goerner, 2000; Morin, 2001), including the educational literature on globalism, postcolonialism, multicultural-ism, and multilingualism.

Deepening Integral Education Pedagogically— Clustering Evolutionary Themes

This section explores the theoretical relationships between the four themes that emerged from the evolution of consciousness discourse and the evolutionary peda-gogies referred to in section two above. Although there is considerable overlap and interpenetration among the evolution of consciousness themes and the evolutionary educational approaches, I cluster the latter under the evolutionary discourse that they appear to most strongly support. (See Figure 28). This clustering is an enactment of my delicate mandalic theorizing and involves a subtle hermeneutic interpretation of both types of discourse. Clustering is to be distinguished from categorization into discrete territories as in formal analysis. My attempts to cohere this diverse literature are a step in deepening integral educational theory so it more explicitly supports the evolution of consciousness. Space does not allow a full scholarly engagement with the literature here, but a more substantial engagement has been undertaken (Gidley, 2008).

The first theme that I identify within the evolution of consciousness literature arises from discourses that promote conscious, active spiritual development, and contemplation.[6] This theme includes religious, and particularly post-traditional, post-secular, and postmodern spiritual approaches. While the term spiritual is still controversial in some continental philosophy, it is arising in the higher education landscape in the United States through the emergence of contemplative studies programs and science/spirituality dialogues. I propose that evolutionary spiritual

Discourses Supporting Evolution of Consciousness	Evolutionary Pedagogies	Intersecting Core Values
Discourses that include notions of conscious, active spiritual development and contemplation	Spirituality in education, transformative and, contemplative studies	Contemplative Love
Discourses that transcend static mechanistic thinking and promote fluid, organic, life-enhancing, thinking and being	Imaginative education, futures education, ecological education, education for sustainability	Life Cultivation
Discourses based on evolutionary/developmental notions of complexification of human thinking	Wisdom education, creative education, complexity education	Creative Wisdom
Discourses that cross linguistic and paradigmatic barriers through reflexivity and deep dialogue	Postmodern, poststructuralist education, postcolonial and critical pedagogy, poetic, aesthetic and dialogic education	Language/ Voice Consciousness

Figure 28. Exploring Lines of Flight between Discourses Supporting Evolution of Consciousness and Evolutionary Pedagogies

development, as identified in this literature, is supported by educational styles that emphasize care, contemplation, empathy, love, and reverence. Such approaches include the spirituality in higher education literature, holistic education, integral education, and transformative/contemplative pedagogies. I cohere these interrelated clusters of evolutionary and educational research under the core value of contemplative love.

Secondly, I identify discourses that transcend static mechanistic thinking and promote fluid, organic, life-enhancing, thinking and being. This new thinking is reflected in organic, process-oriented philosophies and new science theories such as Einstein's theory of relativity, quantum physics, and systems science. The changing consciousness is particularly notable in the shift from simple mechanistic metaphors to life-enhancing, organic metaphors in the new, post-classical, biology theories of chaos, complexity, self-organization, and emergence. Several educational approaches support this movement from static concepts to living thinking. In particular, imaginal thinking is a primary method of bringing concepts to life. Life and its metaphors are also emphasized in pedagogies grounded in ecology, futures thinking, sustainability, complexity, and aesthetics. Such approaches nurture vitality and well-being. I cohere them under the core value of life cultivation.

The third theme I identify is reflected in two discourses, which point to complexification of human thinking and consciousness: cultural evolutionary (phylogenetic) theory and adult developmental (ontogenetic) psychology theory. Both discourses identify the emergence of new stage/s, structures, or movements of consciousness. Adult developmental psychologists link wisdom to creativity and multiperspectivality. The interaction between these features and complexity, paradox, and dialectics is not hard to envisage. Contemporary cultural philosophy and cultural history literature—much of which arises from integral theories—also emphasise creativity, aperspectivality, and complexity. There are specific educational theories addressed to the cultivation of wisdom. However, other postformal approaches that are oriented toward creativity and complexity also facilitate the cultivation of wisdom. I cohere these threads under the core value of creative wisdom.

Finally, I identify discourses that cross both linguistic and paradigmatic barriers through reflexivity and deep dialogue. There is a growing academic and educational movement beyond fragmentation and disciplinary isolationism and toward more integration—through integral and holistic theories, inter- and transdisciplinarity, and dialogic approaches. A challenge that has emerged from the inter- and transdisciplinary literature is the difficulty in communicating across different disciplines, epistemologies, and paradigms. To overcome this challenge requires tremendous sensitivity to linguistic, cultural, and paradigmatic contexts. An important insight of French poststructuralism is awareness of context in terms of how we language the world. I propose that this integrative capacity of language reflexivity is supported by poststructuralist, aesthetic, and postcolonial pedagogies. I cohere these threads under the core value of language and voice consciousness.

A Uni-diversity of Educational Values: Love, Life, Wisdom, and Voice

The clustering of emergent pedagogies within the evolutionary themes revealed a distillation of four core educational values:[7] contemplative love, life cultivation, creative wisdom, and language/voice consciousness. The following four sections expand on these core values providing further theoretical links with the evolution of consciousness literature while grounding the discussion in the more pragmatic orientation of the educational literature. These core values are not mutually exclusive but complexly interconnected.

Contemplative Love and Critical Reverence

> The essence of education is . . . religious [it] . . . inculcates duty and reverence . . . And the foundation of reverence is this perception, that the present holds within itself the complete sum of existence, backwards and forward, that whole amplitude, which is eternity. (Whitehead, 1916/1967, p. 10)

Alfred North Whitehead's words, which affirmed the significance of reverence in his philosophy of education, are aligned to Rudolf Steiner's position. In 1909, Steiner explicitly named love and devotion—which he referred to as the two components of reverence—as educative forces for developing the next stage of consciousness.

> Love and devotion are . . . the best educators of the soul in its advances from the Intellectual Soul to the Consciousness Soul . . . But this reverence must be led and guided from a standpoint which never shuts out the light of thought. (Steiner, 1930/1983, pp. 61–62)

Several holistic educators speak of love and reverence as touchstones for wisdom (Hart, 2001; Miller, 2000). Already we are immersed in the complexly interwoven relationship between love and wisdom. If love and reverence are so significant in the spiritually oriented evolutionary discourses, then we might ask: Why is the word love so out of place in educational circles?

British educator, Maggie MacLure (2006) unpacks the trend to privilege scientific, quantifiable words, such as objectives, outcomes, standards, high-stakes testing, competition, performance, and accountability. She links this to "deep-seated fears and anxieties about language and desire to control it" (n.p.). She sees this resistance to the textuality, complexity, and diversity of qualitative research in the "evidence-based" agendas of the "audit culture" (n.p.). In this context, words like love are likely to create ontological panic in educrats. But the litany of mental health issues among young people suggests we may have pushed them too far (Gidley, 2005). Perhaps new spaces need to be opened up for softer terms, such as love, nurture, respect, reverence, awe, wonder, well-being, vulnerability, care, tenderness, openness, trust. If national governments—as is the case now in the UK and Australia—are serious about well-being and spirituality in education, the reductionism and quantification in language needs to be challenged to support a transition (Woods & Woods, 2002).

Fortunately, in spite of these challenges, the importance of love in educational settings is being re-emphasised through terms such as "epistemology of love" (Zajonc, 2006); "pedagogy of universal love" (Nava, 2001) and pedagogical love (Hatt, 2005). Other educators refer to aligned notions such as "ethics of care" (Noddings, 2005); "heart of a teacher" (Palmer, 1998); and "deep empathy" (Hart, 2001). Nel Noddings and Parker Palmer both link their notions to teacher integrity. While many educators may dismiss notions of love and reverence as being too sentimental, or having too much religious significance for secular education, my dialectical notion of critical reverence may be a way to integrate the critical thinking so valuable for cognitive development with such positive affective states as reverence. Cognitive-affective learning theory is also making moves in this direction.

Life Cultivation through Imaginal Thinking

> The cultivation of imagination does not mean the rejection of hard, lucid thought. It is, rather, the bringing of thought to life, permeating concepts and abstractions with life-giving images and inner energies through which thinking can penetrate and participate in the fullness of reality. (Sloan, 1983, p. 192)

North American educator Douglas Sloan's (1983) characterisation of insight-imagination best approaches my understanding of imagination. Sloan refers to it as a "higher order of consciousness," noting David Bohm's distinction between "the deep act of imagination in insight from what he calls imaginative fancy" (Sloan, 1983, p. 144). This is aligned to Steiner's notion of imaginal thinking and Wilber's vision-logic.

The term imagination can be used disparagingly as meaning inferior to reason—or formal thinking—or to depict complex, higher-order forms of thinking. The significant role of imagination in higher-order thinking, despite its long history has been academically marginalized. The dialectical and synthesizing nature of imagination was identified in the third century CE in Plotinus's conceptual imagination. Steiner—building on Goethe's creative imagination and Schelling's intellectual imagination—explicitly linked Imagination with the evolution of consciousness (Steiner, 1905/1981). The relationship between imagination and post-mechanistic, organic metaphors in philosophical thinking has foundations in the vitality of Henri Bergson's élan vital, Whitehead's process thinking and Giles Deleuze's lines of flight. Philosopher of imagination, Richard Kearney, has researched the major theories of imagination in modern and postmodern European thought. His theory of ethics and narrative imagination provides a philosophical foundation for both imagination and narrative in education (Kearney, 1998). Several philosophers have emphasized the importance of imagination in education (Lyotard, 2004; Nuyen, 1998; Warnock, 1976; Whitehead, 1916/1967).

Imagination as I use the term is an activity that enables conceptual vitality—it can bring concepts to life. I regard it as a core—if tacit—component in the transitions from formal/rational to postformal/postrational thinking. Through imagination in our thinking we not only enliven concepts, but we bring the significance of life back into centre focus in our lifeworld, enhancing vitality and wellbeing.

The cultivation of logic and rationality was significant in overcoming the deficiencies of earlier mythic consciousness, e.g., dogma and superstition. Yet the dominance of narrow forms of rationality, at the expense of other faculties, is arguably a psychic prison for young people and may jeopardize their conscious evolutionary development as adults. Educating with conceptual vitality allows concepts to breathe and grow laying foundations for flexible, complex, process-oriented thinking, and a smooth transition to postformal-integral-planetary consciousness at the appropriate developmental moment.

While formal education seems caught within the inertness of formal thinking, writing stale ideas about the already said (Lyotard, 2004), Deleuze challenges us "to bring something to life, to free life from where it is trapped, to trace lines of flight," (cited in St. Pierre, 2004, p. 287). Could more facility with imagination assist in freeing education from where it is trapped?

Creative Wisdom: Waking Up to Multiplicity

> Education for wisdom is not about simply being taught but about waking up. Waking up requires a certain kind of energy, certain capacities for taking the world into our consciousness. (Hart, 2001, p. 10)

Tobin Hart's words were foreshadowed by Steiner in 1922 when he stated: "what matters is a question of awakening, for evolution has made human beings fall into a sleep that is filled with intellectualistic dreams" (Steiner, 1967, pp. 23–28).

Adult developmental psychologists suggest that wisdom embraces complexity, multi-perspectivity, and creativity (Sinnott, 2005; Sternberg, 2001). Developmental psychologist Robert Sternberg (2001) has proposed a balance theory of wisdom arising from his triarchic theory—comprising analytical intelligence, creative intelligence, and wisdom as practical intelligence. Psychologist Jan Sinnott (2005) views wisdom as a complex and integrative characteristic of postformal thought, explicitly linking it with spirituality and creativity. Arthur Koestler (1964/1989) foreshadowed the notion of creativity as a postformal feature. He claimed creativity is suppressed by the automatic routines of thought and behavior that dominate our lives. Recent psychological research by James Kaufman and John Baer suggests that creativity and imagination are declining during childhood—in contrast to most aspects of cognitive development—perhaps lending support to Koestler's view (Kaufman & Baer, 2006). Kaufman characterizes creativity as the ability to see things from novel perspectives reinforcing Sternberg's and Sinnott's links between wisdom, creativity, complexity, and ability to take multiple perspectives. Sternberg and Sinnott both focus on cultivating wisdom in education.

In the territory of integrating multiple perspectives, Wilber's (2000) Integral framework could contribute significant theoretical coherence to cultivating wisdom in education. Yet there is complexity to how this works in the art of pedagogical practice. Rose and Kincheloe (2003) point to the importance of complex aesthetics in developing and integrating the multiple perspectives of postformal thinking.

Kaufman and Sternberg's (2006) international research on creativity found aesthetic orientation to be a personality trait associated with creativity. This also suggests a role for aesthetic education in cultivating wisdom. Sternberg (2001) pointed to research on wisdom as a balance of cognitive, conative/behavioral, and affective human abilities—echoing Pestalozzi, Steiner, and Sri Aurobindo. Through affect, aesthetic education can contribute to wisdom. Art educators also emphasise the importance of aesthetics in balancing cognicentrism in education (Abbs, 2003; Eisner, 1985; Read, 1943). Through art, drama, and movement, students can see the complex paradoxes of "both/and" relationships, not just the binaries of "either/or."

Voice Consciousness[8] and Language Reflexivity

> The very words and turns of phrase in themselves take on something of a spiritual nature. They cease to be mere signs of what they usually "signify" and slip into the very form of the thing seen. And then begins something like living intercourse with the Spirit of the language. (Steiner, 1929, p. 1)

This statement of Steiner is remarkably similar to the sensibility of Jacques Derrida's deconstruction of language. Both Steiner and Gebser emphasized the significance of language awareness, poetic expression, and creativity as part of the emerging consciousness. The re-integration of philosophy and poetry in western European culture began in the late eighteenth century, initiated by English and German romantic philosopher-poets, such as William Blake, Samuel Taylor Coleridge, Schelling, Novalis, and the brothers August Wilhelm and Karl Wilhelm Friedrich Schlegel. Contemporary philosophical awareness of how we language the world emerged with the linguistic turn (Rorty, 1967). This was influenced by Ferdinand De Saussure's linguistic structuralism, Ludwig Josef Johann Wittgenstein's language-games, and Jean-François Lyotard's notion of metanarratives. French poststructuralists, Deleuze, Derrida, Michel Foucault, and Julia Kristeva deepened linguistic consciousness.

There are also connections between Steiner's and Gebser's notions of language awareness and what Susanne Cook-Greuter refers to as construct-awareness in which awareness of "the language habit" arises (Cook-Greuter, 2000, p. 235). I use the term language reflexivity for this concept. Recent analysis on the relationship between integral theory and postmodernism explored Wilber's vision-logic, Cook-Greuter's construct-awareness and Derrida's deconstruction (Hampson, 2007). Other thinkers have drawn attention to the developmental significance of reflexivity and creativity in languaging (Abbs, 2003; Barfield, 1985).

Steiner (1929) wrote extensively about the conscious development of language and speech, and its significance for human evolution. His emphasis on oral as well as written language has remained a core component of Steiner education, including professional development of teachers. He also developed a complex, enlivening movement art called eurythmy based on his understanding of how consciousness co-evolves with speech and language. Eurythmy is a largely undiscovered postformal movement-art form with the potential to enhance higher order consciousness through complex creativity and body-mind integrality. This language-art form has recently become a focus of university Masters courses in Switzerland and Sweden while research into the potential of eurythmy in systems theory has also begun. It could be philosophically located within the emergent somatic and aesthetic literacies.

In the context of high stakes testing and performativity, pedagogical voice and language reflexivity are not high on educational agendas. More attention to the nuances of the living word could facilitate postformal language sensibility at appropriate developmental moments.

Reflections on Evolving Higher Education Integrally

The development of any educational theory is complex territory and clearly to evolve forms of higher education that are authentically integral is not a simple matter. In my view, the only way that integrally minded educators can muster enough strength to enact the kind of meta-change that is required is through a dialogue of pedagogies. By enacting conversations among the rich pluralism of postformal, integral, planetary pedagogies we can begin to develop an adequate picture of the rich tapestry of evolutionary change that is already happening before our very eyes.

My research interest has been to identify and begin to cohere the plurality of emerging educational approaches that appear to support one or more features identified in the evolution of consciousness literature. By bringing them into dialogic relationship with each other we no longer have one "integral education brand"—whether it be Wilber's or Sri Aurobindo's or any other—but rather a unitas multiplex of postformal-integral-planetary approaches that can learn from each other, inspire each other and give strength to each other. This is what I mean by evolving higher education integrally.

My delicate mandalic theorizing in this chapter has consisted of identifying major themes in the evolution of consciousness literature; hermeneutically analysing a range of emergent pedagogical approaches and clustering them under the evolutionary theme they seem most aligned to; contemplating the qualities that arise at the intersections between the evolutionary and postformal educational discourses; and distilling from this process four core educational values: contemplative love, life cultivation, creative wisdom, and language/voice consciousness. The strengthening of these core values in both integral education theory and practice will not only deepen integral education pedagogically, but will help to ensure that it fulfills the evolutionary promise of its multiple founders.

Notes

1. I have (Gidley, 2010) demonstrated the complementary nature of the integral theories of Sri Aurobindo, Steiner, Gebser, Wilber, and László, and transdisciplinary theorists Morin and Nicolescu (Aurobindo, 1914/2000; Gebser, 1949/1985; László, 2007; Morin & Kern, 1999; Nicolescu, 2002; Steiner, 1904/1993; Wilber, 2000).

2. I use Edgar Morin's complexity-based method of hyphenating linked concepts (Morin, 2001).

3. I am using the term pedagogies as an overarching term to cover both education of children (narrow use of the term pedagogy) and education of adults (andragogy).

4. Other specific approaches such as cognitive-affective learning, gestalt pedagogy, neohumanist education, and transdisciplinary education are included under the notions of wisdom education, holistic education, spirituality in education, and integral education while recognising that these are contestable territories.

5. A notable exception is the broader notion of globalization, which includes cultural and ideological dimensions as well as economic and political (Steger, 2003). Personal communication with Steger (October, 22, 2008) indicates that a forthcoming revised edition will include an ecological focus.

6. These themes are not presented in any particular order.

7. Elsewhere I have explored the significance of these four educational values in relation to nurturing the evolution of consciousness in school education (Gidley, 2009).

8. I am using the term voice consciousness as a broad palette to include postformal developments in language and linguistics, poststructuralism, voice theory, speech and drama development, and language reflexivity.

References

Abbs, P. (2003). *Against the flow: The arts, postmodern culture and education.* London: RoutledgeFalmer.

Aurobindo, S. (1914/2000). *The life divine.* 2nd American Edition. (Originally published in the monthly review Arya 1914–1920). Twin Lakes, WI: Lotus Press.

Barfield, O. (1985). *History in english words.* Herndon, VA: Lindisfarne Books.

Commons, M. L., & Richards, F. A. (2002). Organizing components into combination: How stage transition works. *Journal of Adult Development, 9*(3), 159–177.

Cook-Greuter, S. R. (2000). Mature ego development: A gateway to ego transcendence. *Journal of Adult Development, 7*(4), 227–240.

Davis, B., & Sumara, D. (2006). *Complexity and education: Inquiries into learning, pedagogy and research.* Mahwah, NJ: Lawrence Erlbaum Associates.

Egan, K. (1997). *The educated mind: How cognitive tools shape our understanding.* Chicago: The University of Chicago Press.

Eisner, E. (1985). *The educational imagination: On the design and evaluation of school programs* (2nd ed.). New York: Macmillan.

Elgin, D. (1997). *Global consciousness change: Indicators or an emerging paradigm.* San Anselmo, CA: The Millennium Project.

Esbjörn-Hargens, S. (2005). Integral ecology: The what, who and how of environmental phenomena. *World Futures: the Journal of General Evolution, 61*(1–2), 5–49.

Fien, J. (1998). Environmental education for a new century. In D. Hicks, & R. Slaughter (Eds.), *World Yearbook 1998: Futures Education.* London: Kogan Page.

Gangadean, A. (2006). A planetary crisis of consciousness: From ego-based cultures to a sustainable global world. *Kosmos: An Integral Approach to Global Awakening V,* 37–39.

Gebser, J. (1949/1985). *The ever-present origin.* Athens, Ohio: Ohio University Press.

Gidley, J. (2005). Giving hope back to our young people: Creating a new spiritual mythology for western culture. *Journal of Futures Studies, 9*(3), 17–30.

Gidley, J. (2007). Educational imperatives of the evolution of consciousness: The integral visions of Rudolf Steiner and Ken Wilber. *International Journal of Children's Spirituality, 12*(2), 117–135.

Gidley, J. (2008). *Evolving education: A postformal-integral-planetary gaze at the evolution of consciousness and the educational imperatives.* Unpublished PhD Dissertation. Southern Cross University, Lismore.

Gidley, J. (2010). An other view of integral futures: De/reconstructing the IF brand. *Futures: The Journal of Policy, Planning and Futures Studies, 42*(2), 125–133.

Gidley, J. (2010). Educating for evolving consciousness: Voicing the emergenc-y for love, life and wisdom. In *The international handbook of education for spirituality, care and wellbeing.* New York: Springer.

Gidley, J., & Hampson, G. (2008). Integral perspectives on school educational futures. In S. Inayatullah, M. Bussey, & I. Milojevic (Eds.), *Alternative educational futures: Pedagogies for emergent worlds.* Rotterdam, Netherlands: Sense Publishers.

Glazer, S. (Ed.). (1994). *The heart of learning: Spirituality in education.* New York: Jeremy P. TarcherPutnam.

Goerner, S. (2000). Rethinking education in the light of great change. *New Horizons for Learning* (July).

Hampson, G. P. (2007). Integral reviews postmodernism: The way out is through. *Integral Review. A Transdisciplinary and Transcultural Journal for New Thought, Research and Praxis, 4,* 108–173.

Hart, T. (2001). Teaching for wisdom. encounter. *Education for Meaning and Social Justice,* *14*(2), 3–16.

Hatt, B. E. (2005). Pedagogical love in the transactional curriculum. *Journal of Curriculum Studies, 37*(6), 671–688.

Holborn, H. (1964). *A history of modern Germany, 1648–1840.* Princeton: Princeton University Press.

Holmes, L. (1998). Julia Kristeva: Intertextuality and education. In M. Peters (Ed.), *Naming the multiple: Poststructuralism and education.* Westport, CT: Bergin & Garvey.

Jardine, D. W. (1998). *To dwell with a boundless heart: Essays in curriculum theory, hermeneutics, and the ecological imagination.* New York: Peter Lang Publishing.

Kaufman, J. C., & Baer, J. (2006). *Creativity and reason in cognitive development.* New York: Cambridge University Press.

Kaufman, J. C., & Sternberg, R. J. (Eds.). (2006). *The international handbook of creativity.* New York: Cambridge University Press.

Kearney, R. (1998). *Poetics of imagining: Modern to post-modern.* Edinburgh: University Press.

Kincheloe, J., Steinberg, S., & Hinchey, P. H. (Eds.). (1999). *The post-formal reader: Cognition and education.* New York: Falmer Press.

László, E. (2007). *Science and the akashic field: An integral theory of everything.* Rochester, Vermont: Inner Traditions.

Lyotard, J.-F. (2004). *The postmodern condition: A report on knowledge.* Manchester: Manchester University Press.

MacLure, M. (2006). *The bone in the throat: Some uncertain thoughts on baroque method.* Presented at "Engaging Pedagogies," AARE 2006 International Education Research Conference, Adelaide, November.

Miller, R. (2000). Education and the evolution of the cosmos [Electronic version] [Electronic Version]. *Caring for new life: Essays on holistic education.* Retrieved December 6, 2006 from http://www.ctr4process.org/publications/SeminarPapers/232Miller.rtf.

Montuori, A., Combs, A., & Richards, R. (2004). Creativity, consciousness, and the direction for human development. In D. Loye (Ed.), *The great adventure: Toward a fully human theory of evolution* (pp. 197–236). Albany: SUNY Press.

Morin, E. (2001). *Seven complex lessons in education for the future.* Paris: UNESCO.

Morin, E., & Kern, A. B. (1999). *Homeland earth: A manifesto for the new millennium* (Translated Sean Kelly & Roger Lapoint). Cresskill, NJ: Hampton Press.

Nava, R. G. (2001). *Holistic education: Pedagogy of universal love* (M. N. Rios & G. S. Miller, Trans.). Brandon, VT: Holistic Education Press.

Nicolescu, B. (2002). *Manifesto of transdisciplinarity* (Translated by Karen-Claire Voss). New York: SUNY Press.

Noddings, N. (2005). Caring in education [Electronic Version]. *The Encyclopedia of Informal Education* from www.infed.org/biblio/noddings_caring_in_education.htm.

Nuyen, A. T. (1998). Jean-Francois Lyotard: Education for imaginative knowledge. In M. Peters (Ed.) *Naming the multiple: Poststructuralism and eEducation.* Westport, CT: Bergin & Garvey.

Palmer, P. (1998). *The courage to teach.* San Francisco: Jossey-Bass.

Peters, M. (Ed.). (1998). *Naming the multiple: Poststructuralism and education.* Westport, CT: Bergin & Garvey.

Read, H. (1943). *Education through art*. London: Faber and Faber.

Robbins, B. D. (2006). The delicate empiricism of Goethe: Phenomenology as a rigourous science of nature [Electronic Version]. *Indo-Pacific Journal of Phenomenology, 6*, 13. Retrieved 10 Novemember 2007.

Rorty, R. (1967). *The linguistic turn: Essays in philosophical method*. Chicago: University of Chicago Press.

Rose, K., & Kincheloe, J. (2003). *Art, culture and education: Artful teaching in a fractured landscape*. New York: Peter Lang.

Russell, P. (2000). *The global brain awakens: Our next evolutionary step*. Melbourne: Element Books.

Sinnott, J. D. (2005). The dance of the transforming self: Both feelings of connection and complex thought are needed for learning. *New Directions for Adult and Continuing Education, 108*(Winter), 27–37.

Sloan, D. (1983). *Insight-imagination: The emancipation of thought and the modern world*. Westport, CT: Greenwood.

Sorokin, P. (1941/1992). *The crisis of our age*. Oxford, UK: Oneworld Publications.

St. Pierre, E. A. (2004). Deleuzian concepts for education: The subject undone. *Educational Philosophy and Theory, 36*(3), 283–296.

Steger, M. B. (2003). *Globalization: A very short introduction*. Oxford: Oxford University Press.

Steiner, R. (1904/1993). *Knowledge of the higher worlds: How is it achieved?* (GA 10) (6th ed.) (D. S. Osmond, & C. Davy, Trans.) (Original German work published 1904). London: Rudolf Steiner Press.

Steiner, R. (1905/1981). *The stages of higher knowledge* (GA 12) (L. Monges, & F. McKnight, Trans. 1967) (Original work published 1905). Spring Valley, NY: Anthroposophic Press.

Steiner, R. (1929). Language and the spirit of language (GA 36) [Article] (Original work published in 1922) [Electronic Version]. *Anthroposophy: A Quarterly Review of Spiritual Science, 4*. Retrieved 24 July, 2007 from http://wn.rsarchive.org/Articles/LngLng_index.html.

Steiner, R. (1930/1983). *Metamorphoses of the soul: Paths of experience: Vol. 1* (GA 58) (2nd ed.) (C. Davy, & C. von Arnim, Trans.) [9 Lectures, Berlin and Munich, March 14 to December 9, 1909] (Original work published 1930). London: Rudolf Steiner Press.

Steiner, R. (1967). *The younger generation: Education and spiritual impulses in the 20th century* (GA 217) (R. M. Querido, Trans.) [13 Lectures Stuttgart, October 3 to 15, 1922]. New York: Anthroposophic Press.

Sternberg, R., J. (2001). Why schools should teach for wisdom: The balance theory of wisdom in educational settings. *Educational Psychologist, 36*(4), 227–245.

Warnock, M. (1976). *Imagination*. Berkeley, CA: University of California Press.

Whitehead, A. N. (1916/1967). *The aims of education*. New York: Free Press.

Wilber, K. (1990). *Eye to eye: The quest for the new paradigm*. Boston: Shambhala.

Wilber, K. (2000). *A theory of everything: An integral vision for business, politics, science and spirituality*. Boulder: Shambhala.

Woods, P. A., & Woods, G. (2002). Policy on School diversity: Taking an existential turn in the pursuit of valued learning? *British Journal of Educational Studies, 50*(2), 254–278.

Zajonc, A. (2006). Cognitive-Affective connections in teaching and learning: The relationship between love and knowledge. *Journal of Cognitive Affective Learning, 3*(1), 1–9.

Zimmerman, M. (2005). Integral ecology: A perspectival, developmental, and coordinating approach to environmental problems. *World Futures: the Journal of General Evolution, 61*(1–2), 50–62.

Author Biographies

Listed Alphabetically

Ramon V. Albareda is a clinical psychologist and theologian. He is the founder of ESTEL School of Integral Studies, Barcelona, Spain. He is the cocreator of Holistic Integration, an integral approach to psychospiritual growth and healing, and the coauthor of *Nacidos de la Tierra: Sexualidad, Origen del Ser Humano* (Hogar del Libro, 1990), as well as of many other publications on psychospiritual development and human integration. He is a regular workshop leader at Esalen Institute, Big Sur, California.

Alexander (Sandy) Astin PhD, is the Allan M. Cartter Professor of Higher Education Emeritus at the University of California, Los Angeles. He is also Founding Director of the Higher Education Research Institute (HERI) at UCLA. He has served as Director of Research for both the American Council on Education and the National Merit Scholarship Corporation. Dr. Astin has authored 20 books and more than 300 other publications on higher education, and has received awards for outstanding research from more than a dozen national associations and professional societies.

Matthew C. Bronson PhD, an educational linguist, is Associate Professor of Social and Cultural Anthropology and Director of Academic Assessment at the California Institute of Integral Studies in San Francisco, and a teacher educator at the University of California, Davis. Recent publications include a chapter on language socialization theory in the *Encyclopedia of Language and Education* Research (2008), and a co-edited book, *So What? Now What? The Anthropology of Consciousness Responds to a World in Crisis* (2009). He holds a BA and MA in linguistics from U.C. Berkeley and a PhD in language, literacy and culture from U.C. Davis.

Brent Davis PhD, is Professor and David Robitaille Chair in Mathematics, Science, and Technology Education at the University of British Columbia. His research is developed around the educational relevance of developments in the cognitive and complexity sciences, and he teaches courses at the undergraduate and graduate levels in curriculum studies, mathematics education, and educational change. Davis has published books and articles in the areas of mathematics learning and teaching, curriculum theory, teacher education, epistemology, and action research. His most recent book is *Engaging Minds: Changing Teaching in Complex Times* (2nd edition, 2008; co-authored with Dennis Sumara and Rebecca Luce-Kapler).

Nancy T. Davis PhD, has been a teacher educator at Florida State University for 22 years. Prior to that she taught middle school science for 11 years. Her research interests focus on teachers' professional development, transformational educational reform, integral education, assessment, technology, and environmental education. She has been involved with the Integral Education Group since its inception in 2003 and is on the faculty of the annual Integral Education Seminar hosted by Next Step Integral. Dr. Nancy Davis maintains active involvement with schools and practicing teachers as they adapt to the changing culture of education.

Sean Esbjörn-Hargens PhD, is founding Chair of the Department of Integral Theory at John F. Kennedy University in Pleasant Hill, California. He is founding Director of the Integral Research Center. In addition, he is the founding Executive Editor of the *Journal of Integral Theory and Practice*. Sean is a leading scholar-practitioner in Integral Theory. His articles covering a wide range of applications have appeared in numerous academic journals. Sean is co-author (with Michael Zimmerman) of *Integral Ecology: Uniting Multiple Perspectives on the Natural World*. He lives in Sebastopol, California, on five-acres of redwoods with his wife and two daughters.

Jorge N. Ferrer PhD, is Chair of the Department of East-West Psychology at the California Institute of Integral Studies (CIIS), San Francisco. He is the author of *Revisioning Transpersonal Theory: A Participatory Vision of Human Spirituality* (SUNY Press, 2002) and co-editor (with Jacob H. Sherman) of *The Participatory Turn: Spirituality, Mysticism, Religious Studies* (SUNY Press, 2008). Featured in *The Journal of Transformative Education, Religion & Education*, and *The Journal of Holistic Education*, his integral pedagogy is the focus of *Transformative Inquiry: An Integral Approach* (Kyoto, Japan: Institute of Human Sciences, 2010), an anthology of writings co-edited by Professor Yoshiharu Nakagawa and Yoshiko Matsuda based on Ferrer's visiting teaching at Ritsumekian University, Kyoto. Professor Ferrer offers presentations, seminars, and workshops on integral spirituality and education both nationally and internationally.

Ashok Gangadean PhD, is Professor and Chair of Philosophy at Haverford College where he has taught for the past 40 years. Throughout his career he has focused on clarifying the fundamental common ground across widely diverse worldviews and seeking to expand philosophy and cultural life into a wider global context. He is Founder-Director of the Global Dialogue Institute, Co-Convenor of the World Commission on Global Consciousness and Spirituality, and Co-Chair of the World Wisdom Council. His most recent book is *Meditations of Global First Philosophy: Quest for the Missing Grammar of Logos* (SUNY Press) and introduces new dimensions of ((Integral Reason)).

Jennifer Gidley PhD, is a psychologist, integral educator, and futures researcher. She is a Research Fellow, Global Cities Research Institute, RMIT University, Melbourne, Australia and President of the World Futures Studies Federation. She works globally creating networks between integral studies, futures studies, and innovative education. Jennifer publishes widely in educational and youth futures and evolution of consciousness. Key publications include *The University in Transformation* (2000), *Youth Futures* (2002), *Futures in Education* (2004) and two recent special issues: "The Changing Face of Political Ideologies in the Global Age," *New Political Science* (December, 2009) and "Global Mindset Change," *Futures* (2010).

Olen Gunnlaugson PhD, is presently a SSHRC post-doctoral associate at Simon Fraser University and will soon begin a tenure-track position in leadership and organizational development in the department of Management at Université Laval in Quebec City. Olen has taught undergraduate and graduate courses at the University of British Columbia and Simon Fraser University, as well as the University of Massachusetts (Boston) in the Critical and Creative Thinking Graduate Program. His scholarship in Integral Theory, as well as transformative learning, collective intelligence and presencing has been presented at numerous international conferences and peer-reviewed journals.

Gary Hampson is a scholar, consultant, facilitator and musician. In service of global mindset change, his creative transdisciplinary interests include postconventional poetics, ecosophy, complexity theory, and educational transformation. A member of the World Futures Studies Federation, he is joint winner of the International Association of Universities/Palgrave 2009 essay prize on social inclusion. He has recently submitted his PhD thesis on postconventional integral theory and education.

Katie Heikkinen MA, is a doctoral candidate in human development at the Harvard Graduate School of Education, where she studies with Kurt Fischer, Howard Gardner, and Robert Kegan. Her research focuses on the assessment of adult development. Katie is originally from central Massachusetts. She attended Harvard College from 1998–2002, where she studied cognitive psychology under Stephen Kosslyn. She then spent time in Sweden working in young adult education and nearly three years in Boulder, Colorado working for Integral Institute. She received an EdM in Mind, Brain, and Education from Harvard in 2007.

Irene E. Karpiak PhD, MSW, is Associate Professor of Adult and Higher Education in the Department of Educational Leadership and Policy Studies, University of Oklahoma. Her scholarly interests include adult learning and development, personal and transformative learning, and creating teaching/learning environments that promote integral learning in adult education. In recent years she has focused her teaching and research on the uses of story and autobiography as methods of personal and transformative learning as well as sources of narrative inquiry in the study of adults as learners.

Dr. Joel Kreisberg DC, MA, is the Founder and Executive Director of the Teleosis Institute, an institution dedicated to reducing healthcare's footprint while broadening its ecological vision. Dr. Kreisberg is an adjunct professor at John F. Kennedy University in Pleasant Hill, California. Author of *The Homeopathic Treatment of Poison Ivy and Poison Oak*, and *An Integral Ecology of Sudden Oak Death*, he continues to teach worldwide and maintains a private practice in Homeopathy and Integrative Healthcare in Berkeley, California.

Markus Molz MA, is a psychologist, social scientist, and educator working on human diversity and unity, transformative higher education, and integral meta-studies. Since 1995 he was serving at several higher education institutions in three different countries and he is co-founder and board member of the Institute for Integral Studies (IFIS). His doctorate at the University of Luxembourg is on integral pluralism in sociocultural research.

Terri O'Fallon PhD, in Integral Studies: Learning and Change in Human Systems. She is a principal of Pacific Integral, a consulting, training, and research company. Terri has administered non-profit organizations and public schools, and teaches at the university level. She is a certified scorer and researcher of the SCTi Leadership Development Framework.

Jonathan Reams PhD, is currently an Associate Professor in the Department of Education at the Norwegian University of Science and Technology. He is also Editor-in-Chief of *Integral Review, A Transdisciplinary and Transcultural Journal for New Thought, Praxis and Research* http://integral-review.org. His research interests are in the areas of leadership, integral theory, and the evolution of consciousness. He has presented at a number of international conferences on topics such as leadership, consciousness, transformative learning, spirituality, and science and religion dialogue.

Moshe Renert MA, is a doctoral candidate in Curriculum and Pedagogy at the University of British Columbia. His research centers on ways to relax orthodoxies of math education through increased awareness of the dialectical evolutionary processes that govern the field. As a math educator for the past 20 years, Moshe has worked with thousands of university, high school, and middle school students. He is currently the Director of The Renert Centre, a chain of math schools in Western Canada. Previously, Moshe was an Assistant Professor of Computer Science.

Marina T. Romero is the director of ESTEL School of Integral Studies, Barcelona, Spain, and adjunct faculty at the California Institute of Integral Studies, San Francisco. She is the cocreator of Holistic Integration, an integral approach to psychospiritual growth and healing, and the coauthor of *Nacidos de la Tierra: Sexualidad, Origen del Ser Humano* (Hogar del Libro, 1990), as well as of many other publications on psychospiritual development and human integration. She is a regular workshop leader at Esalen Institute, Big Sur, California.

Jim Ryan PhD, received his doctorate (1985) in South Asian Literature (Tamil) from the University of California, Berkeley. Jim's general interests are in the culture, history, and philosophies of India. He is specifically interested in the various forms of Hindu tantra, particularly the Kashmir Shaiva traditions, the tradition of Sri Aurobindo, and the "modernized" tantra of Haridas Chaudhuri. A secondary interest is in Jainism and the historical interplay between the non-theistic philosophical traditions and Hinduism.

Ed Sarath MA, is Professor of Music in the Department of Jazz and Contemporary Improvisation at the University of Michigan. He divides his time between performing, composing, teaching, and writing about the aesthetic, cognitive, and transpersonal aspects of the creative process. He has performed at jazz festivals worldwide and his most recent CD release is "New Beginnings," featuring the London Jazz Orchestra performing his large-ensemble compositions. His book *Music Theory Through Improvisation: A New Approach to Musicianship Training* is published by Routledge. He is founder and president of the International Society for Improvised Music.

Sue Stack PhD, has been an educator, educational leader, and researcher involved in primary, secondary, and university education for the last 20 years. She is currently Program Manager—Higher Education Strategies—for the Australian Bushfire Co-operative Research Centre and a Research Associate with the University of Tasmania.

Erica Steckler MA, is currently a doctoral candidate in Organization Studies at the Carroll School of Management at Boston College. Her areas of interest include exploring transformational processes related to identity and legitimacy at multiple and intersecting levels of analysis, with a particular focus on the business in society domain.

Bill (William) Torbert PhD, is a professor emeritus of leadership at Boston College and author of such books as The *Power of Balance: Transforming Self, Society and Scientific Inquiry* (1991) and *Action Inquiry: The Secret of Timely, Transforming Leadership* (2004). Currently, he partners with Harthill Consulting UK and serves on the Board of Trillium Asset Management.

Roben Torosyan PhD, has led faculty development at three universities and been invited presenter at 30 conferences and consultant at 13 institutions. Currently Associate Director of the Center for Academic Excellence at Fairfield University, he also teaches undergraduate philosophy and graduate curriculum and instruction. Roben's studies ranged from engineering and studio art to his PhD in cultural studies and education at Teachers College, Columbia University. His scholarship includes six peer reviewed articles and six chapters in books including *The Colbert Report and Philosophy*, and a book-in-progress, *Teaching for Transformation: Pathways and Pitfalls of Integrative Learning*. http://www.faculty.fairfield.edu/rtorosyan/

Carissa Wieler MA, is completing a second Master's Degree in Integral Psychology at JFK University, Pleasant Hill, California. Her master's thesis weaves together two passions: integral psychology and integral ecology. As Associate Director for the newly formed Integral Ecology Center, Carissa leads group events in the San Francisco Bay Area. Past publications include an award-winning essay entitled "A Grandmother's Gift of Story" and a co-authored United Nations training manual for sustainability. Carissa aspires to work locally and globally as a communicator and motivator for healthy, vibrant communities, and emerging leaders.

Index

Note: Page numbers with an *f* indicate figures; those with an *n* indicate notes.